Part-time jobs.
Free-lance assignments.
Temporary positions.
Seasonal work.
Internships.
Volunteer work.

That's what this book covers.

Written for everyone who wants something other than a permanent, full-time job, **989 Great Part-time Jobs in Seattle** is especially oriented to those who are:

- easing back into the work force, perhaps after years at home
- seeking consulting and free-lance assignments
- ready for second jobs that'll show a different industry or job function
- students who need after-school or summer work and an opportunity for "career discovery"
- looking for extra income
- eager for an employer that'll let you work your way up
- retired but not quite ready for complete retirement

How can this book help you? Carefully researched by the only local publisher of job-search guides, **989 Great Part-time Jobs in Seattle** offers you information on:

- Wages and consulting fees;
- 300 joblines accessible from anywhere;
- Temporary agencies;
- In-house temp pools;
- Management training programs;
- Sample resumes, cover letters and thank you notes; and
- No-nonsense advice from recruiters and personnel managers.

An invaluable part of your job search whether you're looking for a first job or a temporary executive position, **989 Great Part-time Jobs in Seattle** is better than any other directory because it's written by a native—someone with 20 years of experience (from internships and summer jobs to corporate management and adjunct teaching) in the Puget Sound job market.

989 Great Part-Time Jobs in Seattle

Linda Carlson

Barrett Street Productions
P.O. Box 99642
Seattle WA 98199
(206) 284-8202

Regarding Telephone Area Codes

In January,1995 western Washington is expected to be divided into two area codes. Many numbers listed in this book will remain in the 206 area code; those further from Seattle will become area code 360. Calls dialed with the wrong area code will be automatically transferred during the period Jan. 15-July 9, 1995. After that date, the correct code will be required. The change in area codes will not affect long distance calling areas.

The 360 area code will be assigned to numbers in such areas as Arlington, Bellingham, Bremerton, Granite Falls, Lacey, Marysville, Olympia, Vancouver and Yelm.

The 206 area code will continue to be used in Seattle, Tacoma, Everett, Bellevue, Redmond, Kirkland (except Ames Lake), Issaquah, Mercer Island, Auburn, Kent, Renton, Federal Way, Des Moines, Burien, Maple Valley, Bothell, Lynnwood, Richmond Beach, Halls Lake and Juanita. It will also be used in Fox Island, Lakebay, Burley, Vashon Island, Bainbridge Island, Puyallup, Sumner, Graham, Silver Lake, Roy and Fort Lewis.

ISBN 0-9627122-3-X

Design by Virginia Hand Graphic Design

Contents

1. Why Consider Part-time Work?

Not every job is full-time and permanent. Employers have many reasons for employing people on a temporary, part-time or project (sometimes called contract) basis. Some organizations only need extra help during certain parts of the day, week or year: restaurants and school districts need extra help at lunch time, fuel oil dealers staff up in the winter and parks departments triple in size for summer. Other employers use temporary assignments to determine whether there's enough additional work—and revenue—to justify new positions. Start-ups use temporary and contract employees until there's sufficient cash flow to commit to regular paychecks and benefits for permanent employees.

Many organizations use people (free-lancers, consultants, interns, volunteers or temps) on a short-term basis to handle special projects—a press conference, a fund-raising drive, a product design—or to fill in for employees on vacation, sabbatical, maternity or sick leave. Finally, some employers use temporary hires and interns as a convenient means of recruiting; employers and employees can evaluate each other with no obligation. Today, temporary jobs are an important part of the labor force; in 1993, *The Wall Street Journal* estimated that 25 per cent of the U.S. work force is made up of temporary, contract and part-time employees.

Why should you consider a part-time or temporary commitment? Maybe for one of the same reasons that people have always sought part-time work: you're a student who needs work after class and on school vacations; you're scheduling around family obligations; you're a stay-at-home parent ready to ease back into the work force; you're a retiree interested in extra income and professional activity; or you're someone who needs—or wants—a part-time job in addition to a full-time position.

Today there are many other reasons to consider something other than a permanent, full-time job. First, it may be the easiest way to work into a permanent position: whether you start as a temporary receptionist or a consultant to senior management, you'll be one of the first to learn about job openings. Or you may find a job created for you. Second, if you are changing career directions, you'll find temporary and project employment an excellent way to test your interest in a new job function or industry, gain valuable experience, make contacts and earn industry-specific references.

Third, if you're new to the Northwest, temping will acquaint you with area employers and give you local references. Fourth, some part-time jobs (for example, teaching skiing) introduce you to people you might otherwise never meet. They also allow you to pursue satisfying activities that may not provide enough income as a full-time job. Fifth, internships, student jobs and volunteer projects are particularly valuable for the person who's never worked or been out of the job market for many years; you can brush up your skills, do some networking and get the references you'll need for a permanent position. Finally, temporary and project assignments can help your morale (and your checking account) even when your job search seems to stall: a temp job gives you somewhere to go every day and offers you the opportunity to network and review professional publications.

How do you find temporary and project assignments? Although not a comprehensive listing of every part-time, consulting or intern opportunity, this book provides several resources for you:

Employers which use only or mostly part-time or project employees, often on a contract (free-lance) basis;

Employers which have a significant number of part-time, temporary or seasonal positions;

Employers which have in-house temporary agencies (where the human resources staff screens applicants for a temporary pool to serve that one employer);

Employers which offer internships that can provide valuable experience, usually at a professional level, as well as references and contacts;

Employers with volunteer programs that can help you brush up your skills, evaluate a job function or industry, try new projects or make contacts and earn references;

Associations with "career discovery," internship, scholarship and mentorship programs;

Community groups with job-search classes, job referral services, training programs and other resources; and

Temporary agencies, especially those that place people in professional and technical positions.

Other means of locating the part-time or short-term opportunity that's right for you:

Telephone established employers and ask if they have in-house temp pools or occasional short-term assignments. Besides calling personnel departments, check with managers in departments where you might want to work: for example, accounting or manufacturing.

Contact new businesses and organizations; you may find their names in newspaper advertising or feature stories or in business newspaper listings of new business licenses or new real estate leases.

Ask your previous employers if they need help part-time or on a project basis—in your old department or in others. Remember, a firm that eliminates jobs for financial reasons sometimes discovers several months later that there's enough work and money for a half-time person.

Expand your network: it should include former employers and co-workers, competitors, professional, trade and alumni association colleagues, civic and social contacts, neighbors, local merchants, your banker and possibly a state job service center specialist. An easy way to open a job-prospecting conversation might be, "If you were looking for a part-time or short-term job today, where would *you* start?"

Most important, be prepared to sell yourself as the ideal candidate. Analyze what you have to offer and sharpen any skills that are outdated or inadequate. Think about what you need (we all like paychecks, but experience, references and industry contacts are often more important). Do a little research (perhaps just an information interview or two) so you know what a prospective employer might need—and be able to offer.

The teenager intent on building a resume can start as a community center recreation program volunteer or stocking shelves for a retailer, volunteer as a photographer for a nonprofit's special event or computerize a small business's mailing list. You can cashier at a ski resort to pay for your own lift tickets or earn your lifeguard certification by assisting with children's swim lessons.

A college student—of any age—should consider an internship. Some are paid, some are not; all offer "real world" experience that'll enhance your resume and make you a favored candidate for career positions. Some, in fact, may work into entry-level jobs with the same employer.

If you're a homemaker who's coming back to work after 10 or 20 years, consider a volunteer stint where you'll get experience with voice mail, E-mail and the latest software packages. Or apply for a seasonal job wrapping packages and running errands during the holiday rush. Transfer your years of volunteer work into a paying job running fund-raisers or editing newsletters.

If you've been in business, put together speeches for local business executives or write business plans for fledgling entrepreneurs. Take up tax preparation—or set up your own business handling inquiry fulfillment ("bingo card" responses). Those who need only occasional employment might teach, either at a local university or through community college continuing education programs.

Be realistic regarding pay; know what you need to make as well as how much the prospective employer can afford. Some people barter, others work on commission or for delayed compensation. (For example, some consultants are paid only when start-up companies are funded.)

2. How to Get Hired for a Part-time or Temporary Job

What does it take to get hired for a temporary job? Here's some suggestions from employers and agency recruiters. Remember, no one candidate is expected to have all these qualifications.

For all positions, you should apply with the following:

An appointment

Resume (excluding consultants, who will have marketing materials)

Current professional references

Pen for completing application

Attire appropriate to the position you seek

Clean and neat appearance

Pleasant and courteous manner

Good eye contact and handshake

Preparation for a screening session (probably including computer testing and an interview)

To be successful as a temp, you also need:

Good interpersonal skills (you've got to be able to get along with others)

Dependable transportation and reliable child care

Flexibility in the hours you're willing to work

A commitment to the job (this means you can't be interviewing elsewhere every day)

For those seeking office jobs:

Computer skills
Each employer's software needs vary, but most expect you to use word processing, spreadsheet management and possibly desktop publishing and database programs. Especially popular: Word for Windows, Access, QuarkXPress and Excel.

Communication skills
Almost every office job will require that you write and speak English well.

Especially important for professional and managerial positions (including consultants):

Standard credentials

A C.P.A. and "Big 6" experience make you more marketable for interim controller and similar positions

Professional appearance

Navy blue suit and pumps and off-white blouse, conservative jewelry and no colored fingernails, says one agency that places accounting supervisors and other professional-level financial people. For men, a suit, white shirt, traditional tie...and no earrings. No perfume, no after-shave. For positions in more creative industries (for example, advertising and retail), temp agencies will consider more "fashion forward" candidates.

An understanding of your role

In most cases, temps—even $50 an hour consultants—are hired as supplemental staff or for special, narrowly focused projects. It's unlikely that you'll be expected to question the company's direction or try to make major changes during your stay.

For those working in home health care:

Compassion toward your patients

The ability to work independently

Other qualifications of value, depending on the position:

Language skills (for example, Mandarin Chinese and Japanese)

Interpreting skills for the hearing-impaired (American Sign Language and closed-captioning)

CPR and first aid training

The ability to lift 40 or 50 pounds

The ability to stand all day (in light manufacturing settings)

3. Where Can You Get Help?
Community Resources
for the Job-Seeker

Looking for a first job? A chance to brush up your skills and return to work after years at home? Or maybe you're leaving a full-time job and looking for something different while you're in school or not quite retired. These are all reasons you may need a little help with your job search: a resume critique, skill-building workshops, a job-search class, a career transition support group. This chapter is intended to help you find some of these resources. Others are described in *How to Network through Professional Associations.*

This chapter describes free or inexpensive workshops and career counseling, community resources and support groups. Some programs have age, income or residence requirements; others are open to everyone. In most cases, the programs are sponsored by nonprofits, schools or government agencies; no for-profit organizations are included.

Many listings refer to libraries. Remember that you can use almost any college or university library regardless of whether you're enrolled there as a student. Although you cannot check out materials, you can research possible new careers and employers through newspapers, locally published news magazines and trade journals. Many libraries also have career development sections with guides to resumes, interviews, cover letters and other job-search concerns.

STATE GOVERNMENT

Washington State Employment Security Department
The state operates 28 Job Service Centers across Washington; besides processing claims for unemployment benefits, these centers offer job-placement help. Assistance is not based on income; everyone is eligible. Services vary by centers; however, all offer a computerized job matching service; job listings; workshops; and referrals to other resources (for example, to training or to veterans' programs). Each center also offers a disability, older worker and veterans placement specialist. The state also operates Job Service Center branches that focus on placement and counseling; these branches do not handle unemployment claims. Employment Security offers other programs for the unemployed, including unemployed middle managers; ask what's currently available for you.

COMMUNITY AND TECHNICAL COLLEGES

Most of the state's community colleges have offices to help adults re-entering the workplace or returning to college. Although often called "women's centers," these serve both men and women. Some schools have "displaced homemaker" programs that focus on those returning to the job market because of separation, death or divorce. Most community colleges also have counseling or career placement offices. Course offerings vary every quarter.

Bellevue Community College Women's Resource Center: 641-2279

Through its Women's Center, BCC offers a 50-hour course for displaced home-makers. These "job readiness" classes for women in transition include testing, confidence-building, career discovery, resume writing and interviewing tech-niques. Cost: $45 maximum (sliding fee scale, depending on your income). "Peer counselors" provide the initial counseling for those considering a career change, a return to school or reentry to the work force. There are also support groups. If you'd like help with your resume, attend one of BCC's occasional resume workshops (about $20 each) or be referred to a private resume specialist ($35-$85 for each one-hour session).

Clover Park Technical College Continuing Education: 589-5671

When funding is available, this vo-tech school offers a free 11-week course, "Getting Ready for the Job Market." It's intended for career changers, re-entering homemakers and others—men and women.

Edmonds Community College

Women's Program: 640-1309
Career Center: 640-1624
Student Employment Office: 640-1561
Continuing Education: 640-1517
The Women's Program offers counseling, workshops, a career discovery and research class, referrals to other community job-search resources, a job board and support groups (some free, some $15 for an eight-week session) on personal and career issues. There's also a displaced homemaker program run in conjunction with Pathways for Women. The Career Center provides a variety of job-search resources, even if you're not a student. If you're a current or former student, the Student Employment Office can help you with your resume. Continuing Education also offers programs to help you brush up skills (for example, computer classes) and an occasional career-oriented class.

Everett Community College: 388-9100

The career center offers the SIGI-Plus programs, WOIS books and other career-search materials in its job-search library and the free weekly "Spotlight on Careers" programs. The counseling center offers life planning and career search classes. You'll also find resume handbooks and other job-search materials in the main campus library.

Green River Community College: 833-9111

From Seattle: 464-6133
From Tacoma: 924-0180
The Women's Center (Ext. 402) offers referrals to community resources and occasional classes. The Educational Planning Center (Ext. 274) provides informa-tion on career exploration, assertiveness training and self-esteem courses; admin-isters interest inventories; and offers free academic advising to prospective students. The Student Employment Office (Ext. 306) is open to the public. Its staff can help you prepare a resume and refer you to the computer lab, where you can

word process your resume. It also offers a four-session "Job Hunters' Workshop." Just inside the office (located in the Lindbloom Student Center) there are free handouts on resumes, interviews and other job-related topics; outside the office you'll find the GRCC job board.

Highline Community College: 878-3710
Women's Programs: Ext. 340
Counseling Center: Ext. 353
Career Center: Ext. 350

The Women's Center offers personal, career, job-search and academic counseling as well as a job search specialist. If you're returning to school while on public assistance, you can attend "Making It Work," a self-help group. A displaced homemakers' program is offered in cooperation with Lake Washington Technical College. The annual "Women's Celebration" usually includes some work-related topics. "Computer Head Start" classes provide an introduction to computers. There are also support groups for women only. Through the Counseling Center, there's a support group for men in employment transition. Prospective students can also get advice about returning to school. The Career Center offers a reference library of books and videos as well as a VCR for viewing the tapes. For $30 a month, you can use the center's computerized job-search programs, including SIGI and WOIS. There's also resume-writing software on a center computer and a laser printer. You can also enroll in the center's career-search workshops and interest-inventory programs.

Lake Washington Technical College
Women's Center: 828-5647
Library: 803-2212
Placement/Job Service Center: 803-2204

The women's center offers a free displaced homemakers program. At press time, the center had applied for a grant to assist single parents and displaced homemakers with child care and transportation costs and tuition waivers while in school. Men and women at any career level can also receive referrals to community job-search resources. The LWTC library offers handouts, videos and workshops on resume writing and interview skills. For information, contact Jeffrey Keuss. The placement center includes a branch of the Employment Security department where you can receive employment counseling. Does not, however, handle unemployment claims.

North Seattle Community College
Career and Employment Center: 527-3685
Women's Center: 527-3696
Continuing Education: 527-3705

Whether or not you're a student, you're welcome to check the job announcement clipboards at the employment center. You can also use the on-site Employment Security office, which provides unemployment claim information and job-search help. The Women's Center offers a variety of programs, including support groups, a free 50-hour job readiness program cosponsored by Lake Washington Technical College's displaced homemaker staff and free weekly lectures. You'll also find career development and planning programs and a job search workshop (including one by the author of this book) taught through Continuing Education.

Olympic College
Career and Job Information Center: 478-4702
Continuing Education: 478-4839
Counseling and Testing: 478-4561
You need not be an Olympic student to enroll in the free resume-writing, interview skills and career development workshops offered by the Career and Job Information Center, which also provides a resource library and the job announcements from the Bremerton Job Service Center. The state Job Service Center also has an employment specialist on campus part-time; call for an appointment. Occasional classes on career search topics are offered through Continuing Education. Considering a return to school? Testing is available through Counseling and Testing.

Pierce College
Career Center: 964-6590
Continuing Education: 964-6600
Special Needs Coordinator: 964-6547
Whether or not you're enrolled at Pierce, you're welcome to use the materials in the Career Center and check the job board. Pierce also offers testing, workshops and a popular credit course, "Human Relations and Career Planning." Through Continuing Education, you can enroll in "How To Find A State Job." A special needs counselor is available for those who have learning or physical disabilities.

Seattle Central Community College
Women's Programs: 587-3854
Women's Programs Hotline: 587-6948
Workshops include one using "SIGI-Plus," an interactive program that suggests career options based on your interests, skills and education. There's a weekly lecture series (topics include work-related concerns) and a resource center, with career information, a job book and information on scholarships.

Shoreline Community College
Women's Programs: 546-4715
Cooperative Education/Career Employment Services: 546-4610
Lectures, workshops and support groups are among the programs offered by the women's center. Topics include "Life Planning and Re-Entry for Women" and "Writing A Resume That Works." Through the career center, "dislocated workers" (those unemployed due to significant changes in their industries) can receive help in pursuing vocational training for new careers. There's also a job board and free employment preparation classes.

South Seattle Community College Career Information and Employment: 764-5304
For those who are not students, there's a package that includes two vocational tests and individual counseling.

Tacoma Community College
Career Services Center: 566-5027
Counseling Center: 566-5122
The career center has SIGI-Plus, a library and the WOIS system. Through the Counseling Center, you can enroll in career development courses. Individual counseling is also available.

PUBLIC LIBRARIES

Everett Public Library Career Center: 259-8012

A computerized assessment program, job resource information and material on training and education are available from career adviser Anita Johansen. Job search skills classes are also offered regularly and there's a free weekly job support group.

King County Library System

Answer Line: 462-9600 (800-462-9600)
Community Relations: 684-6606
All branches of this library system have some career-search materials; the larger facilities (Burien, Fairwood, Federal Way Regional, Bellevue Regional, Kent Regional and Shoreline) have microfiche and computer files on major employers, databases of recent *Seattle Times* issues and Business Index on Infotrac, a CD indexing and abstract service for national business periodicals. Ask librarians to direct you to these and other resources. Free job-search workshops are offered occasionally. Several branches now have PCs with ResumeMaker software and laser printers; you can use the equipment for free, but you'll need your own disk and a reservation.

Pierce County Library: 536-6500

You'll find information on Tacoma-area employers as well as resume-writing and job-search guides in the reference sections of several branches. The two largest reference sections are in the Lakewood and South Hill facilities. To check recent news reports, you can use Data Times, an on-line access to major U.S. newspapers, including the *News Tribune*. In early 1995, the library hopes to offer access to the Internet. For information about programs, call the Public Services or Public Information departments.

Seattle Public Library: 386-4620

The "Career Information and Job Search Center" section (second floor) maintains job-search materials and State of Washington job announcements. The Business Department (also on the second floor) has annual reports, files of clippings from newspapers and many directories, including *Contacts Influential*. On the fourth floor, in the Fine and Performing Arts Department, you'll find the "Arts Opportunities" file, which includes the job and internship openings also listed in the Seattle Arts Commission newsletter as well as notices of competitions and auditions, local to international. The main library and most branches also have WOIS, the Washington Occupation Information System. Many branches also have copies of directories like *Contacts Influential* and *Advanced Technology in Washington State*; these are often kept in the librarian's desk or behind the counter. Through the library's computer system there's some access to the Internet. This includes the On-Line Career Center reached through the Library of Congress, where you can get information on jobs across the country. Getting into this program requires several steps, however, so stop at the career center for help. Once you're familiar with the process, you may prefer to use dial-in access if you have a modem.

Tacoma Public Library

Quick Info: 591-5666

Community Relations: 591-5688

Want to know the largest companies, public and private, in Tacoma, Seattle and Everett? You'll find detailed descriptions when you use Infotrac, a CD-based general business file at the main branch's reference desk on the first floor. The main branch also receives some 800 magazines and trade journals and 150 newspapers to help you in researching prospective employers and job locations. There's a career information file, with resume-writing and other job-search materials. To write resumes and job-search letters, you can use the library's computer lab, which offers Macintosh and PC equipment and word processing software. It's free, but you'll need a reservation (three hours maximum) and your own diskette. A more limited selection of publications and newspapers is available at the Moore and McCormick branches.

OTHER RESOURCES

Senior Centers

If you're 50 or older, you'll find help at several community senior centers. Services vary by center, but most include "Positions Available," usually for part-time handyman or home care jobs. For more information, call: Northshore (Seattle), 486-4564; Greenwood (Seattle), 461-7841; South County (south Snohomish and north King counties), 778-3838 or 774-2921; Des Moines, 878-1642; Pike Market Senior Center, 728-4262; and Maple Valley Community Center Senior Outreach Program, 432-1272.

Center for Human Services: 362-7282

This nonprofit offers free job-search training for youth 14-19 in schools and community centers. For more information about arranging such a program in your community, call the program coordinator.

Central Area Motivation Program: 329-4114

This social service agency's employment program includes skills assessment, interview skills training and help with your resume. Contact Fred Bletson, employment management and training director.

Community Information Line

461-3200 (800-621-INFO)

TTD: 461-3610

This Crisis Clinic service provides information on hundreds of nonprofit and government training and employment programs, including those for youth, senior citizens, displaced homemakers, the disadvantaged and ethnic groups. No referrals to for-profit programs or job openings. Staffed weekdays between 8:30 and 6.

Green Thumb Employment and Training: 923-1038

A federally-funded program for low-income older workers (55 and older), Green Thumb serves nine counties from its western Washington office; in this area, there are Green Thumb participants in Snohomish, King and Thurston counties. Similar to the Senior Community Service Employment Programs, Green Thumb provides on-job training, usually in government agencies and nonprofit agencies.

Jewish Family Services
Seattle: 461-3240
Bellevue: 451-8512
Through its Vocational Guidance Program, which has offices both in Seattle and Bellevue, JFS offers individual career planning and job counseling, testing, coordination of information interviews, support groups, workshops and referrals to other JFS and community services. There's also the Discover computerized career assessment program and a resume writing service. The programs are open to all adults. Fees are on a sliding scale, ranging from $15 to $75 per hour; some financial assistance is available.

Jobline Youth Employment: 362-7282
Individual job coaching and referrals to jobs are provided to Shoreline area youth 14-19 by this program, operated by the Center for Human Services.

King County Human Services, Community Services Division
Employment Training Program: 296-5220
Veterans' Programs: 296-7656
Women's Program: 296-5240
King County's job-training and job-search programs, some limited to those who live within King County but outside Seattle, include Employment Training, the umbrella for the Veterans' Program and the Work Training Program. The Veterans' Programs office offers informal counseling, help with resumes, skills assessment and job placement. You'll need a copy of your DD214. If you're seeking financial help, call for an appointment and information. The Women's Program office maintains files of job announcements and information on other job-search resources and works with the other programs listed below. The Work Training Program provides help for at-risk youth and teen parents. Eligibility requirements vary, but in general, you must live in King County outside Seattle and meet income criteria. Services include:

For youth:
Individual job counseling, help with your job search skills, skills training, work experience, educational and skills assessment, tutoring and referral to GED and high school completion programs. To participate in year around programs, you must be between 16 and 21 years of age; during the summer, 14 and 15-year-olds may also participate. If you're applying only for a summer job, call 296-5220 between mid-March and June 1.

For teen parents:
Help completing your education, job counseling, help finding part-time or full-time work, pre- and postnatal medical services, parenting education, counseling and peer support groups and child care as needed. You're eligible if you're a teenager and pregnant or a parent, if you live in Kent, Renton, Auburn, Enumclaw, Shoreline, Highline or Bellevue and meet income or disability requirements.

Mercer Island Jobline: 236-3530
The City of Mercer Island and King County fund this program, which matches jobs and job-seekers, primarily youth and senior citizens. Priority goes to Mercer Island residents.

Metrocenter YMCA: 382-5011

GED preparation and job training are two of the Y's programs. Both are designed for young people 16-24. The job training programs often include both coursework and work experience. The Y also offers an employment specialist who can help you one-on-one. Call for information on eligibility and the intake process.

National Asian Pacific Center on Aging: 624-1221

A nonprofit federally-funded agency, this center offers two programs for those 55 and older. The Senior Community Service Employment Program is similar to that offered by the AARP; on-job training is provided for low-income residents of King County. The Resource Center's program differs only in that it targets (but does not restrict its help to) Asian Pacific Islanders. The Senior Environmental Program has no income or residency requirements. It places skilled and professional workers (ranging from secretaries to chemical engineers) in Environmental Protection Agency jobs. Each job placement is for a minimum of one year.

Operation Improvement: 258-2766

From Seattle: 745-2636
Operation Improvement provides free and low-cost employment services to Sno-homish County adults. Those 55 or older can receive special help through the "55+" program. Services include job search workshops and seminars, support services (such as financial help with day care and transportation), vocational training, GED-exam preparation and assistance with basic math and reading skills. Programs vary in length to nine months.

Pathways for Women: 774-9843

This group runs three different programs: Saturday workshops on such topics as self-esteem, decision-making and assertiveness; displaced homemakers programs; and job clubs, open to everyone in the job market. Fees for the workshops vary; the displaced homemakers program and job club are free. Counseling is also offered on a sliding scale fee-basis.

Redmond Project Employment: 803-2204

Funded by the City of Redmond, this program helps un- and underemployed Redmond residents. Services include a job-finding workshop, the SIGI-Plus program, individual counseling and placement help.

City of Seattle

Public Access Network (subject to change): 386-1166
Mayor's Office for Senior Citizens: 684-0500
Seattle Veterans Action Center: 684-4708
Information on many governmental and community activities is being made available on the Public Access Network, an on-line service being tested by the city at press time. To be introduced citywide in late 1994 or early 1995, the PAN will include city (and possibly other) job listings by mid-1995. When the PAN is up, you'll be able to access its information via your own computer and modem or through work stations in libraries, community centers, neighborhood service centers and other public buildings. To check on PAN progress, call 684-0552. Through the Mayor's Office, those older than 55 can use "The Age 55+ Employ-ment Resource Center," which offers a job bank, job referral service, jobs hotline

(684-0477), individual counseling, job search workshops and prescreening of candidates for employers. There are only two eligibility requirements: age and residency in King County. The Veterans Action Center maintains a job bank and has a free employment counselor.

Seattle Pacific University
Continuing Studies: 281-2121
Career Development Center: 281-2018
Most Career Development Center programs are for SPU students and alumni. However, the public can visit the library, located on the second floor of the student union at Third and Bertona. SPU also publishes a job bulletin. See *Where Are Jobs Listed?*

Seattle University
Career Development Center: 296-6080
Evening Programs and Continuing Education: 296-5920
If you attended SU or one of several other Jesuit institutions, you can use the career center, which is also open to SU staff and faculty. Through Evening Programs and Continuing Education, SU offers "Leadership Synthesis," which sponsors occasional speakers of interest to job-seekers.

Senior Community Service Employment Program
Seattle: 624-6698
Kent: 859-1818
Funded by a Department of Labor grant and coordinated by the American Association of Retired Persons (AARP), this program for low-income people 55 and older provides on-job training in nonprofits, advice on such job search concerns as resumes and referrals to community resources.

Senior Information and Assistance: 448-3110
A division of Senior Services of Seattle/King County. Serves senior citizens and their families. If you're a senior seeking work, the office staff can refer you to job banks and training programs for which you qualify.

Thurston County Job Search Network: 786-5416
Toll-free: (800) 624-1234, Ext. 5416
A list of joblines, typewriters, a word processor and resume counseling are some of the services offered county residents by this Thurston County-funded office. If you're interested in working for the state, attend one of the workshops explaining the state hiring process. There's also a job bank for older workers. Participates in the annual "Job and Information Fair" sponsored by the Coalition for Older Worker Employment of South Puget Sound. All services free. Call for hours.

University of Washington
Women's Information Center: 685-1090
Center for Career Services: 543-9104
Extension: 543-3900
The Women's Information Center has job boards, library resources that can help you write a resume, information on the agencies and programs that provide aptitude and vocational testing, a directory of women's organizations and profes-

sional associations and a file on women-owned businesses. If you plan to return to school, you can receive help from re-entry counselors. Plus there are workshops and classes, including inexpensive prep courses for the Graduate Record Exam. All services are available to both men and women. The Center for Career Services (formerly called the placement center) is open only to UW students with ID cards (usually those pursuing degrees) and registered alumni (who have paid a quarterly $20 fee), but it publishes job bulletins available to anyone by subscription. See *Where Are Jobs Listed?* If you are an alumnus of the UW, you can also subscribe to the Center's 24-hour jobline for $20 per quarter, which allows you to access all of the job openings listed with the Center; these range from $8 an hour part-time tutoring jobs to executive-level positions. Others can subscribe to the jobline for $40 per quarter. By 1995 the Center expects to be loading approximately 75 new openings into its database each day. (Note that job opportunities for graduates of the law school and MBA program are handled by the respective programs, not the Center for Career Services.) UW Extension offers career counseling, job-search and career assessment courses and tests. For $35 per month, you can use its Resource Center, which offers career choice and resume-writing computer programs; a videotape library, with materials on local companies and job-search techniques; and reference materials.

Youth Employment Project: 526-2992

Individual job coaching and referrals to jobs are provided to University District youth 14-22 by this program, operated by the Center for Human Services.

YWCA of Seattle-King County

Downtown Seattle Employment Services: 461-4862
Eastside: 556-1350, 556-1352
North Seattle: 364-6810
East Cherry: 461-8480
Each Y offers employment help; services and eligibility vary by office. Examples of assistance: assessments by a career specialist, one-to-one counseling, help with resume writing, interviewing techniques and job search skills, job listings from area employers and a typewriter to use for preparing your own resume or job applications. Low-income job-seekers usually are eligible for free individual counseling. At the downtown Seattle office, you'll find brown-bag lunch talks on career-change and job-search topics. The Eastside Y offers a free weekly support group. If you are a low-income single head of household, you may qualify for the Y's "Project Self-Sufficiency." Call the East Cherry office about this program, which provides help with training, housing and placement for as long as two years. The Y also offers vocational testing, which is helpful if you're considering a career change. Fees are based on income.

YWCA of Tacoma-Pierce County: 272-4181

This Y also offers a career resource center open to the public and a displaced homemaker program.

YWCA of Thurston County: 352-0593

Offers a displaced homemakers program, job assistance help and an interview clothes bank.

Washington Human Development: 762-5192

Migrant farm workers and minority and low-income job-seekers can receive medical office assistant, clerical and word processing training and job-search skills through this program funded by the Seattle-King County Private Industry Council. The training program is open-ended; you can start it at any time. Length: nine months to two years. Participants receive several weeks of assistance upon completing the program. Call for eligibility requirements.

Washington Women's Employment and Education

Kent: 859-3718
Tacoma: 627-0527

Helps low-income women and men who face barriers (often resulting from personal crises) to completing their education and obtaining work. This nonprofit provides referrals (for example, to counseling or drug abuse programs) as part of the initial screening. Eligible applicants are enrolled in an intensive three-week program which includes at least a year of followup as participants pursue training or job placement. WWEE can help participants obtain child care, housing, clothing, transportation, and scholarship and loan applications. For eligibility information, call for a telephone interview.

WOIS, Washington Occupation Information System: 754-8222

More than 1,300 careers that exist in Washington state and the training required for these positions are described in the computer program and books produced by a nonprofit. Updated annually, WOIS also provides information on all accredited post-secondary schools, including colleges, universities, vo-tech schools and private vocational courses. The computer program includes a self-assessment component that allows you to match your interests and skills with those required by specific jobs. Available in most community colleges, usually through the career placement or counseling office; some schools charge a fee. Also available free in most branches of the Seattle and King County libraries and in many Job Service Centers and Employment Security offices.

SUPPORT GROUPS

To provide informal guidance and support for those making job changes, many Puget Sound area groups sponsor support groups. Some have met regularly for years; others are made up of people who get together informally until all of them find new jobs. Some groups are free, others have modest fees. Meeting schedules and formats vary. Such groups are offered by many of the programs described in this chapter and by some of the professional organizations listed in *How to Network through Professional Associations*. In addition, the following were at press time offering assistance.

P.O.W.E.R.

Hotline: 885-1163, #600

An informal networking session for executive and managerial women, "Professional Out-of-Work Women Exchanging Resources" meets weekly. At press time, there were three groups, all meeting on the Eastside. This group can help you make contacts, especially if you're considering free-lancing or consulting. Cost: $1 per month.

Professional Educators Resource Seminar: 803-0756

A support group of educators (kindergarten through vo-tech school, community college and university) that meets monthly. Free. Contact: Judith Gray.

Church-sponsored Groups

Several churches have organized employment assistance programs. Formats vary; some include prayers and other religious elements as well as speakers; others, designed to serve the community, are nonsectarian in nature. Unless otherwise noted, telephone numbers are for church offices, which may refer you to volunteer group leaders.

Chapel Hill Presbyterian Church, Gig Harbor, call Wayne "Buck" Buchanan, 756-8094

Mercer Island Covenant Church, 232-1015

East Shore Unitarian Church, Bellevue, 747-3780

First Free Methodist Church, Seattle, call Wray Whitesell, 784-4037

St. John's Episcopal Church, Kirkland, 827-3077

University Presbyterian Church, Seattle, 524-7300

Westminster Chapel, Bellevue, 747-1461

At press time, Overlake Christian Church, 827-0303, was planning an employment ministry similar to that offered by Westminster Chapel; call to see if meetings are currently being held.

The Seattle Church of Religious Science (527-8801) offers a monthly "Business Breakfast" that provides networking opportunities and Overlake Christian Church (827-0303) each week distributes a "Blessing Bulletin" with job listings.

EMPLOYER ASSISTANCE

Today many Northwest employers provide help for employees and family members making career changes. In some organizations this means formal outplacement and relocation centers, complete with computers, telephones and job-search workshops; in others it means referrals to outplacement counselors. Some employers have "transition" libraries, a shelf of books and videos in the human resources office; some refer employees to community college job-search courses. In most cases, help is available both to those who are losing their jobs as well as the "trailing spouses" (and sometimes children) of employees being recruited by the employer.

4. Where Are Jobs Listed?

Whether you're looking for "who's who" in your industry or "help wanted" advertising, you'll find a variety of directories and periodicals. This chapter focuses on those published locally. Some are available free, others by subscription or in libraries. Besides the publications listed here, check *How to Network through Professional Associations* for information on organizations' newsletters. And ask the staff in your library or college placement center about other directories and industry publications. (Editor's Note: unless otherwise noted, all area codes for telephone numbers are 206.)

JOB BULLETINS

University of Washington Job Bulletins

Although use of the Center for Career Services is restricted to UW students with ID cards (usually those with degree-pursuing status) and registered alumni, the public can subscribe to two weekly job listings published by the center. There's also a 24-hour jobline that lists all job openings received by the Center (for more information, see *Where Can You Get Help?*). The bulletin cost is $40 per academic quarter per list (with lower rates for UW alumni). JOB Bulletin #1 includes K-12 and higher education teaching, support services and administrative positions; JOBTRAKKER Bulletin covers career positions in business, industry and the public sector. Most listings are for the Northwest. Contact:

Center for Career Services
301 Loew Hall FH-30, University of Washington, Seattle WA 98195
543-0535

Seattle Pacific University Educational Vacancy Bulletin

This publication lists openings for certified staff. Cost: $35 per quarter (with lower rates for SPU students and alumni). Contact:

Educational Vacancy Bulletin
Career Development Center, Seattle Pacific University, Seattle WA 98109
281-2018

Washington Education Association Position Listing Service

Current job openings for administrators, teachers and support staff in many schools and colleges in the Northwest. A three-month subscription is $10 for WEA members, $35 for nonmembers. Contact:

Washington Education Association
33434 8th S., Federal Way WA 98003
941-6700
Toll-free within Washington: (800) 622-3393

Job Net

Municipal managerial and professional positions are listed in each month's issue of *Job Net*, which costs $8 for a six-month subscription and $15 for a year. For a sample issue and subscription information, contact:

Job Net, Association of Washington Cities
1076 S. Franklin St., Olympia WA 98501
753-4137

Puget Sound Fitness Newsletter

Established in 1987, this twice-monthly newsletter fills half its pages with job listings for fitness-related positions in education, business (for example, in wellness programs), health clubs and physical therapy. Also mentions conferences and workshops. Cost: $33 for 12 issues. Issued by a for-profit publisher:

Puget Sound Fitness Newsletter
P.O. Box 1229, Bothell WA 98041
486-2064

The Employment Paper

Issued by a for-profit publisher, this weekly includes job search advice columns as well as a calendar of job-search events and help wanted ads. Pick it up in your neighborhood or, if out-of-state, request a subscription by contacting the address below. The paper's Job Link service tells you where to find copies of the paper.

The Employment Paper
209 Sixth Ave. N., Seattle WA 98109
441-4545
Job Link: 517-5627 (Touchtone telephone required)

Sound Opportunities

Started in 1989 to advertise openings in regional nonprofit and public sector organizations, this publication is distributed free to placement offices, libraries, nonprofits and government agencies. Includes internships as well as paid positions. Mailed to individuals by subscription ($13 for four months). Contact:

Sound Opportunities
2708 Elliott Ave., Seattle WA 98121
441-8280

DIRECTORIES

Puget Sound Arts Directory lists 353 nonprofit arts organizations. A publication of Business Volunteers for the Arts, a Greater Seattle Chamber of Commerce affiliate. Cost: $12 plus $2 postage. Order from Business Volunteers for the Arts, 1301 Fifth Ave., #2400, Seattle WA 98101.

The Actor's Handbook & Producer's Guide: Seattle, Portland & the Pacific Northwest lists Equity, fringe, community and dinner theaters, corporate video opportunities, production companies, talent agents, casting directors and trade publications. Costs $24.95 (plus $2.25 shipping and, for Washington residents, $1.47 sales tax) from Capitol Hill Press, Inc., P.O. Box 12222, Seattle WA 98102-0222. Bankcard orders are accepted by The Play's The Thing, 323-PLAY.

Advanced Technology in Washington State 1994 Directory lists 1,500 high tech firms statewide. Almost 60 per cent of the listings are for firms along the Interstate 405 belt. Available for $34 in Seattle bookstores or for $36.79 (including tax and postage) from Glenn Avery, Commerce Publishing Corp., P.O. Box 9805, Seattle WA 98109. A DOS-based diskette version is $48. Available in many libraries.

Environmental Services Directory for Washington State, $3 from P.O. Box 99486, Seattle WA 98199. The 1994 directory includes about 45 pages of contact information and brief descriptions of firms offering environmental products, services and information. Companies pay to be listed. Includes environmental and recycling trade and professional associations and locally-published trade journals. The same publisher issues:

The Marine Directory: Puget Sound and Washington Coast. About 40 pages of paid listings, including clubs and professional organizations, trade development groups, consulates, labor unions and steamship operators. Charge: $3.

Where to Turn PLUS, published by the Crisis Clinic. A 250-page directory describing social service agencies in King County. Updated biannually. Price: $20 in bookstores or from the Crisis Clinic, 1515 Dexter Ave. N., #300, Seattle WA 98109.

Referrals and Resources, published by the City of Seattle Office for Women's Rights, lists agencies and associations for women and sexual minorities. Updated in early 1994. Listings include professional associations, social service agencies and crisis lines (e.g., for those being abused). Order for $5 from:

Seattle Office for Women's Rights
700 Third Ave., #220, Seattle WA 98104-1809

Washington Foundation Directory: How To Get Your Slice of the Pie, by Mardell Moore and Charna Klein. More than 250 pages describing foundations plus extensive indexes. Although designed for grant-seekers, it identifies organizations that may have job or internship opportunities. Available for $39.83 (including postage and state sales tax) from Consultant Services Northwest, Inc., 839 N.E. 96th St., Seattle WA 98115.

Washington Education Directory, which lists all state-approved public and private schools, colleges and universities and many professional associations for educators. Available from Barbara Krohn and Associates, 835 Securities Building, Seattle WA 98101-1162, 622-3538. Cost: $13 plus tax and shipping.

Washington State Media Directory lists newspapers, magazines and broadcast stations. Updated monthly. Available for $85 (call 621-6475) and in many libraries.

Directory of Lawyers for King County, which lists 8,000 attorneys and law firms as well as King County courts and bar associations. Compiled by the Seattle Daily Journal of Commerce staff, it's $13 if you pick it up at the newspaper office, 83 Columbia, or $14 if mailed. Contact: Seattle Daily Journal of Commerce, P.O. Box 11050, Seattle WA 98111.

Nonprofit Community Resource Directory, a 125-page listing of nonprofits from the publishers of *Sound Opportunities* (see above). Order from Nonprofit Community Network, 2708 Elliott Ave., Seattle WA 98121, 441-8280. Cost (1995 edition): $16.95.

1993 Charitable Trust Directory, published by the Office of the Washington State Attorney General (call 755-0863), available in many Seattle libraries, lists both grant-makers and nonprofits seeking grants.

Contacts Influential, which includes most King, Snohomish, Pierce and Thurston county firms, public and private. Revised each year, it lists top management, size and SIC (industry) codes. The King-Snohomish version lists 75,000 firms. The Pierce-Thurston version lists 26,000 firms. Available in most Seattle-area public libraries in the reference section or at the check-out counter. Subsets are available in mailing list form. Contact: Contacts Influential, 1001 Fourth Ave., #2727, Seattle WA 98154-1075, 587-6014.

Guide to Business-Related Organizations in Puget Sound, a 69-page list of business, downtown development, professional, alumni and civic groups. Available for $29 from TLS Marketing Consultants, 1321 Queen Anne Ave. N., #209, Seattle WA 98109.

R. L. Polk & Co. City Directories. If you pass a store or firm and want to know who owns it, you may find the answer in the appropriate city directory. Participation is voluntary; listings are incomplete.

Libraries may also have:

The Municipal Year Book, published by the International City Management Association, Washington, D.C.; lists city and county officials.

The Northwest Portrait, a 30-page annual overview of the Pacific Northwest economic situation with a forecast. Written by economists, it offers employment and income trends and an analysis of different sectors, but provides no specifics on where jobs might open up. Covers Washington, Oregon, Alaska, Idaho, Montana and, to a lesser extent, the two western Canadian provinces. Of value to companies considering relocation here. Also available free from:

Economics Department, U.S. Bancorp.
P.O. Box 8837, Portland OR 97208 or

Northwest Policy Center
Graduate School of Public Affairs, University of Washington
327 Parrington Hall, DC-14, Seattle WA 98195

PERIODICALS

For industry information and occasional "help wanted" ads, check:

Puget Sound Business Journal
720 Third Ave., #800, Seattle WA 98104
583-0701

Annual subscription: $49. A weekly, this publication in each issue spotlights several businesses ranging from the very small to the well-established. Five sample issues available upon request.

Seattle Daily Journal of Commerce
P.O. Box 11050, Seattle WA 98111
622-8272
Subscription rate: $60 per quarter. This Monday-Saturday publication provides a different industry focus each day.

Marple's Business Newsletter
17 Mercer St., Seattle WA 98119
281-9609
A six-month subscription for this biweekly, which includes no advertising, is $39. It provides valuable background on Northwest firms and industries. Free sample issue available upon request.

Washington CEO
2505 Second Ave., #602, Seattle WA 98121-1426
441-8415
A monthly designed to reach top executives, this magazine has company and industry features and earnings reports of locally-headquartered public companies. Annual subscription: $19.95.

Business Monthly
15712 Mill Creek Blvd., #6, Mill Creek WA 98012-1260
745-0275
A monthly magazine that describes itself as the business development journal of Snohomish County. Annual subscription: $19.95.

Pierce County Business Examiner
3123 56th St. N.W., #6, Gig Harbor WA 98335-1311
851-3705
Toll-free: (800) 540-8322
This biweekly tabloid and its sister publication, the South Sound Business Examiner, cover Pierce and Thurston counties. Out-of-town subscriptions, annually: $20 each; $36 for both.

Marketing
20300 Woodinville-Snohomish Rd. N.E., Woodinville WA 98072
487-9111
Mailed free within the Seattle area, this monthly tabloid lists staff promotions, awards and the newsletter of the local American Marketing Association chapter. Includes "Positions Available" and "Positions Wanted" in its free "Talent Pool" column. No telephone requests accepted.

Media Inc.
Media Index Publishing, Inc.
P.O. Box 24365, Seattle WA 98124
382-9220

Annual subscription: $25. A monthly focusing on the advertising and entertainment industries. There's also a Portland edition.

Artist Trust
1402 Third Ave., #415, Seattle WA 98101
467-8734
Published thrice yearly by the group Artist Trust, this newsletter advertises internships, grants, awards and shows and galleries where artworks are sold. Available with membership: $25 for artists, $35 for others.

Seattle Arts
312 1st Ave. N., Seattle WA 98109
684-7171
Published by the Seattle Arts Commission, a City of Seattle agency, this newsletter is mailed free within the Seattle area upon request; donations are solicited. There's a charge for out-of-state subscriptions. Includes "Arts Exchange," ads for arts organizations. Job ads range from volunteers to teaching, development and executive director positions.

And don't forget the daily and weekly newspapers

Seattle Times/Seattle Post-Intelligencer
P.O. Box 84647, Seattle WA 98124
Circulation: 464-2121
You'll find most of the employment ads in the Sunday issue (a combined *Times-P-I* publication). A one-month trial subscription is $8 for papers mailed within Washington, $12 for papers mailed to other U.S. addresses.

Journal American
P.O. Box 90130, Bellevue WA 98009
Circulation: 453-4240
The Monday issue includes an employment advertising section, with editorial columns and a calendar of Eastside job-search programs. A one-month daily subscription is $9.50 in King County, $12 elsewhere in Washington and $15 elsewhere in the U.S.

Seattle Weekly
1008 Western Ave., #300, Seattle WA 98104
Circulation: 467-4321
Often described as an "alternative" weekly, this paper includes in-depth analyses of government agencies, arts organizations and an occasional business. A publication of Sasquatch Publishing, which also issues the free *EastsideWeek*. Employment advertising appears in both papers. A six-month subscription to either paper: $15.95 within Washington state, $21 out-of-state.

There's also the Everett *Herald*, Tacoma *News Tribune*, *Olympian*, *Valley Daily News* and Bremerton *Sun*.

CHAMBER OF COMMERCE PUBLICATIONS

Greater Seattle Chamber of Commerce
1301 Fifth Ave., #2400, Seattle WA 98101-2603
389-7256
The chamber sells both publications it produces and those published by others (including this book). Call for a catalog. The relocation packet, which includes state and city maps and an information guide to the economy, housing, schools and recreation, is $9 plus $2.90 postage; the packet with a video, "Step One to Seattle," is $25 plus $2.90 postage.

Tacoma-Pierce County Chamber of Commerce
950 Pacific Ave., #300, P.O. Box 1933, Tacoma WA 98401
627-2175
A variety of materials, some free, some for sale. Most are also available for a quick review if you walk in.

Bellevue Chamber of Commerce
10500 N.E. 8th, #212, Bellevue WA 98004
454-2464
Offers relocation materials (fees vary) and a guide to major employers. The receptionist can also refer you to other sources of information in the community.

Everett Chamber of Commerce
P.O. Box 1086, Everett WA 98206
252-5181
Ask for the checklist of materials currently available and any fees.

Bremerton Area Chamber of Commerce
P.O. Box 229, Bremerton WA 98310
479-3579
This chamber sells demographic information and gives away its membership directory. Write for current prices.

Olympia-Thurston County Chamber of Commerce
P.O. Box 1427, Olympia WA 98507
357-3362
Olympia offers a free relocation packet that provides general information and a list of other materials that can be purchased. A detailed relocation packet offering real estate, school and shopping information, a newcomers' guide and visitor package costs $10.

5. Resumes, Cover Letters and Thank You Notes

Hundreds—even thousands. That's how many unsolicited resumes some Pacific Northwest firms receive every month. And when an employer does advertise an opening, 500 or more responses are not unusual.

With this kind of competition, you need a resume and cover letter that will set you apart. Regardless of your credentials, review these suggestions from managers and recruiters experienced in resume-reading. Recognize that even an Ivy League degree and blue-chip experience cannot compensate for a poorly written resume or unfocused cover letter.

Resumes. In general, you have three resume options. Which you select will depend on how much experience you have and whether you're applying for work in one or many different fields. The person with little experience or a single job objective will have one standard resume that is used for most—perhaps all—applications. The person who has worked in more than one field or is trying to make a career change may have two or more different "standard" resumes, one focusing on one kind of experience (for example, sales) and the others highlighting work in other areas (perhaps teaching). Finally, the person with a great deal of experience in many different areas who is applying for a wide variety of jobs should prepare one very detailed resume. This long document will never be sent out itself, but it will serve as a basis, as the master resume, that is customized for each application. You'll find examples of each at the end of this chapter.

Cover letters. These are the letters you write to express your interest in a position. They have three purposes: to identify the position you seek (remember, some employers have many positions open at one time; you must be specific); to persuade the prospective employer to interview you (usually by citing some experience or credential which makes you an excellent candidate for the job); and to explain how you can be reached regarding an interview. A good cover letter is three or four paragrahs in length. The first paragraph, which notes the job you seek, can be one sentence long. The final paragraph, which says how you can be reached, can also be one sentence in length.

Thank you notes. The thank you note serves three functions: it expresses your appreciation for the interviewer's time, reiterates your interest in the employer and allows you a final chance to emphasize your qualifications. It's a particularly good opportunity to mention experience that was overlooked or not explained in detail during the interview. Again, a good thank you note should be two to four paragraphs in length.

References and applications. Applying for a job may require two other materials.

One is the list of references. The second is the employer's own application form. The best reference is professional, someone who can talk about the kind of worker you are. Your references may include your current or a former boss, although some employers ask for those names in addition to three references. Other possible references include people at your level (preferably people with whom you've worked on projects or on a daily basis) or supervisors in different departments with whom you've closely. You might also use people for whom you've done consulting projects or volunteer work. Before making up a references list, you should contact the people you'd like to include and ask for their permission to be listed. The list itself should have each reference's name, telephone number (office and home numbers, if necessary), current title, employer (or organization, if a contact from volunteer work) and a brief explanation of when and in what setting you worked with this person. Three references is usually adequate. General letters of recommendation will be accepted by some employers, but seldom as a substitute for references. An exception is the application—often for a job in education—that requires letters of recommendation; however, most must be written specifically for that position.

To ensure you have all the information you'll need for an employer's application form, pick up a few applications from government agencies and look at the detail they require. Use these applications to guide you in putting together a complete work history, with employers' official names and mailing addresses, your titles, dates of employment, supervisors' names and telephone numbers, pay rates, duties, skills, awards received, degrees earned, grade point averages, etc. Keep this information on one sheet and take it with you whenever you apply for a job.

Read the ad carefully. Tailor your letter and resume to the job's specific requirements. If you're applying for a lifeguard position, highlight your previous work with water sports and recreation programs and your lifesaving certification; downplay the your restaurant experience and skip the titles of every class you took last semester. If you seek a speechwriting assignment, cite some examples of the speeches you've written and the kinds of meetings at which they were presented. If the ad clearly says this is a temporary position, you shouldn't be asking for a job with advancement opportunity.

Responding to the blind ad. It's always difficult to start the letter that goes to a post office box. Some people use "Dear Sir/Madam." Others try "Dear Sir (or Madam)." Why not skip the salutation? In this context, it's meaningless.

Make your letter visually appealing. Remember, the person reading your application may have already seen 50 or 100. So make your letter and resume especially attractive and easy to read. Use wide margins, short sentences and short paragraphs.

Getting started. Writing to people you don't know isn't easy. It's especially awkward when you're asking for something. Here are examples of openings that are straightforward and identify what you're applying for. (That's important when firms have several openings at the same time or when you're submitting an unsolicited resume.)

When you've seen an advertisement:

"I'd like to know more about your opening for a part-time graphic designer."

"I'm interested in the financial analyst internship you advertised in Sunday's paper."

"I'd like to apply for the seasonal cashier position you posted at the Washington State University career center."

When someone has referred you:

"Lee Smith suggested I contact you regarding possible temporary openings in your accounting department."

When you're "cold calling:"

"I'm interested in a summer internship with your organization, possibly in..."

Avoid the obvious and cute:

"Let me introduce myself. My name is Jane Brown and I am..."

"What will this letter tell you about me? How can it convince you to interview me?"

"Why should you interview me? For one thing, I'm fun to have around."

Watch your ego. Don't underestimate yourself—but don't assume you're the only qualified applicant. Skip openings such as:

"I am an ideal candidate for the position you advertised."

"I am uniquely qualified for..."

Quantify your accomplishments. A resume is more than a list of jobs. For each position you've held (paid or volunteer), describe your accomplishments—in measurable terms. For example:

"Reduced employee turnover 50 per cent in 1989."

"Designed direct mail programs with response rates as high as 5 per cent."

"Staffed busy customer service desk, handling as many as 500 calls daily."

"Planned and implemented art, crafts and sports programs for 20-100 children daily in eight-hour drop-in summer recreation program."

Make your resume concise. The best resume is one page long.

Put the "meat" on top. What makes you valuable to a prospective employer? Is it your education? Your internship? Your fluency in foreign languages? If you haven't had a paid job in years, think about the skills you've developed in volunteer work; some of these may be transferrable to the job in question. (Remember, what's most important to you may not be what an employer values. And what's important to each prospective employer will differ.)

Avoid irrelevant information. Include specifics of your educational program only if you're a student or a recent grad and the program is relevant to the job you seek. The same advice applies to hobbies: the employer looking for a paralegal doesn't really care that you like cats and gardening.

Don't make yourself sound old. It may be illegal, but age discrimination still exists, say recruiters. Avoid use of the word "retired" and consider eliminating the dates of your degrees. Never start your resume with a summary such as "25 years of experience in..."

Use good stationery. Plain white or ivory paper photocopy well (remember, many human resources departments retain original applications and circulate only copies). A smooth finish paper will fold neatly and it's less likely to have laser-printed type crack off the surface. You'll find paper and envelopes at any stationer's. At some discount paper suppliers, you can buy a ream (500 sheets) of paper for about $15 and a box of 500 matching envelopes for about $25. To make sure your resume and stationery match, have a copy shop duplicate your resume on paper you provide.

Use a good typewriter or printer ribbon. Today, with word processing, desktop publishing and laser printing, everyone's letter and resume can have typeset quality. Make sure yours look perfect. A secretarial service will charge about $20 to type your resume. If you have a computer but not a laser printer, look for a secretarial service where you can have your correspondence output. Typical cost: $1 per page.

Consider desktop publishing. Brevity is the key to good resumes, but if you have several jobs to list, the smaller typefaces available with desktop publishing software will help you get all the information on a page or two. Check libraries and job-search programs (see *Where Can You Get Help?*) for computers available for free. Or try the do-it-yourself rentals equipped with desktop publishing software and laser printers at shops like Kinko's and AlphaGraphics. Rental charges vary between $12 and $20 per hour; each laser print is extra.

Include all materials requested. If the ad asks you to submit samples or list specific assignments in a particular function or industry, do so. If you can't, avoid excuses such as "I'd send you samples, but I just moved and I can't find anything." If you ignore a request for salary history or your salary expectations, your application may not even be considered.

Proofread all your materials—at least twice. It's hard to impress someone if you can't spell his or her name correctly. When a job requires accuracy or good written skills, some managers routinely discard every letter or resume with typing or spelling errors. If possible, have someone else proofread your materials.

SAMPLE RESUME, NO PAID EXPERIENCE

Kelly Monsen
123 Ballard Ave. N.W.
Seattle WA 98107
(206) 789-0000

Education:

Washington State University, Pullman, Fall,1993-present. Completing general university requirements in arts and sciences. Current grade point average: 3.5. Planned major: Communications (Advertising).

University of Washington, Seattle, Summers, 1993 and 1994. Intensive language studies in Russian.

Ballard High School, Seattle, 1993. Graduated in top 10 per cent of class. Grade point average: 3.87.

Experience:

Swedish Medical Center, Ballard campus, reception desk volunteer, 1991-93. Worked four hours weekly, directing patients and visitors and answering questions.

City of Seattle Parks and Recreation, Magnolia Community Center summer youth program volunteer, 1989-92. Assisted program coordinator with art, crafts, games and drama projects for 25 preschoolers.

Student Activities

Chair, Recognition Banquet, Russian-American Club, Washington State University, May, 1994. Handled budget, publicity, catering and speakers for 65-member club's annual dinner.

Contributing columnist, *Daily Evergreen*, 1993-present.

SAMPLE RESUME, PAID AND VOLUNTEER EXPERIENCE

Kelly Monsen
123 Ballard Ave. N.W.
Seattle WA 98107
(206) 789-0000

Experience:

Big & Better Computer Sales, Seattle WA, 1984-91.
Sales manager, 1987-91. Managed 20 corporate and retail salespeople for locally-owned computer retailer (now merged into Bigger, Better & Best). Responsibilities: recruiting, training, evaluating, firing, territory assignment, key account sales. Accomplishments: reduced turnover of sales staff by 25 per cent; largest sale in company's 10-year history.

Sales representative, 1984-86. Handled both retail and corporate accounts; consistently outsold other salespeople by as much as 150 per cent.

Sales trainee, A-to-Z Advertising, Kirkland WA, 1982-84.
Through telemarketing and cold calls, sold advertising specialty items (for example, imprinted pens, calendars, T-shirts) to small businesses. Exceeded quota by at least 20 per cent in each sales period.

Other Relevant Experience:

Development Chair, Bright Eyes Preschool, Seattle WA, 1990-present. Created fund-raising program that now provides 30 per cent of budget for 150-pupil cooperative preschool. Developed fund-raising concepts, including special events and corporate solicitation. Organized volunteer committees to manage fund-raisers, including auction, stroll-a-thon and 35-family garage sale. Created corporate matching program through cold calls on corporate personnel directors.

Education:

Washington State University, Pullman, B.A., Communications (Advertising), 1982.

Publications:

"Fundraising on a Shoestring," Northwest Fundraisers Association newsletter, May, 1992.

"Sales Approaches That Work," Marketing News, January, 1991.

SAMPLE MASTER RESUME

Kelly Monsen
123 Ballard Ave. N.W.
Seattle WA 98107
(206) 789-0000

Sales Experience:

Big & Better Computer Sales, Seattle WA, 1985-93.
Sales manager, 1987-93. Managed 20 corporate and retail salespeople for locally-owned computer retailer (now merged into Bigger, Better & Best). Responsibilities: recruiting, training, evaluating, firing, territory assignment, key account sales. Accomplishments: reduced turnover of sales staff by 25 per cent; largest sale in company's 10-year history.

Sales representative, 1983-86. Handled both retail and corporate accounts; consistently outsold other salespeople by as much as 150 per cent.

Teaching Experience:

Marketing instructor, Bellevue Community College, Bellevue, 1993-present. Teach advertising, sales and sales management to classes ranging in size from 25 to 50. Initiated annual sales seminar for business community that now enrolls 250 sales professionals.

Adjunct marketing instructor, Seattle Pacific University Graduate School of Business Administration, 1992-93. Taught advertising and public relations to classes of adults ranging in age from 25 to 45.

Other Relevant Experience:

Development Chair, Bright Eyes Preschool, Seattle WA, 1990-present. Created fund-raising program that now provides 30 per cent of budget for 150-pupil cooperative preschool. Developed fund-raising concepts, including special events and corporate solicitation.

Education:

Washington State University, Pullman

M.B.A., 1983.

B.A., Communications (Advertising), 1982.

Publications and Speeches:

"Sell! Sell! Sell!" Keynote address, Sales & Marketing Executives regional conference, June, 1994.

"Fundraising on a Shoestring," Northwest Fundraisers Association newsletter, May, 1992.

"Sales Approaches That Work," Marketing News, January, 1991.

"Finding the Job You Love in Sales," University of Washington Business Administration Alumni Association career conference, June, 1990.

SAMPLE COVER LETTER

123 Ballard Ave. N.W.
Seattle WA 98107
Jan. 15, 1995

Lee Smith
Northwest Helping Hands
P. O. Box 9067
Seattle WA 98111

Dear Ms. Smith:

I'd appreciate an opportunity to learn more about your opening for a development director.

If you're looking for someone who can plan and implement a fundraising program, you may be interested in my experience. As you can see from the enclosed resume, I have several years of sales and development work. I have the ability to organize a campaign, solicit volunteer help and actually make both cold calls and formal presentations.

If you believe my experience would be of value to your organization, I can be reached at 789-0000.

Sincerely,

Kelly Monsen

SAMPLE THANK YOU LETTER

123 Ballard Ave. N.W.
Seattle WA 98107
Feb. 20, 1995

Lee Smith
Northwest Helping Hands
P. O. Box 9067
Seattle WA 98111

Dear Lee:

It was a pleasure meeting you today. I very much appreciated the opportunity to learn more about your agency.

After our conversation, I realized that the challenges you face in your upcoming fund drive are very similar to the problems I handled with the Bright Eyes Preschool. I also was confronted with a board of directors that had very different ideas about what fund-raising activities were appropriate—and how potential major donors should be contacted. Our cash flow problem was severe, so we couldn't spend much time waiting for consensus. Fortunately, the approach I chose—several individual meetings with board members—resulted in fast approval of my proposal and a solution to the preschool's financial problem.

Once again, my thanks for your time. I look forward to talking to you again about the development director's position.

Sincerely,

Kelly Monsen

6. How to Network through Professional Associations

How do you find a job or consulting assignment? How do you find the employer who will create a position or internship for you? How do you find someone who will give you a chance, even though you have almost no work experience? The answer is networking.

Besides helping you learn of jobs, networking allows you to explore possible new job functions and industries and gather information that will help you evaluate job offers. It's also how you make yourself visible—to prospective employers and clients.

There are many ways to network. Many people start with professional associations. For one reason, such organizations—including many of those selected for this chapter—have programs designed specifically for people making career choices or changes. Second, attending meetings is probably the easiest and most socially acceptable method you'll find of introducing yourself to people you've never met before. Third, the people you'll meet have valuable information: about working conditions in job functions and industries, about the growth or decline of that professional field, about current openings.

So go to association meetings and work at talking to as many members as possible; read the newsletters and use the job banks. Don't hesitate to volunteer; if you work in the association office, you'll be one of the first to see the openings posted in the job bank. If you help on a project, you'll get to know members and you may find yourself on a committee headed by an industry veteran.

Many of the groups described here welcome student participation (sometimes even for high school students). Some sponsor student chapters or student activities. These are also an excellent way for you to network with people in the field you're considering. Introduce yourself to the professionals who speak to your class, for example, and ask about the possibility of an information interview or internship.

If you're self-employed or considering starting your own businesses, this chapter includes organizations you may find helpful. These groups do not have job banks and may require that you be self-employed prior to membership, but they provide valuable continuing education and support for entrepreneurs.

If you are an employment counselor or careers teacher, use this section to find guest speakers and to gather industry information for your clients or students.

A few reminders: when you call association officers, it's usually during their workday. Respect their schedules and keep your calls short. When you attend a meeting, it's your responsibility to introduce yourself and clarify your interest. (Passing out resumes over luncheon is not recommended, but you can collect business cards and make follow-up calls to those who mention openings.)

The contacts below were verified at press time, but changes often occur. You may find more recent information in the meeting announcements published in the *Puget Sound Business Journal* and the business sections of the daily papers. A more complete list of Northwest professional associations is included in *How To Find A Good Job in Seattle*, also by Linda Carlson.

AACE International, Inc., Seattle Section
Contact: Bill Fletcher, Puget Power, P.O. Box 97034, OBC-11-S, Bellevue WA 98009-9734
Serves those who determine how much an architectural or engineering project should cost. Most of the 100 members have a background in construction management, architecture or business; most work for architects or independent cost estimating firms. Nonmembers welcome. For more information: Bill Fletcher, 462-3086, Phil Larson, 451-3881 or Kirk Hennig, 365-0738.

Advertising Production Association
P.O. Box 21407, Seattle WA 98111
448-1501
Includes 150 individuals who work in traffic and production in advertising agencies, design studios and in-house agencies. There's also about 150 corporate members. The job bank includes entry-level to senior positions. Nonmembers can use the job bank for a $15 fee.

AEPUG
Contact: Bill Holt, 119 Pine St., #201, Seattle WA 98101
726-1806
If you're an architect, engineer or planner using computer-aided design, consider this group. It meets for CAD roundtables (novices and students are welcome). Membership is about 45.

African-American Child Care Task Force
Contact: Debbie Lee, 386-1548 or Sandria Woods-Pollard, 386-1003
This task force has several functions, including training and a support group for African-American child care workers. At monthly meetings held at the East Cherry YWCA, job openings are announced.

American Advertising Federation
Three chapters in this area:

Seattle Advertising Federation
800 Fifth Ave., #274, Seattle WA 98104
448-4481
The Seattle chapter offers seminars, a monthly newsletter and regular meetings. Membership: about 500. Nonmembers can receive one complimentary newsletter issue.

Ad 2 Seattle
448-4481
One of 28 Ad2 clubs nationwide. The advertising federation chapter for those younger than 32 sponsors a job bank for members and nonmembers. Membership: about 100.

Tacoma Ad Club
Contact: Lynn Krinsky, 286-8265
The Tacoma chapter, which also draws from Olympia and Bremerton, has about 130 members. Nonmembers can receive the newsletter and attend the monthly luncheons.

American Association of Museums, Western Museums Conference
Contact: Lori Jacobson, executive director, (213) 749-0119, Fax: (213) 939-6493
Information on paid positions and internships is available at the "job marketplace" at annual meetings of this group.

American Electronics Association, Washington Council
11812 North Creek Parkway N., #205, Bothell WA 98011
486-5720
People interested in the software or electronics industry are welcome to attend many AEA meetings; a technical degree is not a requirement. Membership benefits include networking committees (similar to SIGs), some of which meet monthly. Organized by job function (for example, finance, marketing, software engineering), the committees are excellent places to meet people. They are not, however, appropriate places to pass out resumes. If you send a resume to the council office, it will be filed for three months; copies will be available to AEA member firms with openings. By early 1995 the association expects to have a skills bank on-line; job-seekers (including nonmembers) can file their resumes and member firms can search for candidates that meet their needs.

American Institute of Architects, Seattle Chapter
1911 First Ave., Seattle WA 98101
448-4938
Besides the monthly chapter meetings, which attract between 40 and 200 (non-members are welcome), a number of educational sessions are offered, including programs on job-seeking techniques and the variety of jobs available to architecture graduates. Each spring the chapter organizes a career fair, where architectural and engineering firms can explain their specialties and interview job-seekers. As a nonmember, you're welcome to network at chapter and committee meetings and use the job and resume files. You can also attend meetings of the displaced architects' support group, which is organized by volunteers on an as-needed basis. And you can use the Resource Center for Architecture, where member firms provide illustrations of their work. Designed for people planning to hire architects, the Center will let you preview the work of firms.

American Institute of Architects, Southwest Washington Chapter
502 S. 11th, Tacoma WA 98402
627-4006
Nonmembers are also welcome at meetings of this chapter, which serves the area

south of Seattle and north of Vancouver. The resume file includes information on people interested in building design, regardless of position. However, most firms checking the file have openings for architects or draftspeople.

American Institute of Chemical Engineers, Seattle Chapter

217 Ninth N., Seattle WA 98109
623-8632
This group of 250 provides education and networking opportunities for chemical engineers. The monthly meetings usually attract about 40. For job-seekers, there are free "Positions Wanted" ads in the local newsletter and help from the chapter's employment coordinator. During meeting introductions, you can also mention you're in the market.

American Institute of Graphic Artists, Seattle Chapter

1809 Seventh Ave., #500, Seattle WA 98101
624-4950
Includes 375 professional graphic designers. Nonmembers are welcome at most events. The Trapeze Awards include paid six-week internships for students enrolled in graphic design programs; for information, contact Sharon Mentyka, 789-8631.

American Marketing Association, Puget Sound Chapter

217 Ninth Ave. N., Seattle WA 98109
623-8632
One of nearly 100 AMA chapters, this group has more than 425 members. Luncheon meetings are second Wednesdays. Nonmembers are welcome.

American Mathematical Society

(800) 321-4267
This group has only four sections or chapters across the country, but nonmembers are welcome to attend the January joint meeting with the Mathematical Association of America (see later) where an Employment Register is offered. This program, which matches applicants with potential employers, requires that you pay the nonmember registration fee (usually more than $200) as well as an Employment Register application fee of approximately $30. To be placed on the mailing list for this meeting, call the Employment Register coordinator no later than September. Note that most of the jobs at the Register are academic positions requiring a doctorate in mathematics. Most members are university professors.

American Planning Association, Washington State Chapter

Contact: 283-2901
Urban planners may be interested in this chapter of the national association as well as its subgroup, the Puget Sound Section. Members (about 1,100 statewide) include urban planners who work in government agencies, planning consultants, planning commissioners, architects, land use attorneys, planning professors and students. For more information, ask for Roger Wagoner, state chapter president, or Don Erickson or Joseph Scorcio, outgoing and incoming section presidents.

American Society for Information Scientists, Pacific Northwest Chapter

Contact: Bill Hersh, (503) 494-4563 or Jane Starns, (503) 642-6580
An interdisciplinary association for information production and retrieval, this

group includes librarians, computer science engineers, linguists, educators and managers from five western states. Meetings, held at least annually, cover such topics as advances in hardware and software, indexing theories and psycholinguistics. There's a job service through the national.

American Society for Training and Development, Seattle Chapter
217 Ninth N., Seattle WA 98109
623-8632
If you work in human resources or training, either on staff or as a consultant, you may be interested in this group, which boasts 625 members in the chapter serving Seattle, Everett and the Eastside.

American Society for Training and Development, Nisqually Chapter
Hotline: 582-0233
This ASTD chapter announces job openings both in the monthly newsletter and at the meetings. Although passing out resumes during meetings is discouraged, there's a table where you can leave your resume for review and pickup by interested employers. When you're introducing yourself, you can also mention you're in the job market. Serves Pierce, Kitsap and Thurston counties; 60 members.

American Society of Civil Engineers, Seattle Section
About 2,000 members, with meetings attracting 70-100. Contacts: Jill Marilley, newsletter editor, 684-5907; Fred Kern, 632-2664, 1993-94 president; or Jim Thompson, 861-6000, '94-'95 president.

American Society of Interior Designers, Washington State Chapter
5701 6th Ave. S., #427, Seattle WA 98108
762-4313
If you're an interior designer or interested in the field, you're welcome at the chapter's general meetings. The chapter directory is available for purchase; it includes more than 460 members across the state. There's a resume file for members and those who have graduated from college within the past two years.

American Society of Landscape Architects, Washington State Chapter
Contact: The Portico Group, 106 Lenora St., Seattle WA 98122-2210
448-6506
Approximately 280 members. The nonmember fee for the quarterly newsletter is $12. "Positions Wanted" ads are free, even for nonmembers. A valuable resource is a members' handbook issued by the national headquarters. It lists all members and their employers, which include private practices and government agencies. For information: (202) 686-ASLA.

American Society of Media Photographers, Seattle-Pacific Northwest Chapter
Hotline: 527-0632
Serves photographers (free-lance and corporate), photographers' assistants, students and vendors. Membership: 365. The chapter holds meetings monthly; nonmembers are welcome and can subscribe to the newsletter. If you're interested in photography as a profession, consider attending programs for the photographers' assistants.

American Society of Women Accountants, Seattle Chapter
800 Fifth Ave., #101, Box 237, Seattle WA 98104
467-8645
Open to both men and women, this group of 180 meets monthly for dinner and also conducts educational seminars.

American Society of Women Accountants, Tacoma Chapter
Contact: Darlene Riley, 871-4941 or Marti Hilyard, 752-1695
ASWA members from across the country attend the annual seminar at Fort Worden sponsored by this chapter, which has 110 members.

American Society of Women Accountants, Everett Chapter
Contact: Judy Brosius, 653-4454
This chapter has 35 members who meet monthly. Nonmembers are welcome.

American Society of Women Accountants, Bellevue Chapter
15350 S.E. 23rd St., Bellevue WA 98007
Contact: Ann Norman, 455-3200
Founded in 1991, this chapter has 50 members. Nonmembers are welcome.

Apple Network Managers Association, Northwest Chapter
128 N. 82nd St., Seattle WA 98103
Reservations: 789-3111
Systems managers and systems administrators are examples of those who belong to this group for people who manage networks. Established in 1989, it meets monthly. About 120 members in the Pacific Northwest and Alaska. Contact: Chuck Goolsbee, 344-2146.

Appraisal Institute, Seattle Chapter
Contact: Colleen Price, executive secretary, 622-8425
Interested in real estate? If you've worked in appraising or would like to know more about the field, you're welcome at monthly meetings of "candidates," people working on their credentials as appraisers.

Appraisal Institute, South Puget Sound Chapter
Contact: Ann or Gil Wieger, Wieger Appraisal, 566-8885
This chapter, which serves the area between Vancouver and the Pierce-King County line, has 100 members; about 75 per cent work in residential appraising, about 25 per cent in commercial. Nonmembers are welcome at the meetings and can receive the newsletter, which often includes notices of job openings.

Asian Bar Association of Washington
Contact: Dean Lum, 689-8500
Legal issues facing Asian and Pacific-American communities and the concerns of Asian and Pacific-American attorneys are the focus of this group, the local affiliate of the National Asian-Pacific American Bar Association. To be eligible for membership, you must have been admitted to the bar. Nonmembers are welcome at meetings, where job openings are announced.

Asia Pacific Chamber of Commerce
1932 First Ave., #1010, Seattle WA 98101
728-1108
Fostering mutual understanding and encouraging business between Asia and the
U.S. are among the goals of this nonprofit membership organization, which has
corporate, individual and student memberships. You can network at monthly
meetings and students may be able to participate in the business incubator program
planned for 1995.

Associated General Contractors of America, Inc. of Washington
1200 Westlake Ave. N., #301, Seattle WA 98109
284-0061
Looking for a job in commercial construction? The AGC's monthly "Personnel
Mart" publication goes to 625 members in western and central Washington; it
includes free resume summaries from people with industry experience. Write your
own four-sentence description of your credentials and the job you want; it'll be
published without your name. AGC members interested in seeing your complete
resume will then contact the AGC office. Contact the front desk staff.

Association for Computing Machinery, Puget Sound Chapter
Contact: Pete Fox, 670-4641, or Woody Pang, 547-0829
If you're a programmer, a systems analyst or a data programming manager, you're
welcome at meetings of this group. Membership: about 200.

Association for Information and Image Management, Northwest Chapter
P.O. Box 24666, Seattle WA 98124
Serves those who manage records, especially in such electronic forms as scanning
or with LANs. Membership: 145 from Alaska, Montana and Washington. Members include those who use and those who sell imaging equipment, ranging from
corporate records managers and systems engineers to consultants to those with no
computer literacy. Nonmembers are welcome at meetings and can skip the dinner
to reduce costs if desired. Contacts: Forrest Smith, 747-4616 or Patricia Chase,
547-4310.

Association for Quality and Participation, Upper Left Hand Corner Chapter
P.O. Box 58704, Seattle WA 98138
Contact: Alpha and Omega Management, 227-0133
Chartered in 1977 as an affiliate of the International Association of Quality
Circles, this group focuses on the principles of total quality management. Mem-
bership: about 450. Meets monthly; nonmembers welcome.

Association for Services Management International, Puget Sound Chapter
Contact: J. B. Robinson, Intermec Corp., P. O. Box 4280, Mailstop 670, Everett
WA 98203-9280, 348-2600, Ext. 1794
Customer service managers and customer support directors are among the mem-
bers of this group, intended for those who work in management and high-tech
services. Membership: about 50. Meetings are held bimonthly.

Association for Systems Management, Seattle Chapter
P.O. Box 673, Seattle WA 98111
This group for MIS professionals has about 70 members in the local chapter, which

serves the entire Puget Sound area, and 6,000 nationally. Most members are systems analysts or managers at smaller companies. Nonmembers are welcome at the meetings; for a schedule, call Jerry Hillis at 296-0892.

Association for the Care of Children's Health, Puget Sound Affiliate
Contact: Sue Heffernan, Children's Hospital Nursing Staff
Development Department, 526-2096
Doctors, nurses, social workers, recreational therapists, child life specialists and parents are among the 65 members of this group, which focuses on the psychosocial issues in pediatric health care.

Association for Women in Computing, Puget Sound Chapter
P.O. Box 179, Seattle WA 98111
781-7315
Nonmembers are welcome at meetings of this group of 125, part of a national that furthers communication and growth among women in data processing. Meetings attract about 50. If you like, skip the dinner and attend only the speaker's presentation for a reduced fee.

Association for Women Geoscientists, Puget Sound Chapter
P.O. Box 31501 Wallingford Station, Seattle WA 98103
Formed in 1985, this chapter has about 45 members. Members include hydrologists, seismologists, engineering geologists, academics and students. Many work in consulting firms or for government agencies. Nonmembers are welcome. Contact Marsha Knadle, 553-1641.

Association for Women in Architecture
Contact: Karla Forsbeck, 441-1440
A locally chartered group with 145 members between Portland and Bellingham. Includes architects, landscape architects and interior designers; you need not be registered to join. Meets monthly and sponsors several workshops each year. Topics are both creative and business in orientation. Participates in the "Expanding Your Horizons" career discovery program for middle-school girls. There's a mentor program for students and those new to design and a mock licensing exam.

Association for Women in Landscaping
P.O. Box 22562, Seattle WA 98122
Includes about 150. Some are students, instructors and researchers; others are writers, arborists, designers, contractors, consultants and wholesale and retail salespeople. Contact Susan Hanley, Evergreen Services, 641-1905.

Association for Women in Science, Seattle Area Chapter
Contact: Reitha Weeks, 2410 Dexter Ave. N., #102, Seattle WA 98109
286-8787
The Association for Women in Science's only chapter in Washington state. Membership open to men and women, regardless of education or profession, who support the association's goals of furthering science education for women and careers in science for women. Membership: 150, including graduate students, chemists, engineers and those who work in environmental science, biotechnology and computer science. Nonmembers welcome. For students, there's a mentor-protege program.

Association of Northwest Environmental Professionals
2033 Sixth Ave., #804, Seattle WA 98121
441-6020
A new chapter of the National Association of Environmental Professionals, this group requires that a full member have a college degree and employment "principally concerned with environmental issues." Membership: 400. Nonmembers are welcome.

Association of Professional Mortgage Women, National Office
P.O. Box C-2016, Edmonds WA 98020-0999
778-6162
If you work in mortgage banking or a related field, you may be interested in this group, which has several chapters in the Puget Sound area. Members include men and women who process and originate loans, whether in banks, mortgage companies, title insurance or escrow firms. Most chapters have employment chairs who provide informal job-search help.

Seattle Association of Professional Mortgage Women
1851 Central Pl. S., #101, Kent WA 948031
Contact: Kelly Eisaman, 859-0269.
Membership: 75.

Puget Sound Association of Professional Mortgage Women
2101 Fourth Ave., #800, Seattle WA 98121
Contact: Mark Perez, 728-7218
Membership: 30.

Everett Association of Professional Mortgage Women
14503 21st Ct. S.E., Mill Creek WA 98012
Contact: Brian Loth, 258-6450
Membership: 35.

Olympic Peninsula Association of Professional Mortgage Women
P.O. Box 1358, Silverdale WA 98383
Contact: Donna Dana, 830-2252
Membership: 30.

Tacoma Association of Professional Mortgage Women
Contact: Fran Phelan, 582-9560
Membership: about 40.

Olympia Association of Professional Mortgage Women
Contact: Karen Castle, 459-8800
Membership: 20.

Association of Records Managers and Administrators
Jobline: (913) 752-4030
Most members work in records or forms management, handling the paper and electronic files that follow us "from birth to death." Typical employers are

government agencies, bar associations, law firms, educational institutions, insurance companies and major corporations with archives.

Association of Records Managers and Administrators, Greater Seattle Chapter
P.O. Box 84224, Seattle WA 98124-5524
Membership: 150.

Association of Records Managers and Administrators, Greater Puget Sound Chapter
Contact: Carole Blowers, (800) 624-1234, Ext. 5580
Membership: about 75. Serves Pierce, Thurston, Kitsap and Grays Harbor counties.

Association of Records Managers and Administrators, Bellevue/Eastside Chapter
Contact: Barbara Rike, 575-1460 or Steve Morgan, 637-5291
Membership: 45.

Australia New Zealand American Society of Seattle
1420 Fifth Ave., #3300, Seattle WA 98101-2390
340-8789
Focuses on business, government, educational and cultural interchange. There's a monthly social gathering where networking is encouraged; workshops with government and business speakers are offered frequently. Membership: about 100. Nonmembers can attend functions and receive the newsletter by subscription.

Book Publishers Northwest
P.O. Box 99642, Seattle WA 98199
About 40 who work in publishing—as publishers, editors, writers, graphic designers, publicists, marketing and production managers and printing sales reps—belong to this group, which offers informal networking. The directory is for members only, but you can receive meeting notices free. Nonmember meeting fee: $5.

Business and Professional Women's Association
(800) JOIN BPW (564-6279)
BPW has 1,000 members in more than 40 chapters or "local associations" in the Puget Sound area. All working women are eligible for membership. The group's purpose is to further the advancement of women. Nonmembers are welcome at the monthly meetings. No formal job bank, but scholarships are offered to women returning to school. For information on the association in your area, call the number above.

Cartoonists Northwest
P.O. Box 31122, Seattle WA 98103
Contact: Maureen Gibbs, 226-7623
If you're interested in cartooning or humorous illustration, whether as an amateur or professional, you're welcome at the meetings of this worldwide group. Note, however, that many members are self-employed and unlikely to be seeking staff.

Meetings cover such topics as computer graphics, syndication, gag writing and children's books. The $20 dues pay for the monthly newsletter, which sometimes includes job openings. Nonmembers can receive sample issues. Meeting fee: $1.

Chambers of Commerce

Many chambers of commerce now offer special subgroups that provide valuable support or networking contacts. You'll find a detailed list of chambers in *Employers: Business and Tourism Organizations*; also see the descriptions in this chapter for home-based business groups and Small Business Action Council.

Child Care Resources

Interested in child care? This agency offers a Substitute Teacher Referral Service. You can be interviewed in any of the organization's three offices; it's best to interview in the area where you'd like to work. For information in south King County, call Tamara Lamb, Kent, 852-2566; regarding Seattle, call LeiMomi Begay at 461-3708; regarding the Eastside, call Kathy Rinonos at 865-9920. If you'd like to run a day care center, you can obtain technical assistance and training. For family day care help, call Seth Kelsey; regarding day care centers, call Laura Wells; both are at 461-3708.

Child Care Directors Association of Greater Seattle
Contact: Laura Wells, 461-3708
About 90 staff members of child care centers belong to this group. Nonmembers are welcome. Openings are announced at meetings and resumes are circulated by the president.

Chinese American Association for Professionals
P.O. Box 12326, Seattle WA 98111
Networking and recognizing the accomplishments of Chinese-American professionals are among the purposes of this locally-chartered group. About 150 members, including doctors, attorneys, accountants and real estate agents. Four meetings and an annual conference.

Christians in Advertising
Contact: Nienaber Advertising Representatives, 455-9881
Founded in 1976, this local group attracts about 50 to each of its inexpensive monthly luncheons. Many are recent grads networking as they start careers. You can receive the meeting announcements for free.

Coalition of Labor Union Women, Puget Sound Chapter
6910 California Ave. S.W., #13, Seattle WA 98136
Contact: Patricia Agostino, 441-7816
Part of a national that promotes unionism, this group of 100 men and women includes business agents and representatives, the people who negotiate contracts, as well as those who work in industries that are organized.

Commercial and Investment Brokers Association
11422 N.E. 120th St., Kirkland WA 98034
621-7603
If you're considering commercial real estate as a career, plan to attend the "Forum"

conference held every spring. The workshops always include an orientation to commercial real estate and information on how to get started in the field. Cost, even for late registrants: less than $60.

Commercial Real Estate Brokers' Association
Contact: T.J. Woosley, 455-5730 or Scott Evans, 454-8211
Exploring commercial real estate as a career? This Eastside organization includes about 50 representatives of smaller commercial brokerages who gather regularly for morning networking sessions. Perhaps best described as a "leads" group, the association's members are happy to help you evaluate commercial real estate as a career option...but you're unlikely to hear of job opportunities.

Commercial Real Estate Women Northwest
P.O. Box 2016, Edmonds WA 98020-0999
778-6162
An affiliate of the National Network of Commercial Real Estate Women, this chapter serves more than 125 members between Everett and Tacoma. Full membership requires two and one-half years professional experience in commercial real estate and full-time employment. Nonmembers are welcome at luncheons.

Computer and Automated Systems Association, Society of Manufacturing Engineers
P.O. Box 7372-P, Seattle WA 98133
Contact: Rich Murrish, 822-8480
About 130 members. Many programs are tours of manufacturing facilities, so members can see computer-aided design and manufacturing operations.

Construction Management Association of America, Pacific Northwest Chapter
1756 114th Ave. S.E., #210, Bellevue WA 98004
646-8000
This new chapter had about 50 members at press time. Members include project managers and others who work at the management level in commercial, industrial and residential construction. Nonmembers are welcome at the monthly meetings.

Construction Specifications Institute, Puget Sound Chapter
603 Stewart St., #610, Seattle WA 98101
382-3393
An affiliate of the national group for architects and specifications writers. Approximately 400 members.

Consulting Engineers Council of Washington
1809 Seventh Ave., #708, Seattle WA 98101
623-5936
Submit a copy of your resume (indicate discipline) and the council will file it for six months for review by member firms.

Contemporary QuiltART Association
Contact: Karen Soma, 522-8541
About 90 quilt artists from Olympia to Bellingham belong to this group, established in 1986 to focus on contemporary (rather than traditional) quilt art. Purpose:

to further the education and evolution of members both as artists and as business-people. The group sponsors a symposium, critiques and exhibits (including one at the Washington State Convention and Trade Center in late 1994). Monthly meetings.

Craft Networking
Contact: Linda McCarthy, 839-4747
If you work in arts and crafts (ranging from painting and woodworking to quilting, jewelry-making or dollmaking), you can join this informal group, which has a monthly newsletter and quarterly meetings. The 50 members also include craft shop owners, show sponsors and promoters and those who provide professional services (for example, accounting or display construction). Serves crafters from Olympia to the Eastside. Dues: $12.

Credit Professionals International
If you work in credit, you may be interested in this organization. Includes collection agencies, credit bureaus and representatives of retailers, banks, credit unions and real estate firms. Any firm with a credit or collections department is eligible for membership. Nonmembers welcome at meetings.

Credit Professionals International, Seattle
Contact: Mac Wolf, 624-4626
Membership: 25.

Credit Professionals International, North Suburbia
Contact: Carol Kraemer, 774-3521 or Kathy McKee, 745-5933
Membership: 10. Serves north King and south Snohomish counties.

Credit Professionals International, South King County
Contact: Lila Cronyn, 588-1858
Membership: 15. Serves Kent, Renton and Auburn.

Credit Professionals International, Everett
Contact: Dyann Dart, 672-6775.
Membership: about 16.

Credit Professionals International, Bremerton-Kitsap
Contact: Mary Lou Addy, 377-1100
Membership: 30.

Credit Professionals International, Thurston County
Contact: Loretta Watkins, 352-5442
Membership: about a dozen.

Data Processing Management Association, Puget Sound Chapter
P.O. Box 249, Seattle WA 98111
587-3762
If you work in or with data processing, you're welcome at meetings of this group. There's a variety of positions represented in the 140 members, from those who run a single PC in a small office to MIS directors.

Data Processing Management Association, Mount Rainier Chapter
Contact: Jesse Hart, 865-6321 or Gordon Cole, 889-3981
Membership: about 15. Serves Kitsap, Pierce and Thurston counties.

Data Processing Management Association, Evergreen Chapter
Contact: Dave Chapin, 346-9731 or Robbin Boston, 464-2543
Membership: 30. Serves north Seattle, south Snohomish and Kitsap counties.

Employee Assistance Professionals Association, Pacific Northwest Chapter
1902 E. Aloha, Seattle WA 98112
325-4000
If you work with employee problems (for example, chemical dependencies, mental health, career transitions or financial difficulties), you're welcome at EAPA's monthly meetings.

The Engineers Club
217 Ninth N., Seattle WA 98109
623-3250
Engineers of any discipline—including electrical, civil, structural, mining and marine—are welcome at the weekly meetings.

Estate Planning Council of Seattle
Contact: Marjorie Pedersen, Administrative Secretary
3215 N.E. 98th St., Seattle WA 98115
522-2830
If you work in estate planning, you may be interested in this group, which includes attorneys, CPAs, chartered life underwriters, bank trust officers and planned giving directors. Nonmembers can attend as guests of members.

Eastside Estate Planning Council
Contact: Phil Egger, 462-4700
Membership: 115 members.

Snohomish Estate Planning Council
Contact: Virginia Antipolo, 252-5161
Membership: 76.

Estate Planning Council of Tacoma
Contact: Alan R. Zalewski, 752-9400
Membership: 100.

Kitsap Estate Planning Council
Contact: Scott Boyd, 479-1881
Membership: about 25.

Southwest Washington Estate Planning Council
Contact: Ed Holm, 943-6747
Membership: about 45

Executive Women's Golf League

Contact: Nicole Barclay, Echo Glen Country Club, 20414 121st Ave. S.E., Snohomish WA 98290

(800) 377-2420, Ext. 230

Part of a national golf and business networking group formed in 1990 that now has 50 affiliates, this chapter was organized locally in late 1993. About 80 women from King and Snohomish counties participate in activities on and off the golf course. No formal job search programs, but networking is one of the group's stated purposes.

Fashion Group of Seattle

314 Lloyd Building, Seattle WA 98101

Hotline: 624-3136

The regional affiliate of an international, Fashion Group is open to women with at least three years executive experience in retail, wholesale, apparel design, manufacturing and interior design. Nonmembers welcome at meetings.

Federal Way African-American Coalition

Contact: Jay Khalid, Diversified Management Group,

305 S. 9th St., Tacoma WA 98402

946-6256

Established in 1991, this group of more than 100 meets monthly for presentations. Also undertakes community service projects. Some topics are work-related; for example, in 1994 the group sponsored a job-search workshop.

Forty Plus of Puget Sound

300 120th Ave. N.E., Bldg. 7, #200, Bellevue WA 98005

450-0040

Organized to help job-seekers, Forty Plus of Puget Sound is part of a national oriented to those who are 40 or older. Members have made at least $35,000 and held professional, managerial, executive or administrative positions. There are initiation fees, monthly dues and a volunteer work commitment. Services include a class on marketing yourself using the national Forty Plus curriculum. Members can use offices equipped with computers, telephones, fax and copy machines and an answering service. Free orientation sessions.

French-American Chamber of Commerce, Seattle Chapter

2101 Fourth Ave., #2330, Seattle WA 98121

443-4703

Facilitates trade and development with France. If you're interested in international business, attend the luncheons or social events that encourage networking. Nonmembers welcome. Quarterly newsletter and a small resource library. Membership: 125.

Graphic Artists Guild, Seattle Chapter

P.O. Box 31258, Seattle WA 98103-1258

Contact: Chuck Schultz, 443-8209 or Kyle Cruver, 783-2914

Formerly the Society of Professional Graphic Artists. Focuses on the business of design. Open to all graphic designers. Membership: about 45 voting.

Home-Based Business Groups
Although the names are similar, these groups have no affiliation with each other. Some have been started by individuals; others have chamber of commerce sponsorship. Members include home businesses and businesses that serve them; nonmembers are usually welcome. At press time, groups in the Puget Sound area included:

Home-Based Business Association
P.O. Box 24384, Federal Way WA 98093
Contact: (Ms.) Darryl Corfman, 927-9149
If your business is operated from your home, you're eligible for membership in this group, which serves 30-40 of the self-employed in south King County and north Pierce County. Nonmembers are welcome at monthly meetings in Fife.

Home-Based Business Association of Kitsap
Contact: Nellie Fagen, 692-7626.

Home-Based Business Association of South Snohomish County
Contact: Rhonda Delaney, 672-0734
Established in 1992 to serve south Snohomish and north King counties. Membership: about 50 home-based and small businesses. Meets monthly.

Home-Based Business Committee, Greater Redmond Chamber of Commerce
Contact: 885-4014
You need not be a chamber member to attend these monthly meetings; however, the chamber does have a lower membership fee for home-based businesses.

Home-Based Business Roundtable, Mercer Island Chamber of Commerce
Contact: 232-3404
An active group with 45 members and monthly meetings that include speakers.

Home-Based Business Roundtable, Greater Kirkland Chamber of Commerce
Contact: 822-7066
No chamber membership requirements. Meets monthly.

Home Care Association of Washington
P.O. Box C-2016, Edmonds WA 98020-0999
775-8120
Education for professionals in home care and home health care.

Home Economists in Business
Contact: Susan Hatch, Washington Fryer Commission, 226-6125 or Chrish Lind, Better Business Bureau, 431-2227
Affiliated with the American Home Economics Association. Serves about 65 home economists who work in business. Full membership requires a bachelor's degree in home economics and employment in the field. Nonmembers welcome at meetings.

Independent Computer Consultants Association, Seattle Chapter
869-1199
Being included on a consultant referral service is one of the membership benefits of this group of about 50, part of a national. Most members represent one or two-person firms, so the monthly meetings focus on the needs of small businesspeople. Nonmembers welcome.

Independent Insurance Agents and Brokers of King County
778-6162
If you work in insurance, you may find this group's meetings and educational seminars helpful. Nonmembers welcome.

Institute of Business Designers
1808 8th Ave., Seattle WA 98101
622-2015
For commercial interior designers. Serves some 200 in western Washington. Nonmembers welcome at the meetings.

Institute of Environmental Science, Northwest Chapter
2815 106th Pl. S.E., Bellevue WA 98004
The only chapter in Washington state, this group has about 90 members. Most are involved with tests and measurements of contaminates. Many are engineers and "techs," those with associate degrees in related fields; several work for Boeing. Others are chemists, physicists, vendors and students—even high school students. Open to nonmembers.

Institute of Industrial Engineers, Puget Sound Chapter 20
2318 Second Ave., #860, Seattle WA 98121
Hotline: 270-0862
Most of this group's 300 members have degrees in industrial engineering, but that's not a requirement. Nonmembers are welcome.

Institute of Management Accountants
Established as an organization for cost accountants, this group now serves management accountants. Most members come from industry rather than public accounting firms. Membership criteria includes a B.A. in accounting or a related field; a C.P.A. is not required.

Institute of Management Accountants, Seattle Chapter
Contact: Wayne Hays, 224-2122 or Beth Reiman, 345-6533
Membership: more than 500.

Institute of Management Accountants, Bellevue/Eastside Chapter
P.O. Box 40357, Bellevue WA 98015-4357
Membership: 290. Contact Ferrin Lave, 881-6588.

Institute of Management Accountants, Mt. Rainier Chapter
Contact: Mary Cabral, 924-7741 or Larisa Slezak, 627-2133.
Membership: about 300. Serves Federal Way south.

Institute of Management Consultants, Inc., Pacific Northwest Chapter
Hotline: 728-1168
The certifying body for management consulting, this organization includes representatives of large consulting firms (for example, Deloitte + Touche) as well as sole practitioners. Dinner meetings held quarterly; nonmembers are welcome.

Institute of Real Estate Management, Western Washington Chapter
Contact: Nancy LeMay, Executive Administrator, 462-0635
If you're interested in managing multifamily or commercial real estate, you can arrange to attend a meeting of this group, which includes about 200 representatives of large and small firms.

National Association of Insurance Women International
If you work in insurance—in almost any setting, in almost any function—you're welcome at meetings of this association, which has several chapters statewide. Functions are open to men as well as women.

Insurance Women's Association of Seattle
Contact: Dorothy Bunstine, Employment Chair, 727-2011
Membership: 90.

Insurance Women of Puget Sound
Contact: Tina Houston, 448-5500, Marion Alber, 670-9418 or Linda Wickizer, 363-6475
Membership: 43. Serves Snohomish County and north Seattle.

Eastside Insurance Women
Contact: Phyllis Worthington, 889-6456
Membership: 30.

Insurance Women of South King County
Contact: Cindy Hawdon, 682-5656
Membership: 35. Serves Kent, Renton, Auburn and Federal Way.

Insurance Women of Kitsap County
Contact: Dagmar Boldt-Lacey, 871-4512
Membership: 27.

Insurance Women of Tacoma-Pierce County
Contact: Judy Mustin, 591-8721 or Susan Knobeloch, 759-2200
Membership: more than 45.

Insurance Women of Thurston County
P.O. Box 2503, Olympia WA 98507
Membership: 25.

International Association of Business Communicators, Seattle Chapter
217 Ninth N., Seattle WA 98109
623-8632
Public relations, corporate communications, advertising, marketing and technical writing are among the functions represented in this international, which has three

chapters in Washington: Seattle, Eastside and Spokane. Seattle membership: 150. To join IABC, you must be employed in the field; others are eligible for a $30 per year limited membership. This allows you to access the jobline, a 24-hour taped listing of job openings operated with the Washington Press Association and the local chapter of the Public Relations Society of America. Your limited membership also includes monthly job bank meetings, where speakers often make "career discovery" presentations, describing the variety of career paths possible in their industries and how to get started. Nonmembers are welcome at meetings.

International Association of Business Communicators, Eastside Chapter
Hotline: 270-7106
Contact: C. J. Kelly, 773-2746 or Helvi Paterson, 544-1112
Membership: 35. Meetings bimonthly; nonmembers welcome. Cooperates in the jobline with IABC Seattle.

International Career Workshops
A quarterly event sponsored by the International Staff Group, a coalition of international associations (for example, the World Affairs Council and the Trade Development Alliance). Held the third Wednesdays of March, June, September and December in the boardroom of the Greater Seattle Chamber of Commerce. Cost: $5. Includes "Tools of the Trade: A Directory of International Trade Organizations in Washington State." Preregistration required; call the Trade Development Alliance, 389-7296.

International Credit Association
An international with U.S. headquarters in St. Louis, this organization provides education for those who work in credit, including credit managers, credit counselors and sales reps for collection agencies and credit reporting bureaus.

Seattle-King County International Credit Association
Reservations: 483-0522
Membership: more than 100. Nonmembers are welcome. Projects include speaking to civic groups and students regarding the use of credit. President: Gail Fisher, 865-0583.

Pierce County International Credit Association
P.O. Box 977, Tacoma WA 98401
Contact: Merla Bjelland, 383-4537, Ext. 232 or (Ms.) George Battle-Wilson, 589-5652
Membership: 130 firms.

International Facilities Managers Association, Seattle Chapter
Contact: Michael Smith, 477-1870
Established locally about 10 years ago, this chapter includes about 225 who work in a variety of facilities positions ranging from leasing to renovation to management.

International Facilities Managers Association, South Sound Chapter
By 1995 this new chapter should have at least 20 members. Although many of the organizers work in state government, the goal is to also involve private sector

facilities people. Serves Thurston and Lewis counties. Monthly meetings. Call the Seattle chapter for contact names.

International Society for Retirement Planning, Washington State Chapter
Contact: Jim Smith, 564-5980 or Andy Landis, 440-1868
About 50 belong to this group, which meets bimonthly. Some members are self-employed, others work in corporate retirement programs.

International Television and Video Association, Seattle Chapter
217 Ninth N., Seattle WA 98109
623-8632
ITVA has 235 members in Seattle. They include people who work in nonbroadcast television—managers, free-lancers, camera and make-up people, producers, writers, directors and suppliers. The meetings focus on professional development, but there are opportunities for networking. Nonmembers can attend and the newsletter is available by subscription. There is a national job bank for members.

International Trade Institute
527-3732
Affiliated with North Seattle Community College, this organization offers several valuable programs for those in the job market. They include: the International Career Cluster, an informal biweekly session that provides an orientation to international trade (reservations are required); a free quarterly newsletter that lists educational events and conferences; and such conferences as the annual February "Women in International Business." Each year there are also three conferences on regions or countries. For those in small business (or considering it), the Export Trade Assistance Partnership provides specialized training and counseling and there's a free counselor on international trade.

International Women in Boating, Pacific Northwest Chapter
3213 W. Wheeler, #152, Seattle WA 98199
Established in 1990, this organization chartered its first local chapter, the Seattle group, in late 1993. The purpose: to provide for networking among women in the marine industry and, at the national level, to provide education on selling to women. Local membership: about 50. Monthly meetings. Contact Pam Kruger, 285-6941.

Japan-America Society of the State of Washington
1800 Ninth Ave., #1550, Seattle WA 98101-1322
623-7900
Interested in U.S.-Japan relations? Consider this group, an affiliate of the National Association of Japan-America Societies. It has 1,600 members, two-thirds of them representing corporate members. About 50 programs are held each year, many focussing on public affairs (for example, a presentation by a Japanese politician). In addition, the "5:31 Club" meets for informal networking; a nonmember may attend once as a guest of a member. There's also a postings/resume file for members; most jobs require bilingual language skills. In past years the society participated in a seminar for those interested in international careers; the December, 1992 session was videotaped and can be purchased for approximately $20 from Montevideo Teleproductions, 672-2471. Ask for the "International Career Workshop."

King County Nurses Association

9500 Roosevelt Way N.E., #301, Seattle WA 98115
523-0997

Executive director: Sue Vermeulen. An affiliate of the Washington State Nurses Association. Nonmembers are welcome at the SIG meetings (there's a nominal fee), which are organized by such functions as staff development nurses, gerontologists and nurse practitioners. The association also offers a nurse legal consultant clearinghouse, referring nurses to attorneys who need medical advice. Note: if you were licensed in another state or outside the U.S. and need licensing information, contact the Washington State Board of Nursing, 753-2686.

Law Librarians of Puget Sound

Contacts: Peggy Roebuck Jarrett, 543-6794, Brenna Louzin, 389-6226 or Mary Hotchkiss, 553-4475

Formally established in 1991 as an affiliate of the American Association of Law Librarians. Membership: about 100 from King, Pierce and Snohomish counties; about half work in law firms, the other half in academic and government libraries. Most work full-time, although some smaller firms hire part-time librarians or offer job-share options. Nonmembers can attend the monthly meetings and annual professional education seminar.

Lawyers in Transition

Founded by Deborah Arron, the author of *Running From the Law* and *What Can You Do With A Law Degree?*, this program is now run by the Washington State Bar Association's Lawyers' Assistance Program. It helps attorneys looking for jobs outside law and those seeking different positions within the profession. Services include referrals to career counseling, a quarterly newsletter which cites successful transitions and a support group. No placement services. For more information: Joyce Elvin, 727-8268. (Also see the Washington State Bar Association listing later in this chapter.)

Macintosh Downtown Business Users Group

P.O. Box 3463, Seattle WA 98114
Hotline: 624-9329

Nonmembers are welcome at the general meetings of this group, which has some 1,100 members from Everett to Tacoma. There are also more than 25 SIGs covering topics such as accounting, animation and desktop publishing.

Mathematical Association of America, Pacific Northwest Section

Contact: Harvey Schmidt, Lewis and Clark College, Portland, (503) 768-7559 or Larry Curnutt, Bellevue Community College, 641-2412

College teaching is the emphasis of this group, which has 29 sections across North America. However, you need not be a teacher to participate in its annual meeting each spring. The only event for the general membership, the meeting is open to nonmembers and students are especially encouraged to present papers. Members receive the section's semi-annual newsletter and national's monthly newsletter, "Focus," which includes job listings.

Medical Library Association, Pacific Northwest Chapter
Contact: Liza Hanby, Rocky Mountain Laboratory, Biomedical Research Library
903 S. 4th, Hamilton MT 59840-2999
About 225 in five western states and two provinces belong to this group, which lists
its job openings on the Internet. It also participates in a student night each year on
the University of Washington campus. The national offers a career day at its annual
conference and encourages job-oriented networking; most employers are large
academic libraries.

Medical Marketing Association, Puget Sound Chapter
Contact: Kate Larsen, (800) 551-2173
This group of 70 was established in 1990. Members include those who work in the
marketing of health care services and medical equipment as well as representatives
of biotechnology and communications firms.

Meeting Planners International, Washington State Chapter
Contact: Lillian Sugahara, Greendale Associates, 18008 110th Pl. S.E.,
Renton WA 98055
226-9338
More than 200 belong to this organization, which was established to serve those
who plan and manage conventions, trade shows, seminars, sales and other meetings. Nonmembers can attend two monthly breakfasts prior to joining.

Mercer Island Women In Business
Contact: Sharon Setzler, 232-0183
This informal group meets for networking and programs the first Wednesday of
each month at the Island House. Many participants run home-based businesses or
are fledgling entrepreneurs; others are new to the Northwest.

MIT Enterprise Forum
217 Ninth N., Seattle WA 98109
623-8632
If you're interested in high technology, you're welcome to attend the meetings of
this group. At each, presentations are made by start-up firms. Meetings typically
attract 200 to 250. Subscriptions to the newsletter are available upon request.

National Academy of Television Arts and Sciences, Seattle Chapter
217 Ninth N., Seattle WA 98109
623-8632
If you have experience in television, you're welcome to attend many of the
meetings of this group, one of 17 NATAS chapters in the U.S. Membership is about
300. The newsletter is sent only to members.

National Association of Black Accountants, Seattle Chapter
P.O. Box 2562, Seattle WA 98111
Contact: Darryl Harris, 448-5087
Part of a national with both local and student chapters, this group provides career
advancement for its members and encourages minorities to enter accounting. Its
affiliate, the Accounting Career Awareness Program, sends accountants into high
schools to discuss careers with students and also sponsors a week-long summer

workshop for high school students. Through its student chapter at Seattle University, mentoring, including mock interviews and career discovery, is provided. For professional members, there's an informal job referral service.

National Association of Corporate Real Estate Executives, Northwest Chapter
Contact: Valerie Pratt, Transamerica Title Insurance, 1200 Sixth Ave., #605, Seattle WA 98101
628-2820
If you develop or manage commercial, industrial, retail or restaurant real estate, you may be interested in this group. The local chapter has 80 members. Nonmembers are welcome as guests of members. Members include developers, attorneys, architects, brokers and representatives of title insurance firms.

National Association of Legal Secretaries
Affiliated with the Washington Association of Legal Secretaries, this group has several local chapters:

Greater Seattle Association of Legal Secretaries
Contact: Lisa Rudgers, Stanislaw Ashbaugh, 386-5900 or Lisa Miner, Warren Kellogg, 255-8678
Membership: 150.

King County Southern Association of Legal Secretaries
Contact: Mia Pratt, 941-1161, or Kathy Clyde, 591-7465
Membership: 15.

East King County Association of Legal Secretaries
Contact: Shirley "Sam" Schmit, Law Office of Herbert G. Farber, 455-9087, or Tammie Parkinson, 822-2117
Membership: about 30.

Snohomish County Association of Legal Secretaries
Contact: Bernie Heap, Job Placement Officer, 258-3511
Membership: about 55.

Tacoma/Pierce County Association of Legal Secretaries
Contact: Rachelle Tilzer, 597-4182
Membership: about 75.

Thurston County Association of Legal Secretaries
Contact: Jeannie Sockle, 786-1100 or Louise Akramoff, 438-3784
Membership: 22.

Kitsap County Association of Legal Secretaries
Contact: Charlotte Jensen, Newsletter Editor, 479-5111
Membership: 34.

National Association of Purchasing Managers, Western Washington Chapter
800 Fifth Ave., #123, Seattle WA 98104
(800) 223-7629
Established in 1929 as the Purchasing Agents of Washington, this group serves about 700 in western Washington. There's also a Spokane chapter.

National Association of Social Workers, Washington State Chapter
2601 Elliott Ave., #4175, Seattle WA 98121
448-1660
If you have a B.S.W. or M.S.W., you may find job openings posted at the state office or published in the newsletter. The 2,500 members statewide are divided into seven geographic units, some of which meet monthly. For a schedule on the unit in your area, call the state office.

National Association of Women in Construction
Women employed in construction—from pipelayer and secretary to company owner and controller—are eligible for membership in this group, formed more than 50 years ago. Its members across the country include women who work in construction-related fields; for example, architects, engineers, attorneys and insurance brokers. Local chapters include:

National Association of Women in Construction, Seattle Chapter
P.O. Box 81435, Seattle WA 98108
Contact: Tricia Manning, 762-4211
Membership: about 40.

National Association of Women in Construction, Greater Bellevue Chapter
Contact: Judy Jewell, 868-1922 or Rita Morris, 836-0373
Membership: 20.

National Association of Women in Construction, Greater Everett Chapter
Contact: Diane Ferguson, Group Four, Inc., 775-4581
Membership: 20.

National Association of Women in Construction, Tacoma Chapter
Contact: Barbara Williams, 824-6500
Membership: 25.

National Investor Relations Institute, Seattle Chapter
Contact: Susan McPherson, PR Newswire, 624-2414
If you work in investor relations, including finance or communications, you're welcome at this group. There are about 35 members, many from newly public companies. Some local members also offer information interviews and referrals.

National Lawyers Guild, Seattle Chapter
2005 Smith Tower, Seattle WA 98104
622-5144
If you're interested in practicing law with a public service orientation, you can attend meetings of this group, which includes law students, legal workers and

attorneys. The local and national newsletters occasionally list "Positions Available." When staffing permits, the guild handles some cases on a pro bono basis; volunteers can gain experience by working on this litigation. Eventually the chapter hopes to provide a mentoring program for students. The internships once offered through the chapter to law students and paralegals interested in public interest law (the "Summer Project") are now handled through the national: call (212) 966-5000. Positions are available in locations across the U.S.

National Society for Performance and Instruction

Contact: Mark Phillips, 342-0498

An international that strives to improve human performance through technology, this group of 100 established its local chapter in the mid-1980s. Many members have master's degrees in fields such as instructional design or systems design. The focus is on adult learning, often beginning with a needs assessment and working through curriculum design. Recent programs: "Benchmarking" and "Working with Subject-Matter Experts." Meets monthly during the academic year; nonmembers welcome. Job postings are circulated at meetings and openings—for employment or consulting—are announced. The national offers a job bank.

National Society of Fund Raising Executives

2033 Sixth Ave., #804, Seattle WA 98121

441-6020

Nonmembers are welcome at this group, which attracts between 50 and 75 to most meetings. Most of the 200 members are development officers and executive directors of nonprofits.

National Speakers Association, Puget Sound Chapter

Contact: Helen Hesketh, Executive Secretary, 562-0302

If speaking and training are an important part of your business, you may find this group's monthly meetings and special workshops helpful. Speaking techniques and marketing yourself are examples of the topics covered. Nonmembers are welcome. Sample copies of the newsletter are available; a one-year subscription is $25. There are about 100 members. If you join, you can participate in "Showcase," an annual event that helps speakers market themselves.

Netherlands Business Organization

Contact: Mark Roeland, 643-2673

This local organization includes both Dutch natives in business in the Northwest and Washingtonians in business in the Netherlands and other countries. If you're interested in work in the ports or in export-import, you're welcome at meetings. Speakers include ambassadors and members of foreign trade councils. Membership: 100. Meetings attract 20-30.

Network!

Contact: Gail M. Gautestad, 543-1957

If you're a state employee, whether or not you work at the University of Washington, you can network through this event, a monthly breakfast held on the main campus. Typical attendance: 125. Has prompted the organization of several special interest groups (some on business topics, others recreational in nature); contact information for these groups may be on-line by early 1995. Note: only state employees can attend these sessions.

Network of Editors and Writers

Contact: Stephanie Martin, UW College of Forest Resources, Mailstop AR-10, Seattle WA 98195
Open to University of Washington employees and free-lancers doing work for the UW. Members include writers and editors. Because events often focus on concerns specific to UW employees, meetings may provide valuable background for someone considering the university as an employer. Examples of topics: electronic pre-press, readings by campus authors and high-tech scientific illustration. Although job openings are sometimes announced at events, the group offers no placement services or job bank; remember, all permanent UW positions are filled through the campus personnel office.

Nonprofit Direct Marketing Association

260 N.E. 43rd, Seattle WA 98105
Contact: Susan Howlett, 545-8509
An affiliate of the Northwest Development Officers Association, this group of 120 meets monthly to consider the challenges of raising funds with direct mail. Meetings are free and open to guests.

North Seattle Women's Network

Contact: North Seattle Community College Continuing Education, 527-3705
Forty to 60 women, many of them self-employed, attend the breakfasts organized by this NSCC affiliate. Most speakers address business topics (for example, retirement planning).

Northwest Association of Biotechnology Financial Officers

Contact: Washington Biotechnology & Biomedical Association, 235-5154
Affiliated with two groups, the national Association of Bioscience Finance Officers and the Washington Biotechnology & Biomedical Association. Includes CFOs, controllers and accounting managers from about 25 firms. Eligibility requirements for membership. Nonmembers welcome at meetings.

Northwest Association of College and University Housing Officers

Contact: Tina Fuchs, Western Oregon State College, (503) 838-8311
This group helps organize the Western Placement Exchange, an annual conference where Northwest colleges and universities can meet and interview candidates for jobs in student affairs (usually admissions, activities and housing). Most positions are entry-level. In 1994 the event was sponsored by Pacific Lutheran University's Residential Life office and attracted job-seekers from across the country. For more information, see *Employers: Education.*

Northwest Biotechnology Series

A series of breakfasts, not an association—but an excellent place to network with managers in biotech. Held November through April each year, these meetings cover the business side of biotech. Speakers are often presidents of local companies. The first three breakfasts each year are sold as part of a series; you can buy tickets to the fourth through sixth meetings on an individual basis. Brochures on the series are available from Julie Holly, ZymoGenetics (547-8080) or the Washington Biotechnology & Biomedical Assocation (235-5154).

Northwest Customer Relations Group

Contact: Roseann Holowich, 965-8102 or Susan Simpson-Fox, 891-2504
If you work in customer service, customer contact or management, you're welcome at monthly meetings of this locally-chartered group formed in 1992. Nonmember fee: $5. At meetings, there's an information table where job postings and resumes can be left. Sixty members.

Northwest Development Officers Association

2033 Sixth Ave., #804, Seattle WA 98121
441-6020
People at all levels in nonprofits—from volunteers and board members to executive directors—attend the meetings of this local organization. Nonmembers are welcome at the meetings, which attract as many as 140, and can also receive a three-month subscription to the job bulletin.

Northwest EcoBuilding Guild

217 Ninth Ave. N., Seattle WA 98109
622-8350
Sponsored by the Sustainable Design Council, this new group had about 150 members at press time and was developing chapters in Olympia, Bellingham and Portland. Includes contractors, designers, engineers and suppliers interested in ecologically sustainable building practices. Monthly meeting topics have included "Healthful and Recycled-Content Building Materials," "Resource-Efficient Construction" and "Indoor Air Quality." Many members are self-employed and use the networking period for business development.

Northwest Ethics Institute

Contact: Ray Cole, 623-1572
Organized about seven years ago, this local group offers monthly programs on such topics as government, the environment and business and medical ethics. The 90 members include educators, attorneys and accountants as well as those who work in business and health care. There is no job bank and the group does not focus on jobs in any particular industry. Nonmembers can request copies of the newsletter.

Northwest Florists' Association

P.O. Box C-2016, Edmonds WA 98020-0999
778-6162
Nearly 500 retail and wholesale florists and growers from five western states and two provinces are represented in this group, which holds an annual convention and issues a quarterly magazine.

Northwest Human Resource Management Association

Formerly the Pacific Northwest Personnel Management Association. Part of the national Society for Human Resource Management. Includes attorneys and consultants as well as those who work in recruiting, organizational development and corporate personnel in general.

Northwest Human Resource Management Association, Seattle Chapter

Contact: Mary Latham, ADIA, 220 Blanchard, Seattle WA 98121
Hotline: 283-0395
Membership: 750.

Northwest Human Resource Management Association, Lake Washington Chapter
P.O. Box 70305, Bellevue WA 98007
Contact: Shelly Rasmussen, 885-4353
Membership: 300.

Northwest Human Resource Management Association, Snohomish County Chapter
P.O. Box 2992, Everett WA 98203
Contact: Mary Summers, 828-2307 or Calene Jensen, 347-3995
Membership: 100.

Northwest Human Resource Management Association, Tacoma-Olympia
Contact: (Mr.) Le Perry, 586-0052 or Rik Lerbakken, 584-2637
Membership: 200.

Northwest Human Resource Management Association, South King County
Contact: Alesa McCory, 874-2235
Membership: 70.

Northwest Marine Trade Association
1900 N. Northlake Way, #233, Seattle WA 98103
634-0911
If you work in boating, consider this nonprofit, which was founded nearly 50 years ago and now has about 1,000 members. Some are large—for example, boatbuilders Bayliner and Tollycraft—but many are small. You must be affiliated with the marine industry to belong.

Northwest Minority Supplier Development Council
Contact: Clyde Merriweather, 657-6225
If you represent a minority-owned business, consider membership in this group, which allows business owners to network with prospective corporate customers. Membership: 300. Meets monthly. The council also sponsors trade shows and workshops.

Northwest Telemarketing Association
Contacts: Tom Boyd, 640-2004, Linde West, 389-4014, or David Sutton, 775-9164
Attracts 45-60 to quarterly workshops, which have covered such topics as compensation, recruitment, training and motivation and communications. Members include call center directors, inside sales managers, customer service managers and representatives of the state attorney general's office.

Northwest Translators and Interpreters Society
P.O. Box 25301, Seattle WA 98125-2201
Hotline: 382-5642
Bulletin board: 328-6138
Established in 1988. Membership: about 200. Affiliated with the American Translators Association. Objectives include continuing education for working translators, maintaining standards of professionalism and establishing a medium for collaboration among translators and interpreters. Meets about every six weeks.

Mentoring those new to the field is another focus. Its all-day workshops attract participants from as far away as Colorado. Members are listed in a directory that is distributed to agencies and businesses that hire translators and interpreters. Nonmembers can receive the newsletter by subscription ($10). Job opportunities are announced at meetings and on the bulletin board.

Norwegian-American Chamber of Commerce
Hotline: 521-8227
Interested in trade between Washington and Norway? Then consider this group of more than 200, which meets about every six weeks. Speakers include Europeans visiting the U.S. on business. There are also "business after hours" networking sessions. The directory is issued only to members. Contact: Marilyn Whitted, 682-5250, Ext. 214.

Office Support Services Association
Contact Carol Barden, 454-3077 or Carolyn Lacy, 453-1312
Established some 70 years ago, this locally chartered organization has about 35 members, most self-employed. They provide office support services, including word processing, desktop publishing and bookkeeping. Nonmembers can attend two monthly meetings prior to joining.

Pacific Corridor Economics Council (PACE)
720 Olive Way, #1300, Seattle WA 98101
626-5473
(800) 800-PACE
A tri-lateral business council (the U.S., Canada and Mexico) supported by the private sector that organizes forums and provides information on cross-border business. Members include entrepreneurs, bankers, attorneys and tax experts. Nonmembers can attend meetings by arrangement.

Pacific Northwest Association of Church Libraries
P.O. Box 12379, Seattle WA 98111
If you work in a church or religious school's library, whether on a volunteer or paid basis, you're welcome at meetings of this group, which has about 100 members in its Seattle chapter alone. Other Washington chapters include Tacoma, Yakima, Wenatchee, Tri-Cities, Spokane and the Portland-Vancouver area. Contact Nancy Young, 641-4571 or Arlene Nelson, treasurer, 747-1438.

Pacific Northwest Association of Church Libraries, Tacoma-Area Chapter
Contact: Sharone Ketterman, 848-3167
Membership: 25.

Pacific Northwest Booksellers Association
1510 Mill St., Eugene OR 97401-4258
(503) 683-4363
Thom Chambliss is the executive director of this trade association of bookstore owners in Alaska, Washington, Oregon, Idaho and Montana. Also includes publishers, distributors, librarians, reviewers and writers. Members: as many as 600. Membership benefits include a directory and monthly newsletter. The group sponsors spring and fall trade shows, where booksellers (and prospective booksellers) can visit publisher exhibits and attend seminars.

Pacific Northwest Historians Guild

P.O. Box 45687, Seattle WA 98145
Contact: Junius Rochester, 860-2153
Historians, archivists and librarians are among the 100-plus members of this group. Speakers occasionally address job opportunities in the field; informal networking is also encouraged. Nonmembers are welcome.

Pacific Northwest Hungarian-American Chamber of Commerce

Contact: Helen Szablya, Hungarian Consul, 643-0563
Founded in 1992 to encourage trade with Hungary, this growing group is working on such projects as the 1996 world's fair planned in Hungary.

Pacific Northwest Library Association

Contact: Katherine G. Eaton, *PNLA Quarterly* Editor, 1631 E. 24th St., Eugene OR 97403
Jobline: 543-2890
This regional group serves five western states and two provinces. Membership: 800. Its jobline at the University of Washington Graduate School of Library and Information Science lists opportunities for professionals and paraprofessionals in public, academic and corporate libraries in the western U.S. and Canada. A recent PNLA president also advises that librarians in the job market read such national publications as *LJ Hotline*, because many libraries conduct national searches for professional positions.

Pacific Northwest Newspaper Association

P.O. Box 11128, Tacoma WA 98411
272-3611
This trade association represents 58 daily papers in six western states and two provinces. Its bulletins to publishers include free extracts of resumes from those seeking jobs or internships. Simply send your resume to the association and its staff will summarize your qualifications and objective.

Pacific Northwest Organization Development Network

Contact: Pat Christianson, Staff Administrator, 365-3418
Part of a national, this chapter was established in 1988. Membership: more than 200 in Washington and Oregon. Members, many self-employed, include process, quality and organizational development consultants, internal consultants, trainers and human resources staff members. There's a mentorship program for students and those new to the field. Bimonthly meetings. The directory is only for members, but mailing lists can be purchased.

Pacific Northwest PC Users Group

P.O. Box 3363, Bellevue WA 98004
728-7075
Some 1,000—from Everett to Tacoma—belong to this group. Nonmembers are welcome. There are also 40 SIGs, most of which meet at least monthly. You'll find both "Positions Wanted" and "Positions Available" on the club's electronic bulletin board; "Positions Available" are also mentioned in the club newsletter.

Planning Forum, Puget Sound Chapter
Contact: Terry van der Werff, 364-4142 or Peter Spurging, 889-5805
Affiliated with the International Society for Strategic Management and Planning. Membership: 60. Includes consultants and managers with primary responsibility for strategic planning and implementation. Meeting topics range from environmental risk management and new product development to best management practices. Nonmembers welcome.

Professional Environmental Marketing Association, Puget Sound Chapter
P.O. Box 717, Seattle WA 98111
455-3680
"Selling Consulting Services, "Trends in Environmental Legislation" and "Doing Business with Government" are examples of recent programs for this group, which includes business development managers and marketing coordinators for firms in the environmental industry. Other members are attorneys, accountants and public relations agencies that serve environmental consultants. Membership: about 180. The monthly newsletter includes an "Employment Connection" where "Positions Wanted" and "Positions Available" can be listed for a nominal fee (nonmembers can use this service for a slightly higher fee).

Professional Geographers of Puget Sound
401 E. Mercer, #22, Seattle WA 98102
Established about three years ago, this local organization serves geographers from Everett to Olympia who work in government (about half of the membership), research, consulting and such related fields as banking. Although you don't need a geography degree to join, most members have studied the field either as undergraduates or graduate students. Membership: 98. The quarterly newsletter has a jobs column with current openings. The association also allows members to have their resumes inserted with newsletters. Nonmembers can receive one complimentary newsletter. Dues are $12. Call Eric Friedli, 684-8369 or Carlyn Orians, 528-3320.

Professional Secretaries International, Seattle Sacajawea Chapter
Contact: Doris Heistuman-Box, 764-5371
If you work as a secretary or in a similar support role, you're welcome at PSI, which provides education and networking for those making careers as secretaries. The downtown Seattle chapter, which has about 70 members, includes men and women. Services include a job bank.

Professional Secretaries International, Lake Washington East Chapter
Contact: Peggy Knudson, 936-8769 or Lisa Renshaw, 454-6363, Ext. 2224
Membership: 50 members.

Professional Secretaries International, Mount Rainier Chapter
Contact: Lila Licens, 924-3343
Membership: 27. Sponsors student chapters.

Professional Secretaries International, Washington Evergreen Chapter
Contact: Sharon Neilsen, 655-4504
Membership: 30, many of them Boeing employees.

Propeller Club of the United States, Port of Seattle Chapter

Contact: Marine Exchange of Puget Sound, 2701 First Ave., #110, Seattle WA
98121-1123
443-3830
This chapter of an international for the maritime industry has about 300 members.
The meetings attract everyone from accountants and insurance underwriters to
those who manufacture nuts and bolts for ships. The group sponsors Seattle's
annual Maritime Week festivities each May. Nonmembers welcome.

Public Relations Society of America

217 Ninth N., Seattle WA 98109
623-8632
The Puget Sound chapter has more than 350 members. To join, you must be
employed in a professional position in the public relations field. However,
nonmembers are welcome at the luncheons and at professional development
workshops. The day-long "PR Primer" is especially appropriate for people at the
entry level. For a $30 fee, nonmembers can use the jobline cosponsored by the
IABC chapters and the Washington Press Association.

Puget Sound Career Development Association

203 Bellevue Way, #345, Bellevue WA 98004
Started in the 1980s, this local group of about 100 includes career counselors, job
placement specialists and those who work in vocational rehabilitation and
outplacement. Many members are self-employed; others work in Y's, social
service agencies and in school and college placement centers. No eligibility
requirements. Meetings attract about 40. A newsletter is published regularly.
Contact Julie Mellen, 454-1280 or Jennifer Johnson, 455-0585.

Puget Sound Engineering Council

Composed of representatives from 25-plus engineering and technical societies,
this group organizes events like the annual Engineering Fair to promote engineering and math to schoolchildren. It's also active in legislative affairs. Of interest
to job-seekers is the council's newsletter, "Puget Sound Engineering," which
announces the activities of many engineering societies. Available by subscription
for $12 a year: write P.O. Box 7372-P, Seattle WA 98133.

Puget Sound Freelancers Association

Contact: Art Hanlon, 780-1629
A special interest group of the Society for Technical Communication. As many as
20—mostly technical writers and illustrators—attend the monthly meetings. No
dues. Speakers often discuss business topics; for example, how to obtain contracts.

Puget Sound Grantwriters Association

260 N.E. 43rd, Seattle WA 98105
Contact: Susan Howlett, 545-8509
Establishing and maintain liaisons with grantmakers is one of the functions of this
group, which has about 700 members. Some are free-lance grantwriters, others
work for nonprofits. At the bimonthly meetings, job openings are announced. If
you're a grantwriter, you can also have your name added to a list that is sent to
prospective employers upon their request; cost: dues ($30 per year) plus a $25 fee.

Puget Sound Research Forum
P.O. Box 12796, Seattle WA 98111
Contact: Rob Coughlin, Pacific Rim Resources, 623-0232
Started by market researchers, this group now represents both the public and
private sectors. Membership: 120. Student dues, $20; full memberships, $30.

Robotics International, Society of Manufacturing Engineers
Contact: Mary Lynch, P.O. Box 872, Issaquah WA 98027
391-5379
Includes engineers and engineering managers, manufacturing supervisors and
designers; employers represented include the underwater warfare station at Keyport,
Hanford, Boeing and PACCAR. Nonmembers and students welcome.

Seattle Area Computer-Aided Publishers
P.O. Box 40134, Bellevue WA 98015-4134
SEACAP's 50 members range from magazine art directors and corporate desktop
publishers to newsletter publishers and service bureaus. Many work in corporate
marketing departments. Both Mac and PC users are represented. You can receive
the newsletter free for three months; a year's subscription is $15. For more
information, call Lynn Mead at 271-9717 or check the *Puget Sound Computer User*
calendar.

Seattle Association of Women Economists
Contact: Elizabeth Morrison, 283-0634
If you're interested in economics, you're welcome at the meetings of this locally-
chartered group, which has about 30 members. Job openings are announced at
meetings and in the monthly newsletter. The newsletter and directory are sent only
to members; annual dues are $10.

Seattle Design Association
P.O. Box 1097 Main Branch, Seattle WA 98111
448-5251
Graphic designers, illustrators, photographers, copywriters, printers, production
managers, architects, interior designers and fine artists are welcome to join this
group of 200. Newsletters are sent to members.

Seattle Direct Marketing Association
217 Ninth N., Seattle WA 98109
623-8632
Direct response marketing and telemarketing are the focus of this group of 150,
which meets monthly and conducts an annual seminar. Meetings are announced in
Marketing. There's also a monthly newsletter.

Seattle Economists Club
P.O. Box 1113, Fall City WA 98024
467-8404
Economists from business, utilities and government join economic consultants and
academics in this group, which has about 150 members. Nonmembers are
welcome. Resumes of job-seekers can be inserted with the monthly meeting
notices ($10 fee for nonmembers). Openings are occasionally announced at
meetings. Dues: $20.

Seattle Professional Photographers Association
Contact: Eric Droz, 745-0698
About 50 commercial, architectural and portrait photographers—most self-employed—belong to this group, an affiliate of the Professional Photographers of Washington and the Professional Photographers of America. Nonmembers are welcome at the monthly meetings.

Seattle Storytellers' Guild
P.O. Box 45532, Seattle WA 98145-0532
621-8646
Professional and amateur storytellers as well as those interested in the art are among the 400-plus members of this locally chartered group, which draws most of its membership from King, Snohomish and Pierce counties. If you'd like to promote yourself as a storyteller, the group also compiles a directory for distribution to schools and libraries. Open to nonmembers. Dues are about $15.

School Health Association of Washington
22323 Pacific Highway S., Seattle WA 98198
An affiliate of the American School Health Association, this chapter has about 350 members statewide. Members include school health educators, nurses and counselors as well as representatives of nonprofits and social service agencies. Two conferences are held each year; nonmembers are welcome and there's ample opportunity to network. Dues are $15. Call Karen Dalton, executive director, 824-2907.

Service Quality Network
Contact: Barbara Emmons, 956-5838
If you'd like to network with state employees, consider this group. Established in 1991, it emphasizes the continuous improvement of services by streamlining processes and focusing on customer needs. Attracts 75-150 to monthly meetings in Olympia; members represent state and municipal government, with a few from the private sector. No dues. Meetings are usually announced in the calendar published by the state personnel office. Or call Ms. Emmons for the new member packet.

Small Business Action Council, Greater Seattle Chamber of Commerce
Contact: Susan Meadows, 389-7246
A dozen roundtables are organized by this arm of the chamber; two of particular interest to readers of this book are Women In Business and Micro Business. Both are open only to members of the Seattle chamber. Meeting dates are announced in the chamber newsletter. Women In Business has two groups: one meets afternoons, the other evenings. Founded in 1993, the sessions attract as many as 30. The Micro Business group, which includes many home-based businesses, meets monthly.

Society for Intercultural Education, Training and Research, Cascadia Chapter
8236 23rd Ave. N.E., Seattle WA 98115
Open to anyone with an interest in the Pacific Rim or intercultural communication. Meetings and workshops often attract 30-50. Many of the founding members were

teachers of English As A Second Language; current members also work in diversity training and cross-cultural communication. Meeting topics include business development. The SIETAR newsletter is available to nonmembers by subscription. Contact Albertine Smit, 523-3711 or Mary Tatone, 277-9534.

Society for Marketing Professional Services, Seattle Chapter
Contact: Diane Kinman, 232-9583 or Kathy Beckley, 623-5736
For those who'd like to market professional services, especially for architectural, engineering or interior design firms.

Society for Public Health Education, Pacific Northwest Chapter
P.O. Box 24973, Seattle WA 98124-0973
One of 20 U.S. chapters, this group welcomes you to its meetings if you're pursuing or have received a degree in health education or a related field (for example, nursing or dietetics), or if you work in health education or promotion.

Society for Technical Communications, Puget Sound Chapter
217 Ninth N., Seattle WA 98109
623-8632
If you work in technical communications—writing, editing, graphic design or illustration—you can ask that your resume be included in the STC chapter's resume book, which is available for review by firms with openings. Or, for $25, you can access the STC jobline. One reminder: most jobs in technical communications require some computer knowledge and a background in at least one technical field (for example, computer science, engineering or medicine). Nonmembers can receive a complimentary three-month subscription to the newsletter. You're also welcome at meetings. Membership: about 500.

Society of Architectural Administrators
Contact: Michelle Wyden, Dodd Pacific, 682-1500 or Linda Flynn, NBBJ, 223-5555
If you're interested in working in the design profession in a support role, consider this group. One of the largest SAA chapters, it has about 50 members representing architectural, engineering, interior design and cost estimating firms in western Washington. Nonmembers are welcome.

Society of Government Meeting Planners, Pacific Northwest Chapter
1812 S. E. 166th Pl., Seattle WA 98166
227-2127
Making government meetings more productive and cost-effective is one of the goals of this group, founded on the national level in 1981. The 85 local members include government meeting planners, contract planners, suppliers (for example, hotels) and educators and students. Eligibility requirements for membership; nonmembers welcome at meetings.

Society of Medical Interpreters
c/o Cross-Cultural Health Care Program
Pacific Medical Center, 1200 12th Ave. S, Seattle WA 98144
Established in 1993 for interpreters who work in medical and social service settings. This group helps establish standards for interpreters and provides training. Quarterly general meetings. Most members have high levels of expertise

in both language and culture; many work as independent contractors. Contact: Martine Pierre-Louis, 328-2850.

Society of Plastics Engineers, Pacific Northwest Chapter
P.O. Box 88929, Seattle WA 98138
Membership: nearly 400. Most members work in manufacturing; some hold jobs in distribution or design. About half are engineers. Contact Laura Turner, 284-9963.

Society of Professional Journalists, Western Washington Chapter
217 Ninth N., Seattle WA 98109
623-8632
Nonmembers are welcome at meetings of this chapter of 200.

Society of Women Engineers, Pacific Northwest Section
P.O. Box 31910, Seattle WA 98103
Contact: Laura Ritzow, 342-2115 or Sandra Schaffer, 644-4010
Such educational programs as "Math Counts" and "Expanding Your Horizons" are two projects of this organization, which serves 145 women who work in engineering. Its mission: interesting more women in engineering. All engineering disciplines are represented in the group, which also offers a speakers bureau for elementary through high school classes.

Special Libraries Association, Pacific Northwest Chapter
P.O. Box 127, Seattle WA 98111
Contact: Laura Lipton, 543-0415
Corporate, nonprofit, specialized academic and government libraries are represented in this group, which serves those librarians who do not work in public or general academic libraries. Serves Washington, Oregon, Idaho, Montana, Alaska and parts of British Columbia. Membership: about 350, nearly all librarians or library students. No placement help for professionals, but there is a student liaison coordinator and each year the chapter co-sponsors a student night with the American Society of Information Scientists.

Structural Engineers Association of Washington
P.O. Box 4250, Seattle WA 98104
682-6026
Providing education and promoting the engineering profession are two missions of this organization, which has 675 members and three chapters in the state. The Seattle chapter serves King County and north; the Southwest chapter Tacoma and south. Most members are in private practice.

Successor's
Contact: Ann Copeland, 566-1611
About 20 Tacoma women attend the twice monthly meetings in University Place of this informal networking and referral group. No dues, no formal membership, no newsletter. Most members are self-employed; they range from doctors and accountants to a career counselor, a financial planner and an Avon salesperson.

Swedish-American Chamber of Commerce

Contact Leif Larsson, Crown Travel, 462-0666

Encouraging trade between Sweden and the U.S. is the primary mission of this group, part of a national. There are 42 corporate members in addition to individual and student members. You can network at luncheons and the "business after hours" functions; members can also use the directory.

Washington Association for the Education of Young Children

827 N. Central Ave., #106, Kent WA 98032

854-2565

Part of the National Association for the Education of Young Children, which supports those who educate and care for children from birth to age 8. Members include day care providers and directors and those who teach in preschools and elementary schools. There are 20 "affiliates" in the state; they range in size from 175 to 300 members. For information on your affiliate, call the state office.

Washington Association for Financial Planning

217 Ninth N., Seattle WA 98109

623-8632

This group emphasizes education for financial planners. Offers four symposiums each year; nonmembers are welcome. Membership: about 200.

Washington Association of Health Underwriters

(800) 995-2024, 236-3214

If you work in insurance, especially in individual or group health insurance or disability, you'll find this association of interest. Statewide membership: about 400. Two chapters in the Puget Sound area. To reach the chapter in your area, call the numbers below or contact the state office.

King County Health Underwriters

Contact: Jan Chapman, 226-2953 or Dave McNichols, 443-2505

Membership: about 200.

Southwest Washington Association of Health Underwriters

P.O. Box 196, Tacoma WA 98401-0196

Contact: Steve Williams, 582-8302 or Nancy Giacolone, 272-2228.

Membership: 90. Serves those south of King County and north of Lewis County.

Washington Association of Landscape Professionals

P.O. Box 729, Mercer Island WA 98040

236-1707

This group, which includes about 200 landscape contractors, designers and suppliers, now has chapters; in the Puget Sound area, they include North Puget Sound, serving Seattle and Everett, and South Puget Sound, serving Pierce and Thurston counties. For chapter meeting information, call the state office.

Washington Association of Marriage and Family Therapy

217 Ninth N., Seattle WA 98109

623-1820

Education is the primary goal of this group, which has 500 members. Most are self-employed, although a few work for institutes. A chapter of the American Association of Marriage and Family Therapy.

Washington Association of Personnel Services
P.O. Box 129, Bellevue WA 98009
If you work in personnel placement, either permanent or temporary, or as an executive recruiter, you may be interested in this affiliate of the National Association of Personnel Services. Membership is corporate. Meetings attract 50 to 100. Contact Dave Salzberg, 455-2141.

Washington Biotechnology & Biomedical Association
P.O. Box 58786, Renton WA 98058
235-5154
Organized to promote the continued growth of the biotechnology industry in this state, the WBBA includes about 110 corporate members. Student memberships are also available. Many focus groups, including some that are also affiliated with other professional associations. A resume database may be operating by early 1995. Executive director: Sue Charrier.

Washington Community College Mathematics Conference
Contact: Doug Mooers, Whatcom Community College, 676-2170, Ext. 285
An event, rather than a group, this conference has been held annually since the 1960s. The 1995 session will be hosted by Whatcom Community College. No officers and no mailing address; the community college math departments rotate the responsibility for organizing the meeting. An excellent place to network with college math teachers and learn of job openings. No eligibility requirements.

Washington Council on International Trade
2615 Fourth Ave., Seattle WA 98121
443-3826
If you want to work with international trade policies (perhaps as an executive in governmental affairs or international sales and marketing), consider this group, which has 200 corporate members and about the same number of individual members, including students and academics. The council also mails two free publications: "Some Thoughts on Looking for Jobs in the International Sector," by Dr. Robert Kapp, and "Tools of the Trade: A Directory of International Trade Organizations in Washington State."

Washington Film and Video Association
217 Ninth N., Seattle WA 98109
623-8632
A locally-chartered organization of 200, this group serves free-lancers in film and video production. Nonmembers are welcome; the directory is distributed only to members. The bimonthly newsletter is available upon request.

Washington Home Economics Association
Contact: Diane Grossenbacher, 6911 189th Pl. S. W., Lynnwood WA 98036
778-7147
Affiliated with the American Home Economics Association. Membership: 380. They include cooperative extension agents, teachers, fabric store owners and day

care center operators as well as people who work in commodity commissions, communications and other businesses. Active membership requires a degree in home economics and employment in the field; other membership categories are open to students, graduates of other college programs, graduates of associate programs and home ec graduates who work part-time. Chapters in King and Pierce counties; call for contact names.

Washington Library Association
747-6917
An affiliate of the American Library Association. Membership: about 1,300. Open to everyone who works in a library as well as students and members of Friends of the Library groups.

Washington Library Media Association
Contact: Barbara Baker, treasurer, P.O. Box 1413, Bothell WA 98041
About 1,200 elementary and secondary school librarians belong to this group, which has five "regions" (chapters) in the Puget Sound area. The treasurer can refer you to your closest region.

Washington Mathematical Association of Two-Year Colleges
Contact: Paul Casillas, Math-Science Department, Clark College, 694-6521
An affiliate of the American Mathematical Association of Two-Year Colleges, this group includes those who teach math in the state's community colleges. There's an annual meeting, a directory and a newsletter. Membership is $5.

Washington Medical Librarians Association
Contact: Marcia Batchelor, Madigan Army Medical Center, 968-0118
A local group of about 100, WMLA has an annual meeting where programs occasionally focus on the job market. One association member describes this field as "very competitive," with many jobs part-time.

Washington Museum Association
Contact: Ellen Ferguson, 543-5115
The 250 members of this group include volunteers and representatives of both small and large museums across the state. You must be a member (dues are $20) to attend the two annual functions. A resource available from the WMA is its "Directory of Museums of Washington State," with more than 400 entries; the cost is $13.95 to nonmembers.

Washington Newspaper Publishers Association
3838 Stone Way N., Seattle WA 98103
634-3838
Want to work on a newspaper? WNPA, which represents 135 community newspapers (most of them weeklies), includes brief summaries of resumes from jobseekers in its newsletter, sent to newspaper publishers every month. To have your qualifications and career objective listed, contact WNPA for its resume form. There's no charge.

Washington Organization of Nurse Executives
190 Queen Anne Ave. N., Third Floor, Seattle WA 98109
285-0102
Serves nurses who are executives, managers and other administrators in hospitals, long-term care facilities, public health, universities and risk management. For specifics on the council in your area, call Karen Haase-Herrik. Note: WONE cannot provide information on licensing requirements; you must contact the Washington State Board of Nursing, 753-2686.

Washington Press Association
217 Ninth N., Seattle WA 98109
623-8632
A statewide group with about 150 members. Primarily serves writers: journalists, publicists and free-lancers. Participates with the IABC chapters and PRSA on a jobline, open to nonmembers for $30. The jobline fee also entitles you to attend the monthly job bank meetings. Each spring there are print and broadcast media forums that can introduce you to local media figures.

Washington Recreation and Park Association
350 S. 333rd St., #103, Federal Way WA 98003
874-1283
Both parks and recreation departments and individuals are among the 1,200 members of this group, which provides several services for job-seekers. The monthly newsletter includes a "jobs" section and there are job boards at the two annual conferences. You can also network at workshops held throughout the year. Nonmembers can attend all programs (there's a slightly higher fee); to receive the newsletter, you can join as a student ($20) or associate ($25). You need not be a state resident to join.

Washington School Public Relations Association
Contact: Mary Wagoner, Wenatchee School District, (509) 663-8161 or Jackie Smith, Renton School District, 235-2441
An affiliate of the National School Public Relations Association. About 100 members statewide.

Washington Society of Certified Public Accountants
902 140th Ave. N.E., Bellevue WA 98005-3480
644-4800
Jobline: 641-4832
An affiliate of the American Institute of Certified Public Accountants. Fifteen chapters and 8,000-plus members. About half the members work in public accounting. For information about Puget Sound chapters, contact John Mix, chapter relations director.

Washington Software Association
10940 N.E. 33rd Pl., #206, Bellevue WA 98004
889-8880
Jobline: 889-8880, Ext. 3
The WSA has more than 375 corporate industry members in addition to supplier, individual and student members. To learn more about the software industry in this

area (reportedly it's the third largest software center in the country, second only to Silicon Valley and Route 128), you can attend meetings and any of the 15 SIGs: topics range from technical support and object-oriented programming to human resources and finance and operations. For information about SIGs, call Barb Cummelin, the WSA's programs manager. Students can ask about the chapter at the University of Washington. There's also an Inland Northwest chapter serving Spokane.

Washington Speech and Hearing Association
2033 Sixth Ave., Seattle WA 98121
441-6020
If you're a speech pathologist or audiologist, consider this group, which has 900 members statewide, divided into six regions.

Washington State Association of Black Professionals in Health Care
1110 Lake Washington Blvd. S., Seattle WA 98144
Includes more than 450 doctors, dentists, social workers, nurses, educators and other health care professionals. Meets quarterly. A spin-off is Blacks in Science, a project to encourage black children's participation in the sciences. For more information, contact Millie Russell, secretary of the WSABPHC and finance officer for Blacks in Science.

Washington State Association of Broadcasters
924 Capitol Way S., #104, Olympia WA 98501
705-0774
An organization for broadcast stations, this group provides such station services as help with broadcast license renewals and lobbying. It also maintains a "job bank" list of openings at member stations across the state; call Mark Allen to discuss current opportunities.

Washington State Association of Life Underwriters
4201 Roosevelt Way, #206, Seattle WA 98105
632-4330
If you're a life insurance agent, consider this group, part of the National Association of Life Underwriters. It has 2,200 members across the state; the Puget Sound area has seven chapters. The Seattle chapter (see below) has its own office. Information on these following chapters is available from the state office: Snohomish (serving Snohomish County), Cascade (serving Bellevue, Redmond and Kirkland), Rainier (serving south King County and north Pierce County), Tacoma, Olympic Peninsula and Southwest (serving Thurston County).

Seattle Association of Life Underwriters
P.O. Box 99266, Seattle WA 98199
623-9265
This group has some 550 members. Most are life and health insurance brokers and agents. About 40 per cent are self-employed. Nonmembers are welcome at meetings. There are also regular continuing education programs.

Washington State Bar Association
2001 Sixth Ave., Fourth Floor, Seattle WA 98121-2599
727-8203
Jobline: 727-8261
Both resumes and notices of openings for attorneys are kept in notebooks in the
foyer of the bar association office. You can consult the book weekdays between
8 and 4:30. To submit your resume, mail it to "Resume Service," Communications
Department. The jobline carries only positions for attorneys; no managerial,
paraprofessional or support positions.

American Culinary Federation, Washington State Chefs' Association
Hotline: 725-1545
Nonmembers are welcome at most meetings of this group, which has 300 members,
mostly between Mount Vernon and Olympia. They work in catering, restaurants
and hotels, health care and educational institutions, clubs and airlines. There's an
apprenticeship chair to help those entering the industry. At meetings, you can also
introduce yourself and describe your job objective.

Washington State Court Interpreters and Translators Society
P.O. Box 1012, Seattle WA 98111
382-5690
Established in 1988. Locally chartered. Includes 150 who work (most on a free-
lance basis) in many settings, including law. The purpose: education and standards. No eligibility requirements for membership, although the chapter's mission
statement clarifies that the court interpreter and translator is a specially trained
professional, as distinguished from someone who simply speaks two languages.
Nonmembers are welcome at meetings, held five or six times annually. No job
bank or clearinghouse, but postings regarding job openings are sometimes circulated to members and prospective clients can be informally referred to members
working with a particular language.

Washington State Dental Hygienists Association
P.O. Box 389, Lynnwood WA 98046
771-3201
There's no formal job bank in this organization of 1,100, but networking takes
place at the local level. There are 14 component societies in the state, including
groups in Seattle, Snohomish County, the Eastside, Tacoma, South King County,
Kitsap County, Olympia and the Olympic peninsula. Call the state office for
information on the society in your area.

Washington State Hispanic Chamber of Commerce
P.O. Box 24623, Seattle WA 98124
340-1556
Part of the U.S. Hispanic Chamber of Commerce, this group was founded in 1983.
It now includes 100 firms, both small businesses and large corporations. You need
not be Hispanic to join.

Washington State Paralegal Association
(800) 288-WSPA
Jobline: 938-4355
The state office, located in Spokane, can provide information on a chapter in your

area. The jobline lists upcoming Puget Sound events as well as job opportunities.

Washington State Tax Consultants, State Support Office
Contact: Roy Scruggs, P.O. Box 4097, Bremerton WA 98312
674-2552
If you're a tax preparer, whether self-employed or employed by a firm, you're welcome at this group, which has nearly 400 members in 16 chapters across the state.

Washington State Veterinary Medical Association
2050 112th N.E., #115, Bellevue WA 98004
454-8381
Veterinarians new to the Northwest can receive a sample copy of the association newsletter, which includes listings of both openings and people seeking work. New graduates of Northwest vet schools can request a complimentary six-month subscription.

Washington Women in International Trade
P.O. Box 1136, Seattle WA 98111
Contact: M. Martha Ries, Bogle & Gates, 621-1517
Affiliated with the Organization of Women in International Trade, this group has about 180 members, including customs brokers, attorneys, accountants, importers, exporters and freight forwarders. Nonmembers welcome.

Washington Women in Timber
Contact: Kristin Butterfield, 943-7631
Includes natural resource attorneys, governmental affairs specialists, foresters and those who work in family-owned forest products companies. Its purpose is education—especially public education about forest management. Statewide, about 200 members.

Washington Women Lawyers
P.O. Box 25444, Seattle WA 98125
622-5585
Chartered to further the integration of women in the legal profession and to promote equal opportunities for women, this statewide group has nine chapters. All meet regularly. Members include attorneys and those working in related fields, legislators, bar association officials and law students. Both men and women are eligible for membership. Job openings sent to the state office are also listed on the office voice mail. For the contact in your area, call Tiffanie Kilmer, state executive director.

Women and Mathematics
Contact: Sara Selfe, 543-7835
Affiliated with the Mathematical Association of America, WAM has about 15 chapters across the U.S. Its members strive to help children recognize the importance of math. WAM has no regular meetings; instead, men and women who work in math, science, computer science and engineering volunteer as mentors and speakers.

Women Business Owners
217 Ninth N., Seattle WA 98109
624-4075
Established in 1979. Membership: 150. Nonmembers are welcome at meetings and functions; full membership requires that you have an equity position in a business and a state business license.

Women Entrepreneurs Network
P.O. Box 3522, Bellevue WA 98009
340-1679
This group is for women who have—or want—their own businesses. The meetings are designed to provide support and information, especially for the many one-person firms represented. Nonmembers welcome.

Women In Communications, Inc.
217 Ninth N., Seattle WA 98109
623-8632
For women in all areas of communications—journalism, advertising, public relations and marketing. Meetings are open to everyone, although the job bank is reserved for members. Membership: about 250.

Women in Engineering
101 Wilson Annex, Mailstop FC-08, University of Washington, Seattle WA 98195
543-4810
Under this title, the UW holds an annual conference, a one-day session each April that provides students, faculty and professionals with professional development and opportunities to network, explore career options and form mentor relationships. Many of those attending work in engineering, although students from the sciences are encouraged to participate. Attracts as many as 250 from a 14-state region. Sponsored by the Women in Engineering Initiative, a UW program founded to help women and minorities pursue engineering careers. The office also sponsors other programs open to the public. For example, "Discover Engineering," a free, one-day winter session offered in conjunction with the Freshman Intervention Project which explains the variety of careers available in engineering. Appropriate for teenagers; for a schedule, call the number above. The Community College Bridge Program, held in cooperation with five local community colleges, helps lower-division students explore and evaluate engineering careers.

Women In Film/Seattle
2318 Second Ave., #348-A, Seattle WA 98121
Hotline: 477-1537
Chartered in 1990, this chapter of a national now has about 100 local members. They work in motion pictures, broadcast television and video, as producers and directors, screenwriters, post-production editors and supervisors and production assistants. Some do corporate work; others make documentaries, commercials or features. Membership requires three years paid experience in the field. Nonmembers can attend many events. Besides screenings of members' work and talks by women filmmakers there are seminars on business and technical topics.

Women's Business Exchange
382-1234
This organization of business people encourages business and personal growth through networking, professional education, leadership training and mentoring. Nonmembers welcome. Offers a monthly career support group.

Women's Fisheries Network
Contact: Christy Suelzle, administrator, 742-2810
Members work in fishing, processing, cold storage and equipment as well as in financial services, insurance, government and education. Nonmembers welcome.

Women's Food Industry Network
P.O. Box 58687, Seattle WA 98138
Contact: JoAnne Gallagher, 413-1422
Founded in 1989, this local organization has about 75 members from Olympia to Bellingham. They work in hotels and restaurants, as dieticians, food brokers and manufacturers, and as equipment dealers. Its mission: to support women in an industry that has traditionally been male-dominated. No formal job-search programs, but the organization provides scholarships for women returning to school and each meeting begins with an introduction period, where job-seekers can describe their goals.

Women's Math Network
Contact: Vicky Ringen, 528-4511
An informal group with no official name, this includes women who teach math or computer science at the college level in the Puget Sound area. Through it women new to the area may learn of part-time teaching jobs at two or four-year colleges. Responsibility for organizing meetings is rotated; for information, call a community college math department and ask for a woman instructor.

Women's Transportation Seminar
Contact: Judy Leslie, 464-7079 or Marjorie Press, 382-5216
One of 27 chapters of a national, this group of 180 men and women includes transportation professionals and others concerned about transportation. The local chapter's focus is on "people moving," with many members working in transit engineering and transportation planning. Meetings open to nonmembers.

World Affairs Council
515 Madison St., #501, Seattle WA 98104
682-6986
Affiliated with the National Council of International Visitors, this group of 1,000 provides opportunities for international education. It regularly sponsors lectures by well-known policy-makers. You can network at the council's many special events and by volunteering in the council offices. Members can also host foreign visitors at meals and on sightseeing trips. The newsletter lists events sponsored by many local international groups. There's a special $15 student membership.

World Trade Club
P.O. Box 21488, Seattle WA 98111
448-8803
Nonmembers are welcome at this group of 600, which allows networking and

provides information about international business. There's a newsletter and directory for members and monthly educational meetings. Club members also organize "country forums." Some meet irregularly, others as often as monthly. These free programs, which may feature bankers, consultants and businesspeople working in import-export, are often mentioned in the club newsletter. Or call the club secretary for information.

World Trade Club of Snohomish County
c/o Port of Everett, P.O. Box 538, Everett WA 98206-0538
Established in 1990, includes bankers, freight forwarders, entrepreneurs, attorneys, manufacturers, educators and representatives of government agencies. Membership: about 50. Nonmembers are welcome at monthly meetings. Contact: Helen Hankwitz, 338-1985.

7. Temporary Agencies

Why temp through an agency? In many situations, that's how you get certain kinds of jobs—or jobs with particular employers. Some firms simply don't hire their temporary people directly; they don't use their personnel staff to recruit, interview and check references on those who provide extra help during rush projects or vacations. Other advantages of temping through agencies: you may not have to interview for each assignment (the agency will simply send you out); you can evaluate employers on a "no-obligation" basis while temping and decide whether to pursue any of the permanent jobs you see posted; and, if you work enough hours with a single agency, you may earn such benefits as health insurance, vacation pay and a 401(k) retirement account.

In general, there are three kinds of opportunities available through temp agencies. Temp assignments may be as short as four hours, often fill-in work for absent employees, rush work or special projects. "Temp-to-hire," sometimes called "temp-to-perm," means you start on a temporary basis, working for the agency, with the understanding that you might later be transferred to the employer's payroll, in a permanent position. Whether this transfer takes place may depend on how well you do your job and fit into the company—or whether the employer sees a need for (and can afford) another position. Finally, there are contract employees, people who usually work full-time, but only for a specified length of time. These are often project assignments such as the writing or translating of software documentation.

How can you work with an agency most successfully? Here's some suggestions from agency recruiters. You'll find more specific guidelines in *How to Get Hired for a Part-time or Temporary Job.*

First, appearance: be well-groomed (neat and clean), in attire appropriate for the job you seek.

Second, skip the scent. No perfume for women, no cologne or heavy after-shave for men. (Some recruiters—and some clients—have allergies.)

Third, show up for appointments and assignments—and show up on time.

Fourth, be able to articulate your objective; what do you want to do? Be prepared to discuss your skills and how they match the requirements of the jobs you seek.

Fifth, be honest. Your references will be checked and your degrees and work history may be verified.

Sixth, stay in touch with the agency. Let your contact person know when you're not available for work or if you're having difficulty with an assignment.

Most important, remember the agency works for the client. Don't undersell your abilities, but don't expect a recruiter to act as your personal agent.

Here are examples of the agencies that make placements in the Puget Sound area. For more contacts, see "Employment Agencies," "Employment Contractors-Temporary Help" and "Speakers' Bureaus" in your Yellow Pages.

Accountants On Call
601 Union St., #1665, Seattle WA 98101
467-0700
A division of ADIA, which also includes Accountants Executive Search, Nursefinders, Lee Hecht Harrison and ADIA Information Systems. Places on temp, temp-to-hire and permanent basis. Specializes in accounting personnel who usually make the annual equivalent of $25,000 or less. Typical positions: junior accountants, staff accountants, controllers and credit managers. A junior accountant, who need not have a degree, can make $8 an hour; a staff accountant, for which a degree and one to four years experience is ideal, can make $9 to $12. A controller, who needs an accounting degree and preferably a C.P.A., should expect about 75 per cent of what would be paid in the position if permanent—perhaps $10 to $15 an hour to start. To apply, call for an appointment; bring your resume and references to the interview and be prepared to be assigned quickly, sometimes within a week or two. You can interview at either the Seattle or Bellevue office and be placed from both.

AccounTemps/RHI Consulting
600 Stewart St., #800, Seattle WA 98101
443-8840
Divisions of Robert Half, which places clerical staff through its Office Team division. AccounTemps handles both temp and temp-to-hire. Typical positions: controllers, accountants, bookkeepers, collections and banking people. Requirements for the higher level positions: three years recent experience, spreadsheet management program skills (Lotus 1-2-3 and Excel) and the ability to motivate and manage staff. A C.P.A. and "Big 6" experience are preferred for controllers. What can you earn? A controller with a C.P.A. and three years experience working temp-to-hire might earn $35,000 to $40,000; on a temporary basis, expect $18 to $30 an hour. An accounting supervisor might make $15 to $18 an hour. Through the same office you can apply for work with RHI Consulting, which places people on a temp, contract and permanent basis in information technology. Positions might involve networks, mid-range to PC-driven. Typical positions: systems analyst, project managers, technical trainers and technical writers. RHI has a small but growing need for people bilingual in English and such languages as Mandarin Chinese and Japanese.

Accounting Partners
500 108th Ave. N.E., #1640, Bellevue WA 98004
450-1990
Specializes in accounting and finance, doing both temporary and permanent placement. Positions range from accounting clerk to controller, from data entry to financial analyst. Most upper level accounting positions are for staff accountants; you should have an accounting degree and one to three years of experience. A C.P.A. is an excellent credential, but not as important as the appropriate experience. Such positions pay between $11 and $15 an hour. A financial analyst should have at least two years experience; a degree is preferred. You'll also need skill with

such spreadsheet programs as Lotus 1-2-3 and Excel. Almost all jobs require DOS or Windows skill. A junior analyst might make $10 to $12 an hour, a more senior person $15 to $25. To apply, call for an appointment and a telephone screening; qualified candidates will later complete applications, be interviewed and tested. Your degree will be verified and references will be checked before you're sent out on a job.

Act Media
11807 North Creek Parkway S., #111, Bothell WA 98011
487-6792
Ever wondered how people get hired to pass out coupons in Safeway stores? Or demonstrate new products at QFC? This is one of the agencies that places "in-store representatives" in grocery and drug stores in most of western Washington, including King, Pierce, Thurston, Kitsap and Snohomish counties. Shifts range from three to eight hours. Hours are usually 10 a.m. to 5 p.m. or 11 to 6. Assignments almost always include weekends; they may involve only Fridays or Thursdays through Sundays. Depending on the project or promotion, you might work one weekend a month—or three. Schedules are available a week in advance. Many workers are retirees or homemakers. Qualifications: an outgoing personality, with a sales attitude, the ability to stand for several hours, reliable transportation and a neat appearance. You'll probably be asked to wear black slacks and a white shirt with tie and apron. Reps make $6.50 an hour to start. To apply, call and ask for an application to be mailed.

Brown Bag Bookings
2133 E. Interlaken Blvd., #1, Seattle WA 98112
329-3095
Marguerite Peterson runs this speakers' bureau, which also places people in training and consulting assignments, including facilitation of retreats. Because she markets to conventions, associations, corporations and public agencies, she receives many requests for business-related topics. You are most likely to make money as a speaker, she advises, if you are one of a few experts in your field or if you have expertise that you can adapt for many different audiences (for example, the communications skills speaker who can address the concerns of business-people, parents and teachers). Brown Bag represents only Puget Sound-area speakers and consultants and also looks for speakers who are polished and experienced and provide some substance in their presentations. You need not be an entertainer, says Peterson, but you cannot be boring. Peterson, who takes a percentage of the fee the speaker is paid, rarely places a speaker for a fee less than $100; some experienced speakers ask for $600 or more. To be considered for the Brown Bag speaker pool, send Peterson a short biography, a list of your recent speaking appearances, samples of your titles, references with telephone numbers and a list of upcoming presentations where she might preview you. If accepted for her agency, you'll be contacted only when clients express interest in your talks; this may take a few days—or several months.

General Employment Service, Inc.
600 University St., #2525, Seattle WA 98101-3129
623-1750
Established in 1945, this agency offers temporary, temp-to-perm, contract and

regular opportunities in some of the area's largest companies. Some examples: administrative/clerical, accounting, law, customer service, insurance, human resources, information technology and light industrial (including production, warehouse, packaging and maintenance). Assignments range from a half day to a year. What does General look for? It's easier for you to be placed if you have good computer skills and type at least 40 words per minute. Other plusses: experience with a multi-line phone system, public relations skills and excellent grammar. Most applicants take a basic math, spelling and filing test. The agency's recruiters recommend that you be dressed professionally when you come in to inquire about positions; you should also bring a resume and a list of your skills. No fees to applicants.

Gilmore Temporary Personnel
2722 Colby Ave., #414, Everett WA 98201
252-1195
A subsidiary of the Gilmore Research Group. Applicants must be at least 18 and have word processing skills, preferably with WordPerfect or Word. Minimum typing speed: 60 words per minute. Good telephone skills are also helpful. Assignments can range from four hours to several months.

HandyMac PC
316 Occidental Ave. S., #308, Seattle WA 98104
682-6005
Computer graphic design and production, multimedia, presentation, desktop publishing and illustration software assignments are what this agency places for. The ideal candidate has at least three to five years full-time, paid experience with a traditional graphic design background (training in a college or university graphic design program). The software experience most in demand at press time included MacroMedia Director and Photoshop, three-dimensional illustration programs, PageMaker, QuarkXPress, Freehand, PowerPoint and Persuasion. Most clients use Macs, although there are some Windows jobs. What else do you need? A strong portfolio, with "real world" samples of everything you've done, and the ability to work in stressful situations. What can you make? For desktop publishing and production people, $14 to $25 an hour; for multimedia and illustration, $25 to $60. How should you apply? Resume and cover letter first, please. You'll be interviewed if your skills match the agency's needs.

Janet Church & Associates
101 Stewart St., #300, Seattle WA 98101
443-9673
This high-tech marketing and event management firm hires consultants on a per job basis. Some work for a few days, others for a year. Positions range from project management to marketing director. Pay usually is at least $50 an hour. To apply, you must be an experienced manager or executive in the software industry; five or more years experience is preferred. Candidates also need a thorough understanding of software distribution channels. Experience with software publishers and a marketing degree are helpful. Contact: Randy Broad, business development manager.

MacTemps
520 Pike St., #1340, Seattle WA 98101
622-2800
One of 20 MacTemps offices across the country, this branch employs 50-70 people a week. About half work in computer graphics and desktop publishing, the balance in clerical, database or data entry work. The most commonly requested expertise: QuarkXPress, Adobe Illustrator, Microsoft Access and Word 6.0. You'll be easier to place in a professional position if you have two to four years of experience with one or more of these programs and a degree. If your experience is more limited but you type at least 65 words per minute, you can make $9-10.50 an hour using Access or Word 6.0. Pay averages $13.50 an hour and benefits are paid or partly paid for employees who work at least 1,000 hours in a 52-week period. Branch manager: Anne Webster.

Manpower Temporary Services
1420 Fifth Ave., #1850, Seattle WA 98101
583-0880
Jobline: 447-JOBS
This Wisconsin-based firm has several offices in the Puget Sound area; apply in the city where you'd like to work because that's where your records will be kept. Year around Manpower needs people with word processing (the latest releases of Word and WordPerfect) and spreadsheet management (Excel) skills. For warehouse work, you must be able to lift 50 pounds; for light industrial (assembly), you must be prepared for a fast-paced environment and be able to stand all day. Also places some grocery store demonstrators and summer landscaping workers.

Olsten Accounting Services
2033 Sixth Ave., #777, Seattle WA 98121
441-6648
Places professional and managerial-level financial people on a temp, temp-to-hire and permanent basis. At least 30 per cent of the positions require a C.P.A. An experienced CFO will usually be placed on at least a temp-to-hire basis; the typical opening calls for someone to manage a staff of three to six and will pay $30,000 to $60,000. A C.P.A. with "Big 6" experience and an M.B.A. will be paid on the higher end of the range. The "ideal" candidate? A well-rounded accountant, with experience in accounts payable and receivable, spreadsheet management software, bank auditing and real estate loan packaging.

Olsten Kimberly Quality Care
155 N.E. 100th, #306, Seattle WA 98125
528-1551
Places homemakers, home health care aides, RNs, LPNs, physical therapists, occupational therapists, speech therapists and M.S.W.s. About 60 per cent of assignments are temporary, the balance permanent. Because this division provides home health care, especially to AIDS, cancer and stroke patients, the ability to work independently is important. Olsten also looks for compassion. You must have a minimum of a year's experience at the level you'll be working. (For example, an LPN who has just qualified as an RN cannot yet work at the RN level.)

Olsten Staffing Services

2033 Sixth Ave., #910, Seattle WA 98121

441-2962

Handles placements for warehouse, light industrial, clerical and office automation. Office automation applicants should have Windows experience; they'll be tested on all major software programs.

Pyramid Technical Services Inc.

40 Lake Bellevue, #100, Bellevue WA 98005

454-7515

Jerry Reed, president, accepts applications for high tech professionals seeking contract and permanent work in engineering, computer software or data communications. Most jobs involve software. Places technical writers, especially experienced writers (with a related degree) with a technical background. No sales jobs.

Rho Company, Inc.

4034 148th Ave. N.E., Redmond WA 98052

883-2233

Places people in positions ranging from entry-level clerical and light industrial to professional and technical. Most positions are in the software industry, in such jobs as tester or software developer. Most upper level positions require at least two to four years of experience. Assignment length: one week to ongoing. To be added to Rho's database, direct a cover letter identifying the positions you'd like and a resume to "Recruiting." Because your resume will be scanned, use a chronological format and key words about your responsibilities and skills.

S & T Onsite

4464 Fremont Ave. N., #200, Seattle WA 98103

632-6931

Specializes in technical communications, placing technical writers, copy editors, proofreaders, indexers, graphic designers and multimedia whizzes. Most work is in software documentation and on-line help. You need experience in commercial (rather than in-house) software documentation and, in most jobs, Word for Windows. At press time, one of the greatest needs was for experienced writers with programming experience (for example, C++ or Visual Basic). To apply, send Dan Green a resume (preferably on diskette, in Word for Windows) that calls out your technical skills in a section separate from your experience.

Snelling Personnel Services

15 S. Grady Way, #246, Renton WA 98055

228-6500

Haven't worked in years? Even if you don't type and have no computer skills, account manager Stacy Winslow says a good attitude and good references (possibly from volunteer work) may get you placed in an entry level job such as filing or labeling merchandise. If you have no work experience and are unsure how to put together a resume, Winslow said her staff will try to help you evaluate your volunteer and personal experience to develop a resume. To get you "computer friendly," Snelling will refer you to computer classes and let you spend a few hours on its word processor. To apply, call to schedule an interview; you should bring along a resume and at least two professional references. Most Snelling positions are in word processing, legal transcription, reception and other office support, warehouse, computer programming (DOS and Windows) and accounting (both bookkeepers and C.P.A.s are placed). Assignments range from a half day to a year.

Special Assignment, Inc.
6523 California Ave. S.W., #299, Seattle WA 98136
938-0630
Founded by Robin Rypinski in early 1992. Provides high-level help for special short-term projects. She often assembles a team of people, including herself, to handle such projects. Most of the people in Special Assignment's database are self-employed, seeking additional work through the agency. Rypinski describes her ideal candidate as the individual with at least 10 years of specialized management experience, especially in finance, human resources or marketing. The people she places usually earn between $20 and $75 an hour. No temp placements.

Wasser Inc.
2005 Fifth Ave., #201, Seattle WA 98121
441-0707
A temporary placement agency, this firm most often uses people with technical backgrounds. For example, at press time, it was most in need of writer/programmers, people with experience in Windows-based programming, C++ or Visual Basic who could also write and edit. Often places people when a particular expertise is needed on a short-term basis, in overload situations, for rush jobs, vacation relief or maternity leave. Typical projects are computer software documentation and maintenance manuals for equipment. Technical writers can expect to make $20-$45 an hour, proofreaders and editors $15-$40 and graphic designers (with expertise with CorelDraw, Freehand and FrameMaker) $20-$35. Desktop publishing specialists should have experience in PageMaker, Ventura Publisher, QuarkXPress or Word for Windows. Computer graphics specialists, who are often hired for on-line documentation work, need Windows Help. Also places instructional designers, people who can design training materials, both for computer-based and traditional programs. Occasionally needs foreign language skills (with technical and writing background). Employs 15 permanently, maintains 200-300 on contract. Established in 1980. To apply, send a resume detailing your experience. If called for an interview, bring in samples that demonstrate the breadth of your experience.

The Write Stuff
5508 35th Ave. N.E., Seattle WA 98105
524-4423
An agency that specializes in technical writing and translating, this firm uses technical writers and editors, people who can create or translate software documentation. Most positions require programming background (usually Windows-based). Pay depends on several factors, including whether the client requires the work to be done on-site, the length of the assignment and its complexity. Contacts: Linda Werner and (Ms.) Beryl Gorbman.

8. Joblines
300 Recorded Job Listings

How can you quickly learn of job openings—wherever you are, whatever time or day? Take advantage of the special telephone lines that many employers use to provide application information and updated lists of job openings. In most cases, these lines connect you to taped messages that provide brief descriptions of the employer, the application procedure and the positions currently open. Some firms list all openings on their joblines; others list only entry-level positions. Some include internship information.

Most messages are available 24 hours a day; many require the use of a touchtone telephone. The messages are usually revised weekly when positions are open. Some joblines allow you to request application forms or leave other messages. A few firms have lines staffed with personnel specialists who can discuss openings with you.

The joblines are typically easier to reach before and after regular working hours. Calling before 8 a.m. or on weekends will also reduce toll charges if you must call long distance. Unless otherwise indicated, all numbers can be reached using area code 206 until at least mid-1995. (For more information on new area codes, see the front of the book.)

BUSINESSES AND ORGANIZATIONS

Accountants (Washington Society of Certified Public Accountants): 641-4832

Advanced Technology Laboratories: 487-7799

Airborne Freight: 281-4815

Alaska Airlines: 433-3230

Alaskan Copper: 623-5801, Ext. 639

Aldus Corp.: 622-5500, Ext. 7000

Alliant Techsystems: 356-3024

Applied Voice Technology: 820-6000, Ext. 3980

Arts and Model Auditions (a service of the *Seattle Times*): 464-2000, Ext. 2787

Associated Grocers Inc.: 767-8788

Asymetrix: 462-0501, #5

AT&T
Management: (800) 348-4313
Nonmanagement: (800) 562-7288

Attorneys (Washington State Bar Association): 727-8261

Auburn General Hospital: 833-7711, Ext. 429

Bartell Drug Co.: 763-2626, #1

Battelle: 528-3090

Blue Cross of Washington and Alaska: 670-4773

Boeing: 965-3111 (Toll-free within Washington: 800-525-2236)

Boeing Employees Credit Union: 439-5725

Bogle & Gates: 621-2639

Bristol Myers Squibb: 727-3779

Burlington Environmental: 442-8170 (800-882-9785)

Cascade Savings Bank: 339-5500, Ext. 814

Cascade Valley Hospital: 435-0505

Cell Therapeutics: 270-8382 (800-656-2355)

Chateau Ste. Michelle: 488-1133, Ext. 500 (During office hours only)

Children's Hospital and Medical Center: 526-2230

Claircom, see McCaw Cellular

Cucina! Cucina! See Schwartz Bros. Restaurants

Darigold: 286-6730

Data I/O: 867-6963

The Defender Association: 447-3900, Ext. 513

Digital Equipment: (408) 748-4222

Drug Emporium: 646-1629 (800-526-JOBS)

Eddie Bauer: 861-4851

Edmark (Product development positions): 556-8845

Egghead Software: 391-6316

Eldec Corp.: 743-8215

Enchanted Parks:
From Seattle: 661-8027
From Tacoma: 925-8027

Ernst: 621-6880

Everett Clinic: 339-5400

Everett Mutual Savings Bank (When positions are open): 258-0527

Evergreen Hospital Medical Center: 899-2502

Federal Reserve Bank: 343-3634

Film Industry (Washington State Film and Video Office): 464-6074

First Interstate Bank of Washington: 292-3111

Fisher Broadcasting Co. (KOMO): 443-6444

Fluke Corp.: 356-5205

Food Services of America: 251-1413

Four Seasons Olympic Hotel: 682-9164

Frank Russell Co.: 596-5454

Fred Hutchinson Cancer Research Center: 667-2977

Fred Meyer: (800) 401-5627

Gai's Bakery: 726-7517 (During office hours)

Genetic Systems/Sanofi: 861-5045

Genie Industries: 881-1800 (Through operator)

General Employment (Placement agency): 467-1255

Good Samaritan Hospital: 848-6661, Ext. 1905

Greater Seattle Chamber of Commerce: 389-7300, Ext. 506

Great Western Bank: (800) 367-5545

Group Health Cooperative of Puget Sound: 448-5100

GTE Northwest
Management positions: 261-5667
Hourly positions: 261-5777

Harborview Medical Center (Nursing positions): 223-8409

Harrison Memorial Hospital: 792-6729

Heath Tecna: 395-HIRE

The Herald: 339-3009

Hewlett-Packard Co.: 334-2244

Highline Community Hospital: 431-5325

Holland America Line-Westours: 286-3496

IBM: (800) 831-2303

Icicle Seafoods: 281-5331

ICOS Corp.: 485-1900 (Through operator)

Immunex: 389-4060

InControl: CHECK

Intermec: 348-2820

Interpoint Corp.: 882-3100 (Through operator)

InterWest Savings Bank: 679-4181, Ext. 888 (Toll-free within Washington, 800-422-0235, Ext. 888)

Kaiser Aluminum: 383-1461 (Through operator)

KCTS/9: 443-4800

KeyBank of Puget Sound: (800) 677-6150

King Broadcasting Co.: 448-3915

King County Medical Blue Shield: 464-5588

KIRO, Inc.: 728-5205

Laidlaw Transit: 365-7300, #4

Lamonts: 644-5700 (Through operator)

Leviton Manufacturing: 485-5100, Ext. JOBS

Magnolia Hi-Fi: 623-7872 (Through operator)

Manpower Temporary Services: 447-JOBS

MarkAir: (907) 266-6731

McCaw Cellular Communications Inc. (Includes Lin Broadcasting, Claircom and Cellular One): 828-8484

McChord Credit Union: 589-8012

Microsoft: 936-5500 (800-892-3181)

Mount St. Vincent: 938-8998

MultiCare Medical Center: 594-1256

Mutual of Enumclaw (Live voice): 825-2591
From Seattle: 623-7855, Ext. 181

News Tribune: 597-8590

Nintendo of America: 861-2170

Northwest Airlines: (612) 726-2111, #2

Northwest Hospital: 368-1791

Northwest Kidney Center: 292-2771, Ext. 6924

Olin Aerospace: 885-5000, Ext. 5132

Overlake Hospital Medical Center: 688-5150

Pacific Medical Center: 326-4120

Paralegals (Washington State Paralegal Association): 938-4355

PEMCO Financial Center: 628-8740

PepsiCola: 326-7436

Physio-Control Corp.: 867-4130

Precor: 486-9292, Ext. 444

Price/Costco: 803-6416

Princess Tours (Shipboard positions): (310) 553-1770, Ext. 4095

Print Northwest:
From Tacoma: 922-9393, Ext. 365
From Seattle: 621-1943, Ext. 365

Providence Hospital, Centralia: 330-8584

Providence General Medical Center, Everett: 258-7562

Providence Medical Center: 320-2020

PTI Communications: 851-1376

Puget Sound Blood Center: 292-2302

Puget Sound Hospital
From Tacoma: 474-0561, Ext. 103
From Seattle: 623-1417, Ext. 103

Puget Sound Power & Light Co. (Puget Power): 454-3540

Recreational Equipment Inc.: 395-4694

Red Lion Hotel, Bellevue: 450-4104

Red Lion Hotel, Sea-Tac: 439-6102

Restaurants Unlimited: 634-3082, Ext. 777

Royal Seafoods, Inc.: 285-1105

R.R. Donnelley: 222-0328

R.W. Beck: 727-4524

Safeco: 545-3233

Safeco Life Insurance and Property and Casualty: 867-6100

Safeway: 455-6501

St. Claire Hospital: 581-6419

St. Francis Community Hospital
From Seattle: 838-9700, Ext. 7930
From Tacoma: 952-7930

St. Joseph Hospital and Health Care Center: 591-6623

St. Peter Hospital: 493-7779

Schwartz Bros. Restaurants (Includes Cucina! Cucina!): 647-4864, #6

Seafirst Corp.: 358-7523

Sea-Land Service Inc.: 593-8042
From Seattle: 233-3299

Seattle Federal Credit Union: 340-4500, #5 and #5

Seattle FilmWorks: 281-1390, Ext. 241

Seattle Lighting: (800) 689-7505

Seattle Sheraton Hotel and Towers: 287-5505

Seattle Pacific Industries (Unionbay): 282-8889 (Through operator)

Seattle Times
General: 464-2118
News jobs/internships: 464-3124

Shurgard Storage Centers: 624-6610, Ext. 377

Siemens Medical Systems: (800) 458-6503

Software Industry (Washington Software Association): 889-8880

Solectron Washington: 335-3180

Space Needle Corp.: 443-2161, Ext. 3

Starbucks Coffee Co.: 447-4123, Ext. 2

Stevens Memorial Hospital: 640-4194

Stouffer Madison Hotel: 583-0300 (Through operator)

Sun Sportswear: 251-1845

Swedish Medical Center: 386-2888

Targeted Genetics: 623-7612, Ext. 5000

TRAMCO: 347-6969, Ext. 2600

Trident Seafoods Corp. (Hourly positions): 783-3818 (Through operator)

Unigard: 644-5236, #1

UniSea Inc. (Hourly positions): 883-0884

United Airlines: (708) 952-7077

University of Washington Medical Center
Nursing positions: 548-4470
General positions: 543-6969

U.S. Bank: 344-5656

USTravel: 224-7715

U S West Communications: 345-6126

U S West New Vector: 644-3994 (Through operator)

Valley Medical Center: 251-5190

Virginia Mason Medical Center: 223-6496

Visiting Nurse Services of the Northwest: 548-2398

Washington Natural Gas: 622-6767, Ext. 2800

Washington Mutual Savings Bank: 461-8787

West Coast Grocery: 593-5876

Westin Hotel: 728-1000, Ext. 5766

West One Bank: 585-2714

Weyerhaeuser Co.: 924-5347

WRQ: 217-7411

ZymoGenetics: 547-8080, #7

GENERAL

Senior 55+ Hotline (A service of the Mayor's Office, City of Seattle): 684-0477

University of Washington Center for Career Services
See *Where Can You Get Help?*

GOVERNMENT AGENCIES

City of Auburn: 931-3077

City of Bellevue: 455-7822

City of Bothell: 486-9473

City of Bremerton (Civil Service): 478-5241

Community Transit: 348-2333

City of Edmonds: 771-0243, #1

City of Everett: 259-8768

City of Federal Way: 661-4089

City of Kent: 859-3375

King County: 296-5209

City of Kirkland: 828-1161

Kitsap County: 876-7169

City of Lacey: 491-3213

Libraries (Pacific Northwest Library Association): 543-2890

City of Mercer Island: 236-5326

METRO: 684-1313

Metropolitan Park District: 305-1009

City of Mukilteo: 290-5175

City of Olympia: 753-8383

Pierce County: 591-7466

Pierce Transit: 581-8097

City of Puyallup: 841-5596

City of Redmond: 556-2121

City of Renton: 235-2514

City of Seattle: 684-7999

Seattle Center: 684-7218

Seattle City Light: 233-2181

Seattle Housing Authority: 443-4376

Port of Seattle: 728-3290

Seattle Public Library: 386-4120

Snohomish County: 388-3686

Snohomish County PUD: 347-5599

City of Tacoma: 591-5795

Port of Tacoma: 383-5841, Ext. 2

Thurston County: 786-5499

City of Tukwila: 433-1828

FEDERAL EMPLOYMENT

Bonneville Power Administration: 553-7564

McChord Air Force Base: 984-2277

Army Corps of Engineers: 764-3739

Fort Lewis Army Base: 967-5377

Central Intelligence Agency: (800) JOBS-CIA

Department of Commerce: 526-6294

NOAA: 526-6051

Environmental Protection Agency: 553-1240

Federal Aviation Administration: 227-2014

Federal Emergency Management Agency: 487-4783

General Services Administration: (415) 744-5182, (800) 347-3378

Housing and Urban Development: 220-5132

Internal Revenue Service: 220-5757

Labor Department: (800) 366-2753

National Park Service: 220-4000

Navy Fleet and Industrial Supply Center Puget Sound: 476-2889

Puget Sound Naval Shipyard: (800) 562-5972

Naval Station Everett: 304-3598

Naval Submarine Base/Bangor: 396-4779

Naval Undersea Warfare Center/Keyport: 396-2433

Office of Personnel Management (General federal openings): 220-6400

Postal Service
Seattle and Everett positions: 442-6240
Tacoma, Bremerton and Olympia positions: 756-6148

STATE EMPLOYMENT

Washington State Convention and Trade Center: 447-5039

State of Washington: 586-0545
From Seattle: 464-7378
From Spokane: (509) 456-2889

SCHOOLS, COLLEGES AND UNIVERSITIES

Antioch University-Seattle
General application information: 441-5352, Ext. 5033
General openings: 441-5352, Ext. 5031
Adjunct faculty: 441-5352, Ext. 5032

Bates Technical College: 596-1652

Bellevue Community College: 643-2082

City University: 649-4625

Cornish College: 323-1402, Ext. 312

Edmonds Community College: 640-1510

Everett Community College: 388-9229 (Live voice)

The Evergreen State College: 866-6000, Ext. 6361

Green River Community College: 833-9111, Ext. 86

Olympic College: 792-2078

Pacific Lutheran University: 535-8598

Pierce College: 964-7341

Renton Technical College: 235-2354

Seattle Community Colleges (All campuses): 587-5454

Seattle Pacific University: 281-2065

Seattle University: 296-6363

South Puget Sound Community College: 754-7711, Ext. 360

Tacoma Community College: 566-5014

University of Puget Sound: 756-3368

University of Washington and UW Medical Center: 543-6969

University of Washington Temporary Services: 543-5420

Washington State University: (509) 335-7637

Auburn School District: 931-4916 (Live voice)

Bainbridge Island School District: 842-2920

Bellevue School District: 455-6009

Bethel School District: 536-7270

Central Kitsap School District: 698-3470

Clover Park School District: 589-7436

Edmonds School District: 670-7021

Everett School District: 339-4346

Federal Way School District
Certified positions: 941-2058
Classified positions: 941-2273

Fircrest School: 364-0300, Ext. 244

Franklin Pierce School District: 535-8829

Highline School District: 433-6339

Issaquah School District: 557-5627

Kent School District (Classified positions): 859-7508

Lake Washington School District: 828-3243

Marysville School District: 653-0807

Mercer Island School District: 236-3302

Mukilteo School District: 356-1237

North Kitsap School District: 779-8914

Northshore School District (May-September): 489-6381

Peninsula School District: 857-3565

Puyallup School District: 841-8666

Renton School District: 235-5826

Riverview School District: 883-0854

Seattle Public Schools: 298-7382

Shoreline School District: 361-4367

South Central School District: 244-2100 (Live voice)

South Kitsap School District: 876-7389

Sumner School District: 863-2232

Tacoma School District
Certified positions (June-August): 596-1300
Classified positions: 596-1265

University Place School District: 566-5605

King's Schools: 546-7533 (Live voice)

NONPROFITS

Catholic Archdiocese of Seattle: 382-4564

Crista Ministries: 546-7202

Fremont Public Association: 548-0331

League of Fringe Theaters: 637-7373

Planned Parenthood of Seattle-King County: 328-7721

YWCA of Greater Seattle: 382-5335

9. Employers: Businesses and Organizations

When we say "jobs," many of us think first of business. And that's where many of the best jobs are. Some businesses have huge part-time staffs, others just a few positions. Some offer seasonal employment; others provide valuable work experience through internships. Some businesses hire temps and free-lancers directly; others contract through employment agencies or other vendors. (For example, you may write speeches or do design an annual report for a newly public company for its corporate communications department—or as a subcontractor to the investor relations consultant.).

This chapter lists businesses and many nonprofits that provide business-like services (for example, medical care, publishing and recreation). The organizations included in this chapter have indicated they *at least occasionally* have opportunities that are part-time, seasonal or temporary. In many cases, the employers listed here are only representatives of their industries; do not hesitate to contact other firms in the same field regarding work. This chapter does not include franchises (for example, McDonald's) for which you must apply at each outlet.

A & H Stores
1420 Maple Ave. S.W., #201, Renton WA 98055
255-7083
This retail drug and Hallmark store chain employs about 150. Stores hire their own staff.

Active Voice Corp.
2901 Third Ave., Seattle WA 98121
441-4700
Makes voice-mail and call-processing systems run by PCs. Employed 150 at press time, with most working in the Puget Sound area. Some part-time professional opportunities in quality assurance, especially for computer science students. Human resources manager: Debbie Faulkner.

Advanced Technology Laboratories
22100 Bothell-Everett Highway S.E., P.O. Box 3003, Bothell WA 98041
487-7000
Jobline: 487-7799 (Touchtone telephones only)
Manufacturer of medical diagnostic ultrasound equipment (used by obstetricians, cardiologists and other specialists).

AEI Music Network Inc.
900 E. Pine St., Seattle WA 98122
329-1400
Provides foreground and background music. Employs 300. Internships possible through college and university programs in fields such as accounting, human resources, customer service and broadcast technology. Human resources manager: Nancy Maio.

Aetna Life & Casualty Co.
1501 Fourth Ave., #1000, Seattle WA 98101
467-2640
Shelley Jacobson handles personnel for this insurance company, which employs 635 locally. At-risk high school students intern through a Chief Sealth High School program; the only college interns are taken through a Washington State University insurance program.

Agro-Biotech Corp.
P.O. Box 2622, Woodinville WA 98072
487-6011
Michael Banfield founded this biotech, which moved to the Puget Sound area from Oregon in 1992. According to the *Puget Sound Business Journal*, its principal product will be a nontoxic, bacteria-based pesticide for agriculture. Employs seven on a permanent basis, with contract employees added as needed. May take students in the sciences as interns starting in mid-1995.

AIDS Impact Inc.
P.O. Box 9443, Seattle WA 98109
284-3865
Created in 1989 to provide health-care professionals with self-study materials on HIV/AIDS that meet continuing education requirements. Now also provides training materials on bloodborne pathogens. Employed eight at press time; uses interns from community colleges and area universities. Also offers work-study opportunities for students. Founder: Madeline Beery.

Airborne Freight Corp.
P.O. Box 662, Seattle WA 98111
285-4600
Jobline: 281-4815
Employs more than 1,100 locally. Corporate job openings are posted in the human resources office at headquarters, 3101 Western Ave., second floor. Just ask the receptionist for help. Many part-time customer service and clerical positions; these are permanent positions with partial benefits. There's also an in-house temporary pool for short-term clerical jobs; applicants should have 10-key skills and be able to type at least 35 words per minute. Experience with PCs and Word is helpful. Temps work on an on-call basis, but many assignments are several weeks in length. Temp pay ranged from $6 to $8 an hour at press time.

Alaska Airlines
P.O. Box 68900, Seattle WA 98168
433-3200
Jobline: 433-3230

This airline's jobline lists job titles, qualifications and, in the case of group interviews, where interviews will be held. Hires nonsmokers only.

Alaska Highway Cruises
3805 108th Ave. N.E., #204, Bellevue WA 98004
828-0989
Gary Odle and Brent Hobday recently launched this tour company, which combines an Alaskan cruise with sightseeing in a rented RV. Seasonal positions, appropriate for college students, include guest services administration, meeting tour members at airline or cruise terminals, troubleshooting and technical services for the RVs. The season: early June through August.

Alaska Sightseeing/Cruise West
2401 Fourth Ave., #700, Seattle WA 98121
441-8687
Runs seven boats and employs as many as 200 on a full-time, seasonal basis (April-November). Most work aboard ship; others drive buses and handle baggage in Alaska. As much as two-thirds of the seasonal work force returns every year. Also some part-time seasonal jobs in Seattle, working two to four days a week with passenger embarkation and boat loading and unloading. These are laborer positions, requiring people who can lift at least 60 pounds. For students, some accounting jobs that are part-time during part of the winter and full-time during the summer. Apply by letter or by completing an application in the office. Applications will be mailed only to those who provide a self-addressed, stamped No. 10 envelope. Human resources manager: (Ms.) Kit Timmons.

Albertsons Food Centers Inc.
11000 N.E. 33rd Pl., #102, Bellevue WA 98004
827-8070
Most hiring is done in the stores, where openings are often posted. Many part-time retail opportunities. This regional office employs only sales managers and their support staff.

Aldus Corp.
411 First Ave. S., Seattle WA 98104
622-5500
Jobline: Ext. 7000
This desktop publishing and graphics software firm has agreed to be taken over by Adobe Systems, Inc. of Mountain View, Calif., creating one of the world's largest software companies specializing in personal computer software for editing and publishing. Layoffs are expected locally.

Alki Software Corp.
300 Queen Anne Ave. N., #410, Seattle WA 98109
286-2600
About 25 work for this software developer. Some part-time employment, both for professional and support staff.

Allenmore Hospital
South 19th and Union, Tacoma WA 98405
572-2323

Job openings are posted in a glass case outside the personnel office and advertised in the *News Tribune*. Employs 420; some full-time, some part-time, some pool (on-call relief positions).

AlliedSignal Commercial Avionics Systems

15001 N.E. 36th St., P.O. Box 97001, Redmond WA 98073-9701
885-3711
Formerly Sundstrand Data Control, Inc. Manufactures electronic equipment. Employs about 900. Job openings can be reviewed at the reception desk. Occasional internships; in 1994 there was one in engineering. Human resources manager: Tim Sprake.

American Airlines

Seattle-Tacoma International Airport, Seattle WA 98158
433-3951
Personnel inquiries should go to L.W. Cooper, the general manager of AA's regional operations. The airline employs about 500 here.

American Inventory Service

5900 4th Ave. S., #202, Seattle WA 98108
762-1205
This firm contracts to count things, especially merchandise for retailers and wholesalers. Employs about 45 in permanent, part-time positions. Because turnover is common, 100 to 150 positions are filled each year. Unsolicited applications are kept on file; the firm advertises every couple of months when it's recruiting and training new employees. Ten-key skill is required; many employees are accountants and bookkeepers. The company employs some parents who work only during the school day; however, about 50 per cent are full-time students or have other full-time jobs and rely on the part-time work only as an income supplement. Peak periods include the end of each quarter, the last week of December and the first week of January, the last week of June and the first week of July. President: Sue Banks.

Andrew Corp.

19021 120th N.E., Bothell WA 98011
485-8200
Develops communications software for minicomputers. Employs 100 locally. Occasional part-time professional positions. Engineering students can work as interns in software engineering. Personnel manager: Amy Wilson.

Applied Microsystems Corp.

P.O. Box 97002, Redmond WA 98073-9702
882-2000
Gale Mowrer is the human resources manager for this high tech electronics manufacturer. Rarely has entry-level opportunities. No unsolicited resumes are accepted; openings are posted in the lobby at 5020 148th Ave. N.E. Internships are seldom available; candidates must be upper division students in electrical engineering or computer science.

Arthur Andersen & Co.

Personnel
801 Second Ave., #800, Seattle WA 98104
623-8023
This "Big 6" accounting and consulting firm employs about 300 locally. Internships possible. Contact: Tamara S. Young, human resources director.

Arctic Alaska Fisheries Corp./Tyson Seafood Division

P.O. Box 79021, Seattle WA 98119
282-3445
This bottom fishing firm employs more than 200 in its Seattle office. Internships may be possible. If you'd like to work on one of the fishing boats, applications are accepted year around. Seasonal positions on boats require that you be on the boat for 30 to 90 days.

Asia-Pacific Economic Cooperation (APEC) Forum

See the Pacific Corridor Enterprise Council (PACE) and the Washington Council on International Trade (WCIT).

Asia Pacific Chamber of Commerce

1932 First Ave., #1010, Seattle WA 98101
728-1108
Goals: mutual understanding and increased trade with Asia. Employs only five but takes interns (on an unpaid basis) and uses free-lance writers on the quarterly *Pacific Economic Review*. If you're a writer with experience on Asian topics, contact (Mr.) Chris Beer.

Associated Grocers Inc.

P.O. Box 3763, Seattle WA 98124
762-2100
Jobline: 767-8788
Val Thoreson is the personnel director for this grocery co-op, which employs more than 1,000. Openings are posted in the human resources office. AG location: 3301 S. Norfolk, at the south end of Boeing Field. Interns may work in such departments as advertising or, if they're already working in a member store, in retail operations. Part-time opportunities exist for warehouse workers and truck drivers, all of whom start on a casual basis. (These are union positions.)

Associated Press

P.O. Box 2144, Seattle WA 98111-2144
682-1812
Interested in writing for the AP? You'll need at least two years of journalism experience. The Seattle bureau has 14 news employees and the Olympia bureau four; the Seattle staff also includes 11 employees without newswriting responsibilities. There are both internship and temporary opportunities; most temps work in Olympia during the legislative session or as vacation relief. Contact: Dale Leach, bureau chief.

Associated Vintners

Owns Columbia Winery (see later in this chapter) and recently purchased Paul Thomas Winery.

Asymetrix Corp.
110 110th Ave. N.E., #700, Bellevue WA 98004
462-0501
Jobline: #5
ToolBook and Multimedia ToolBook are among the software programs marketed by this firm, established in 1985 by Microsoft co-founder Paul Allen. Employs 300 in the Puget Sound area. Some part-time clerical jobs. Internships for students who want to work in software development. Recruiter: Brian Hoffman.

AT&T
Joblines:
Management: (800) 348-4313
Nonmanagement: (800) 562-7288
In this area, AT&T employs hundreds, but personnel is centralized in Oakland, Calif. The only recent openings on the jobline were for account executives.

Auburn General Hospital
20 Second St. N.E., Auburn WA 98002
833-7711
Jobline: 833-7711, Ext. 429
A 100-bed hospital with two outpatient clinics for physical and occupational therapy. Many part-time opportunities in medical services. Internships arranged through university nursing programs. Job applications available from the switchboard operator. Human resources director: Brenda Kennedy.

Automobile Club of Washington
1745 114th Ave. S.E., Bellevue WA 98004
462-2222
Employs about 360 statewide and 175 in its headquarters. Other Puget Sound facilities are in Bellevue, Tacoma, Lynnwood, Everett, Bremerton, Renton and Olympia. If you're interested in a summer job, call Human Resources about the temporary counter and Triptik assembly positions.

AVTECH Corp.
3400 Wallingford Ave. N., Seattle WA 98103
634-2540
About 220 work for this manufacturer of electronic components for aircraft. Internships may be possible. Personnel manager: Stan Hiraoka.

Bader Martin Ross & Smith, P.S.
1000 Second Ave., #3400, Seattle WA 98104-1022
621-1900
Accounting firm formed by six former partners in the local office of the now dissolved firm of Laventhol & Horwath. Employs about 40. Limited opportunities for part-time professionals. Personnel contact: (Ms.) Pat Rylander, office administrator.

Ballard Computer
5424 Ballard Ave. N.W., Seattle WA 98107
781-7000
Largest computer retailer in the Pacific Northwest. Expects to employ 400 by 1995

in as many as 13 stores. Most employees start in sales, with about 20 per cent working part-time. Many jobs are held by college students. Especially for management, the firm promotes from within. No significant seasonal hiring; for the holiday rush, a couple of "greeters" may be hired for each store. Recruiting gears up in the fall. Resumes can be directed to human resources when positions are advertised; no unsolicited resumes or telephone applications are accepted.

Barnes & Noble
District Office
626 106th Ave. N.E., Bellevue WA 98004
451-4420
This New York City-based bookstore chain expects to have a minimum of five stores open in the Puget Sound area by the end of 1995. Locations either open or verified at press time: Bellevue, Crossroads, University Village (Seattle), Silverdale and Southcenter. Most staff is hired at the store level. Emphasis on promoting from within; for example, when the Crossroads store opened, several management slots were filled with staff from the Bellevue store. Store recruiting starts at least three months prior to the opening; ads are run and a job fair is usually scheduled. For a new store, you can also apply at an existing store and ask that your resume be held for the new store's recruiting period. Each store employs 35 to 50; about half work full-time. Part-time employees must be prepared to work evenings and weekends. Some jobs are appropriate for teenagers, although those under a certain age cannot legally work until the 11 p.m. store closing. The stores also recruit senior citizens. Entry-level employees must be outgoing and provide good customer service; a knowledge of books is valuable, but secondary to the customer contact skills.

Bartell Drug Co.
4727 Denver Ave. S., Seattle WA 98134
763-2626
Jobline: Ext. 1
Most employees work full-time. Holiday seasonal workers begin in October and work into January, usually on a full-time basis. The only interns are pharmacy students attending the University of Washington or Washington State University.

Battelle Seattle Research Center
4000 N.E. 41st, Seattle WA 98105
525-3130
Jobline: 528-3090
Battelle Memorial Institute is a nonprofit research organization that employs 8,400 worldwide. Its goal is to generate, apply and commercialize technology. Locally, Battelle employs 170. Some part-time research positions exist; they're usually filled by graduate students at the University of Washington. In 1994, Battelle started a summer internship program for social science graduates who work part-time on a paid basis in research.

Bellevue Square Managers, Inc.
P.O. Box 908, Bellevue WA 98009
454-2431
A division of Kemper Development, this is the management firm for Bellevue

Square's 1.3 million-square-foot shopping center. Employs fewer than 10 in the office and nearly 200 in maintenance and security.

Berger/ABAM Engineers, Inc.

33301 9th Ave. S., Federal Way WA 98003
241-2040
Ann Kennedy is the personnel director for this 75-employee structural engineering firm. Engineering students are sometimes hired as summer interns.

Better Business Bureau

4800 S. 188th St., #222, SeaTac WA 98188
431-2222
Affiliated with the Council of Better Business Bureaus, this organization employs 28 and offers internships. Departments include sales, arbitration, publications and public information. President and chief executive officer: Robert W. G. Andrew.

BioControl Systems Inc.

19805 North Creek Parkway, #101, Bothell WA 98011
487-2055
Manufactures diagnostic kits for detecting salmonella, E. coli and listeria. Biosciences students can work as interns, usually during the summer, part-time or on an on-call basis. Human resources manager: Susan Rippy.

Biomembrane Research Institute

210 Elliott Ave. W., #305, Seattle WA 98119
285-1309
Tracy Little, controller, handles recruiting for this organization, spun off from Oncomembrane to do studies relating to cancer. Internships may be possible for graduate students in chemistry or immunology.

Blue Cross of Washington and Alaska

7001 220th St. S.W., Mountlake Terrace WA 98043
670-4000
Jobline: 670-4773
This provider of group and individual insurance plans employs about 1,000. Some clerical positions are part-time or temporary. Interns, usually graduate students (for example, in business or health care administration), sometimes work on a project basis, often during summers. These paid positions are usually posted at university placement offices.

Bob Walsh & Associates

3131 Elliott Ave., #240, Seattle WA 98121
285-3212
This event-planning and public relations firm is an affiliate of Bob Walsh Enterprises, which focuses on sports marketing and international affairs, with an emphasis on Russian business development. Employs six full-time. Internships often available on a project basis, usually in event management.

Boeing

Always ranked near the top on the annual "Fortune 500" list, Boeing has hundreds of different kinds of positions, both permanent and free-lance, even during periods of cutbacks. The largest divisions are: Commercial Airplane; Defense and Space; and Computer Services.

Boeing Employment Office
Mailing Address:
P.O. Box 3707 MS 68-PL, Seattle WA 98124-2207
Jobline: 965-3111
Toll-free within Washington: (800) 525-2236
The jobline describes the Puget Sound positions for which applications are currently being accepted. Applications can be picked up at the employment office (hours are limited) in the East Valley Office Center, 1601 East Valley Frontage Rd., Bldg. 7-22, Renton, reached via Lind Avenue (near the intersection of Highway 167 and Interstate 405). Or you can mail in a resume. For information about Spokane jobs, call (509) 623-8700.

Bogle & Gates
601 Union St., #4700, Seattle WA 98101
682-5151
Jobline: 621-2639
This law firm employs 150 attorneys and 300 staff in Seattle. Some part-time opportunities for both lawyers and paraprofessionals. Openings are posted in the human resources office. Human resources director: Leann Carden.

The Bon Marche
Third and Pine, Seattle WA 98181
344-2121
This upscale retail chain has always been a star for its parent company, Federated Department Stores, Inc. The 42-store retailer (with 23 stores in Washington) is headquartered above its flagship store in the heart of Seattle's retail district. There's a corporate personnel staff (that's where interns are hired) as well as the store personnel manager, Andrea Hosfild. For the holiday season, temporary help works October into January.

Boyer Children's Clinic
1850 Boyer Ave. E., Seattle WA 98112
325-8477
Runs outpatient programs for children who have cerebral palsy and other neuro-muscular delays. The 25 employees include the program staff (doctors, nurses, speech therapists, physical therapists, occupational therapists and certified special education teachers who provide services) as well as those who provide administrative services. Internships available. No unsolicited resumes.

Bremerton Sun
P.O. Box 259, Bremerton WA 98310
377-3711
From Seattle: 842-5696
Mike Phillips is the editor and Tim Lavin the personnel director for this 40,000-circulation daily newspaper. Its job openings are advertised in its own classified pages. The editorial staff occasionally takes college seniors as summer interns; elsewhere in the paper, high school students are selected for internships through

the Kitsap County-based P.O.W.E.R. program, which works with at-risk youth.

Bright Star Technology Inc.
400 Lake Bellevue, #350, Bellevue WA 98005
451-3697
An educational software developer that employs more than 40. Takes an occasional intern in a technical or engineering discipline. Nini James, office manager, routes resumes to the appropriate department heads. Owned by Sierra On-Line Inc.

Bristol-Myers Squibb Pharmaceutical Research Institute
3005 First Ave., Seattle WA 98121
728-4800
Jobline: 727-3779
Employs 260, most in technical positions. Most staff members have degrees (ranging from B.S. to Ph.D) in the sciences. Students in the sciences are employed through work-study programs with area universities; openings are posted on campuses. Human resources director: Judy McGough.

Broadcast Stations
Because few of the stations listed below have personnel departments, resumes can be directed to the general manager unless otherwise indicated. There's a limited number of positions at smaller stations, although many welcome interns (usually unpaid). Note that ownership of several stations was in transition at press time.

KCIS/KCMS
See Crista Ministries

KCPQ/13
P.O. Box 98828, Tacoma WA 98499
582-8613
From Seattle: 625-1313
This television station offers four or five internships each quarter—and you need not be a student to qualify. Usually 12 weeks in length and often requiring at least 30 hours of work per week, these unpaid stints are available in a variety of departments, including research, marketing, sports programming and research and public affairs programming. The internships occasionally develop into entry-level paid positions. Contact: Adele Hauck.

KCTS/9
401 Mercer St., Seattle WA 98109
728-6463
Jobline: 443-4800
Internships: 443-4822
Seattle's public television station employs about 150; only 10 or 15 work part-time. However, there are 80-90 hourly staff; many work on-call, some on short-term projects, others on long-term productions. Virtually no openings for inexperienced staff. As many as 50 unpaid internships (at least 20 hours a week for a three-month period) are offered each year to those with aptitude in broadcast journalism or production (you need not be a student). Only occasionally do the internships result in paid positions at Channel 9; however, the former interns are those likely to be considered for such entry-level positions as receptionist.

KEZX-FM
Park Broadcasting
2615 Fourth Ave., #150, Seattle WA 98121
441-3699
Employs 20. Occasional internships; contact the department in which you'd like
to work (for example, traffic).

KING 5
See King Broadcasting Co.

KING-AM/KING-FM
Classic Radio, Inc.
333 Dexter Ave. N., #400, Seattle WA 98109
448-3666
Spun off from King Broadcasting when that firm was sold, these radio stations
were retained by the Bullitt sisters. In spring 1994, however, the owners announced that they were donating KING-FM, a classical music station established
by their mother decades ago, to a nonprofit corporation to be called Beethoven Inc.
and run by a board to benefit several arts organizations. KING-AM is to be sold
to KIRO Inc., which has announced it also will manage the sale of advertising for
KING-FM.

KIRO TV, KIRO-AM/FM
See KIRO, Inc.

KISW-FM
Nationwide Communications, Inc.
712 Aurora N., Seattle WA 98109
285-7625
Employs 40. Part-time internships are sometimes available in promotions or
research. For information on these unpaid stints, contact Gus Swanson (promotions) or Stacy Koontz (research).

KMPS
113 Dexter Ave. N., Seattle WA 98109
443-9400
This radio station employs 50. Offers unpaid internships, usually in promotions
(contact Karen Macisaac, promotions director) or sales (contact Fred Schumacher,
general manager). KMPS also runs what it calls a relationship marketing program
that includes event marketing, a monthly magazine and direct mail services to the
station's "loyal listeners." The magazine is published by Fivash Publishing but all
editorial work is handled by the station; journalism students interested in interning
can contact B. Jean O'Flynn, magazine director.

KMTT-FM/AM
1100 Olive Way, #1650, Seattle WA 98101
233-1037
Employs about 20. Students can intern in promotions.

KZOK-AM/FM
200 W. Mercer, #304, Seattle WA 98119
281-5600

KJR-AM/KLTX-FM
190 Queen Anne Ave. N., #100, Seattle WA 98109
285-2295
Ackerley Communications, which has owned KJR and KLTX, contributed its
stations to a new company, New Century Radio Partners, in which Ackerley will
be the largest single shareholder. Cook Inlet Radio, an Alaska-based Native-
American corporation is selling all of its radio stations; its Seattle property, KUBE,
is being purchased by New Century. KUBE's former general manager, Michael
O'Shea, is president and chief operating officer of New Century. At press time, the
stations were expected to operate in their existing facilities until late 1994, when
a common location (possibly the address above) would be secured. No personnel
changes are planned as part of the new combination. KJR/KLTX are expected to
continue to employ about 60, with unpaid internships available both on a full-time
and part-time basis. KUBE is expected to employ about 40 full-time, with
internships (some paid, some not) available in all departments. Both stations will
also have part-time jobs.

KRWM-FM
Brown Broadcasting
1109 First Ave., #300, Seattle WA 98101
292-8600
Employs 20. Interns can work on a part-time basis. Contact: Russ Block, program
director.

KPLU-FM
Tacoma WA 98447
535-7758
Toll-free within Washington: (800) 677-5758
Public radio. Employs 25 full-time; some part-time professional positions,
including on-air jobs. Interns might work in news or promotions. Located at
Pacific Lutheran University; posts its openings at the campus personnel office.
You can also mail a resume to the station.

KPLZ-FM/KVI-AM
Golden West Broadcasting
1809 Seventh Ave., #200, Seattle WA 98101
223-5700
Sale to Fisher Broadcasting pending at press time. Prior to the sale, employed 50
and used student interns.

KSTW/11
2320 S. 19th, P.O. Box 11411, Tacoma WA 98411
572-5789
About 125 work for this local television station. Some part-time opportunities. For
information on openings, check with the receptionist; she'll have the postings.
Interns can work in the news department; contact Gary Conner.

KTZZ/22
945 Dexter Ave. N., Seattle WA 98109
282-2202
This local television station employs about 50. For information on openings, call
the receptionist. Community college and university students may be eligible for
unpaid internships in production or public relations; contact (Ms.) K.D. Smith,
internship coordinator.

KUBE-FM
Cook Inlet Radio Partners
120 Lakeside, #310, Seattle WA 98122
322-1622
See KJR/KLTX above.

KUOW-FM
A National Public Radio affiliate at the University of Washington. See *Employers: Education.*

KXRX-FM
3131 Elliott Ave., Seventh Floor, Seattle WA 98121
283-5979
At press time, a sale to Alliance Broadcasting was pending. Employs about 35. Uses unpaid interns, usually in promotions. Contact: Ken Cardwell, promotions director.

Brown & Haley
P.O. Box 1596, Tacoma WA 98401
593-3000
If you've tasted Almond Roca, you've sampled one of the many products this pioneer Tacoma firm (still family-owned) manufactures or distributes internationally. Employs 300. Adds about 75 full-time between August and December for seasonal work. No internships, but students in chemistry, biology and microbiology are occasionally hired to work part-time in quality control. Personnel director: Debbie Schrader.

Buttonware Inc.
P.O. Box 96058, Bellevue WA 98009
865-0773
Develops software for IBM-compatible personal computers. Internships possible. Personnel contact: Steve Knops.

The Callison Partnership
1420 Fifth Ave., #2400, Seattle WA 98101
623-4646
This architectural and interiors firm is one of Seattle's largest. Interns can work part-time or full-time, some on a paid basis, in architecture, interior design and possibly the in-house graphic design department. Must be upper division students. Internship opportunities are usually posted at the University of Washington, Washington State University, University of Oregon, Montana State University, Cornish College and the Art Institute of Seattle. Human resources manager: Katie Grabow.

Care Computer Systems Inc.
636 120th Ave. N.E., Bellevue WA 98005
451-8272
Provides computer hardware and software for nursing homes. Employs 100. Kim Allen, administrative assistant, coordinates personnel. Internships (paid, full-time) may be possible in software development.

Care Unit Hospital of Kirkland

10322 N.E. 132nd, Kirkland WA 98034
821-1122
Donna Allen-Thompson is the personnel coordinator for this 83-bed chemical
dependency care facility, which added a sub-acute psychiatric care unit in late
1994. Employs 85, including full-time, part-time and on-call. Internships are
possible by late 1995.

Carver Corp.

P.O. Box 1237, Lynnwood WA 98046
775-1202
This manufacturer of high-end audio components, founded in 1978, suffered
several years of losses but is redefining its product line and cutting costs in a
turnaround campaign led by Robert Fulton, named president in late '93. By 1995
it's expected to employ 130. Openings are posted at the front desk. Human
resources administrator: Carol Hodgen.

Cascade Valley Hospital

330 S. Stillaguamish, Arlington WA 98223
435-2133
Toll-free: (800) 272-0115
Jobline: 435-0505
This 48-bed hospital employs 300, including full-time, part-time and on-call
employees. In clinical areas, interns include student nurses and technicians. Also
allows students to "shadow" professionals for career discovery purposes. Openings are posted across from Human Relations.

Cascadia Revolving Fund

157 Yesler, #414, Seattle WA 98104
447-9226
Patricia Grossman is the executive director of this nonprofit, which provides loans
and technical assistance to socially and environmentally responsible small businesses and nonprofits in Washington and Oregon. Employs six; uses volunteers
(including VISTA) and interns, especially in administrative support.

Catapult, Inc.

405 114th Ave. S.E., #100, Bellevue WA 98004
646-6767
Markets and delivers personal computer software training, usually to corporate
clients. Employs about 75 locally, plus individual contractors to teach some
classes. Total employment: about 400. Occasional internships, for example, in
curriculum development. Most openings are advertised; unsolicited applications
should be sent to personnel.

CellPro

22215 26th Ave. S.E., Bothell WA 98021
485-7644
This growing biotech company employs 150. Occasional temporary assignments
at a professional level. Internships may be possible for students in the sciences.
You'll find job announcements in the lobby.

Cell Therapeutics Inc.

201 Elliott Ave. W., #400, Seattle WA 98119
282-7100
Jobline: 270-8383
Toll-free: (800) 656-2355
This biopharmaceutical will employ 140 by 1995. Interns are usually college
juniors or seniors majoring in the sciences; they work summers, either full-time or
part-time. Human resources contacts: Susan Moore and Vonnie Sytsma.

CF2GS

1008 Western Ave., #201, Seattle WA 98104
223-6464
Formerly Christiansen & Fritsch Direct Response Advertising, now a unit of
Foote, Cone & Belding. Ron Christiansen, Bill Fritsch, David Giersdorf, Cynthia
Grant and Tom Sperry head this 37-person agency, which has both Seattle and
Portland offices. In early 1994 added Cynthia Hartwig and Dave Sharp, founders
of the now-dissolved Sharp Hartwig. Uses advertising students as interns.

Chateau Ste. Michelle

P.O. Box 1976, Woodinville WA 98072
488-1133
Jobline: through operator (office hours only)
A division of Stimson Lane (which itself is owned by U.S. Tobacco). Other
Stimson Lane operations in Washington are Columbia Crest Winery (in eastern
Washington) and Whidbey's Greenbank Farm (which currently employs only
about 10). The Woodinville facility employs about 150 in administrative, bottling,
public relations and tour operations. Internships are possible. Seasonal opportunities both in Woodinville and Patterson, the eastern Washington community
where the grapes are grown. At the chateau, about 15 are hired to work June
through mid-September as tour guides, retail clerks and to pour at private tastings.
This is considered a part-time job, although some employees will work 40 hours
some weeks. The jobs involve weekend and evening work. You must be at least
21 and have customer service experience (perhaps from retail, restaurant or
catering work). Wine experience is valuable; so is experience with tours (from
museum work, perhaps). Because employees must feel comfortable speaking to
large groups, teachers are often hired. An excellent means of learning more about
the wine industry, said the Ste. Michelle staff, because of the training manuals
provided and the opportunity to work with experts in the field. Pay is based on
proficiency; starting pay is $6 an hour but it's possible to receive your first raise
within weeks. Recruiting for these seasonal positions is handled with a March job
fair; watch for advertisements or call Ste. Michelle for information. In Patterson,
temporary field work is available at different times throughout the year; the busiest
season is January, when pruning and trellising are done. Between 50 and 100
laborers are often hired for this. Previous experience with pruning is preferred.
Human resources director: Deborah Milter.

Childhaven

316 Broadway, Seattle WA 98122
624-6477
Deals with abused, neglected or drug-addicted infants and toddlers and provides

parent education and crisis intervention, so most staff members need specialized training and experience. Some part-time positions are appropriate for college students, especially those considering careers in social services. For therapeutic day care centers, Childhaven hires people with early children education.

Children's Alliance
172 20th Ave., Seattle WA 98166
324-0340
This child-advocacy organization works with government agencies and other decision-making bodies to encourage pro-child policies. No direct services. Employs five; uses interns. Executive director: Peter Berliner.

Children's Hospital and Medical Center
P.O. Box 5371, Seattle WA 98105
526-2000
Nurse recruiter: 526-2112
Jobline: 526-2230
Employs approximately 2,400. Full-time and part-time opportunities. Standby and on-call work is now handled through an agency. You'll find a variety of positions described on the jobline. If you cannot apply in person, mail a resume and cover letter to the Human Resources office. If you're a registered nurse, call the nurse recruiter for an application packet. Applications are accepted only for open positions.

CH2M Hill
P.O. Box 91500, Bellevue WA 98009
453-5000
This engineering consulting firm employs 330 locally. Recruiting is handled by Eric Berberich, human resources administrator. Paid internships during the summer (some full-time, some part-time) are occasionally available for students in engineering or the sciences.

CityBank
P.O. Box 7028, Lynnwood WA 98046
745-5933
This locally-owned bank serves north King County and Snohomish County. Eight branches. Openings are posted in the third floor personnel office at the main office, 14807 Highway 99, Lynnwood. Personnel contact: Belinda Faylona.

Claircom Communications
700 Fifth Ave., #2100, Seattle WA 98104
621-7174
Jobline: 828-8484, #9
A fast-growing subsidiary of McCaw Cellular, Claircom provides in-flight digital communication services in aircraft. Will employ 240 by 1995. Interns have worked in international marketing (where bilingual skills are valuable) and in technical jobs (where UNIX and C programming is needed).

Clark, Nuber & Co.
P.O. Box 3844, Bellevue WA 98009
454-4919

This accounting and consulting firm employs about 70. May accept interns in accounting. Personnel manager: Ann Rael.

Cole & Weber Inc.
308 Occidental Ave. S., Seattle WA 98104
447-9595
The local affiliate of New York-based Oligvy & Mather, this advertising agency is one of Seattle's largest. It employs approximately 125. Interns sometimes work in client services. Personnel contact: Dolly Chale, vice president, administration.

College Planning Network
914 E. Jefferson, Seattle WA 98122
323-0624
Doug Breithaupt is president of this organization, which offers publications, workshops and individual counseling about post-secondary education. Free-lance opportunities for graphic designers, artists and editors. Interns can research financial aid programs or provide general office support.

Columbia Winery
P.O. Box 1248, Woodinville WA 98072
488-2776
A unit of Associated Vintners. About 60 (full-time and part-time) work at the headquarters. Besides the administrative staff, there's a bottling crew. Columbia has no personnel manager, but inquiries can be directed to the appropriate department head. For part-time banquet work, contact Lori Reeder, banquet/events manager. Interns sometimes work in sales; for infomation, contact Joann Fjellman, national sales manager.

Commerce Bank of Washington
601 Union St., #3600, Seattle WA 98101
292-3900
John Kephart, director of administration, handles personnel for this single-branch bank established in 1988. Focus: business customers. Total employment: 32. Uses interns from community colleges and local universities.

Common Ground
107 Cherry St., #410, Seattle WA 98104
461-4500
Established in 1980 to provide fund-raising expertise to other nonprofits, this housing developer employs 13 and uses VISTA volunteers. Executive director: Carlos Telleria.

Community Health Centers of King County
1025 S. 3rd St., #A, Renton WA 98055
277-1311
Two dental clinics and six medical clinics for the low-income and homeless are operated by this agency, which serves about 15,000 a year. Volunteers welcome. Unpaid internships possible; for information, contact Jan Williams, clinical services manager, regarding medical internships, or Kate Kadoo, resource development director, about internships in social work, public health, public relations or

development. Paid medical personnel is handled by Patricia Wendt, operation/facilities manager; administrative staff is hired by Jayne Leet, executive director.

Community Home Health Care
200 W. Thomas, Second Floor, Seattle WA 98119
282-5048
This private not-for-profit provides in-home health, mental health and social services in King and Snohomish counties. Employs 325, about one third working part-time. Occasional interns in such fields as nursing. Human resources manager: (Mr.) Sandy Ward.

Community Memorial Hospital
P.O. Box 218, Enumclaw WA 98022
825-2505
Roseanne Martin handles personnel for this 28-bed facility. Part-time and full-time opportunities.

Comprehensive Health Education Foundation (CHEF)
22323 Pacific Highway S., Seattle WA 98198
824-2907
Carl Nickerson is president of this nonprofit, which publishes a variety of health education materials for schoolchildren. Employs 65. Students in social work, health education and public health can work as interns (some paid, some not).

Connelly Skis
P.O. Box 716, Lynnwood WA 98046
775-5416
Dana Sprouse is the human resources manager for this manufacturer of water skis. Employs about 100. Internships may be possible.

Consolidated Restaurants Inc.
P.O. Box 380, Mercer Island WA 98040
232-9292
This restaurant chain includes the Metropolitan Grill, Union Square Grill, Quincy's, Hiriam's at the Locks, Elliott's and five Steamer's outlets. Employs about 500, with seasonal hiring dependent on the weather. Apply at the restaurant where you'd like to work or, for management positions, contact Molly Hancock, operations director. Hancock also handles management recruiting for Metropolitan Catering; those interested in part-time catering work can contact the catering office at 2601 Elliott Ave., #4135, Seattle WA 98121.

Continental, Inc.
601 Union St., #2000, Seattle WA 98104
623-3050
Includes Continental Savings Bank, Continental Mortgage, property management, casualty and liability insurance and escrow companies. Employs 465. Occasional interns in the Seattle mortgage banking department. Vice president, human resources: Ann Hedquist.

CPC Fairfax Hospital
10200 N.E. 132nd St., Kirkland WA 98034
821-2000
Peggy Trachte is director, business services, for this 133-bed acute psychiatric care facility. Employs 210, including full-time, part-time and on-call. Each hospital department handles its own hiring; for mental health or nursing positions, contact Julie Callebert, director, nursing services.

Crowd Management Systems (CMS)
2727 E. D St., Tacoma WA 98421
272-0551
Employs only three full-time, but keeps as many as 500 on its on-call list for security, parking and ticket-taking assignments at the Tacoma Dome, security at University of Washington football, basketball and soccer games and Seattle International Raceway events. Much work is seasonal; for example, there's little at the Dome between May and September, but the Raceway season runs April through September. As many as 250 might work a single event. You might work 70 hours one week and none the next, depending on events; many employees average 15 or 20 hours weekly. Openings are usually advertised. You must be 18 or older and have good customer service skills. Applicants attend a training session, complete applications, undergo a background check and then, if hired, complete a 90-day probation period. Manager: Joe Nolan.

Crystal Mountain
P.O. Box 158, Enumclaw WA 98022
825-3865
This ski resort has a 38-person permanent staff. In the winter, the staff swells to about 500, with about half the crew working part-time (for example, weekends). About 75 people work the summer season. To apply for a ski season job, watch for advertisements of the October job fair. Some winter employees return for the summer season; other summer slots are filled with applications that are on file. Human resources director: Ted Lewis.

Crystal Point Software
22232 17th Ave. S.E., #301, Bothell WA 98021
487-3656
(Ms.) Chris Stephens, president, heads this start-up, which will employ 20 by 1995. LAN packages include PC Term, Ace and Outside View. Some permanent part-time opportunities in shipping and bookkeeping. Unpaid internships possible in software engineering.

Cucina! Cucina! Inc.
1745 114th Ave. S.E., Bellevue WA 98005
Jobline: 637-4864, #6
A 10-outlet Italian restaurant chain recently spun off from Schwartz Brothers Restaurants. See Schwartz Brothers Restaurants for more information. At press time, was still using the Schwartz Brothers telephone system.

Daly's Home Decorating Centers
3525 Stone Way N., Seattle WA 98103
633-4200

Paint, stain, wallpaper, window coverings and decorating accessories are among the products retailed by this company, which also offers "how to" classes. All instructors are regular Daly's employees, usually managers. A few summer seasonal opportunities. Retail applicants should have experience with paint, a customer service orientation and be self-motivated; technical training (for sales and teaching) is provided. Contact: (Mr.) Chris Miller, general retail manager.

Dan Flickinger Inc.
1505 Western Ave., Seattle WA 98101
623-7795
Owns two Kasala furniture stores. It was included on *Inc.* magazine's list of the 500 fastest growing private companies in 1992. The tiny corporate staff maintains its office in the downtown Kasala space.

Darigold Inc.
P.O. Box 79007, Seattle WA 98119
284-7220
Jobline: 286-6730
In western Washington, 600 work for this co-op, which manufactures and distributes dairy products. Occasional internships in sales and distribution and, for daily science students, in research and development. Personnel director: Thomas Lee.

Data I/O Corp.
10525 Willows Rd. N.E., Redmond WA 98053
881-6444
Jobline: 867-6963
James Russell is vice president, human resources for this electronics firm, which employs about 350 locally. Openings are posted in the lobby. Internships are arranged through university co-op programs.

Davis Wright Tremaine
1501 Fourth Ave., #2600, Seattle WA 98101
622-3150
Carol Yuly recruits attorneys and Alma Perez handles administrative personnel for this law firm, which employs 375 in its Seattle and Bellevue offices.

The Defender Association
810 Third Ave., #800, Seattle WA 98104
447-3900
Jobline: Ext. 513
Robert Boruchowitz directs this nonprofit, which contracts with governments to provide defense representation to 17,000 people annually. Employs 135. Of the staff, 92 are attorneys. Other professional staff members include paralegals, investigators and social workers. The association recruits attorneys nationally; each summer it brings clerks to Seattle. There are legal, social work and investigative internships. Legal interns work full-time; others work part-time.

Deloitte + Touche
700 Fifth Ave., #4500, Seattle WA 98104
292-1800
Martha Tanner, human resources manager, is responsible for all recruiting—

accountants, consultants and support staff—at this "Big 6" firm's offices in Seattle and Anchorage. Upper division accounting students can sometimes work as interns in the tax department during the busy January-April season; MBA candidates are occasionally taken as summer interns by the consulting department. No internships in audit.

Delta Airlines
Applications for this airline are available at its offices at the Seattle-Tacoma International Airport and at Delta ticket offices. Or call the central personnel office in Atlanta at (404) 715-2600.

Dilettante Inc.
2300 E. Cherry, Seattle WA 98122
328-1530
Family-owned manufacturer of premium chocolates. Employs 50, mostly full-time. Frank Myhre staffs the retail shops.

Drug Emporium Northwest
12515 116th Ave. N.E., Kirkland WA 98034
820-1616
Jobline: 646-1629
(800) 526-JOBS
This high-volume discount retailer specializes in health and beauty aids, cosmetics, over-the-counter drugs and pharmacy services. The corporate staff of about 40 includes people in advertising, accounting and human resources. The chain will start 1995 with 17 stores in the Puget Sound area. An additional two or three stores are planned for each of the next several years. There's a management training program that combines a retail rotation with 120 hours of classroom training; candidates must have at least one year of retail supervisory or management experience. If you'd like to work in a store, you'll find openings advertised on the jobline or announced in the stores. Some positions have unusual hours; for example, the night stockers work 10 p.m. to 6 a.m., the morning stockers 5 a.m. to noon. Many store positions are part-time or seasonal (summer or holiday); in fact, more than 70 per cent of Drug Emporium's work between 15 and 35 hours a week. Applications are always accepted for cashier and merchandiser positions. If you're interested in health care and customer service, consider the pharmacy technician positions; the retailer provides the training you need and you have the opportunity to work side-by-side with pharmacists. Looking for a summer job? You can apply as early as May. For the holiday season, many stores start accepting applications about Oct. 1.

Eagle Hardware & Garden Inc.
101 Andover Park E., #200, Tukwila WA 98188
431-5740
David Heerensperger, formerly head of Pay 'N Pak, has established a new retail chain, which at press time expected to have 24 stores open by January, 1995. Direct resumes regarding management positions to Bryan Price; for store positions, apply in a store. For new stores, recruiting begins three months in advance of the opening and usually includes a job fair.

Eccentric Software
P.O. Box 22777, Seattle WA 98111
628-2687
Produces A Zillion Kajillion Rhymes, a rhyming dictionary, with other products scheduled for release in late 1994. Employed only five at press time. May take interns in late 1995. President: David Goldstein.

Economic Development Council of Seattle-King County
701 Fifth Ave., #2510, Seattle WA 98104
386-5040
A private nonprofit consortium of private firms and several government agencies. Focuses on stimulating and maintaining growth in King County. Its current emphasis is on regional economic strategy, transportation planning and training and education. Employs 10; limited turnover. Occasional project employment for such projects as the annual report. Internships, usually unpaid, are sometimes available for upper division or graduate students in such disciplines as business or public administration. Contact: Jennifer Johnston, business manager.

Eddie Bauer Inc.
Human Resources
14850 N.E. 36th, Redmond WA 98052
882-6100
Jobline: 861-4851
This specialty retailer employs about 2,200 locally in the corporate headquarters, catalog sales and Seattle-area stores. Openings are posted in the lobby of the corporate office. Also advertises its temporary part-time employment, available during the holiday season (recruiting begins in September for work between September and January) and summer (recruiting begins in April for work through June). Most temps work in catalog sales and "customer satisfaction," a telephone troubleshooting position. Both jobs require a good phone voice, customer service attitude, typing (40 words per minute minimum) and some computer experience. Temps can work "short" (four or five-hour) or "long" (six and one half to nine-hour) shifts.

Edmark Corp.
P.O. Box 3218, Redmond WA 98073-3218
556-8400
Jobline (product development positions only): 556-8845
Publishes educational software and printed reading materials. Employs 120. Internships possible. Sally Narodick is chief executive.

Egghead Software
22011 S.E. 51st St., Issaquah WA 98027
391-0800
Jobline: 391-6316
A large software retailer. Employs 2,000 total, about 600 locally. Job postings are available for review in the headquarters reception area.

Elgin Syferd/DDB Needham
1008 Western Ave., #601, Seattle WA 98104
442-9900

Ron Elgin heads this advertising and public relations firm, which employs about 95. The public relations department uses at least one intern each academic quarter; to apply, you must be an upper division student in a related major. Some interns work full-time, others part-time; they're paid a stipend. For PR internships, contact Laura Ames. Regarding an account services internship in advertising, contact Patti Frey; regarding a production or creative assignment, contact Melissa Stalsberg. Accounting interns are handled by Sharon Ohm.

ElseWare Corp.
101 Stewart St., #700, Seattle WA 98101-1048
448-9600
FontWorks, released in spring, 1994 is the first product of this firm, established by two former Aldus Corp. employees. President: Ben Bauermeister. Employed 36 at press time. Job openings are posted at the front desk. Uses paid interns on a full-time basis in such areas as testing.

Emerald City Arts
P.O. Box 20146, Seattle WA 98102
323-0750
This nonprofit, the parent of the Seattle Men's Chorus, also publishes programs for the Seattle Children's Theatre, Intiman Theatre, Seattle Lesbian/Gay Chorus, the Village Theatre and the Alice B. Theatre. It handles advertising sales and printing of the programs, but no editorial work. Employs three. Contact: Paul Bauer.

EMF
15110 N.E. 95th St., Redmond WA 98052
883-0045
This manufacturer of high-volume sorting equipment for the reprographic and printing industry employs 44. No unsolicited resumes. The receptionist has a list of job announcements. Internships are possible; contact Tom Chudecke, vice president, finance and administration.

Enchanted Parks Inc.
36201 Enchanted Parkway S., Federal Way WA 98003
661-8000
From Tacoma: 925-8000
Joblines:
From Seattle: 661-8027
From Tacoma: 925-8027
This amusement park can see its winter staff of 25 increase to as many as 800 during the spring and summer. Permanent positions include maintenance, advertising, accounting, human resources and administrative. Seasonal positions, which can be full-time or part-time, include camp counselors (for the day camp), ride and game operators, pony ride leaders, lifeguards, costumed characters, food service workers and caterers and gift shop clerks. Also seasonal openings in telemarketing, group sales, switchboard operations, ticket sales, locker and equipment rentals and grounds maintenance. Most seasonal jobs start on a part-time basis on weekends prior to Memorial Day and end on the weekends following Labor Day; the facility operates daily between June and September. Many schedules are flexible. Some positions require a driver's license; others require security checks. You must be

16 to work, although you can be interviewed prior to your 16th birthday. Every qualified applicant is interviewed, if schedules permit. Human resources director: Keith Liebetrau.

Encore Publishing Inc.
87 Wall St., Seattle WA 98121
443-0445
Encore is a small firm that produces—but does not write—the performing arts programs and magazines for such organizations as A Contemporary Theatre, Seattle Opera, Seattle Repertory Theater and the Pacific Northwest Ballet. All writing and editing is done by the arts organizations. Regarding advertising sales or administrative positions, contact Paul Heppner, publisher.

Entenmann's/Oroweat Foods Co.
1604 N. 34th, Seattle WA 98103
634-2700
Job openings at this bakery are often posted on the window by the retail outlet. Resumes can be sent to "Personnel." The corporate staff is small (about 40) and turnover is very limited; many clerical positions are union. Bakery employees, all union, start as "jobbers," an on-call position. Some work two years in that temporary status before a permanent position becomes available.

The Enterprise
P.O. Box 977, Lynnwood WA 98046
775-7521
Joe Pitt heads this publishing company, a unit of Lafromboise Newspapers. Publishes weekly newspapers serving Edmonds, Lynnwood, Mountlake Terrace and Mill Creek. Interns are accepted through college journalism programs.

Enumclaw Courier-Herald
P.O. Box 157, Enumclaw WA 98022
825-2555
A weekly newspaper edited by Kitty Saunders, this is published in combination with the Buckley *News-Banner*. Owned by the Longview *Daily News*, it has a small staff.

Enviros Corp.
25 Central Way, #210, Kirkland WA 98033
827-5525
Jim Quarles is president of this environmental remediation firm. Employs 20 locally. Occasional internships.

Ernst & Young
999 Third Ave., #3500, Seattle WA 98104
621-1800
If you're applying for a professional position at this "Big 6" accounting and consulting firm, contact the human resources director. If you're a recent college grad, contact Vic Breed, campus recruiter. For administrative positions, contact Lynn Howe, administrative director. Current employment: 250.

Ernst Home Centers
1511 Sixth Ave., Seattle WA 98101
621-6700
Jobline: 621-6880
An 80-store home improvement chain. Employs about 300 in the corporate offices. If you're interested in working in one of the 30 stores in the Puget Sound area, you can in a store. Positions range from cashier and receiver to signmaker and kitchen and bath design specialist. The Kent distribution center employs 120.

ESCA Corp.
11120 N.E. 33rd Pl., Bellevue WA 98004
822-6800
Manufactures integrated computer systems for utilities. Internships are possible for upper division students in electrical engineering or computer science. Human resources manager: Diane Coblentz.

Evans Group
190 Queen Anne Ave. N., Seattle WA 98109
285-2222
One of Seattle's oldest and largest advertising agencies. Also offers public relations, food publicity and test kitchens. Interns are taken in most departments from university programs; for information, contact Megan Parker.

Everett Giants
2118 Broadway, Everett WA 98201
258-3673
Established in 1984, this minor league ball club satisfies those who prefer an authentic outdoor baseball experience. Employs seven full-time year around. Seasonal employment is primarily for game-day operations; there are about 60 jobs, but many workers return year after year. Openings are most likely in concessions; employees can then work into jobs in ticketing, gates, security or ushering. Unusual positions include scoreboard operator, mascot and cotton-candy maker. Game-day employment is a minimum of three hours and usually a maximum of four. Pay: minimum wage. You must be at least 16 to apply. Interns are occasionally taken on a seasonal basis, usually for field preparation and game-day clean-up; the rare office internship involves administrative support. To apply, write Melody Tucker, general manager.

Everett Mutual Savings Bank
P.O. Box 569, Everett WA 98206
258-3645
Jobline (when positions are open): 258-0527
Lori Christenson is vice president, human resources, for this nine-branch Snohomish County thrift.

Evergreen Community Development Association
1310 Smith Tower, Seattle WA 98104
622-3731
A private nonprofit that provides small business loans, usually construction and capital loans guaranteed by the Small Business Administration. Employs 10 in Seattle and one in Portland. Unpaid internships sometimes available for those with financial experience or training and computer skills. Some previous interns have worked into paid positions. Executive director: Robert Wisniewski.

Evergreen Hospital Medical Center
12040 N.E. 128th, Kirkland WA 98034
899-1000
Jobline: 899-2502
Employs about 1,500 in a 153-bed hospital, hospice, home health care and related programs. Openings are posted in the human resources office. Personnel contact: Cindy Johnson, associate administrator, human resources.

Evergreen Legal Services
101 Yesler Way, #300, Seattle WA 98104
464-5933
Represents the poor in civil legal actions. Law students are welcome as summer interns. Director: Ada Shen-Jaffe. Personnel contact: Sue Encherman, program administrator.

Evergreen Services Corp.
12010 S.E. 32nd St., Bellevue WA 98005
641-1905
Offers commercial landscaping and landscape management services. Employs a maximum of 80 (including seasonal workers) in such positions as administrative, marketing, horticulturists and field managers. For mid-level and above positions in the field, vocational training is preferred. Susan Hanley is human resources manager.

EVS Consultants, Inc.
200 W. Mercer St., #403, Seattle WA 98109
217-9337
This environmental consulting firm is headed by Robert N. Dexter. Employment: about 20.

Executive Consulting Group
1111 Third Ave., #2700, Seattle WA 98101
689-2200
Andrew MacDonald is the president of this 20-year-old consulting group, which employs about 40. Occasional internships. (Ms.) Lee Kowbel handles recruiting.

Express Systems Inc.
2101 Fourth Ave., #303, Seattle WA 98121
885-5550
Formerly hDC Computer Corp. This software developer, which offers software utilities for Windows applications, employs 10. President: Brian Conte.

The Fearey Group Inc.
1809 Seventh Ave., #1111, Seattle WA 98101
343-1543
Pat Fearey heads this public relations firm. At press time, the firm employed 10. Applicants should have a background (either education or experience) in public relations, marketing or journalism. Interns should be majors in one of these areas.

Federal Home Loan Bank of Seattle
1501 Fourth Ave., #1900, Seattle WA 98101-1693
340-2300
A federally chartered wholesale bank that serves housing lenders in eight western states. Similar to a "banker's bank," the FHLB has the unique advantage of federal status in the capital markets. It raises funds that are then loaned to member institutions. Besides serving as a credit facility, the FHLB offers correspondent banking services. New emphasis on community lending supporting affordable housing programs. Employs 102, most full-time. Occasional interns. Contact: Darren Hamby, human resources director.

Federal Reserve Bank of San Francisco, Seattle Branch
1015 Second Ave., Seattle WA 98104
343-3600
Jobline: 343-3634
The Federal Reserve, the seller of savings bonds and T-bills, is a government-regulated private corporation which also functions as a banker's bank. Many functions have been centralized in San Francisco. Most openings here are entry-level.

Festivals Inc.
P.O. Box 1158, Mercer Island WA 98040
232-2982
An outgrowth of the Bite of Seattle, begun in the early 1980s. Employs seven year around and is expanding outside Washington. Emphasizes food and beverage festivals, including the Bite and the Taste of Tacoma, Coffee Fest and the Great Northwest Microbrewery Invitational and Brewstock. In 1995, will do festivals in Philadelphia, Atlanta and Minneapolis. Offers summer internships to college communications students, who handle projects such as press releases. Interns often come from Washington State University, because the students are available in May, when the seasonal work starts. Also hires between 25 and 75 temporary employees for each festival to handle projects ranging from grounds maintenance to supervision. Some laborer positions are appropriate for high school students and the developmentally disabled; many supervisory positions are filled by people who return each year. Some jobs involve incentive pay; others offer tips. Temps may be hired for one festival—or several. Openings are advertised each spring. Or send a letter of interest, indicating the dates you're available. Interviews are conducted in June.

First Interstate Bank of Washington
P.O. Box 160, Seattle WA 98111
292-3111
Jobline: 292-3551

Employs 2,450 in its Washington corporate headquarters, the Tukwila operations center or the branches. Many branch opportunities are part-time or summer relief. Job openings are posted in the human resources office, located on the sixth floor of the First Interstate Building in downtown Seattle, 999 Third Ave. Applications are available at every branch.

First Mutual Bank
P.O. Box 1647, Bellevue WA 98009
455-7300
Robin Carey handles personnel for this thrift, which employs about 100.

Fisher Companies Inc.
600 University St., #1525, Seattle WA 98101
624-2752
This privately-owned holding company employs fewer than 10. Most job opportunities are at the units, which include Fisher Broadcasting and Fisher Mills.

Fisher Broadcasting Inc.
100 Fourth Ave. N., Seattle WA 98109
Jobline: 443-6444
Fisher owns KOMO radio and television and at press time was purchasing radio stations KVI and KPLZ. Openings are described on the taped message. Many are for part-time or on-call jobs. You can pick up an application at the station's front desk.

Fisher Mills Inc.
P.O. Box C-3765, Seattle WA 98124
622-4430
This flour milling company, which also owns Sam Wylde Flour, employs about 130 total. Occasional part-time and casual jobs in the mill. Personnel contact: Gloria Peterson, executive assistant.

FishPro Inc.
3780 S.E. Mile Hill Dr., Port Orchard WA 98366
871-2727
An environmental and engineering consulting firm with an emphasis on aquaculture and wetland permitting projects. Employs about 25. Each division hires its own staff; resumes of qualified applicants are kept on file.

Fivash Publishing Group
2505 Second Ave., #602, Seattle WA 98121-1426
441-8415
Issues *Washington CEO*, a slick monthly magazine distributed free to company presidents and top managers. Free-lance writers can query editor Kevin Dwyer regarding writing assignments. *PS* (formerly *Peninsula*), a glossy guide to the Olympia Peninsula, is edited by Joy Cordell. *KCTS/9*, the public television guide, is edited by Peter Potterfield. Unpaid internships are available in the editorial staff; contact the editor of the magazine that interests you. The company publishes, but does no editorial work for, a magazine issued by KMPS radio. (See the listing for KMPS earlier in this chapter under Broadcast Stations.)

Fleetfoot Messenger Service

227 9th N., Seattle WA 98109
728-7700
Two openings a month is typical at this company, which delivers small parcels in Seattle, Tacoma and Everett. Employs about 75, about 55 working either full-time or part-time as couriers. Some positions are appropriate for college students. If you're applying for a bicycle courier position, be prepared for hours of nonstop riding each day; if you seek a job driving a car or truck, you'll need a good driving record. Applications are available from the receptionist.

Floathe-Johnson Associates

P.O. Box 97050, Kirkland WA 98083
822-8400
Maury Floathe heads this advertising and public relations firm, which specializes in high technology clients. Besides Kirkland, where it employs 42, the firm has an office in Boise. Clients include Hewlett Packard, Morrison-Knudson, Kenworth Trucks and ATL. Occasional internships are available for public relations students.

Flow International Corp.

P.O. Box 97040, Kent WA 98064-9740
872-4900
Develops ultrahigh-pressure waterjets and abrasive-jets for industrial cutting and milling. Also manufactures, sells and services power scaffolding equipment for commercial and industrial use. Employs 275 locally. Internships are occasionally available. Human resources manager: John Hopp.

Food Services of America

Corporate Office
P.O. Box 84628, Seattle WA 98124
933-5000
FSA employs about 75 in its headquarters; turnover is limited.

Food Services of America, Kent Branch

18430 E. Valley Highway, Kent WA 98032
251-9100
Jobline: 251-1413
Openings are usually listed in a notebook available at the reception desk. Most opportunities are in warehousing and truck driving. All warehouse staff and drivers work on a casual, on-call basis through the Teamsters union. Five or six temporary clerks work in the offices. Limited turnover. Occasional internship opportunities.

Foster Pepper & Shefelman

1111 Third Ave., #3400, Seattle WA 98101
447-4400
This law firm employs about 300 in Seattle and Bellevue. There's also a Portland office; legal recruiting for it is also handled in Seattle. Human resources director: (Mr.) Carroll Livingston.

FourGen Software
115 N.E. 100th St., Seattle WA 98125-8098
522-0055
Sells modifiable financial applications software worldwide. Internships possible
in 1995, probably in software development or technical writing. Human resources
manager: Cindy Ruiz.

Frank Russell Co.
909 A St., P.O. Box 1616, Tacoma WA 98401
Human Resources: 596-3056
Jobline: 596-5454
International financial consulting and investment management are offered by this
financial services firm, which includes Frank Russell Trust Co., Frank Russell
Investment Management Co., Russell Analytical Services and Frank Russell
Securities. Local employment: about 850. Also has offices in London, Toronto,
Sydney, Tokyo, Zurich and New York. Offers monthly information sessions
(similar to information interviews). Informal internships may be possible for
upper division finance students.

Fran's Chocolates
1300 E. Pike, Seattle WA 98122
322-0233
This specialty candy company sells its chocolates across the country. Employs 20
year around; about half are part-time. Seasonal hiring starts in October. General
manager: Cindi Todo.

Fred Hutchinson Cancer Research Center
1124 Columbia St., Mailstop LV-201, Seattle WA 98104
667-5000
Jobline: 667-2977
About 1,800 are employed by this research center, which has an international
reputation for its work in bone marrow and peripheral blood stem transplantation.
Job openings are posted in the personnel office at 1300 Valley St., on the Lake
Union campus. Occasional internships in labs and also formal programs in social
work and basic sciences. The social work internship usually involves one student
at a time; it's arranged through area universities. Interested M.S.W. candidates
should contact their school internship coordinators. As many as 10 undergraduate
students participate in the summer internship program offered through the Basic
Sciences Division (call 667-4617). Fred Hutch recruits nationally for this program, for which you should apply during your holiday vacation or at the beginning
of Winter Quarter. The ideal candidate is a sophomore with biological sciences
background who, although not planning on medical school, expects to attend
graduate school in the sciences. Volunteers do not work on site or in counseling;
however, through the Patient-Family Volunteer program, they provide compan-
ionship and practical help (for example, with housing). Volunteer van drivers
provide transportation. Both volunteer programs involve a one-year commitment.
For those interested in the hospitality industry, volunteers are sought for the
outpatient concierge program, which involves a minimum six-month commitment.
All volunteers receive training; you must be at least 21 and able to provide
consistent support. For information, contact Anne Vedella, 667-4529.

Fred Meyer Inc.
433-6404
Jobline: (800) 401-5627
For information about openings in a Fred Meyer store, stop at the customer information desk of the appropriate store. Opportunities often increase in spring. Most retail positions start as part-time; some are appropriate for 16-year-olds. Seasonal hiring begins in September; the temporary staff works into January. To apply for the entry-level store manager training program, for which previous retail experience is helpful, write:

Christi Grossman
Fred Meyer Inc.
P.O. Box 42121, Portland OR 97242

French Creek Cellars
17721 132nd Ave. N.E., Woodinville WA 98072
486-1900
This winery employs three full-time, seven part-time. Very occasionally there is short-term seasonal work in production.

Funtasia Inc.
7212 220th St. S.W., Edmonds WA 98026
775-2174
If you're a high school or college student looking for a part-time job, consider this indoor/outdoor family amusement park. At press time, it employed 60, nearly all students working while attending school. Employment may increase on a seasonal basis in 1995. Some positions are appropriate for 16-year-olds; others require that you be at least 18. Dependability and honesty are important; the managers also like cashiering experience and, in the food concessions, restaurant experience. Contact: Jenny Mackie, manager.

Gai's Bakery
2006 S. Weller, Seattle WA 98144
322-0931
Personnel/jobline: 726-7517
The management staff is very small; many office jobs are union and have almost no turnover. To work in the bakery, you must start on a part-time, on-call basis; positions may become full-time within a year or so. Occasional summer opportunities as vacation relief.

Generra Sportswear Co. Inc.
Once a leading fashion sportswear manufacturer, this firm has become a licensor and reduced its staff to five. No openings expected.

GeoEngineers
8410 154th Ave. N.E., Redmond WA 98052
861-6000
John Cykler Jr. is human resources manager for this 150-employee Northwest-based environmental, geological and geotechnical engineering consulting firm. Headquartered in Redmond, the firm also has offices in Tacoma, Bellingham, Spokane, Portland and Anchorage. No formal internships, but occasional summer

openings for upper division or graduate civil engineering students pursuing geotechnical engineering.

Gilmore Research Group
2324 Eastlake Ave. E., #300, Seattle WA 98102
726-5555
This market research firm employs approximately 400 nationwide and 100 locally. It provides field audits, telephone surveys and product demonstrations. Student interns sometimes work summers, assisting analysts; for information, contact JoElla Weybright. For part-time employment as a telephone interviewer (a job appropriate for students), contact Cathy Peda.

Giant Pacific Companies
P.O. Box C-3637, Seattle WA 98124
628-6222
Pacific Fabrics and Crafts, a fabric and craft retailer, Pacific Iron & Metal, a scrap recycler, and Pacific Building Materials are the divisions of this firm. Expects to establish a new division to distribute fabrics and garments made of recycled materials (for example, plastic soda bottles). Employs more than 200. Carol Canfield handles personnel.

GMA Research Corp.
11808 Northup Way, #270, Bellevue WA 98005
827-1251
Jamie Baba, director, client services, handles personnel for this market research firm, which employs about 20 full-time. Telephone interviewers work on a project basis; for information, contact Cheri Williams.

Golden Grain Macaroni Co.
4100 Fourth Ave. S., Seattle WA 98134
623-2038
This division of Quaker Oats makes rice mixes and pasta. Employs about 85. Occasional interns in quality assurance. Employee and community relations manager: Gloria Ang.

Good Samaritan Hospital
407 14th Ave. S.E., Puyallup WA 98372
848-6661
Jobline: 848-6661, Ext. 1905
About 2,100 work in this health care organization's two divisions: the 225-bed hospital and the outreach programs. Many work part-time; some work on-call. Occasional seasonal openings for students who help with summer grounds maintenance. Openings are posted in the human resources office and near the cafeteria. Internships occasionally available in such departments as the pharmacy, physical therapy, mental health, social work, public relations, community development and accounting. You must be enrolled in a college program to apply for an internship; in most cases, interns are paid.

Group Health Cooperative of Puget Sound
521 Wall St., Seattle WA 98121
Human Resources: 448-2728
Jobline: 448-5100
This health maintenance organization employs 9,500 in its hospitals and clinics in the Puget Sound area. For more information on the positions listed on the jobline, you can visit the Human Resources offices in Seattle, 521 Wall St., or Tacoma, 124 Tacoma Ave. S., second floor, 383-4883. If you're a free-lance writer, direct inquiries regarding assignments (health topics only) to *View*, the magazine sent to Group Health members. Contact the editor, Jan Short, at 448-5648.

GTE Northwest
1800 41st St., Everett WA 98201
261-5321
Joblines:
Management positions: 261-5667
Hourly positions: 261-5777
The second largest telephone company in Washington. Offers internships most years; openings are posted in college placement offices. The number and type of internships depends on company needs; in 1994, there were only six and most were for technical majors.

Hagen, Kurth, Perman & Co.
601 Union St., #2700, Seattle WA 98101-2392
682-9200
This firm offers audit, tax and advisory services as well as network integration systems, a part of the firm affiliated with USConnect. It also provides computer training on such systems as Novell and Microsoft NT. Limited seasonal employment in accounting (December through April). Occasional internships for upper division accounting students. Recruiter: Bruce Larson, administrator.

Half Price Books
If you're looking for a company where you can work your way up, consider this used book, record and software company. Started in 1972, it now employs 500 across the country—and only two didn't begin shelving books. Another plus: Half Price is recognized for its "family friendly" policies, including maternity, paternity and elder care and full-time benefits for everyone who's worked three years. In this area, the chain now has five stores, with a sixth planned for late 1995 or early '96. The stores employ a total of 55, about 80 per cent working full-time. Seattle's U District store, with 16, is the largest. There are also three regional employees. The workforce is fairly stable, but turnover is estimated at about 20 per cent a year; for application information, stop at the store of your choice. You must be 16 or older and retail experience is preferred; a customer service orientation is a must. Pay starts between $5 and $6 an hour, but there's also a profit-based bonus. Internships may be offered locally by 1995; they also are available in the Dallas corporate headquarters in such departments as marketing.

Harrison Memorial Hospital
2520 Cherry Ave., Bremerton WA 98310
377-3911
Jobline: 792-6729

This 297-bed facility posts its openings just outside the personnel office. Limited turnover; inquiries can be directed to Kathy Mork, human resources director, or Vicki Lee, nurse recruiter.

Hart Crowser
1910 Fairview Ave. E., Seattle WA 98102
324-9530
Paula Houston is the human resources manager for this engineering consulting firm. Internships possible for students in programs with an environmental emphasis; for example, chemical or geotechnical engineering, hydrogeology, geochemistry or geology.

Health and Hospital Services Corp.
15325 S.E. 30th Pl., Bellevue WA 98007
747-1711
This nonprofit owned by the Sisters of St. Joseph of Peace operates hospitals, nursing homes, a health maintenance organization and a chemical dependency treatment firm in the Northwest. The only local facility is the Marionwood nursing home in Issaquah. Thirty-eight work in the corporate headquarters, a few on a part-time basis. Contact: Scott Houston, vice president, human resources.

Heart Technology Inc.
17425 N.E. Union Hill Rd., Redmond WA 98052-3376
869-6160
Makes a device that cleans the plaque from arteries, creating a less expensive alternative to bypass surgery. You can learn of most openings by stopping at the main reception desk, where applications are also available. Interns are usually upper division students; in 1994, four summer interns worked in human resources, manufacturing operations, engineering and information services. Human resources manager: Karen Grosz.

Hebert Research Inc.
13629 N.E. Bellevue-Redmond Rd., Bellevue WA 98005
643-1337
Employs 25, about 15 part-time. If you're interested in a research analyst position at this market research firm, direct your inquiry to John Burshek, vice president. For jobs in data collection (often with telephone surveys), contact the data collection supervisor. Most telephone survey jobs are part-time permanent.

Helly-Hansen (U.S.) Inc.
P.O. Box 97031, Redmond WA 98073
883-8823
This activewear designer and manufacturer employs about 50 in its corporate office; the staff is stable, so openings are limited. An occasional internship for a student in accounting or design; high school students can sometimes work in clerical positions.

Henry Bacon Building Materials
P.O. Box 7012, Issaquah WA 98027-7012
Human Resources: 391-2075, Ext. 356

This building materials chain emphasizes contractor sales. It employs about 300, most of those full-time. Some part-time opportunities for weekend work, either in the lumberyards or as a cashier. May add 20 or 30 summer employees in the stores; most work between 25 and 40 hours weekly, usually on weekends. Seasonal recruiting starts in May; you must be 18 or older. To apply, contact any store or the Issaquah headquarters.

The Herald
P.O. Box 930, Everett WA 98206
Human Resources: 339-3024
Jobline: 339-3009
This 60,000-circulation daily is owned by the Washington *Post*. Stan Strick is executive editor. Employs 300. Openings are posted in the front lobby at California and Grand in downtown Everett. Internships are often available during the summer in both editorial and advertising operations for upper division students.

Herring/Newman Direct Response Advertising
414 Olive Way, #300, Seattle WA 98101
343-9000
This direct response advertising agency now employs about 75, with others working in the small offices in Boston and San Francisco. Intern applicants should contact Sandy Brown.

Hewitt/Isley
119 Pine St., #400, Seattle WA 98101
624-8154
Tim Spelman handles personnel for this architectural firm, which employs about 30. Graduate students in architecture are occasionally taken as interns.

Hewlett-Packard Co.
8600 Soper Hill Rd., Everett WA 98205
335-2000
Jobline: 334-2244
The Lake Stevens Instrument Division of this national electronics firm employs about 350. Upper division engineering students can apply for summer internships through this office or the corporate headquarters:

S.E.E.D. Recruiting
3000 Hanover St., Palo Alto CA 94304-1181

Highline Community Hospital
16251 Sylvester Rd. S.W., Seattle WA 98166
244-9970
Jobline: 431-5325
Provides a variety of programs, including senior citizen health care and alcohol and drug abuse treatment. For information about volunteer opportunities, which can provide both valuable experience and a look at health care as a career, contact Cathy Kalin, 244-9970, Ext. 298. Volunteers can work in areas as diverse as the emergency room, occupational and recreational therapy and the pharmacy. Some volunteer positions are appropriate for those as young as 14; others require that you

be at least 18. Some specialized positions, including peer counseling in the geriatric psychiatry unit, use people 55 and older. Volunteers are interviewed just as job applicants are; they receive hospital and safety orientation, on-job training and, in some cases, classroom training.

Hillhaven
1148 Broadway Plaza, Tacoma WA 98402-2264
572-4901
This public company, which operates long-term care facilities, retirement housing and pharmacies, employs 1,720 in the Puget Sound area. Job openings are posted in the fourth floor personnel office.

Holland America Line-Westours
300 Elliott Ave. W., Seattle WA 98119
281-3535
Jobline: 286-3496
Interested in cruises and tours? Holland America owns Windstar Cruises, Grayline of Seattle and Grayline of Alaska, charter bus operator Cascade Trailways and the Westmark Hotels in Alaska. Full-time, part-time and seasonal positions, some in Seattle, some in Alaska and others aboard cruise ships. Internships may be possible in 1995 in such corporate departments as human resources and accounting; these may be paid, unpaid or work-study positions. Many shipboard positions are filled by concessionaires (e.g., photographers) or by foreign unions; detailed information is available on the jobline. Seasonal jobs often require early applications; for example, if you'd like to escort bus tours in Alaska between May and September, you should apply between October and February for the next year. Bus drivers for the same tours should apply before year end.

Home Depot
District Office
6810 S. 180th St., Tukwila WA 98188
Human Resources: 394-0371
This national warehouse-style home improvement center may have as many as 12 stores in the Seattle area in 1995. A typical store employs 180, with about 15 per cent working part-time. No seasonal hires; business peaks are handled by increasing the hours of part-timers. To groom management candidates from within, Home Depot provides a 12-week training program for every salaried new hire. There's also a 12-18-month training program for other management recruits. Management candidates should apply to Steve Cope at the address above. If you're seeking an hourly position at an existing store, apply in the store of your choice; when new stores are opened, there's usually a job fair where applications are accepted. For nonmanagement positions, experience is preferred but not required for all positions; you must be 18 or older and able to lift 50 pounds. Pay is based on merit; the average hourly rate is estimated at more than $10.

Hornall/Anderson Design Works Inc.
1008 Western Ave., #600, Seattle WA 98104
467-5800
If you're a graphic designer, your inquiry should go to John Hornall. Employs 31. Internships possible for graphic design students.

H.O. Sports Inc.
17622 N.E. 67th Ct., Redmond WA 98052
885-3505
Water ski manufacturer. Employs about 100. Employment contacts: Brian Gardner, sales manager, for outside sales; Jack Sappenfield, vice president, customer service, for inside sales; Bob McKeeman, shop supervisor, for manufacturing jobs; and Brenda Marty, shop supervisor, for receiving and shipping positions. Seasonal workers are usually hired through a temporary agency. Interns can sometimes work summers in such areas as customer service.

Host International, Inc.
Seattle Tacoma International Airport, Seattle WA 98158
433-5611
Operates restaurants, catering and in-flight kitchens for airlines. Local employment: about 575, mostly full-time. There are seasonal positions before Christmas and during the summer. Openings are posted in the state Job Service Centers and in the Host office on the mezzazine level of the main terminal. Recruiter: Mary Lee Tabora.

Howard Needles Tammen & Bergendoff
600 108th Ave. N.E., #405, Bellevue WA 98004
455-3555
Carol Pomeroy is the personnel director for this architectural and engineering firm. Interns can sometimes work in computer-aided design, as engineering technicians or assisting an architect; they can be either community college or university students.

Humongous Entertainment
13110 N.E. 177th Pl., #180, Woodinville WA 98072
485-1212
This young software developer has received favorable notices in *The Wall Street Journal* as well as industry publications for its children's computer games. Will employ about 35 by 1995. Founded by Ron Gilbert and Shelley Day.

Iasys Corp.
Backed by Immunex Corp., this new biotech is being organized to develop diagnostic tests, therapies and vaccines for infectious diseases. At press time, was raising funds and did not yet have employees. President: John Calvert.

IBM
Jobline: (800) 831-2303
Through consolidation and downsizing, IBM's local staff is expected to continue to decline. No applications or job postings are available in Seattle. Recruiting is now handled by a wholly-owned subsidiary, Employment Solutions Corp.

Icicle Seafoods Inc.
4019 21st Ave. W., Seattle WA 98199
282-0988
Jobline: 281-5331
Julie Aydelotte is the human resources manager for this seafood processor. One of Seattle's largest, with operations in the Northwest and Alaska. The corporate

staff is small (about 50) and there's limited turnover; many of the positions require employees to spend part of the year in Alaska. The company hires as many as 400 from Seattle to work on a seasonal basis, but all of these positions are hourly (starting at $5.25) and aboard processing vessels in Alaska. The number of openings each year depends on how many previous employees return; some years there are no opportunities. Prospective employees can attend an orientation session that explains living and working conditions.

ICOS Corp.
22021 20th Ave. S.E., Bothell WA 98021
485-1900
Jobline: through operator
This biopharmaceutical is working on medications for such chronic inflammatory diseases as asthma, multiple sclerosis and arthritis. College students are often hired for summer projects. Positions are filled prior to April 1. To apply for a student internship, you should send a resume and letter of interest, describing what you'd like to do and the value of your project to the company. Human resources representative: Diane Murphy.

Immunex Corp.
51 University St., Seattle WA 98101
587-0430
Jobline: 389-4060
Anita Williamson is the human resources director for this biotech, which focuses on the research, development, marketing and manufacture of immunological therapeutic products. Job openings are posted at the reception desk (use the 1201 Western Ave. entrance). Or visit the Bothell operation at 21511 23rd Dr. S.E. Employs 800, most of them in the Puget Sound area. There's no formal internship program, but students are often employed, some part-time, some full-time.

Imre Corp.
401 Queen Anne Ave. N., Seattle WA 98109
298-9400
Develops immunoabsorption treatments. Internships possible in 1995 for science students. Personnel contact: Alex de Soto, chief financial officer.

InControl
6675 185th Ave. N.E., Redmond WA 98052
861-9800
This start-up is researching an implantable heart pacemaker. Employs 90. Internships are occasionally available for college students in the sciences. Human resources manager: Kay Hannah.

Interlinq Software Corp.
11255 Kirkland Way, Kirkland WA 98033
827-1112
Sandy Daubenspeck is personnel manager for this developer of PC-based software for the mortgage banking industry. Occasionally offers paid student internships in such departments as MIS and product development; applicants usually need to be studying a technical discipline (for example, computer science). Applicants for marketing internships should be majors in related fields.

Interpoint Corp.

P.O. Box 97005, Redmond WA 98073-9705

882-3100

Jobline: through operator

Manufacturer of communications and military microelectronics. Interns are hired for clerical work in many departments; a few are also taken in engineering. Human resources director: Shannon Dillingham. A wholly owned subsidiary is:

Advanced Digital Information Corp.

14737 N.E. 87th St., P.O. Box 97057, Redmond WA 99073-9757

881-8004

A manufacturer of tape backups. Employs 70. At press time, personnel was handled by the office manager.

InterWest Savings Bank

P.O. Box 1649, Oak Harbor WA 98277

679-4181

Toll-free within Washington: (800) 422-0235

Jobline: Ext. 888

This thrift will have 28 branches statewide by early 1995, including several offices in the Seattle area. Employs 375, including branch relief staff who work on an on-call basis. Occasionally hires college students for summer work. Resumes should be directed to Human Resources at the corporate office or to the branches specified on the jobline.

Jay Jacobs, Inc.

1530 Fifth Ave., Seattle WA 98101

622-5400

This publicly held specialty retailer has expanded from Seattle across the country. In May, 1994, however, *The Wall Street Journal* noted that Jay Jacobs had filed for reorganization under Chapter 11 of the bankruptcy code, citing the financial burden caused by several unprofitable stores. In western Washington, it has 27 stores and a distribution center. Employs about 2,000 total. For corporate management positions, contact Human Resources. For retail positions, apply in any store. For warehouse positions, apply at the distribution center at 19821 89th Ave. S., Kent WA 98031 (872-5730). Stores increase their staffs about 10 per cent during the summer (recruiting begins in May) and holiday (recruiting begins in November) seasons. For entry-level positions in the stores, sales experience is preferred, although high school students are occasionally hired to start in shipping and receiving. A customer service orientation and interest in clothing is important. Occasional unpaid internships.

J.C. Penney Co., Inc.

District Office

P.O. Box 24087, Seattle WA 98124

575-4865

If you'd like to work in sales at Penney's, you can pick up an application in any store, usually at the switchboard. Stores often have sales support, warehouse and alterations positions, too. Many jobs are part-time. If you're interested in management in the 13-store district extending from Northgate to Aberdeen, submit a resume to Jerry Ulsund, district personnel manager, at the address above. College students pursuing retailing should inquire about summer internships; many former interns return to Penney's as management trainees or assistant buyers. Interested in seasonal employment? The stores hire both for "back to school" and Christmas. For "back to school," hiring starts in June; a large store like Southcenter may employ as many as 50, mostly part-time. Holiday hiring starts in October, with 150 or more being added to the staff. Again, most work part-time. (Many are professionals with other full-time positions.)

John Graham Associates

900 Fourth Ave., #700, Seattle WA 98164
461-6000
John Pettit handles personnel for this architectural, engineering and planning firm, which employs 55. Upper division and graduate students can sometimes work as interns. Occasional openings for high school students.

Jon Rowley & Associates

3916 15th Pl. W., Seattle WA 98119
283-7566
This food and beverage consulting and marketing firm has national clients and receives much media attention, but it employs only two. Unpaid internships are possible, especially for public relations students. Contact Jon Rowley.

Journal American

P.O. Box 90130, Bellevue WA 98009-9230
455-2222
The Eastside's daily newspaper, with a circulation of about 35,000. Affiliated publications: the Mercer Island *Reporter*, the Bothell-Woodinville *Citizen,* the Snohomish Valley *News*, all weeklies, and the Port Angeles daily and the *Valley Daily News.* Editor: Jack Mayme. Vice president, human resources: Nick Chernock. Job announcements are available from the receptionist.

Junior Sports Publishing Inc.

P.O. Box 9921, Seattle WA 98109
284-4574
A small new firm that publishes *Junior Tennis* magazine five times a year. Hires free-lancers. Takes editorial and production interns. President: Emily Smith.

KCM Inc.

1917 First Ave., Seattle WA 98101
443-5300
Formerly Kramer, Chin & Mayo, Inc. Sharon Webb is the human resources coordinator for this engineering firm. Upper division engineering students can apply at any time for the occasional internship.

KeyBank of Puget Sound

P.O. Box 11500, Mailstop 0250, Tacoma WA 98411-5500
Jobline: (800) 677-6150
The second largest bank in Washington. Now has about 200 branches and 4,000 employees. Many part-time opportunities in entry-level positions (teller, recep-

tionist, customer service). Some summer relief positions possible in 1995. Applications can be mailed to the address above or delivered to either human resources office: in Tacoma, 1119 Pacific Ave., eighth floor; in Seattle, 700 Fifth Ave, arcade level.

Kidder Peabody & Co. Inc.
700 Fifth Ave., #5400, Seattle WA 98104-5054
628-8575
This stock brokerage and investment banking firm employs about 110 in Seattle. College students are hired for part-time work as sales assistants, the mailroom or for computer work. Industry interest is helpful, as is previous office experience and computer skills. Human resources contact: Cheryl Archer, vice president and branch administrator.

KidStar 1250 AM/Children's Media Network
1334 First Ave., #150, Seattle WA 98101
382-1250
This new multimedia network for children and adults offers a radio station, a magazine and a phone system (KidZone) that allows children to participate in radio broadcasts and telephone in ideas for future magazine features. Will employ 45 full-time by 1995; also employs about a dozen part-time. Few employment opportunities; applications are accepted only for open positions. Interns are welcome, especially in radio broadcasting, print production and promotions. Contact: Diane Gary, director of administration.

KidSwim
23509 32nd Ave. W., Brier WA 98036
485-2289
This swimming program for children employs both swim instructors and registration clerks on a part-time basis, often 20 hours a week. Employs about 18 permanently, with an additional 10 hired during summer. Many instructors are college students; others are housewives and retirees. Requirements: lifesaving and water safety instructor (WSI) certification, plus the ability to work with small children. Experience as a camp counselor or working with preschoolers is valuable. All instructors start as aides. You can volunteer as an aide to earn swim lessons, either for yourself or your children. Instructors must be at least 17. The office staff, which takes lesson registrations by telephone, includes some high school students. No computer skills are required, although swimming ability and WSI certification are preferred. President: Joan Breda.

King Broadcasting Co.
333 Dexter Ave. N., Seattle WA 98109
448-5555
Jobline: 448-3915
Sold by the founding Bullitt family to the Providence (R.I.) *Journal*, this broadcasting company now includes KING-5 television, the Puget Sound-area NBC affiliate, and several other television stations. College juniors or seniors interested in unpaid internships (full-time during the summer, part-time during school terms) may contact Human Resources regarding these quarter-long programs in such areas as news, marketing, sales and broadcast production. You need not be a communications major to apply.

King County Medical Blue Shield
P.O. Box 21267, Seattle WA 98111
Human Resources: 464-3654
Jobline: 464-5588
Health-care insurance firm. Employs 1,500 here and in four branches: Snohomish, Lewis, Cowlitz and Yakima. No unsolicited resumes. Applications are available at the customer service desk at 1800 9th Ave. There are occasional project opportunities, but most recruiting is done internally or among former Blue Shield employees.

KIRO, Inc.
2807 Third Ave., Seattle WA 98121
728-7777
Jobline: 728-5205
Owned by Bonneville International Corp., Salt Lake City, KIRO operates KIRO-TV, Channel 7 television, the CBS affiliate; KIRO-AM, 710: KIRO-FM, 100.7; and Third Avenue Productions. Has announced plans to buy KING-AM and with that deal, would assume advertising sales responsibilities for KING-FM. Pick up a job application in the KIRO lobby. If you're a college junior or senior or in your final year at a vocational or community college student, you may be eligible for a three-month unpaid internship in radio, television, marketing, public affairs, accounting or human resources; for details, write Jane Martin.

Kits Cameras
6051 S. 194th St., Kent WA 98032
872-3688
Photographic gear retailer; 115 locations in several western states. If you'd like to work in a store, apply with the store manager. Very limited seasonal opportunities—perhaps only 25 chain-wide.

Kitsap Federal Credit Union
1025 Burwell St., Bremerton WA 98310
478-2200
Claire Lucas is vice president, human resources, for this seven-branch thrift. Total employment: about 175. Part-time opportunities are expected to increase in 1995. Students can work at KFCU through high school and community college co-op programs.

Knight Vale & Gregory
1145 Broadway Plaza, #900, Tacoma WA 98402
572-7111
Michelle Chopp handles personnel for this public accounting firm. Employs as many as 90 in its three offices: Tacoma, Olympia and Renton. Some seasonal opportunities.

KP Corp./Impression Northwest, Inc.
2001 22nd Ave. S., Seattle WA 98144
328-2770
Chuck Parsons is president of this large commercial printer. Internships possible.

KPMG Peat Marwick

601 Union St., #3100, Seattle WA 98101
292-1500
Public accounting and consulting firm. Maggie Ethington handles administrative recruiting. Because "alumni" of the office often return during tax season, there are no seasonal opportunities.

K2 Corp.

19215 Vashon Highway S.W., Vashon WA 98070
463-3631
Alpine ski and snowboard manufacturer. Few openings other than entry level because of internal promotions. No seasonal hiring. Occasional internships. Contact Robert Moynan or the personnel office, open Monday through Thursday.

Laidlaw Transit Inc.

13525 Lake City Way N.E., Seattle WA 98125
365-7300
Jobline: #4
The yellow buses that criss-cross Seattle daily with schoolchildren are from Laidlaw. The firm also operates a charter department. Most openings are for bus-driving, a part-time position with split shifts. Most drivers work only the academic year, with some on-call work during the summer. In mid-1994, starting hourly pay ranged between $7 and $12.75. Laidlaw employs 300 drivers. Applicants must be at least 21 and have at least three years driving experience; you'll be trained for the commercial driving license you must obtain.

Lamonts Apparel Inc.

3650 131st Ave. S.E., Bellevue WA 98006
644-5700
Jobline: through operator
This regional retailer operates 56 stores in eight states. Its management training program, which involves six to 18 months of on-the-job training, is open to recent college graduates and to internal candidates. Seasonal hires can work part-time during November and December. Internships are available in such departments as advertising, MIS and stores operation; these paid assignments are full-time, usually 12 weeks in length.

Landau Associates, Inc.

P.O. Box 1029, Edmonds WA 98020
778-0907
Environmental and geotechnical engineering consulting firm. Internships are possible. Personnel contact: Julie Stutz.

Larry's Markets

16000 Christensen Rd., Bldg. 2, #300, Seattle WA 98188
243-2951
By mid-1995 this upscale grocer will operate six stores and a catering division that serves everything from box lunches to banquets. Will employ about 950. About 25 per cent of the staff is part-time. All openings are posted in the stores. Occasional internships in departments such as advertising and environmental.

Learning World
17500 W. Valley Highway, Tukwila WA 98188
656-2900
Beth Lyden handles personnel for this 10-store chain of educational toy stores. Some seasonal opportunities for "back to school" and Christmas; some part-time opportunities in the stores.

Leviton Manufacturing, Inc.
Telcom Division
2222 222nd St. S.E., Bothell WA 98021-4422
486-2222
Jobline: 485-5100, Ext. JOBS
About 120 work in the Canyon Park operation of this data and voice communications firm. Professional recruiting is the responsibility of Joy Adamson-Clark. High school and college students can intern in human resources, marketing and engineering; in most cases, these positions start as unpaid but may work into paid assignments.

Livingston & Co.
800 Fifth Ave., #3800, Seattle WA 98104
382-5500
Advertising agency. Employs 30. The occasional internship in research is posted on university campuses. Personnel manager: Holly Nottingham.

Lone Wolf Inc.
2030 First Ave., Third Floor, Seattle WA 98121
728-9600
A Redondo, Calif. firm that announced a move to the Seattle area after a significant investment by Paul Allen, Microsoft co-founder. The *Puget Sound Business Journal* describes Lone Wolf's MediaLink software as a means of networking CD players, power amplifiers, equalizers, mixers, laserdisc players, monitors and video cameras. Employs 35; internships possible in marketing and technical support. Chief operating officer: Byron McCall.

Lumberman's
3773 Martin Way E., Bldg. A, Olympia WA 98506
456-1880
This building supply firm is the only Puget Sound-area division of Lanoga Corp. Operates 30 stores in Washington, Idaho and Oregon, about a third of them in the Puget Sound area. Each store hires its own staff.

Lutheran Alliance for Transitional and Community Housing (LATCH)
6532 Phinney N., Seattle WA 98103
789-1536
This independent housing group currently employs two and uses interns. Also offers volunteer opportunities. Operates both multi-family and single-family low-income housing. Executive director: Katherine Roseth.

Mach Publishing
P.O. Box 499, Snohomish WA 98291
258-9396
This job printing and publishing firm issues three weeklies, the Everett *News Tribune*, the Snohomish County *Tribune*, and the Monroe *Tribune*. Employs 33; occasionally takes an intern in editorial. Contact: Dave Mach, publisher.

Manson Construction & Engineering Company
P.O. Box 24067, Seattle WA 98124
762-0850
Turnover is limited at this marine construction firm. About 25 salaried employees. The field work force is unionized. If you're an engineer, contact Robert Stevens, chief estimator. Some other personnel is handled by (Ms.) Pat Gage, controller. Internships possible; inquiries should be directed to Stevens.

Manus Services Corp.
P.O. Box 440406, Seattle WA 98114-4406
325-2200
This firm now has only one division, Manus Direct Response Marketing, which employs 75. Manus Temporary Services has been sold to General Employment. Internships possible in 1995. Human resources manager: Dawn Ross.

Marine Digest
P.O. Box 3905, Seattle WA 98124
682-3607
This monthly magazine focuses on the marine industry. Employs eight full-time. Buys some free-lance pieces. Internships possible. Contact: Alec Fisken, publisher.

Mariposa/Savannah
P.O. Box 40, Woodinville WA 98072
483-6556
These divisions of Charles F. Berg Inc. retail women's junior fashions in 11 stores in the Puget Sound area. For a sales position, you should have a customer service attitude, the ability to sell and a sense of professionalism. Retail experience is preferred, but not required. For part-time positions, you must be at least 16; for full-time positions, those 18 or older are preferred. Three primary management levels: assistant manager, the entry level; a "manager in training," someone who has retail experience and is receiving training for three or four months; and store manager, a position usually filled by promotion from within. The warehouse crew varies from four to 13, depending on the season. For seasonal sales positions, Mariposa recruits in June and July (for "back to school") and in October and November for holiday. The staff can easily increase by 75 per cent during each of these rush periods. Seasonal warehouse recruiting is earlier: May for "back to school" and September for holiday. Internships are possible in the corporate offices. Personnel director: Susan Sturholm.

Market Spice
85-A Pike Pl., Seattle WA 98101
622-6340

Runs a retail store in the Pike Place Market and a warehouse in Redmond. Retail, mail order and wholesale operations. Employs 25 total, of whom 10 are part-time. Adds some part-time staff in the store during the tourist season (Memorial through Labor days) and, for the holidays, October through December. A must: strong sales ability and maturity. There's limited turnover and only occasional seasonal opportunities in the warehouse, where the employees include senior citizens who work part-time. Contact: Judy Dawson, manager.

Marriott International
110 110th Ave. N.E., #220, Bellevue WA 98004
453-1521
Besides hotels, Marriott runs food and facilities management programs for schools, colleges, businesses and health-care facilities.

McCann-Erickson
1011 Western Ave., #600, Seattle WA 98104
682-6360
A unit of the Interpublic Group of Companies, New York, this advertising agency employs 50 in Seattle. Interns can often work in account services or media; contact Michelle McEttrick, account supervisor.

McCaw Cellular Communications Co. Inc.
5400 Carillon Point, Kirkland WA 98033
827-4500
Jobline: 828-8484
McCaw employs 400 in its corporate office and Lin Broadcasting, in the same offices, employs 30 locally. To learn of openings, use the jobline or check at the front desk, where there's a notebook with job announcements. Internships are possible for 1995. Resumes should be directed to "People Development." A McCaw-AT&T merger is pending; after the deal closes, McCaw's rapid growth is expected to continue.

McChord Credit Union
P.O. Box 4207, Tacoma WA 98438
584-6413
Jobline: 589-8012
With four branches, this credit union employs 145. It accepts applications only for open positions. You can pick up an application form at the personnel office on the second floor of the Lakewood branch, 6019 Lake Grove S.W., Tacoma.

McCullagh Leasing
415 Baker Blvd., #110, Seattle WA 98188
431-8332
A unit of General Electric Capital Fleet Services, this office employs only about 15. Occasionally, however, it needs part-time mechanics and drivers to handle rental cars. Work may be on-call.

McHugh Restaurants
419 Occidental S., #501, Seattle WA 98104
223-9353
This upscale restaurant chain, which runs six restaurants including New Jake's, the

Leschi Lake Cafe, F. X. McRory's and the Roost, has a very small corporate staff, but resumes are always welcome. If you're interested in a restaurant management position, contact Michael Douglas, operations manager; for other restaurant positions, you can apply with the restaurant manager. Seasonal opportunities vary by location. New Jake's is busier at Christmas while Leschi boosts its staff significantly for summer. At McRory's, part-time wait staff is added during Mariner and Seahawk season for game days. Because the Sonics will be playing in the Tacoma Dome during Coliseum renovation, T.S. McHugh's is expected to need fewer staff. A catering operation is being established and some provide some on-call opportunities.

Media Index Publishing, Inc.
P.O. Box 24365, Seattle WA 98124
382-9220
Publishes *Media Inc.*, a monthly tabloid for the Washington and Oregon advertising, entertainment and production industries and annual indexes for the film production, creative and advertising industries. Staff writing positions; free-lance material is also purchased. Internships are possible in editorial, sales or production. Contact Richard K. Woltjer, publisher, regarding production internships; Paul Gargaro, editor, regarding free-lancing and editorial internships; and Jim Baker regarding sales internships.

Medio Multimedia Inc.
2643 151st Pl. N.E., Redmond WA 98052
867-5500
Publishes CD-ROMs on such subjects as ancient architecture, the assassination of John F. Kennedy and old movies. By 1995, a dozen titles may be in distribution. At press time, employed 15, seven of whom were former Microsoft colleagues. Also hires professionals on a contract basis. Interns can work in marketing. Contacts: Steve Podradchik, founder and president; Lisa Malkoff, office manager.

Mercer Island Reporter
P.O. Box 38, Mercer Island WA 98040
232-1215
This weekly has an editorial staff of six headed by Jane Meyer. Free-lance and intern opportunities.

Message!Check Corp.
P.O. Box 3206, Seattle WA 98114
463-3299
Toll-free: (800) 243-2565
This Vashon Island firm is credited with transforming checks into a fund-raising vehicle for nonprofits. No free-lance opportunities. Will consider interns; however, candidates must be aware of the location's distance from Seattle and the very technical nature of the work. Owner: Priscilla Beard.

Metropolitan Federal Savings and Loan Association
1520 Fourth Ave., Seattle WA 98101-1648
625-1818
This 11-branch thrift employs 100. There are part-time opportunities in entry-level

positions in the branches. You'll find a sheet describing current openings on the fourth floor. Human resources director: Cathy McAlhaney.

MicroDisk Services
15530 Woodinville-Redmond Rd., Bldg. B, #100, Woodinville WA 98072
881-1609
One of two local subsidiaries of the Prism Group, MicroDisk offers high volume disk duplication and software packaging. Full-time employment is about 250. On a temporary basis, MicroDisk may hire as many as 300—all through agencies. However, temps have access to the internal job postings and so can see what permanent positions are available. Openings are also posted at state Job Service Centers and often advertised. Also see Software Production Inc.

MicroProbe Corp.
1725 220th S.E., Bothell WA 98021
485-8566
This biotech develops diagnostic and therapeutic DNA probes. In mid-94 a patent dispute forced the company to remove from the market its major revenue-generating product; as a result, several employees were laid off and growth slowed. No internships, but post-doctoral positions are available. Human resources director: Nancy Ryan.

Microscan Systems Inc.
1201 S.W. 7th St., Renton WA 98055
682-5293
Designs and manufactures bar-code scanners. Employed 72 at press time, with some growth expected. Applications available at the reception desk. Inquiries regarding jobs and internships can be mailed to Lynn LaDou, benefits administrator. Internship applicants should be upper division engineering students.

Microsoft Corp.
One Microsoft Way, Redmond WA 98052-6399
882-8080
Jobline: 936-5500
(800) 892-3181
This large software firm posts job openings—but not summer jobs for college students—in its recruiting office, Bldg. 24. Postings are updated each Monday. You'll also find openings, both permanent and contract, advertised in the Seattle papers. Resumes are always accepted; address yours to "Recruiting." College students and those enrolled in graduate school will find special listings for them on the jobline; summer opportunities are also posted in campus recruiting offices. Or you can apply through College Relations.

Midisoft Corp.
P.O. Box 1000, Bellevue WA 98009
881-7176
Develops software for Windows multimedia applications using MIDI (musical instruments digital interface) standards. Employs 35, with growth expected to continue. Accepts occasional student interns in engineering. To inquire about openings, you can send your resume to the address above (it'll be held on file for

a year) or visit the company offices at 15379 N.E. 90th, Redmond WA 98052. Human resources director: Bonnie Seefeldt.

Milliman & Robertson, Inc.
1301 Fifth Ave., #3800, Seattle WA 98101
624-7940
This firm of consulting actuaries employs 150 locally. Internships are possible for 1995. Personnel contact: Sharon Barker, administrative director.

Molbak's Greenhouse & Nursery
13625 N.E. 175th, Woodinville WA 98072
483-5000
Kathy Kemper handles personnel for this large nursery and retail operation. Molbak's also owns a Pike Place Market retail store:

Seattle Garden Center
1600 Pike Place, Seattle WA 98101
448-0431

Morning Sun
P. O. Box 2945, Tacoma WA 98401
922-6589
This firm, which sells screen-printed activewear, employs 300 at peak season. Located at 3500 20th St. E., Bldg. C, Tacoma 98424.

Moss Adams
1001 Fourth Ave., #2900, Seattle WA 98154
223-1820
Public accounting and consulting firm. Employs 100 in Seattle; there are also small offices in Bremerton, Tacoma and Everett. Recently acquired Management Advisory Services Inc., which specializes in business valuation and financial-management training. Seniors in accounting are often hired for tax season, January through mid-April. Occasional seasonal openings for support staff. Personnel director: Sue Carpenter.

The Mountaineers
300 3rd Ave. W., Seattle WA 98119
284-6310
Steve Kostie, member services manager, handles most personnel inquiries for this nonprofit. The main office employs about 17, mostly in member services (which takes reservations for outings). There's also a small deli and room rental staff. Internships may be available in the conservation department; for information, contact Maryann Mann, conservation division manager (281-8509). The Mountaineers publishing operation hires separately:

Mountaineers Books
1011 S.W. Klickitat, #107, Seattle WA 98134
223-6303
Donna DeShazo heads this division, which issues approximately 30 titles a year. There's a staff of about 20 and free-lance opportunities.

Mount Baker Recreation Co., Inc.

1017 Iowa St., Bellingham WA 98226

734-6771

Duncan Howat manages the operations company for the Mount Baker ski resort, which employs about 20 year around and adds another 100-125 during the winter. Most jobs are in lift operation, ski instructing and the ski shop. Applications are accepted starting in mid-August and interviews are conducted about Oct. 1. The ski patrol is all volunteer; food concessions are run by High Mountain Management in Lynden, (206) 354-3455, which hires about 50 each season.

Mount St. Vincent

4831 35th Ave. S.W., Seattle WA 98126

937-3700

Jobline: 938-8998

Part of the Sisters of Providence Health System, this includes a long-term care facility, assisted living, Arise, a stroke rehabilitation center, and an intergenerational day care center for children and the elderly. Employs 450, of whom an estimated 50 per cent work part-time. Openings are posted in the Resource Center.

MultiCare Medical Center

409 S. J St., P.O. Box 5299, Tacoma WA 98405

594-1250

Jobline: 594-1256

Tacoma General and Mary Bridge Children's hospitals are the major units of this medical center.

Multicom Publishing Inc.

1100 Olive Way, #1250, Seattle WA 98101

622-5530

"You've never gotten so much information in such an entertaining way," announces a sales brochure for Multicom, which produces CD-ROMs with such titles as "Wines of the World," "Better Homes and Gardens Guide to Gardening" and "National Parks of America." Founded by Tamara Attard. Employs 40.

Multiple Zones International

17411 N.E. Union Hill Rd., #A-140, Redmond WA 98052

883-1975

Mail order software company. Salespeople, who work full-time, need computer hardware and software knowledge. There's some seasonal employment; extra help is recruited in November and works December and part of January in telemarketing. Internships are possible. The firm was to relocate in late 1994 to Bellevue. Personnel director: Kathy Salopek.

Musicware Inc.

8654 154th N.E., Redmond WA 98052

881-9797

Founded in 1993, this software developer markets programs that teaches you how to play the piano. Employed 15 at press time. Internships in software development may be possible. President: Dan Peterson.

Mutual of Enumclaw
1460 Wells St., Enumclaw WA 98022
825-2591
From Seattle: 623-7855
Jobline (Live voice): Ext. 181
Enumclaw's largest employer is this insurance company. Limited part-time opportunities. Occasional summer internships in claims or personal lines for college students. All western Washington recruiting is handled in Enumclaw; resumes directed to "Personnel" will be retained on file.

Muzak Limited Partnership
400 N. 34th, #200, Seattle WA 98103
633-3000
Thinking elevator music? Muzak is also "foreground" music, business messaging services, in-store advertising and video programming. Employs 600 total, 125 in its corporate office. Human resources manager: Matthew McTee.

Nalley's Fine Foods
P.O. Box 11046, Tacoma WA 98411
383-1621
Produces potato chips, pickles, salad dressings and canned beef stew. Jacqueline Bateman, personnel director, handles inquiries regarding professional and administrative positions. There's an occasional internship in the corporate offices. Production jobs and seasonal openings are posted at the state Job Service Center. Seasonal work is for pickle packers, usually mid-July through September.

National Frozen Foods Corp.
P.O. Box 9366, Seattle WA 98109
322-8900
This privately-held food processor employs as many as 1,000 in its three Washington plants (Burlington, Chehalis and Moses Lake) but most employment is seasonal. Each plant handles its own recruiting. At the Eastlake corporate office, there's only about 30 on staff.

National Health Laboratories
21903 68th Ave. S., Kent WA 98032
395-4000
Headquartered in La Jolla, Calif., this clinical laboratory employs 460 in five Northwestern states, with the most jobs in Washington. Occasional interns in labs. Human resources manager: Gini Bushmaker.

The NBBJ Group
111 S. Jackson, Seattle WA 98104
223-5555
Scott Johnson handles personnel for this firm, one of the area's largest architecture and interior design firms. Upper division students are eligible for summer internships in design departments.

Neopath, Inc.
1750 112th Ave. N.E., B-101, Bellevue WA 98004
455-5932

This biotech firm is developing an automated Pap smear screening system. No internships, but students can often work part-time; applicants should be bio-sciences or technical majors (engineering or computer science, for example). Human resources manager: Jean Berry.

Newcomers Service
879 Rainier Ave. N., #D-203, Renton WA 98055
772-9250
Like to chat up your new neighbors? This firm employs only part-timers who work eight to 12 hours a week contacting (by phone or in person) new residents from Everett to Olympia. Employees are paid on a unit basis for each visit conducted. To apply, you'll need a Washington state driver's license, dependable transporta-tion and thorough knowledge of your neighborhood. Applicants should also be neat and well-groomed. Contact: Debbie Paul.

The News Tribune
P.O. Box 11000, Tacoma WA 98411
Human Resources: 597-8575
From Seattle: 447-0541
Jobline: 597-8590
Tacoma's daily paper. If you are applying in person, you must complete your application at the Tribune office at 1950 State St. or at the Federal Way office at 32050 23rd Ave. S. Openings are posted in a notebook available in the front office. Part-time jobs exist in classified advertising sales, newspaper delivery and cus-tomer service. Some of these jobs have unusual hours; for example, working from 1 to 5 a.m. Internships are often available in the newsroom and in advertising, accounting, marketing, human resources and circulation. Some interns are work-study students. Another McClatchy subsidiary, which hires its own staff, is the twice-weekly:

Pierce County Herald
P.O. Box 517, Puyallup WA 98371-0170
841-2481
Employs 27. Occasional internships during summer and spring vacations in the newsroom and advertising sales.

Nintendo of America
P.O. Box 957, Redmond WA 98052
882-2040
Jobline: 861-2170 (Touchtone telephones only)
Helping customers play games is one of the jobs at this video-game developer, a subsidiary of the Kyoto-based Nintendo Co. Ltd. that dominates the U.S. home video game market. Two Puget Sound locations: 4820 150th Ave. N.E., in Redmond, and the North Bend shipping facility.

Nordstrom
628-2111
This specialty retailer, now expanding across the U.S., employs about 1,700 in its corporate offices and another 3,400 in western Washington stores. No internships, but students can apply for employment. Seasonal opportunities include the summer sales and the November sale through Christmas. If you're interested in

working in one of the stores, apply at the appropriate store's personnel office.

Northwest Airlines
Employment Department
5101 Northwest Dr., Mailstop A-1410, St. Paul MN 55111-3034
Jobline: (612) 726-2111, #2
You can request applications for specific open positions by sending a self-addressed No. 10-size envelope with two first class stamps. You must specify a job posting number with your request.

Northwest Emergency Physicians
2001 Western Ave., #610, Seattle WA 98121
441-8614
A multi-hospital emergency physician group that subcontracts with nearly 150 emergency room doctors who work in the emergency departments of such hospitals as St. Claire in Tacoma. Northwest administrator: Sharon Monaghan.

Northwest Folklife
305 Harrison St., Seattle WA 98109
684-7300
The private nonprofit corporation that produces the Folklife Festival also runs catalog sales (of Folklife music and handcrafts), a teacher training program in ethnic culture, an ethnic music touring program and a festival consulting service. Publishes the *Washington Festival Directory and Resource Guide* and produces the Festival of World Traditions. Temporary employees are recruited in early spring for the Families Together summer arts program; between January and June temporary assistants are hired to prepare for Folklife. Interns are welcome. Some internships later result in paid positions. Unsolicited resumes are discouraged. Executive director: Scott Nagle.

Northwest Hospital
1550 N. 115th St., Seattle WA 98133
364-0500
Jobline: 368-1791
Job announcements are posted near the human resources office, located in Suite 17 in the professional center, and the cafeteria. Internships possible in administrative departments.

Northwest Kidney Center
700 Broadway, Seattle WA 98122
292-2771
Jobline: Ext. 6924
This outpatient dialysis center has several satellite operations. Employs about 350. Job openings are posted in the human resources office; applications are accepted between 1 and 4 p.m. weekdays.

Northwest Mobile Television
12698 Gateway Dr., Seattle WA 98168
242-0642
Purchased by three former King executives as part of the sale of King Broadcasting

assets in 1992. Five branch operations; employs a total of 84. Many opportunities for free-lancers; you should apply with the operations manager in your area. Internships possible.

Northwest Parent Publishing
2107 Elliott Ave., #303, Seattle WA 98121
441-0191
Ann Bergman heads this firm, which publishes *Seattle's Child, Eastside Parent, Pierce County Parent* and *Portland Parent* for educators and families with small children. Also publishes books for children and families. Small staff. If you're a free-lance writer or photographer, query before sending material.

Northwest Strategies
111 Queen Anne Ave. N., #500, Seattle WA 98109
282-1990
Ron Dotzauer heads this public affairs, governmental relations and lobbying firm, which at press time employed 15. Occasional internships. Established in 1985.

O'Brien International Inc.
P.O. Box 97020, Redmond WA 98073-9720
881-5900
Manufactures water skis, ski boards, knee boards and other water recreational equipment. May hire as many as 100 seasonal workers through temp agencies between January and May. Internships possible in 1995. Human resources manager: Annaly McPherson.

Ocean Beauty Seafoods Inc.
P.O. Box C-70739, Seattle WA 98107
285-6800
One of the largest fish processors. Between July and November, may add 30-50 employees in Seattle in entry-level seasonal fish processing jobs. Openings are posted at state Job Service Centers or advertised.

Olin Aerospace
11441 Willows Rd. N.E., Redmond WA 98052
885-5000
Jobline: Ext. 5132
In early 1994 Pacific Electro Dynamics (PED), which makes aviation electronics, and Rocket Research, which manufactures jet engines, were merged together by their owner, Olin. Internships not offered in 1994, but may be available in 1995. Recruiter: John Knapp.

The Olympian
P.O. Box 407, Olympia WA 98507
754-5490
Toll-free within Washington: (800) 869-7080
Vikki Potter is executive editor and Len Bruzzese managing editor of this daily, a Gannett publication. Dan Walker is advertising director and Carol Achatx personnel director.

One Reel
P.O. Box 9750, Seattle WA 98109-0750
622-5123
This event producer employs about 15 on a permanent basis. Internships available; contact Terri Hiroshima, public relations manager. During events such as Bumbershoot, Summer Nights at the Pier and the Lake Union Family Fourth, extra staff is hired on an independent contractor basis.

Optiva Corp.
13222 S.E. 30th St., Bellevue WA 98005
957-0970
This 10-year-old company makes the Sonicare brand electronic toothbrush. Employs 80, about half in production. Many of the production workers are hired through temporary agencies. Human resources manager: Maureen Webb.

Outdoor Empire Publishing Co., Inc.
511 Eastlake Ave. E., Seattle WA 98109
624-3845
The weekly *Fishing and Hunting News*, with a circulation of nearly 140,000, is the flagship publication of this printing and publishing firm. Part-time positions include 30 in telemarketing and others in production (for example, an artist and data entry crews). Free-lance work is purchased from columnists and other writers. Editorial internships are possible for 1995; applicants should be upper division journalism students with experience or an interest in fishing and hunting. Internships will be part-time (probably 20 hours per week) and include a stipend. Human resources director: Margaret Durante.

Overlake Hospital Medical Center
1035 116th Ave. N.E., Bellevue WA 98004
Human Resources: 688-5201
Jobline: 688-5150
This 225-bed facility posts its job openings outside the personnel office and on a board near the cafeteria. Both full-time and part-time opportunities. Occasional student internships. Employs 1,650.

Pabst Brewing Co.
P. O. Box 947, Olympia WA 98507
754-5000
About 40 are added on a seasonal basis most years; they work between May and September. Some tour guides may continue on into winter, working one weekend a month. You can apply between Christmas break and early spring for the seasonal jobs. The receptionist has applications for open positions. Located in Tumwater at the intersection of Schmidt Place and Custer Way

PACCAR, Inc.
This Fortune 500 firm is the corporate parent for Kenworth and Peterbilt trucks as well as the Al's Auto Supply retail chain. PACCAR operates worldwide, so it's a company to consider if you have (or would like) international experience. Besides the Bellevue corporate headquarters, locations in the Puget Sound area include Kirkland, Seattle, Renton and the PACCAR Technical Center in Mount Vernon.

Personnel contacts in the Seattle area include:

Corporate
P.O. Box 1518, Bellevue WA 98009

Regarding mid-management and professional positions:
Julie Horsman, human resources manager, 455-7547

Regarding support positions:
Kathy Eagle, human resources specialist, 455-7423

PACCAR Leadership Development Program (Internships)
P.O. Box 1518, Bellevue WA 98009
In its divisions, PACCAR uses graduate students, especially those with engineering undergraduate degrees. Usually candidates for master's degrees, these students work full-time during the summer or part-time during academic years on special projects. In some cases they then return to the company in permanent positions upon completion of graduate school. Contact: Julie Marshall, director, organizational development, 455-7403

Kenworth Division Headquarters
P.O. Box 1000, Kirkland WA 98083
Dan Snell, human resources director, 828-5750

Kenworth Seattle Plant
8801 E. Marginal Way S., Seattle WA 98108
Jim Britton, personnel manager, 767-8577

Kenworth Renton Plant
1601 N. 8th St., Renton WA 98055
Jim Britten, personnel manager, 227-5825

PACCAR Parts
750 Houser Way N., Renton WA 98055
Sue Neil, human resources manager, 251-7028

PACCAR Management Information Systems
P.O. Box 1518, Bellevue WA 98009
Regarding managerial positions:
Ree Laughlin, human resources director, 251-7297

PACCAR Financial
P.O. Box 1518, Bellevue WA 98009

Regarding managerial positions:
Ree Laughlin, human resources director, 251-7297

Regarding professional and technical positions:
Cheryl Nishimoto, human resources manager, 462-6231

PACCAR Leasing
P.O. Box 1518, Bellevue WA 98009

Regarding professional and technical positions:
Chuck Gerringer, human resources manager, 462-6239

PACCAR Automotive, Inc.
(Al's Auto Supply)
1400 N. 4th, Renton WA 98055
Bill Meyers, human resources director, 251-7692

Pacific Corridor Economic Council (PACE)
720 Olive Way, #1300, Seattle WA 98101
626-5473
This tri-national business council, a membership organization supported by the private sector, was organized in 1990. Small staff, internships a possibility. Also see *How To Network through Professional Associations*. President: Peter Fraser.

Pacific Interactive
1460 4th St., #200, Santa Monica CA 90401
Seattle telephone: 324-5584
With new projects for Disney in the wings, this firm expects to move most of its staff from Los Angeles in late 1994 and add significantly to its employee count by the end of 1995. Products include interactive CD-ROMs. Will consider applications for internships from upper division graphic design and software development students. Chief executive officer: Jonathan Strom.

Pacific Linen Inc.
22032 23rd Dr. S.E., Bothell WA 98021
481-2221
This home textiles chain has about 50 stores. Stores hire their own retail clerks. Unpaid internships are possible in such corporate departments as human resources and marketing; the minimum requirement is 10 hours per week. The distribution center at 22105 23rd Dr. S.E. hires its own staff and for the Tukwila distribution center; together, they employ about 90. Seasonal employment includes jobs in the stores at Christmas and during the summer and occasional work in the distribution centers in October.

Pacific Media Group
2314 Third Ave., Seattle WA 98121
461-1300
This printing and publishing firm includes 10 weeklies, two monthlies and specialty publications. Also runs a web and sheet-fed print shop. There are four publishers, each with responsibility for several publications; each is aware of openings throughout the firm. Internships are often arranged through the Washington Newspaper Publishers Association. For information about newspaper jobs, contact Denis Law, one of the publishers. For opportunities in the printing operation, contact Tom Haley, president.

Pacific Medical Center
Quarters 5, 1200 12th Ave. S., Seattle WA 98144
Human Resources: 326-4111
Jobline: 326-4120
This outpatient facility has six clinics, employing about 900. Openings are posted in the human resources office as well as on the jobline.

Pacific NorthWest Economic Region
999 Third Ave., #1080, Seattle WA 98104
464-7298
Roger Bull is the director of this nonprofit group, established in 1991 to help five states (Washington, Oregon, Idaho, Montana and Alaska) and two Canadian provinces (British Columbia and Alberta) compete in the world marketplace as one entity. Employs four full-time, with additional part-time help. Graduate students from the Northwest Policy Center, located in the University of Washington's Graduate School of Public Affairs, serve as interns.

Pacific Northwest/Seattle Magazines
701 Dexter Ave. N., #101, Seattle WA 98109
284-1750
Publishes two glossy regional magazines: *Pacific Northwest* and *Seattle*. Both publications have small staffs supplemented by free-lancers. At press time, *Pacific Northwest* was edited by Ann Naumann and *Seattle* by Giselle Smith. Part-time unpaid internships are available on both magazines; minimum commitment is 20 hours per week. You need not be a student to apply. For editorial internships, contact Molly Anderson; for marketing internships, contact Lisa De Vogel.

Panlabs Inc.
11804 North Creek Parkway S., Bothell WA 98011
487-8200
This contract research lab provides research for pharmacology and fermentation industries. Employs about 150. Occasional summer internships. You can ask the receptionist about current openings. Human resources manager: Jane Ramsey.

Paradigm Press
2701 First Ave., #250, Seattle WA 98121
441-5871
Mimi Kirsch heads this firm, which publishes the Alaska, Horizon and Midwest Express airlines in-flight magazines. Employs 25. Occasional free-lance writing opportunities exist; contact Paul Frichtl, who edits the publications. Unpaid editorial internships are available for three-month periods; commitment is 10-20 hours per week. You need not be a student; an interest in writing is the primary requirement. Apply in writing to Bryon Ricks. Sales and marketing internships may be in place by 1995.

Parametrix Inc.
This Sumner-based environmental and engineering consulting firm has seven locations in Washington, Oregon, Texas and Hawaii. The two largest, in Sumner and Kirkland, each employ about 130. Paid internships are occasionally available on a part-time or full-time basis for upper division students in the sciences; contact Human Resources.

Parametrix Inc.
P.O. Box 460, Sumner WA 98390
863-5128
From Seattle: 838-9810

Parametrix Inc.
5808 Lake Washington Blvd., #200, Kirkland WA 98033-7350
822-8880
Personnel contact: Cathy Seeley.

Parametrix Inc.
5700 Kitsap Way, #202, Bremerton WA 98312
377-0014
Employs about 25.

Parenting Press
11065 5th Ave. N. E., #F, Seattle WA 98125
364-2900
Specializes in books for families. Employs eight, several on a part-time basis; some free-lance art opportunities. Occasional internships, usually for editorial and usually unpaid. Contact: Carolyn Threadgill, associate publisher.

Path
4 Nickerson St., Seattle WA 98109-1699
285-3500
Makes medical technology available to developing countries. Develops diagnostic and health-care devices and trains native health care educators. Jackie Sperry, senior human resources officer, says staff falls into three categories. The program staff usually has public health training and experience in developing countries. The technical staff members have bioscience or engineering training and work on diagnostic and preventative product development. The third category is the administrative staff (personnel, purchasing, accounting, etc.). Check the job listing book at the receptionist's desk. Unsolicited resumes are welcome. All clerical applicants should have excellent communications and computer skills. Some part-time opportunities, especially in such jobs as lab assistant and clerk. Consultants are occasionally hired to work on specific programs, usually involving health-care delivery overseas. Occasional internships (unpaid or stipended), usually for students planning a career in public health.

PathoGenesis Corp.
201 Elliott Ave. W., Seattle WA 98119
467-8100
A biotech pursuing infectious disease research. Summer internships sometimes available for upper division or graduate students in the sciences. Some paid, others unpaid. May be full-time or part-time.

Pemco Financial Center
325 Eastlake Ave. E., Seattle WA 98109
Personnel: 628-4090
Jobline: 628-8740
Pemco Mutual Insurance, Pemco Corp., Evergreen Bank and Washington School Employees Credit Union share a personnel office. Some student employment in accounting and the credit union's loan department; in most cases, you must be majoring in a related discipline. High school and college students also work for Pemco companies through summer programs. Many student jobs are listed on the jobline.

Peninsula Gateway

P.O. Box 407, Gig Harbor WA 98335
851-9921
A weekly paper published by Thomas Taylor. Employs 40 total, with an editorial staff of six. Occasional internships in editorial.

Perkins Coie

1201 Third Ave., #4000, Seattle WA 98101
583-8888
For this law firm, one of Seattle's largest, Janet Hall is director, lawyer personnel. She handles both summer associates and career positions. Administrative staff is recruited by Ann Mary Oylear, employment administrator.

PGL Building Products

P.O. Box 1049, Auburn WA 98071
941-2600
Now a unit of Huttig Sash & Door, St. Louis. Occasional temporary assignments (usually two or three weeks in length) in the warehouse. Some opportunities for high school students arranged through the Auburn schools. Personnel contact: Teresa Kaelin.

Phamis, Inc.

401 Second Ave. S., #200, Seattle WA 98104
622-9558
Develops integrated hospital information systems. A jobline is to be installed soon. Rare internships, usually in product development. Human resources director: Kathy Dellplain.

PhotoDisc Inc.

2013 Fourth Ave., Second Floor, Seattle WA 98121
441-9355
Supplies digitized photography for desktop publishing and multimedia productions. Occasional interns, usually in technical areas or marketing. Applicants must be upper division or graduate students. Occasional project employment.

Physio-Control Corp.

P.O. Box 97006, Redmond WA 98073-9706
867-4000
Jobline: 867-4130
Produces cardiac care systems. Occasional internships during the summer, usually for upper division engineering or finance students.

Pinnacle Corporate

2334 Elliott Ave., Seattle WA 98121
728-0507
About 50 work for this firm, which through Pinnacle Post Production provides film to tape transfers and editing, including on-line editing, and through Pinnacle Effects provides such special effects for film and television as motion control, 3-D animation, cell animation and 2-D graphics. Hires free-lancers. Occasional internships in production.

Plum Creek Timber Co.

999 Third Ave., #2300, Seattle WA 98104

467-3600

One of the largest private owners of Northwest timberland. Employs about 50 in the corporate office. Most operations are in Montana. Occasional internships in wildlife biology, finance, legal (for law students only) and in marketing and corporate affairs (for students—often at the graduate level—with a public affairs background). Intern openings are posted at local campuses; you can also call in February to inquire whether any will be offered the next summer.

Polymer Technology International Corp.

1871 N.W. Gilman Blvd., Issaquah WA 98027

391-2650

Manufactures First Choice Test Strips, which measure sugar levels for diabetics. Uses temporary agencies for both production and clerical help.

POSdata

P.O. Box 1305, Gig Harbor WA 98335

851-6500

Supplies point-of-sale code scanning equipment. Internships may be possible in 1995 for students in business or technical majors. Human resources manager: Sherryl Peterson.

Preston Gates & Ellis

701 Fifth Ave., #5000, Seattle WA 98104

623-7580

Susan Jones is the hiring partner, handling the recruiting of attorneys. Nancy Sullivan, human resources administrator, recruits for administrative staff. Besides the permanent full-time staff, there are summer associates, summer support jobs and a few permanent part-time positions.

Price/Costco, Inc.

10809 120th Ave. N.E., Kirkland WA 98033

Human Resources: 803-6156

Jobline: 803-6416

Formerly Costco Wholesale, a warehouse retailer opened in Seattle in 1983. Merged with Price Club in 1993. Apply for retail positions at the store in your neighborhood or use the jobline to learn of corporate positions. Publishes *The PriceCostco Connection*, a monthly tabloid for customers.

Princess Tours

2815 Second Ave., #400, Seattle WA 98121

728-4202

Shipboard jobline: (310) 553-1770, Ext. 4095

Owned by P & O, Ltd., this firm runs cruises and land tours to Alaska. Seasonal opportunities occur primarily between May and September, but jobs do come up year 'round; some people work most of the year on a temporary basis, applying for new assignments as others end. (For example, someone might start in reservations and then move to an air ticketing job.) Because of a policy of promoting from within, these temps have an opportunity to apply for the few permanent positions that open. Although the company employs about 1,000 on a seasonal basis, only 50-150 of those jobs are filled in Seattle. No shipboard hiring is done here. Jobs range in length from two to five months. Examples of summer jobs:

Accounting, for which you usually must be at least a junior in finance or accounting. Positions are posted at the University of Washington.

Reservations—for many different programs, including cruise reservations for the Los Angeles operations.

Tour guides, for Alaska and the Canadian Rockies.

Bus drivers, for which you must complete a 10-week training program.

Hotel jobs, especially for seasonal positions on the Kenai peninsula and in Denali National Park.

General requirements for seasonal jobs: you must be at least 18 and in some cases, 21 or older; you must be available all or most of the May 1-Sept. 30 season; and you must be familiar with Alaska for some jobs (Alaska residents receive hiring preference for Alaska-based positions). For some jobs, language skills (especially Japanese, Chinese or Korean) are a plus. You may apply as early as Christmas vacation; all applications must be in by mid-February. Prospective employees receive an orientation packet with job offers; this explains pay rates (not especially high, Princess warns), living conditions (remote, for the two hotels that operate on a seasonal basis) and benefits (including discounts on a cruise after two seasons).

There are no formal internships in the corporate office, but students occasionally work on special projects for department heads. Personnel director: Lynne Gold-smith.

ProCyte Corp.
12040 115th Ave. N.E., #210, Kirkland WA 98034-6900
820-4548
A biotech developing peptide-copper compounds to promote healing, tissue repair and hair growth. Also has an anti-viral drug in research. Openings are posted at the front desk. Occasional internships, usually for full-time summer work, for students in such sciences as chemistry. Human resources manager: Craig Lawson.

Providence General Medical Center
916 Pacific, P.O. Box 1067, Everett WA 98206
258-7267
Jobline: 258-7562
Formerly Providence Hospital. Merged with General Hospital Medical Center in 1994. At press time, the hospitals had just begun consolidation and both personnel offices remained open. However, by early 1995 all recruiting may be handled through the address above. Due to the consolidation, job opportunities are very limited. Providence posts its job openings in the personnel office, located on the main floor. At the Colby campus (formerly General), located at 1321 Colby Ave. (telephone 261-2000) openings are posted outside the personnel office (enter from Fourteenth Street).

Providence Medical Center

500 17th Ave., Seattle WA 98122
Personnel: 320-2464
Nurse recruiter: 320-2476
Jobline: 320-2020
Review the postings in the personnel office, located on the main floor near the gift shop. Occasional internships in the pharmacy and administrative departments. Providence also operates Hospice of Seattle and 15 clinics. For those interested in volunteering, whether for career discovery purposes or to enhance skills, there are two volunteer programs, one for the hospital and one for the hospice.

PTI Environmental Services

15375 S.E. 30th Pl., #250, Bellevue WA 98007
643-9803
Environmental consulting firm. Focuses on natural resource damage assessment, human health and ecological risk assessment, water quality and sediment management and industrial compliance and waste management. Occasional project employment. Some on-call work, both for technical and support employees.

Puget Consumers Co-op

4201 Roosevelt Way N.E., Seattle WA 98105
547-1222
This eight-store natural foods retailer employs 285; 40 per cent work part-time. All candidates apply at the corporate office; those who pass the initial screening are then interviewed at the store level. For an application, call or stop by the address above. Occasional work-study opening for a student to assist the nutrition educator.

Puget Sound Blood Center

921 Terry Ave., Seattle WA 98104-1256
292-6500
Jobline: 292-2302
Nonprofit clinical and research medical facility serving 11 northwest Washington counties. Facilities: Seattle, Bellevue, Southcenter, Everett and near Northgate. Employs 490. Part-time openings are limited; most such positions are support. Occasional internships for vocational college students; some work-study opportunities for Seattle University students. Job openings are listed on a sheet available from the receptionist. Human resources manager: Don Anderson.

Puget Sound Business Journal

720 Third Ave., #800, Seattle WA 98104-1811
583-0701
Mike Flynn is publisher and Donald Nelson executive editor. Employment: 33 full-time, six part-time. Free-lance opportunities. Unpaid internships available in editorial, advertising and production; applicants must be college students. They can work part-time or full-time for an academic term.

Puget Sound Hospital
215 S. 36th St., Tacoma WA 98408
474-0561
From Seattle: 623-1417
Jobline: Through operator, Ext. 103
This 160-bed hospital offers general services as well as drug abuse treatment and mental health care. Employs 400 part-time and full-time. Occasional internships in administrative departments. Openings are posted outside the human resources department on the main floor.

Puget Sound Power & Light Co. (Puget Power)
Employee Services
P.O. Box 90868, Bellevue WA 98009-0868
454-6363
Jobline: 462-3540
An investor-owned electric utility. Entry level openings are posted at the state Job Service Centers. Apply by sending a resume to the address above; no application forms are provided. Occasional internships.

Puyallup Valley Bank
P.O. Box 578, Puyallup WA 98371
848-2316
David Brown is president of this four-branch local commercial bank. Occasional part-time opportunities.

Quality Classics
3000 Lind Ave. S.W., Renton WA 98055
251-0320
Established in 1980, this locally owned imprinted sportswear company has moved from an emphasis on custom work to preprint. It creates and sells both "souvenir" attire (San Juan Islands T-shirts, for example) to shirts with the work of recognized artists (Ray Troll, for one). A few summer openings. Opportunities for artists, on staff, on contract and on a royalty basis. Occasional opportunities for interns, especially in accounting and marketing. Job and intern applicants should contact Kathy Rossol, human resources manager; artists should contact Scott Duttry, art director, or Connie Lanigan, merchandising director. The company only adds about 60 designs a year; currently, it emphasizes designs in four areas: natural (including preservation, wildlife and ecology), humor, Southwest art; and warm water (in other words, designs that can be sold in such winter vacation areas as Hawaii and Florida). Artists should review the company's brochure and have a good understanding of how artwork is reproduced on fabric before submitting proposals.

Quality Food Centers (QFC) Inc.
10116 N.E. 8th, Bellevue WA 98004
455-3761
Concentrated in King County, this upscale supermarket chain had 45 stores at press time following the acquisition of Johnny's Food Centers in south King County.

Ragan MacKenzie, Inc.

999 Third Ave., #4300, Seattle WA 98104

343-5000

Brooks Ragan heads this investment banking and brokerage firm, which employs about 150 in the area. Small mergers and acquisition and research staffs. Personnel director: Judy Sterling.

Recreational Equipment Inc.

P.O. Box 1938, Sumner WA 98390

395-3780

Jobline: 395-4694

The country's largest consumer cooperative. Operates retail outlets, a mail order sales department and a distribution center in Sumner. Openings can be reviewed in the foyer of the headquarters office, located at 6750 S. 228th, Kent, or at the distribution and catalog sales center, at 1700 45th St. E., Sumner. About 80 per cent of the jobs are in the stores; many are part-time. (Overall, 60 per cent of the REI employment is part-time.) Store positions, for which you should apply in the store of your choice, include cashiers, clerks, bike and ski technicians and salespeople. Distribution center jobs also include part-time and full-time positions; the jobline will occasionally list a seasonal opportunity. (For example, at press time there was one packing catalog orders which started at $6.90 per hour.) Apply in person at the distribution center. All jobs in the international mail order operation are also located in Sumner; again, you must apply in person. Jobs are part-time and full-time and include sales and customer service. Recruiting for seasonal jobs starts in August, with work starting in September. Especially in mail order, seasonal employees may be able to continue as permanent part-time.

Restaurants Unlimited, Inc.

1818 N. Northlake Way, Seattle WA 98103

634-0550

Jobline: 634-3082, Ext. 777

Cutter's Bayhouse, Palomino, Palisade and Kayak Lakefront Grill are just four of the 24 full-service restaurants owned by this regional chain. A subsidiary, Cinnabon, operates 400 cinnamon roll bakeries in the U.S., Canada and Mexico. There's also a catering operation, Triples, located at the Kayak (formerly Triples restaurant). You can apply directly at the catering office or check the jobline for catering openings. Corporate recruiter Tom Griffith emphasizes that RU is always hiring. The first step in the application process is a screening interview. These interviews are held regularly at most restaurants, usually once or twice weekly; you'll hear the schedule on the jobline. Different restaurants have different seasonal loads; for example, Palomino has more Christmas business, while the waterfront restaurants hire more people for summer. Positions can be part-time or full-time. Some entry-level jobs pay $5 per hour.

Robbins Co.

P.O. Box 90927, Kent WA 98064-9727

872-0500

Products include machines for cutting round tunnels through mountains as well as rectangular holes on mining sites. Many openings are advertised; you can also visit the reception desk at the office, located at 22445 76th Ave. S. Occasional temporary assignments in production and engineering.

The Rocket
2028 Fifth Ave., Seattle WA 98121
728-7625
This free bimonthly music and entertainment magazine has a press run of 75,000 and two editions, but the full-time staff is small (less than 10). If you're interested in free-lance writing, check a sample issue and contact Charles Cross, managing editor. Little unsolicited material is purchased. Unpaid internships.

The Rockey Co. Inc.
2121 Fifth Ave., Seattle WA 98121
728-1100
One of Seattle's oldest and largest public relations agencies. Public relations and support staff recruiting is handled by Mimi Dukes, support staff manager, and design recruiting by Gail Lansing. Occasional opportunities for free-lancers, especially in design. Unpaid internships (full-time, usually for an academic term) are available; most are filled by upper division students in related majors. (However, you need not be a student to apply.)

Roffe Inc.
808 Howell St., Seattle WA 98101
622-0456
Markets skiwear and sweaters under the Roffe and Demetre names. Also manufactures on contract. Each department hires its own staff, but resumes can be directed to Sandra Andresen, controller. Occasional internships in advertising.

Royal Seafoods, Inc.
1226 16th Ave. W., P.O. Box 19032, Seattle WA 98109
Jobline: 285-1105
Royal catches and processes bottomfish in Alaska, with final processing completed in Seattle plants. Employs about 150 permanently, with another 200 working seasonally. All seasonal positions are in Alaska. Most are entry-level, in processing plants. Recruiting depends on when fishing seasons open, but generally the company recruits in January and again in June.

R. R. Donnelley & Sons Co.
8166 304th Ave. S.E., Preston WA 98050
222-4711
Jobline: 222-0328
This large commercial printer in 1993 opened a facility to duplicate computer software and assemble software manuals. By 1995, expects to employ about 120, all full-time. Occasional internships. Human resources administrator: Karen Boone.

R.W. Beck & Associates
2101 Fourth Ave., #600, Seattle WA 98121
441-7500
Jobline: 727-4524
Provides engineering consulting services in planning, technical and financial feasibility, design and construction management. Internships may be possible in engineering, economic analysis and environmental studies. Human resources director: (Mr.) Van Finger.

Ryder
130 S. Kenyon St., Seattle WA 98108
763-2222
You can work part-time nine months of the year—with a split-shift—getting schoolchildren to and from school with Ryder. The firm employs about 150, some of whom also drive charter buses. Applicants must be at least 21, with Washington driver licenses and good driving records. Ryder provides the training necessary for a commercial driver license with passenger endorsement. Apply in person.

Safeco Insurance Corp.
Safeco Plaza, Seattle WA 98185
545-5000
Jobline: 545-3233
One of Seattle's major service industry employers, Safeco is headquartered in the University District.

Safeco Life Insurance Co.
15411 N.E. 51st St., Redmond WA 98052
Personnel: 867-8101
Jobline: 867-6100
Safeco's Redmond campus is the headquarters for its life insurance company, which employs approximately 725 in such areas as pension administration, information systems, accounting, underwriting and claims.

Safeco Insurance Co. (Property and Casualty)
4909 156th Ave. N.E., Redmond WA 98052
881-4500
Jobline: 867-6100 (shared with Safeco Life Insurance Co.)
About 500 work in the regional and branch offices of the property and casualty subsidiary, which also has offices in Portland and Spokane. Most positions are in claims, underwriting and customer service.

Safeway Stores Inc.
1121 124th N.E., Bellevue WA 98005
455-6444
Jobline: 455-6501
Many Safeway positions, including those at the Bellevue division office and distribution center, are filled through referrals from the state Job Service Centers; for some entry level positions, apply directly at stores.

St. Claire Hospital
11315 Bridgeport Way S.W., Tacoma WA 98499
588-1711
Jobline: 581-6419
Employs 485. Part-time and full-time opportunities. Posts openings on a bulletin board outside Human Resources and the cafeteria.

St. Francis Community Hospital
34515 9th Ave. S., Federal Way WA 98003
838-9700
Jobline:
Seattle: 838-9700, Ext. 7930
Tacoma: 952-7930
This 110-bed hospital is owned by Franciscan Health Services. Employs 675.
Openings are posted in Human Resources.

St. Joseph Hospital and Health Care Center
P.O. Box 2197, Tacoma WA 98401
Human Resources: 591-6622
Jobline: 591-6623
Owned by Franciscan Health Services of Washington. Special programs include
a burn center and kidney renal dialysis. Part-time and full-time opportunities.
Internships may be possible in administrative departments. Openings are posted
outside Human Resources.

St. Peter Hospital
413 Lilly Rd. N.E., Olympia WA 98506
Human Resources: 493-7439
Jobline: 493-7779
Owned by the Sisters of Providence. Approximately 350 beds. More than 2,100
employees. Openings are posted on the second floor near Human Resources.

Salmon Bay Communications
1515 N.W. 51st, Seattle WA 98107
789-5333
This firm has two units. It publishes *Pacific Fishing*, a periodical for commercial
fishermen, and organizes the Northwest Flower and Garden Show each February.
The publishing staff is small, but articles and photos are purchased from free-
lancers. Contact Steve Shapiro, editor. The garden show staff adds about 45 part-
time employees for the show's five-day run. Each works four to six hours per shift
in information booths, selling such merchandise as souvenir T-shirts, handling
"will call" and assisting show attendees. The number of openings depends on how
many previous employees return. Applicants must have good customer service
skills; gardening experience is not necessary. Many positions are held by retirees.
Some positions are appropriate for teenagers (16 or older). Recruiting begins in
January; you can call and ask to receive a mailing.

Saros Corp.
10900 N.E. 8th, Bellevue WA 98004
646-1066
This software developer markets two products, Mezzanine, an electronic library
system, and SDM (Saros Document Manager). Employs 100. Occasional stipended
internships, most often in marketing or engineering; summer or academic year.

Sasquatch Publishing Inc.
1008 Western Ave., #300, Seattle WA 98104
623-0500

Publishes weekly news and arts tabloids, the *Seattle Weekly* and *EastsideWeek*, as well as several books about Northwest living and entertainment (the Best Places series, for example, as well as many new titles). David Brewster is publisher of the *Seattle Weekly*; Knute Berger is editor-in-chief and Katherine Koberg managing editor. Opportunities for free-lance writing; inquire before submitting material. The book publishing staff is small; Chad Haight is publisher.

Satisfaction Guaranteed Eateries
419 Occidental S., Seattle WA 98104
625-9818
Headed by Tim Firnstahl, this upscale restaurant chain includes Von's and Jake's. The corporate staff is very small, but the restaurants employ hundreds.

Schuck's Auto Supply Inc./Northern Automotive Corp.
2401 W. Valley Highway N., Auburn WA 98002
833-1115
Schuck's is based in Phoenix, but Harry Lang, the human resources manager in this office, handles much of the recruiting for regional offices and stores in the Northwest.

Schwartz Bros. Restaurants
300 120th Ave. N.E., Bldg. 3, #200, Bellevue WA 98005
455-3948
Jobline: 637-4864, #6
Includes 12 restaurants (for example, The Butcher and Benjamin's), some of which offer catering, and two separate catering operations, Gretchen's Of Course and The Atrium. The firm also markets fresh pasta, sauces, gourmet pizzas and biscotti in some retail outlets (for example, QFC). The 10 Cucina! Cucina! cafes have been spun off into a separate company, which moved into its own facility in late '94. Within Cucina! Cucina! there's a small staff handling such retail items as souvenir T-shirts. Although the two companies together employ as many as 1,200 during the peak summer season, the corporate staff is small; most openings are entry-level. Many seasonal opportunities, most part-time. Because many of the Schwartz Bros. restaurants have deck service, employment can increase by as much as 300 during the summer. You should apply after April 1 in the restaurant where you'd like to work. For the holiday rush, you can apply in November. For entry-level catering positions, apply with a restaurant or at the catering offices:

Gretchen's Of Course
1333 Fifth Ave., Seattle WA 98101
623-8194
Located next to the Schwartz Bros. cafe on the top retail level of Rainier Square.

The Atrium
5701 6th Ave. S., Seattle WA 98108
763-0111
Located next to The Butcher restaurant in the Seattle Design Center.

Science Applications International Corp.
10260 Campus Dr. Pt., San Diego CA 92121
(619) 546-6000
In the Puget Sound area, the San Diego-based SAIC has several offices, most

focusing on environmental consulting. The Bellevue and Bothell offices also have marine consulting operations. Total local employment is about 150; however, some offices (for example, Seattle) are very small and have virtually no openings. Addresses for the larger offices:

Science Applications International Corp.
18706 North Creek Parkway, #110, Bothell WA 98011
485-5800
Employs about 55.

Science Applications International Corp.
13400-B Northup Way, #36, Bellevue WA 98005
747-7152
Employs about 30.

Science Applications International Corp.
606 Columbia St. N.W., # 300, Olympia WA 98501
754-7077
Employs 15.

Scott Worldwide, Everett Operations
P.O. Box 925, Everett WA 98206
259-7333
This paper mill employs more than 1,200. Hourly positions posted at the Everett Job Service Center; resumes accepted for salaried positions. Students can work at Scott through college cooperative education programs. Contact: Veralee Estes, staffing and compensation administrator.

Seafair
2001 Sixth Ave., #2800, Seattle WA 98121-2574
728-0123
Kate Hastings is managing director of Seafair, a Seattle summer festival that includes neighborhood parades, downtown parades, special events and hydroplane races. Permanent staff: 10. Unpaid internships are available year around; especially for summer, applicants should be willing to work full-time on event planning, marketing and operations.

Seafirst Corp.
P.O. Box 3977, Seattle WA 98124
358-3000
Jobline: 358-7523
Washington's largest commercial bank. As much as 30 per cent of the work force may be part-time—working 20 or more hours a week. There are also "casual" positions, on-call jobs that include no benefits. Recent part-time openings listed on the jobline included customer service representative, starting at $7.24 per hour, and branch teller, starting at $6 per hour. Detailed descriptions of job openings are available in the employment office, 800 Fifth Ave., 33rd floor. Internships are occasionally available in branches and corporate administration; when a need is identified, Seafirst recruits on college campuses for intern candidates. Most students are upper division or in graduate school; most work summers. Some internships are paid. In the past, internships have been offered in such areas as computer operations, statement operations and international.

Sears, Roebuck & Co.
Most hiring is now done at the stores. Because Sears promotes from within, most openings are entry-level. Many are part-time. For example, at the Aurora Avenue store in north Seattle, one of the larger stores, all entry-level positions are part-time. Despite the store's size (about 280 employees), there is almost no seasonal hiring; some years one or two people may be added in "lawn and garden" for summer and an extra cashier or two for Christmas. For information about college recruiting, call (708) 286-7016.

Seattle Biomedical Research Institute
4 Nickerson St., #200, Seattle WA 98109-1651
284-8846
This nonprofit research group employs about 60. Occasional internships, some paid.

Seattle Commons
2201 Ninth Ave., Seattle WA 98121
628-8245
Joel Horn is director of this mostly volunteer organization that wants to develop an 85-acre park surrounded by a new neighborhood of business and residential development. The staff of 18 is supplemented with interns in such disciplines as architecture, urban planning and accounting. Also 300 volunteers working on the project. Personnel contact: Barbara Feasey, development director.

Seattle Daily Journal of Commerce
P.O. Box 11050, Seattle WA 98111
622-8272
Phil Brown is the managing editor of this 9,000-circulation business publication. Small staff.

Seattle Federal Credit Union
P.O. Box 780, Seattle WA 98111-0780
340-4500
Jobline: 340-4500, #5 and #5
Formerly City Credit Union of Seattle. This three-branch credit union employs 80. Uses contract employees as branch representatives during peak periods. Recruiter: Bettina Julio, personnel specialist.

Seattle FilmWorks
1260 16th Ave. W., Seattle WA 98119
281-1390
Jobline: Ext. 241
This mail-order film processing firm has few part-time positions, but often full-time seasonal jobs. The company starts recruiting in April for the summer season, which extends from Memorial Day to two weeks after Labor Day. There's also a couple of weeks of temporary work after each major holiday; most of those jobs are filled by summer workers who return. Some weekend work and many evening positions; 80 of the employees work nights. Announcements are posted in the human resources office on the first floor. Human resources director: Annette Mack.

Seattle Harbor Tours
Pier 55, #201, Seattle WA 98101
623-1445
With a business that relies on charters and tours (usually for visitors), this firm maintains a permanent staff of about 45, including skippers, supervisors and sales staff. There's limited turnover and the company tries to promote from within; often an opening will be filled by a former seasonal employee. Seasonal (April 1-Sept. 30) hiring can easily increase the staff by 75, although many of the positions are filled by returning seasonals. In recent years, for example, there have only been about 25 newcomers hired each summer. Seasonal employees all work in customer service in such positions as ticketing, photography and deckhand. Most work full-time. Many positions are entry-level; the primary requirements are customer service or sales background and a customer service attitude (for example, an enthusiastic, outgoing personality) and physical fitness. You must be 18 or older to work aboard boats. The ideal candidate, says the company recruiter, is a recent high school graduate or college student, someone taking a quarter or two off from college or someone between careers. Pay starts at $5.50 or $6 an hour. Most uniform items are provided. For seasonal work, you can apply starting in February; you're encouraged to stop by the tour office to pick up the official application form. Personnel director: Ralph Pease.

Seattle Lighting Fixture Co.
222 Second Ave. Ext. S., Seattle WA 98104
622-1962
Jobline: (800) 689-7505
This retailer employs 230 in 15 locations from Bellingham to Silverdale to Salem, Ore. Besides the 13 stores, there's a commercial department and a distribution center. Most positions are full-time; there are, however, part-time weekend and evening sales jobs. Internships are available in the marketing department; the ideal candidate would be an upper division student or recent grad in a related major (e.g., advertising). Personnel manager: Stephanie Harper.

Seattle Mariners Baseball Club
P.O. Box 4100, Seattle WA 98104
628-3555
Love sports? Try for one of the occasional unpaid internships in sales or such marketing-related areas as public relations. Also a few part-time seasonal jobs, often for high school students, during games or game preparation: for example, some teenagers chase balls, deliver messages, babysit players' children or assist the team mascot. Occasional work moving equipment prior to games. Personnel contact: Shirley Ward, executive assistant to the president.

Seattle Pacific Industries
P.O. Box 58710, Seattle WA 98138
282-8889
Jobline: Through operator
Unionbay is the major label at this large sportswear manufacturer. Between its Seattle and Kent operations, it employs about 200. Starting in mid-May, there are temporary jobs (lasting until August or September) in the Kent distribution center; you can apply at 21216 72nd S. Human resources director: Kimberly Daughenbaugh.

Seattle Post-Intelligencer
P.O. Box 1909, Seattle WA 98111
Human Resources: 448-8076
Owned by Hearst, this morning daily functions under a joint operating agreement
with the *Seattle Times*, which handles all advertising sales, production and
distribution. This means that virtually all of the 160 employees are editorial. Free-
lance material is occasionally purchased. Most summers there are one or two paid
editorial interns; college students can apply at Christmas break or in January.
Managing editor: Kenneth Bunting.

Seattle Seahawks
11220 N.E. 53rd St., Kirkland WA 98033
827-9777
Employs about 55. All positions full-time permanent except for the intern who
works in the public relations department. If you're a college student in PR or
marketing who'd like to apply for the internship, you should submit your resume
to the public relations director after March 1.

Seattle Sounders
1560 140th Ave. N.E., #200, Bellevue WA 98005
622-3415
Re-established recently, this team played its first American Professional Soccer
League season in 1994. Scott Oki, a former Microsoft executive, is the major
owner. All profits will support innner-city and youth programs in the Puget Sound
area. Started the season with seven permanent employees. Employs only a few
game-day workers; most such jobs are filled by volunteers and interns. During the
season, interns are used in game-day operations, public relations, marketing,
summer day camps for children and clinics. Regarding internships, contact
Stephen Brezniak, public relations director.

Seattle Thunderbirds Hockey Club
2505 Third Ave., #150, Seattle WA 98121
728-9121
Seattle's professional hockey team employs about 12 in administrative positions,
including the marketing and finance staff, the coaches and scout. On rare
occasions, there's an opportunity for an intern in sales; apply to the sales manager.

Seattle Times
P.O. Box 70, Seattle WA 98111
464-2111
Jobline: 464-2118
News/Internship Information: 464-3124
Seattle's evening newspaper. The newsroom employs about 300, with opportunities very limited (perhaps no more than 12 or 13 a year) in recent years due to staff
reductions. Each summer the newsroom hires 12-15 students for paid internships;
applicants are usually upper division or graduate students or recent graduates. The
paper recruits nationally for these interns. There's also a minority internship
program that accepts four participants each year; the interns rotate through
assignments at the *Times,* the *Yakima Herald-Republic* and the *Walla Walla Union-
Bulletin.*

Part-time opportunities:

You may have started your career carrying papers—and you can do it again, especially if you're looking for a part-time job or supplemental income. Today about 40 per cent of the *Times* carriers are adults earning $4,000 to $12,000 annually; nearly all copies of the Seattle *Post-Intelligencer*, which is also distributed by the Times, are delivered by adults. When the economy worsens, carrier turnover drops, but 40-60 routes for adults open each month. Requirements: a commitment, preferably for six months or a year; a reliable vehicle that can accommodate papers (adult routes can be as large as 250 papers); and a good driving record. How do you apply? Call 464-2121, explain where you live or want to work and ask for an application. Or apply in person at the Times human resources office. After your application has been reviewed, it'll be forwarded to one of 80 district advisers. If you're not called within three weeks, you can apply again; it's at the first of each month when the Times knows which routes will be available. Making yourself available to substitute for other carriers before you get your own route will increase your chances of a job.

Other part-time jobs exist in customer service, classified advertising, circulation, the mailroom and the pressrooms. You can apply at either plant, Fairview and John in downtown Seattle or the North Creek facility at 19200 120th Ave. N.E., in Bothell. At the main entrances of each facility, the security staff will either have applications or will direct you to Human Resources. Some positions require Class B endorsements on driver licenses; others require fast, accurate typing (for example, while customer service positions require that you type 25 words per minute, classified advertising requires 50 words per minute). Many positions offer at least 20 hours of work a week, with the hours increasing seasonally. (Production and mailroom work increases in mid-November; classified advertising and customer service work increases in the summer.) Some positions offer regular shifts and so are appropriate for those with other jobs or classes to attend; other departments schedule workers as needed, so shifts fluctuate.

Jobs at subsidiaries:

Local Times subsidiaries include Rotary Offset Press, which offers printing and mailing services, Times Information Services, an electronic and video information service, and Times Community Newspapers, which publishes weekly papers in the south end. The Walla Walla and Yakima papers do their own hiring. With the subsidiaries, most positions are filled directly. For more information, contact:

Times Community Newspapers

207 S.W. 150th, Burien WA 98166
242-0100.

The *Highline Times* and *Des Moines News*, published twice weekly (Rob Smith, editor), share space with the subsidiary headquarters. In total, the community newspaper division employs 113, of whom 80 are full-time. In circulation there are part-time opportunities in telemarketing (selling subscriptions 20 hours a week, usually evenings) and as "bundle drop drivers," delivering papers to pickup points for the 700 youth carriers. Most bundle drop drivers work about 15 hours a week, usually as a second job. The kids who deliver papers often work before school and are paid on a piecework basis. During the summer, there are also internship opportunities, usually one per paper; college students or recent graduates work full-time on a paid basis on the news staffs. Human resources manager: Cathleen Pickett.

Times Distribution Inc.

Both part-time and full-time opportunities exist with this subsidiary, which delivers "Sound Values," a Times advertising section, and other publications in King and Snohomish counties. All delivery is done by independent contractors, people who work one day a week, each delivering material to about 550 homes. Delivering by foot requires about four hours and pays eight to 10 cents per piece; motor routes pay slightly more. Requirements: a commitment of at least three months, dependable transportation, insurance and a Washington state driver's license. You must be 18 or older. Because deliveries can be completed any time between 7 a.m. and 7 p.m., these positions are appropriate for students. TDI also employs more than 45 people, including 20 who each work only 13 hours a week to verify deliveries. These positions pay about $6 an hour and require dependable transportation. To request an application for independent contracting or verification, call 872-7009 or, in north Seattle, 362-2852.

Shannon & Wilson Inc.

P.O. Box 300303, Seattle WA 98103
632-8020
This geotechnical and foundation engineering firm employs about 100 in its Seattle headquarters. Occasional project employment (for example, for CAD operators). Human resources director: Harvey Parker.

Sheraton Seattle Hotel and Towers

1400 Sixth Ave., Seattle WA 98101
621-9000
Jobline: 287-5505
If you're interested in the hospitality industry, consider hotels. Applications are accepted for open positions only. At press time, the jobline included such entry-level openings as part-time deli server, starting at $6.55 an hour.

Sheraton Tacoma Hotel

1320 Broadway Plaza, Tacoma WA 98402
572-3200
Virtually no seasonal hiring. Openings are posted in the human resources office off the employee entrance. Applications are taken from 9 a.m. to noon weekdays.

Shuttle Express Inc.

805 Lenora St., Seattle WA 98121
622-1434
By 1995 this locally-based airport transportation company expects to employ 225 drivers, nearly all full-time, as well as 25 in "guest services" (dispatch and reservations). Driver applicants must be at least 25 and have good driving records and a customer service attitude. No special license is required. What else is important? Good arithmetic skills, for making change and finding locations; a knowledge of the area; verbal skills, for communicating with customers and over radios to the dispatch crew; and physical ability. Beginning drivers usually start with the overnight shift; more senior drivers can select their shifts. You're encouraged to apply in person. Mailed applications can be sent to Bob Myles, transportation and safety director.

Sisters of Providence in Washington, Inc.
P.O. Box 11038, Seattle WA 98111-9038
464-3355
This corporate office of a Catholic health care system employs about 100. Its units (most of which you'll find listed elsewhere in this chapter) include Providence Medical Center, St. Peter Hospital, Mount St. Vincent and low-rent housing projects.

Ski Lifts, Inc.
7900 S.E. 28th St., #200, Mercer Island WA 98040
232-8182
Interested in working at Snoqualmie Summit, Ski Acres, Hyak or Alpental? This firm operates these four Snoqualmie Pass ski areas. The corporate staff is small. About 1,000 seasonal positions, some part-time, some full-time, exist at the pass: you can work in lift operations, the restaurants, child care, rental shops, ski instruction, ski patrol or in the offices. Some jobs can be filled by 16-year-olds; others require that you be at least 18. Work starts when the resorts open, sometimes by Thanksgiving, and end in early April. You can call the corporate office and ask about the job fair, usually held in October on the pass.

Skyhawks Sports Academy
(800) 804-3509
This Spokane-based organization operates summer soccer, basketball and baseball camps for city recreation departments, Y's and other youth groups from Olympia to Bellingham. In 1995, it expects to employ 550 college students who have sports backgrounds (perhaps even in intramurals) and the ability to work well with children 4 to 14. Contracts range from four to 10 weeks in length. Depending on the camp, instructors work from 8:30 a.m. until 1:30 or 3:30. In 1994, pay ranged from $170 to $200 a week. To apply, call for an application before Dec. 1; interviews start in December and January. Last-minute openings will be filled as late as May.

Smith Brothers Farms
27441 68th Ave. S., Kent WA 98032
852-1000
Delivers milk door-to-door from Olympia to Marysville. Employs about 150 at three farms and two depots. Truck drivers are independent contractors rather than employees.

Software Production Inc.
13312 S.E. 30th St., Bellevue WA 98005
746-7467
Another subsidiary of Prism Group (see MicroDisk Services earlier in this chapter), this is a software duplication house. Employs 100 plus temps hired through agencies. Human resources manager: Della Anderson.

Solectron Washington
8600 Soper Hill Rd., #A, Everett WA 98025-1256
335-3130
From Seattle: 622-7139
Jobline: 335-3180

A subsidiary of Solectron Corp. which purchased part of Hewlett-Packard's local custom-printed circuit board assembly business.

Space Needle Corp.
203 6th Ave. N., Seattle WA 98109
443-2161
Jobline: Ext. 3
This restaurant and tourist attraction employs about 270 during the winter, adding 30-50 during the summer. Applications are accepted even if no openings exist; however, you must apply at the corporate office, not at the Needle. There's limited turnover in the full-time staff; you may find more openings for part-time assignments during winter. Recruiting for seasonal employment begins in April (college students can apply while on spring vacation); work starts in June. Most summer employees work full-time. Unpaid internships sometimes available in marketing for college students. At press time, the Space Needle was recruiting for positions including busser (starting at $4.90 an hour plus tips), sales clerk (starting at $6 per hour) and elevator operator (starting at $6.85 per hour)

Starbucks Coffee Co.
P.O. Box 34067, Seattle WA 98124
447-1575
Jobline: 447-4123, Ext. 2
This fast-growing coffee roaster and retailer has more than 320 stores here and elsewhere in the country. Rather than submit a general application, recruiters suggest that people interested in retail positions (where most jobs exist) apply in the stores of their choice; for seasonal jobs, especially in mail order, for roasting plant jobs and for corporate positions, use the jobline. (If you're interested in working for Starbucks elsewhere in the country, there are regional joblines to check.) The company also recruits on selected university campuses and at community job fairs. Of the approximately 5,000 employees, about 600 work at corporate headquarters, most full-time. Most retail positions are part-time and require experience, especially restaurant or retail. If you work 20 or more hours a week, you're eligible for benefits; the company also strives to promote from within. There are two management training programs: one for store employees and a second for external candidates, usually those with restaurant management experience. Seasonal work is available for the Christmas season; recruiting usually begins in October. Check the jobline for specific openings. An in-house temporary pool is being developed. An internship program may be in place by 1996.

Stevens Memorial Hospital
21601 76th Ave. W., Edmonds WA 98026
Human Resources: 640-4190
Jobline: 640-4194
Nurse Recruiter: 640-4193
This 217-bed facility has a variety of nursing, professional and support positions. Employs 1,100. Openings are posted in the human resources office, located at 21727 76th Ave. W., #102, in the Warren Medical Bldg. one block south of the hospital. Occasional opportunities for interns in the administrative department; you can apply directly to it.

Stevens Pass

P.O. Box 98, Leavenworth WA 98826
(206) 973-2441

This ski resort employs about 40 on a permanent basis and adds as many as 500 during the winter. You can work in accounting, administration, day care, food services, ticket sales, equipment sales, lift operations or the ski patrol. Ski schools are operated by concessionaires; see Professional Ski Instructors of America. You can apply at the annual job fairs, held in October in Monroe (Oct. 15 in 1994) or at the pass (Oct. 22 in 1994). Or contact the administrative office, open Monday through Thursday during the off season.

Stoddard-Hamilton Aircraft Inc.

18701 58th Ave. N.E., Arlington WA 98223
435-8533
From Seattle: 622-1789

Ted Setzer is president of this employee-owned firm, which produces small airplane kits and offers catalog sales of parts for existing planes. Internships possible. Contact: Cheryl Valliant, controller.

Stouffer Madison Hotel

515 Madison St., Seattle WA 98104
583-0300
Jobline: Through operator

Job openings are posted in the human resources office, entered at the back of the hotel off the alley. If you're graduating from college (especially in a business or hotel administration program) and interested in the corporate management training program that rotates trainees through positions in different properties, write Jeanne Hartman, human resources director. Interested in a summer job? The hotel adds about 50 seasonal positions throughout its operations.

The Stranger

1201 E. Pike, #1225, Seattle WA 98122
323-7101

Described as a "gutsy, irreverent" free weekly, this publication launched by Tim Keck in fall, 1992 had by press time a circulation of 33,000. The target audience, according to the staff: "urban hipsters." The staff of 10 includes advertising sales reps; most editorial material comes from free-lancers.

Stratos Product Development Group

2025 First Ave., #PH-B, Seattle WA 98121
448-1388

Allan Stephan and Mike Nelson head this firm, which designs such high-tech products as mouse-style pointers for computers. The staff of 29 includes electrical, software, mechanical and manufacturing engineers. Internships may be available in 1995.

Summit Savings Bank

400 112th N.E., Bellevue WA 98004
451-3585

In mid-1994 announced plans to merge with Washington Mutual Savings Bank.

Sun Dog Inc.
6700 S. Glacier, Seattle WA 98188
547-2270
Makes such soft-sided carriers as fanny packs and backpacks. No seasonal employment. Internships may be available in 1995. Contact: Trev Cookson, controller.

Sun Sportswear
6520 S. 190th St., Kent WA 98032
251-3565
Jobline: 251-1845
One of the largest producers of screen-printed casual sportswear for such discount chains as Wal-Mart. No seasonal hiring. Internships, paid and unpaid, for students in such areas as art, design, merchandising and human resources. Job openings are posted in the reception area. Most recruiting is handled by Jeff Williams, employment specialist.

Sunset Magazine
500 Union St., #600, Seattle WA 98101
682-3993
Part of Time Warner, Sunset maintains a small editorial and advertising sales office in Seattle. No internships. All hiring for permanent positions is done through Sunset headquarters:

Sunset Publishing Co.
80 Willow Rd., Menlo Park CA 94025
(415) 321-3600

Swedish Medical Center
Personnel Office
601 Broadway, First Floor, Seattle WA 98104
Personnel: 386-2141
Jobline: 386-2888
One of Seattle's most specialized medical centers. First Hill and Ballard campuses. Openings are posted outside the First Hill hospital cafeteria and in personnel offices. You can apply at either facility (in Ballard, at 5223 Tallman Ave.; call 781-6366 to check hours). Volunteer work can help you brush up skills needed for paid positions or help you determine whether you'd like to pursue a health-care career. Examples of opportunities identified by Volunteer Services (call 386-2090): data entry in administrative departments; filing or data entry in the library; or clerking in the gift shop. Students considering medical careers can help in the emergency room, usually transporting patients to surgery or other floors, or in the pharmacy. You must be 14 or older to apply. Volunteers are asked to commit to four hours per week for six months (adults) or three months (teenagers). To be considered, complete an application, including references, be interviewed by the Volunteer Services staff and then be referred to a department supervisor for an additional interview. You'll receive a general hospital orientation, including safety and CPR training, and you may receive more training in the unit you join.

Tacoma Dome

2727 E. D St., Tacoma WA 98421
272-3663

The dome is a city facility, with its employees hired through the city personnel office. (See *Employers: Government Agencies*.) However, three concessions offer other employment opportunities: Ticketmaster, which sells admission tickets; Ogden, which runs the concession stands, catering and restaurants; and Crowd Management Services (CMS), which provides security. All can be reached by telephone from the main Tacoma Dome number or written at the address above.

Ticketmaster

Employs about 30 part-time; you can apply at the office, located next to the Dome's administrative offices. Openings are also advertised. Manager: Gina Lanza.

Ogden Services

Depending on events, Ogden employs between 20 and 100. Part-timers only work during events. The peak season is September-April. You must be 18 or older. You can apply by mail or in person; visit the Ogden office, located at the back of the exhibition hall near the 24-hour security office.

Crowd Management Services (CMS)

See listing earlier in this chapter.

Tacoma Rockets Hockey Club

222 E. 26th, #104, Tacoma WA 98421
627-3653

Employs 12 in its administrative office. Students interested in working as unpaid interns in marketing can contact Gavin Hamilton, sales director.

Tacoma Tigers Baseball Club

P.O. Box 11087, Tacoma WA 98411
752-7707

Tacoma's pro baseball team employs 12 full-time. Game-day staff, people who work only when home games are scheduled, include ushers, ticket sellers and takers, vendors, concessions workers, security and clean-up crews. Some work only an hour and a half per game; others (for example, concessions) may work four hours per day. You must be 16 or older to apply. Recruiting begins in February; you can apply by mail or in person at Cheney Stadium, 2501 S. Tyler.

Targeted Genetics Corp.

1100 Olive Way, #100, Seattle WA 98101
623-7612
Jobline: Ext. 5000

This biotech focuses on gene therapy. Spun off from Immunex in early 1992. Occasional opportunities for students through work-study programs.

TCI West, Inc.

2233 112th Ave. N.E., Bellevue WA 98004
462-2620

About 60 work in this regional headquarters for the Denver-based TCI, a cable television operation. More job opportunities occur in the system offices, which each hire their own staff.

TCI Cablevision of Washington, North Seattle
1140 N. 94th St., Seattle WA 98103
525-0332
Along with South Seattle and Auburn, this is one of the larger system offices, employing 130. Positions (most are full-time) include customer service, installation, marketing, telemarketing, direct sales, human resources, MIS, dispatch and office administration. You can apply at any time (resumes are held for six months); new positions are most likely to be created early in the year. Personnel coordinator: Melody Brown.

For information on opportunities in other system offices, call:

South Seattle, 433-3434

Auburn, 228-1101

Tacoma, 383-3961

Marysville, 659-7047

Olympia, 754-3455

Bremerton, 337-2059

Teledesic Corp.
At press time, located in the McCaw Cellular Communications offices in Kirkland. Founded by Craig McCaw and Bill Gates. The goal: to deliver high-end communications to many remote parts of the earth using satellites in low-Earth orbits. President: Russell Daggatt.

Teltone Corp.
22121 20th Ave. S.E., Bothell WA 98021-4408
487-1515
Manufactures electronic telecommunications equipment that's used by telephone operating companies and by large companies. Employs about 75 locally. Occasional temporary opportunities. Interns usually work in engineering; you must be an upper division student to apply. Human resources manager: Marnie Vitt.

That Patchwork Place
P.O. Box 118, Bothell WA 98041
483-3313
The country's largest publisher of quilt books. Offers submission guidelines for quilt designers preparing manuscripts. Publisher: Nancy J. Martin. Personnel contact: Marta Estes, assistant to the publisher.

Thaw Corp.
P.O. Box 3978, Seattle WA 98124
624-4277
A subsidiary of Recreational Equipment, Inc. Manufactures and imports recreational apparel and equipment. The receptionist at the main entrance (1212 First Ave. S.) has job announcements; they're also posted outside the reception area.

Thousand Trails/NACO
12301 N.E. 10th Pl., Bellevue WA 98005
455-3155
This campground company has positions in 60 recreation sites across the U.S.
Total employment: 1,500, increasing to 2,000 during summers. Most local
openings are advertised. For seasonal positions in the seven campgrounds in this
area, apply directly at the campground. John Powers, the editor of *Trailblazer*, the
membership magazine, buys an occasional free-lance piece.

Tim Girvin Design Inc.
1601 Second Ave., Fifth Floor, Seattle WA 98101
623-7808
An award-winning firm with clients across the country, this 36-person agency is
headed by Tim Girvin. Occasional internships for graphic design students.

Todd Pacific Shipyards Corp.
P.O. Box 3806, Seattle WA 98124
623-1635
Personnel: Ext. 256
Todd is seeking more commercial ship repair business to compensate for the
reduced military business. Most positions are union; the taped message from the
personnel office lists how to apply for these jobs.

Tosco Northwest Co.
601 Union St., #2500, Seattle WA 98101
Human Resources: 442-7110
This division of a Fortune 500 petroleum refining company, recently bought the
assets of BP Northwest, including the Ferndale refinery and 500 service stations
and convenience stores. The corporate office employs 90; turnover is limited.
Both entry-level and management positions are available in the 43 Tosco-operated
gas stations; they employ managers, assistant managers and cashiers. No mechanics. In Washington, all stations are self-service. Openings are posted in stations;
you can write the corporate office if you like, but you must indicate the stations or
geographic area in which you'd like to work. If you work more than 20 hours a
week, you're eligible for the 401(k); there's also a tuition reimbursement program
that pays for the first $2,500 of school expenses each year.

TRA
215 Columbia, Seattle WA 98104
682-1133
Provides architectural, engineering, planning and graphic and interior design
services. Occasional student internships. Human resources director: Wendy
LeClaire.

Traveling Software Inc.
18702 North Creek Parkway, #102, Bothell WA 98011
483-8088
Openings are posted at the reception desk. Occasional internships in marketing or
product development; contact Margaret Sisneros, human resources generalist.

Trident Seafoods Corp.
5303 Shilshole Ave. N.W., Seattle WA 98107
783-3818
Jobline (Hourly positions): Through the personnel office.
Operates in both the Northwest and Alaska. Employs about 100 in the administrative offices. Also hires as many as 3,000 seasonals, but many of these Alaskan positions are filled by returning employees. Some years the return rate on vessels is as high as 90 per cent; some shore plants have 50 per cent of the previous season's employees return. All positions are entry-level and pay about $5 an hour (in addition, the company provides room and board and such services as laundry). Locations are remote and there are often "down" days, periods when there's no fishing work (and thus no pay). To apply, you must be at least 18, have legal authority to work in the U.S. and speak English. The Alaska employment manager says he looks first for good attitude, second for good health and third for a good work history. Applicants must attend an orientation session and be interviewed; the best candidates then must pass physical exams and drug tests.

UniSea Inc.
15400 N.E. 90th St., Redmond WA 98073
881-8181
Jobline (Hourly positions): 883-0884
Openings—for both Alaska and Redmond operations—are listed on the jobline or advertised. Employs 350 in Washington; only about 60 work in the corporate office. Internships may be possible in the administrative departments. The Redmond processing plant positions are usually full-time and year around; there's limited turnover. In Alaska, many of the positions are seasonal, but they're often filled by returning employees. (For example, in 1993, for the second pollock season, only one new person was hired.) Recruiting begins in October, for the January pollock season, when most openings occur. Most of the processing positions are entry-level; pay starts at $5 an hour. To apply, you must have some work history and references. UniSea also runs two hotels in Dutch Harbor; employees sign six-month contracts, but most work year around.

United Airlines
Employment Office
P.O. Box 66100, Chicago IL 60666
Jobline: (708) 952-7077
This jobline provides information on "ground support" positions, including reservations agents, food service workers and accounting support staff in regional offices. To apply for a position at UA's local offices, request an application by mailing a postcard to the office above.

United Press International
110 Cherry St., #200, Seattle WA 98104
283-3262
This wire service offers free-lance reporting opportunities (hard news only). Also takes interns; to apply, you must be an upper division journalism student with experience. Northwest regional manager: Stuart Glascock.

United States Arbitration & Mediation

601 Union, #4300, Seattle WA 98101
467-0794
This firm employs only nine full-time but contracts with more than 30 other attorneys and retired judges to serve as mediators and arbitrators. Contract staff are selected based on recommendations and referrals; if you'd like to be considered, you can submit a letter outlining your credentials to Michael Gillie, the firm founder and executive director. You should have at least five years experience after passing the bar.

University Savings Bank

6400 Roosevelt Way N.E., Seattle WA 98115
526-1000
This 25-branch thrift employs about 270. Many part-time opportunities. Job openings are advertised and posted at state Job Service Centers. A jobline may be installed soon. Mail inquiries to Barbara Bales, human resources manager.

University of Washington Medical Center

1959 N.E. Pacific, Seattle WA 98195
Joblines:
Nursing: 548-4470
General: 543-6969 (Touchtone telephones only)
A unit of the University of Washington, this medical center employs 3,300 excluding doctors and the staff at Harborview. Job openings, which include positions at Harborview Medical Center, are posted at:

University Hospital Personnel
BB130 University Hospital, 1959 N.E. Pacific St.

UW Staff Employment Office
1320 N.E. Campus Parkway

Harborview Medical Center
319 Terry Ave.

U.S. Bank

P.O. Box 720, Seattle WA 98111-0720
Human Resources: 344-3619
Jobline: 344-5656
Employs 2,500 in the Puget Sound area. You can use the jobline or apply in person at any branch or at the corporate headquarters staffing office, 1420 Fifth Ave, 10th floor. Summer internships are occasionally available for those who are at least college juniors. You should apply no later than February, through Human Resources; for more information, call (503) 275-6118.

U.S. Marine

17825 59th Ave. N.E., Arlington WA 98223-8796
435-5571
Produces Fiberglas boats, including the well-known Bayliners. No seasonal employment. Many openings are advertised in the Seattle Sunday papers. You can also check at the reception desk.

U S West Communications

Employment Office
1600 Seventh Ave., Room 2110, Seattle WA 98191
345-1234
Jobline: 345-6126
To learn about part-time telephone company jobs in the Puget Sound area and elsewhere in the state, use the jobline. An application booth is also scheduled to be installed in the building lobby. At press time, U S West was downsizing.

U S West NewVector Group

3350 161st Ave. S.E., Bellevue WA 98008-1329
644-3994
Jobline: Through the operator
To review opportunities at this cellular telephone and mobile communications company, check the postings book in Human Resources, Suite 150. Employs about 1,700. No unsolicited resumes. Student interns are recruited for by U S West University Relations, which posts openings on several local college campuses.

UTILX Corp.

22404 66th Ave. S., Kent WA 98032-4801
395-0200
This utility renovation firm provides a trenchless service with its own technology. During "build" cycles, the completion of major projects, hires technicians (for example, hydrology technology technicians, quality assurance staff, purchasing assistants) on a temporary basis. Occasionally uses high school students as interns through programs arranged by local high schools. Recruiter: Gail Carter-Lindberg, human resources administrator.

Uwajimaya Inc.

A family-owned retailer and wholesaler of Asian groceries and gifts. Apply at either the Seattle or Bellevue store if you're interested in a retail position; about 40 per cent of the retail jobs are part-time, with hours increasing during the summer and holiday season. Seasia, which imports and distributes Asian foods, is a division that employs about 45; positions include sales, order entry and warehouse. Corporate recruiting is handled by the human resources manager, who maintains her office at Seasia. Resumes are always accepted.

Seasia

Diane Rasmussen, Human Resources Manager
4601 6th Ave. S., Seattle WA 98108
624-6380

Valley Daily News

P.O. Box 130, Kent WA 98032
872-6600
The 33,000-circulation newspaper serving Kent, Renton and Auburn. If you're a journalist, contact Bob Jones, executive editor, who also screens internship applicants. If you're interested in working as a carrier, an independent contractor position (either motor or youth position), call the circulation department for more information. Advertising sales is managed by Rick Riegle. Some entry-level positions such as selling classified ads are handled at the *Journal American* in

Bellevue, an affiliate. The paper offers some part-time opportunities, especially in the mailroom, where you can work graveyard shift inserting or stacking.

Valley Medical Center
400 S. 43rd, Renton WA 98055
251-5160
Jobline: 251-5190
Full-time, part-time and on-call opportunities. Internships possible in departments such as public relations, pharmacy and food service.

Vectra Technologies Inc.
1010 S. 336th, #220, Federal Way WA 98003
874-2235
Hazardous waste engineering services firm. Employs 1,300 total, but only 16 in this headquarters office. Occasional internships: engineering students preferred; a few possibilities in administrative departments. Contact: Alesa McCrory, human resources generalist.

Vernon Publications Inc.
P.O. Box 96043, Bellevue WA 98009
827-9900
Vernon has sold some of its business periodicals and moved into more consumer-oriented publications, including the annual *Puget Sound Homeowners' Guide* and four former Alaska Northwest publications, including *The Milepost* and *The Alaska Wilderness Guide*. The editorial staff is small (four); regarding full-time positions and free-lance writing and photography, contact Michelle Dill, editorial director.

Videodiscovery
1700 Westlake Ave. N., #600, Seattle WA 98109
285-5400
Develops interactive videodiscs and CD-ROMs for science educators. All video production is handled in-house. Employees include software developers, graphic designers and sales; functions such as writing are often contracted out. Chief executive officer: Joe Clark.

Virginia Mason Medical Center
P.O. Box 900, Seattle WA 98111
Human Resources: 223-6757
Jobline: 223-6496
Virginia Mason Clinic and Virginia Mason Hospital have merged recruiting, with this office handling hiring for the 4,000 positions in the clinics, hospital, research center, health plan (an HMO) and the Bailey-Boushay House for AIDS patients. Operations include a day care center for employees' children and the Inn at Virginia Mason, a 79-room hotel (with Rhododendron Restaurant) open to the public. Full-time, part-time, temporary and on-call positions. No unsolicited resumes. Apply by mail or in person, at 909 University, on the third floor of the Health Resources Bldg. Human Resources may also know of internships, sometimes available in such departments as public relations or pharmacy. The center also uses about 140 volunteers; Carol Severson, director, Volunteer Services (call

583-6507) can place volunteers who are at least 14 1/2 years old. Volunteer assignments can be used to brush up skills or for career discovery. Some examples: office support, including clerical work, reception, telephones and data entry; gift shop; such administrative departments as accounting, public relations and human resources; patient care, including visiting patients and refilling water pitchers, sitting with patients in recovery rooms of the "short stay" areas; and helping in the occupational medicine clinics. The application process includes an interview and an application form with references.

Visiting Nurse Services of the Northwest
400 N. 34th St., #306, P.O. Box 300317, Seattle WA 98103-9717
548-8100
Jobline: 548-2398
Offers home health services in King, Snohomish and Skagit counties, including specialized nursing care, speech, physical and occupational therapy and medical social work. Its clinic program employs RNs who provide health care in community settings such as senior centers. Visiting Nurse Supportive Services employs chore workers, respite care workers and home helpers. Employs nurses (both visiting and private), therapists, medical social workers, a nutritionist and home health aides. Employs 800, about half on a part-time basis. Internships are possible. Human resources generalist: Cathy Ivers.

Walker Richer & Quinn Inc. (WRQ Inc.)
1500 Dexter Ave. N., Seattle WA 98109
217-7100
Jobline: 217-7411
Reflection, connectivity software, is the primary product of WRQ, often cited as one of the country's fastest growing software firms. Expects to employ 350 by 1995. Internships may be possible in 1995. Employment manager: Norris Palmanteer.

Wall Data Inc.
17769 N.E. 78th Pl., Redmond WA 98052
883-4777
Wall markets Rumba, a software program that connects personal computers with mainframes and allows applications from mainframes to be accessed with Microsoft Windows. Internships are occasionally possible in such areas as technical writing and product development; contact Human Resources for details. Scheduled to relocate in late 1994.

Washington Community Reinvestment Association
2001 Western Ave., #350, Seattle WA 98121
728-8088
A nonprofit mortgage banking corporation established in 1991. Provides permanent financing for multi-family housing for low and moderate-income families. Internships possible. President: Judy Reed.

Washington Council on International Trade
2615 Fourth Ave., Seattle WA 98121
443-3826
Patricia Davis was recently named president of this membership group, called the

leading trade policy organization in the state. Former president Robert Kapp is considered instrumental in arranging the APEC forum in Seattle in 1993. The council employs three and accepts one intern each quarter, usually an upper division or graduate student. Also see *How to Network through Professional Associations*.

Washington Dental Service
P.O. Box 75688, Seattle WA 98125
522-1300
Dental insurance firm. Employs 190. Internships are sometimes available in marketing, finance, public affairs and human resources.

Washington Education Association
33434 8th Ave. S., Federal Way WA 98003
941-6700
The professional association for education employees and the union for state school employees. Employs 65 in its Federal Way office. There's a legal internship program, for which WEA recruits at local law schools. Also employs a few high school students, often arranged through Federal Way schools. Personnel director: Kristi Bruhahn Mills.

Washington Energy Co.
This firm has two subsidiaries (see below).

Washington Natural Gas
P.O. Box 1869, Seattle WA 98111
622-6767
Jobline: 622-6767, Ext. 2800
Distributes natural gas. Employs 1,400. No unsolicited applications.

Washington Energy Services Co.
P.O. Box 91060, Seattle WA 98111
521-5400
A new subsidiary formed to handle the sales and installation of replacement windows, gas furnaces and home security systems. The most likely openings will be for commission salespeople; experience is required. Limited turnover in other positions. Human resources manager: Carol Briant.

Washington Farm Bureau Federation
P.O. Box 2009, Olympia WA 98507
357-9975
Purpose: legislative advocacy and service to ranchers and farmers. It employs 10 in Olympia plus two in the field; the county offices are usually staffed by volunteers. Unpaid student internships possible. Executive vice president: Ray Poe.

Washington Federal Savings
425 Pike St., Seattle WA 98101
624-7930
This thrift has 73 branches in four states, including 23 in Washington. You can send a resume to Laurie Ware, vice president, personnel, or call the personnel office to check on openings. You can also inquire in branches regarding openings.

Washington Mutual Savings Bank
Employment Department
P.O. Box 834, Seattle WA 98111
Human Resources: 461-6400
Jobline: 461-8787
Internship Information: 461-6418
Washington's largest independently owned bank, this firm also offers insurance, travel planning, securities and brokerage services. Subsidiaries include Murphey Favre, Inc., Composite Research and Management and Mutual Travel. Offers PACE, an 18-month management training program with a sales orientation for those interested in careers in the bank's financial centers (branches); applicants should have a B.A. and two or three years of work experience. Hires permanent staff for its in-house temp pool, which at press time included about 25 who worked in different departments of the bank on assignments ranging from one day to six months. You can check listings for most open positions, including the temp pool, in the personnel office (located at 1191 Second Ave., first floor), open Monday through Thursday. For students, work-study opportunities and two internship programs. Twelve to 15 students (usually college, but occasionally high school) can work summers in departments and branches that require extra help; examples include educational loans, home loan centers, accounts payable and customer service. Recruiting begins on college campuses in February, with applications due in early April. The Diversity Advisory Group internship is a year-long program for students of color who are entering their final year of college or community college. Students work full-time during the summer and then part-time during the last year of school. The program's goal is to identify prospective candidates for permanent employment. Involves five or six students a year. Recruiting is handled through campus minority affairs offices.

Washington State Bar Association
2001 Sixth Ave, #500, Seattle WA 98121-2599
727-8200
Employs about 70—and many are not lawyers or paralegals. This nonprofit administers the bar exam, handles the discipline process, provides continuing legal education and publishes a monthly magazine and many different pamphlets. Interns are taken only in the legal department; they're usually paralegal students with internships arranged by their schools. Personnel: Pat Dieken, controller and director, administration.

Washington State Labor Council
314 First W., Seattle WA 98119
281-8901
The umbrella organization for the AFL-CIO in Washington. The staff includes the directors of such programs as education, which conducts workshops and provides materials on workplace issues; political action; research, which studies issues and pricing for members; public relations; and job training, which works with apprenticeship programs and encourages the development of both apprenticeship and alternative training programs. Interns are welcome. Contact: Rick Bender, president.

Washington Wine Institute
1932 First Ave., #510, Seattle WA 98101
441-1892
Trade association for state wineries. Staff of two. Uses unpaid interns, especially
for special events. Shares space with the Washington Wine Commission, the
promotional agency for state wineries, which employs three.

Washington Winestyle
P.O. Box 1512, Mercer Island WA 98040
232-8681
Introduced in September, 1993, this bimonthly has a very small permanent staff,
but it uses interns and buys free-lance work. Editorial interns should be upper
division journalism students; graphic design interns should be familiar with Adobe
Photoshop and QuarkXPress. Writers need not be previously published, but they
should be able to report quotes accurately and provide product or winery history
in their stories. Submissions (write for guidelines first) are preferred on PC-
formatted diskettes, but typed material will be accepted. Photographs should be
transparencies, shot in color in at least full-frame 35mm format.

Waterfront Press
1115 N.W. 46th, Seattle WA 98107
789-6506
Seafood Leader, which covers the commercial seafood industry, *Simply Seafood,*
a new consumer-oriented magazine, and *Alaska Fisherman's Journal* are the three
publications of this firm. Peter Redmayne is editor of the first two; contact him
regarding free-lance opportunities. The *Journal* is edited by John van Amerongen.

Watts-Silverstein & Associates
1921 Second Ave., Seattle WA 98101
443-4200
Charlie Watts and Bruce Silverstein head this firm, which produces film, video and
computer-generated multimedia presentations. Employs 22 and uses free-lancers,
especially producers and computer multimedia specialists.

West Coast Grocery Co.
P.O. Box 2237, Tacoma WA 98401
593-3200
Jobline: 593-5876
About 1,000 are employed by this wholesale grocery supplier, part of Super Valu.
Part-time positions include order selecter, a warehouse laborer position, and truck
driver (a union position). Occasional internships. Contact: Les Soltis, human
resources manager. Applications are accepted only for open positions. Openings
are posted in the HR office at 1525 E. D St., fourth floor.

Western Washington Fair
P.O. Box 430, Puyallup WA 98371
845-1771
This nonprofit fair association has limited turnover in the permanent staff of 55, but
internships are possible, especially for college students majoring in public relations; they can work summer through September. Contact: Karen LaFlamme,

public relations manager. Come September, you can work at the fair—either for the fair board itself (which hires about 1,500) or for those who operate food or ride concessions or sponsor exhibits. The fair's own hiring is handled by the state Employment Security's Lakewood Job Service Center, which opens a branch on the fairgrounds Aug. 1. To apply, enter at the Yellow Gate on 5th Street Southwest. Minimum age for some jobs is 16, for others 18. There is no other seasonal hiring; the events that occur on the fairgrounds throughout the rest of the year are staffed by permanent employees.

Westin Hotel
1900 Fifth Ave., Seattle WA 98101
728-1000
Jobline: 728-1000, Ext. 5766
One of Seattle's largest hotels, the Westin offers a variety of job opportunities, both managerial and entry-level, full-time, part-time and seasonal. Pick up an application at the employee entrance between Fifth and Sixth avenues on Virginia. Internships are sometimes available in corporate departments; they're not listed on the jobline, but you can write or call Human Resources for information.

West One Bank Washington
P. O. Box 1987, Seattle WA 98111
Human Resources: 585-2709
Jobline: 585-2714
This bank employs about 1,000 statewide. Part-time teller positions available in branches; most other employment is full-time. Occasional internships in the corporate offices. Openings are posted in the personnel office at 1301 Fifth Ave., 20th floor. Applications—for any position—can be picked up in any branch. Human resources manager: (Ms.) Lynn Garrison.

West Seattle Herald, Inc.
P.O. Box 16069, Seattle WA 98116
932-0300
Two community papers published by Jerry Robinson. Editor: Ann Holiday.

Weyerhaeuser Co.
Recruiting and Staffing CH1J26, Tacoma WA 98477
924-2345
Jobline: 924-5347
Established as a timber company, Weyerhaeuser planted the country's first tree farm and has been recognized for its programs in fire prevention, perpetual-harvest forestry and intensive forest management. Today this Fortune 500 firm remains one of the largest forest products companies. This address is for Weyerhaeuser's central screening office; you can send it your resume with a cover letter explaining the kind of position you seek. Many positions are also advertised.

Weyerhaeuser Temporary Services
Tacoma WA 98477
924-3063
An in-house employment agency. Most of the 70 employees work in clerical positions. What's important? Good phone skills and excellent computer skills, including word processing (especially Word for Windows), Excel and Microsoft

Mail and Schedule Plus. There's no minimum typing speed for applicants; accuracy's more important.

Whidbey Press Inc.
7689 N.E. Day Rd., Bainbridge Island WA 98110
842-8305
Community newspaper organization with four weekly newspaper units and two printing plants. The newspaper groups include Kitsap, which publishes such Seattle-area papers as the *Bainbridge Island Review*; Cascade, which issues the *Lakewood* (Tacoma) *Journal*; Whidbey, which publishes the Oak Harbor paper; and the San Juan unit, which handles the *Island Sounder*. Occasional entry-level positions on the news side. Openings are advertised in the papers, at the front desk of the corporate headquarters and in the Washington Newspaper Publishers Association newsletter (see *How to Network through Professional Associations*). Student internships in editorial. Human resources director: Sherry Havens.

Zenith Administrators, Inc.
201 Queen Anne Ave. N., #100, Seattle WA 98109
282-4100
A third party administrator of employee health and pension plans. The receptionist has a list of current openings. Internships may be possible in 1995. Human resources administrator: Gail Stewart.

Zimmer Gunsul Frasca Partnership
1191 Second Ave., #800, Seattle WA 98101
623-9414
This branch of a Portland architectural firm employs about 40 in Seattle. For information about internships, contact the Portland headquarters, (503) 224-3860.

ZymoGenetics, Inc.
1201 Eastlake Ave. E., Seattle WA 98102
547-8080
Jobline: #7
This biotechnology firm employs about 200. Most openings are in research and development and require training in the sciences. Limited part-time opportunities. Occasional temporary assignments. Internships sometimes available for upper division or graduate-level students in the sciences. Openings are posted at the reception desk. Human resources manager: (Ms.) Kim Kimbell.

10. Employers:
Government Agencies

In King County alone, government agencies—federal, state, county, city and tribal—employ more than 100,000. Many of the jobs are in downtown office buildings; others are on research vessels or disaster sites, in parks, classrooms or test labs. Some government emloyees work full-time; others have part-time, seasonal, on-call or intermittent positions. Some agencies have in-house temp pools; some hire independent contractors. As a "less than full-time" government employee, you might plant trees, teach swimming, write and design publications, run preschool programs or explain income tax regulations. You might be a reserve police officer, volunteer zookeeper, legal intern, playground leader, nurse or umpire.

ACTION
See Corporation for National Service.

City of Auburn
25 W. Main St., Auburn WA 98001
Personnel: 931-3040
Jobline: 931-3077
A city of about 34,000, Auburn employs about 360. There are part-time, full-time and seasonal opportunities. On the jobline, you'll learn of administrative positions and receive instructions for applying for the police and fire jobs that require civil service tests. Openings are posted in the personnel office, where detailed job descriptions are available.

City of Bainbridge Island
625 Winslow Way E., Bainbridge Island WA 98110
842-7633
Formerly Winslow, a city which encompassed only part of Bainbridge Island, this community in 1991 annexed the rest of the island and changed the city name. It now has a population of 17,000 and employs 95, nearly all full-time. Some additional summer positions. Job openings are posted at the city hall.

City of Bellevue
11511 Main St., Bellevue WA 98004
Personnel Services: 455-6838
Jobline: 455-7822
Employs about 1,000 work full-time and an additional 40 part-time (most part-timers are support staff). As many as 300 more positions are added during the summer. Permanent job opportunities and many temp openings are posted in the personnel services office on the third floor of City Hall. If you are an undergradu-

ate or graduate student, you can apply for an internship; some are paid (as much as $14 an hour), some offer academic credit. Many departments participate. All internships are coordinated by colleges and universities.

City of Bellevue Parks and Recreation Department

11511 Main St., Fourth Floor, Bellevue WA 98004

Bellevue hires as many as 300 for summer positions as day camp counselors and pony ride instructors (call the Recreation Division at 455-6885 for more information), lifeguards, swimming and aerobics instructors (call the Athletics Division, 455-6887) and in grounds maintenance (call the Resource Management Division, 455-6855). Some of these openings are listed on the city jobline, but you should also check postings in the city personnel services department (see above); apply directly to the appropriate division; or call the director of the facility (for example, Kelsey Creek Park) where you'd like to work. Year around the Recreation Division employs professional instructors to teach classes on such topics as painting, aerobics and foreign languages. These teaching positions, which pay at least $11 per hour but are limited to less than 69 hours per month, are seldom listed on the jobline or posted. They are occasionally advertised and you can file an application at any time, even if a position is not open. You can also apply at the facility where you'd like to teach. There are also part-time and temporary jobs (which may be full-time for as long as four months) with Parks and Recreation; some of these provide valuable experience for permanent positions.

City of Black Diamond

P.O. Box 599, Black Diamond WA 98010

886-2560

Population: 1,520. Staff: eight full-time, plus six reserve police officers.

Bonneville Power Administration

Puget Sound Area Office

201 Queen Anne Ave. N., #400, Seattle WA 98109

Personnel: 553-2539

Jobline: 553-7564

In western Washington, this federal agency employs about 250, about 150 of them hourly journeymen. About 10 per cent of the total staff works part-time, in both professional and support positions. Some hiring through the Office of Personnel Management (see later). Engineers and some economists can submit applications directly to the BPA.

City of Bonney Lake

19306 Bonney Lake Blvd., P.O. Box 7380, Bonney Lake WA 98390

862-8602

When this city of 8,500 has job openings, they're advertised in the local papers and posted in City Hall. Employs 60 full-time and seven part-time (for example, as the senior center director and court clerk) plus two or three summer public works employees.

City of Bothell

18227 101st Ave. N.E., Bothell WA 98011

489-3437

Jobline: 486-9473

Population: 25,000. Employs 155, including two part-time. There are also two to 12 seasonal jobs in public works and parks maintenance. Openings are posted in the personnel office and at city hall. Applications are accepted only for open positions. Internships and work-study positions are arranged through the sponsoring universities.

City of Bremerton
Personnel
239 4th St., Bremerton WA 98310
478-5283
Jobline: 478-5241
Population: 38,000. Permanent city work force of about 300; only about five work part-time. Because most nonmanagerial city positions are civil service, openings are posted in the civil service department. There's also a bulletin board outside the personnel office. Most summer jobs are offered by the Parks Department, which also hires lifeguards and continuing education instructors year around (see below).

City of Bremerton Parks Department
680 Lebo Dr., Bremerton WA 98310
478-5305
Hires rec leaders, maintenance people and swimming pool staff for its summer program; students interested in these jobs should stop by the Parks Department office in January or during spring break. These positions are not always listed on the city jobline. Lifeguards are hired year 'round; some are full-time, others part-time. If you have a skill you'd like to teach—in athletic, senior citizen or art programs—the city may organize a class for you. Contact Jodi Wroblewski, assistant director.

Port of Bremerton
8850 S.W. State Highway 3, Port Orchard WA 98366
674-2381
Port openings are advertised in the Bremerton *Sun* and the Port Orchard *Independent*. Two to four summer openings appropriate for college students.

City of Buckley
P.O. Box D, 933 Main, Buckley WA 98321
829-1921
This city of 3,700 employs 39, plus two part-time summer helpers in parks and public works. For 1995 the city expects to have a youth employment program employing four to six teenagers on a part-time basis. Openings are posted at the post office, multipurpose center and City Hall.

CASU
See Cooperative Administrative Support Unit under Federal Government.

Community Transit
1133 164th St. S.W., #200, Lynnwood WA 98037
348-7100
From Seattle: 745-1600
Jobline: 348-2333
The bus service for Snohomish County residents, Community Transit employs

380. About 185 are bus drivers (20 part-time). The administrative staff includes eight part-time phone assistant positions and a paid planning intern. Unpaid internships are possible in other departments. Job openings are posted in the office and at Employment Security offices. If you're interested in a position for which there are currently no openings, complete a "job interest" card so you'll be notified when there is a vacancy. Applications are accepted only for open positions. For internship information: Pat Olafson, personnel analyst. At press time, a merger with Everett Transit (see the City of Everett) was under discussion.

Congress
All members of the U.S. Congress maintain local offices in their districts. If you'd like to work or intern for a member of the Senate or House of Representatives, you'll find the offices listed in the telephone book under "U.S. Government-Congress." Considering a career in government? Remember these positions in the offices of members of Congress are not civil service and carry no seniority within the federal system. You may also be interested in a position on a campaign staff. These jobs are temporary, usually starting in April or June (depending on the position) and continuing through November. Senate races, like such other state-wide races as governor, require larger staffs. Members of the House of Representatives, who have smaller districts, will have fewer people on their campaign staffs. Typical positions: campaign manager, finance manager, district organizer, press secretary, bookkeeper and data entry clerk. Some are part-time or combined with other jobs. To inquire about campaign positions, call the member of Congress' local office. The campaign office will not be located there, but the staff will be able to refer you.

Cooperative Extension
Run in cooperation with Washington State University's College of Agriculture and Home Economics, extension offices provide information on agriculture and family life (through the Master Gardener program, for example) and run educational programs (4-H is the best known). Most support personnel are hired through county personnel offices; in King, Pierce and Snohomish counties, openings are listed on county joblines. For minority college students (juniors, seniors or graduate students), there is a summer internship program. For details, write

Barbara Scott, administrative assistant
Washington State University
305 Hulbert Hall, Pullman WA 99164-6230
(509) 335-2888

Corporation for National Service
The federal agency which many of us know as VISTA but was later named ACTION is now being merged into CNS along with the Commission on National and Community Service and the White House Office of National Service as part of the Clinton administration's national service program. VISTA remains one of several employment opportunities under CNS, the umbrella for AmeriCorps. Through AmeriCorps agencies, people earn stipends through three different programs. Except for VISTA (see below), there are no local administrative jobs, only the short-term stipended positions. The AmeriCorps programs include one called AmeriCorps, which provides grants to community groups which provide stipends to people doing community service; the National Civilian Community

Corps, a residential program for youth; and Vista. This reorganization is designed to increase the number of people working in community service, especially in direct services. At press time recruiting was just beginning for some AmeriCorps programs, with enrollees expected to start work in late 1994. For more information, contact:

AmeriCorps, Washington, D.C., 1 (800) 94ACORPS or,

VISTA
915 Second Ave., #3190, Seattle WA 98174
553-1558
If you're interested in public service, consider a year (the minimum) in VISTA. You'll receive a stipend, usually $600 to $700 monthly. In addition, VISTA service counts toward seniority for other federal government positions. May also result in deferment or forgiveness of certain government student loans. In screening prospects, recruiter Simon Conner looks for people with volunteer experience who demonstrate a commitment to alleviating the problems of poverty. Examples of VISTA jobs in Seattle: setting up recreational programs for the elderly; establishing family centers for the homeless; and handling such projects as youth mentoring, literacy, legal advocacy, small business development, infant mortality prevention and AIDS education.

City of Des Moines
21630 11th S., Des Moines WA 98198
878-4595
Population: 21,000. Seasonal positions in the parks, public works and at the marina appropriate for college students. Openings are posted at the library and in the courtyard outside City Hall.

City of Edmonds
Personnel Office
505 Bell St., Edmonds WA 98020
775-2525
Jobline: 771-0243, #1
As many as 20 full-time summer positions exist in the parks; another 100 students are hired on a part-time basis to work in recreational programs. Other part-time opportunities exist with the police reserves, who are paid when they work, often directing traffic, and with the fire department, which uses unpaid volunteers as backups on an on-call basis.

Port of Edmonds
336 Admiral Way, Edmonds WA 98020
774-0549
About 15 work full-time for this port, with summer employment adding as many as another 20 temporary positions. Permanent positions are advertised in the *Seattle Times*; for a summer job, apply after January.

City of Enumclaw
1339 Griffin Ave., Enumclaw WA 98022
825-3591
This growing community (9,300 population at press time) employs more than 90 full-time and 30 to 40 part-time and seasonal. Part-time positions include

maintenance, parks and library positions; summer jobs are in public works and the parks. Also about 50 volunteer firefighters. Openings are posted in City Hall and advertised. Applications accepted only for open positions.

City of Everett
Mailing Address
3002 Wetmore, Everett WA 98201
Personnel: 259-8767
Jobline: 259-8768
More than 73,000 live in Everett, where the city employs about 1,000. Most permanent positions are full-time. There are also summer jobs with the parks and public works departments; library pages work part-time year around. The city runs Everett Transit, which may eventually be merged with Community Transit. Job openings, permanent and seasonal, are posted at the personnel office, located at Wetmore and Wall, on the sixth floor of the Wall Street Building.

Everett Museum
2915 Hewitt Ave., Everett WA 98201
259-8873
Rotating exhibits interpreting Northwest history and its impact on the city of Everett are provided by this facility, which opened in 1992. The director is paid; other staff are volunteers. Student interns are welcome; curatorial collection experience is preferred. Director: Donna Chase.

Everett Public Library
Mailing Address
2702 Hoyt, Everett WA 98201
259-8000
Of the library's 80 employees, most are hired through the City of Everett personnel office. You can complete a "job interest card" and when an opening in that function occurs, you'll be notified. Openings are also posted on the city jobline. If you're interested in part-time work, you can apply at the library for a "page" position. These are support jobs involving shelving and checking out books. Applications are available at the downtown and Evergreen branches.

Port of Everett
P.O. Box 538, Everett WA 98206
259-3164
Most port openings are posted at the Job Service Centers and advertised in the Everett *Herald*. Some part-time jobs, usually for summer.

Federal Government
Federal agencies are listed alphabetically throughout this chapter, with most listings under "U.S.," beginning on page 211. The number of full-time permanent openings has declined recently. For one reason, as the Department of Defense downsizes, many DOD civilian employees move to the openings that do occur. Some other agencies (the forest service, for example) are in transition as responsibilities change. Federal personnel staff also describe the Northwest as a very stable work area, with limited turnover. If you'd like to temp for a federal agency, especially in a clerical role, contact:

Cooperative Administrative Support Unit (CASU)
915 Second Ave., #309, Seattle WA 98174
220-6129
You may file an SF 171, the standard federal application, at any time with the CASU office. Computer literacy, especially in word processing, is important. Veterans and previous federal employees have hiring preference. Most employees are paid at the GS 4 or 5 level, with wages (on a full-time, annual equivalent basis) starting at about $17,000.

City of Federal Way
33530 1st Way S., Federal Way WA 98003
Human Resources: 661-4083
Jobline: 661-4089
This community of 75,500 just north of Tacoma was incorporated in 1990. Temporary positions, both full-time and part-time, usually are in summer park maintenance and recreation programs. Openings are posted on a counter in the back lobby in City Hall.

City of Fife
5213 Pacific Highway E., Fife WA 98424
922-2489
Openings are posted outside City Hall. Even when no openings exist, you can complete an application. Summer jobs, usually for students, are in maintenance and at the pool.

City of Fircrest
115 Ramsdell St., Fircrest WA 98466
564-8901
Adjacent to Tacoma, this city of 5,300 employs 41 full-time, four part-time and about 45 on a seasonal basis. The seasonal jobs are at the pool (about 25), in park maintenance and with the fire department, in such jobs as fire hydrant testing (usually handled by volunteer firefighters). Job openings are advertised and listed on a clipboard in City Hall.

City of Gig Harbor
P.O. Box 145, 3105 Judson, Gig Harbor WA 98335
851-8136
Students are hired for summer jobs in the office, maintenance and in the parks. Openings are posted on a bulletin board at City Hall.

Intercity Transit
P.O. Box 659, Olympia WA 98507
786-8585
Thurston County's bus service will employ more than 300 by 1995. Most employees are bus drivers, both full-time and part-time. Openings are posted in the front lobby and at several agencies, including the Olympia Job Service Center. Applications, available from the Intercity receptionist, are accepted only for open positions; however, driving positions are usually open, even if not advertised.

City of Issaquah
P.O. Box 1307, Issaquah WA 98027-1307
391-1000
Openings for permanent positions are posted in the lobby at City Hall South, 135
E. Sunset Way. For part-time or seasonal jobs, contact:

City of Issaquah Parks and Recreation
P.O. Box 1307, Issaquah WA 98027
391-1008
Issaquah contracts out some youth camp operation to the Skyhawks Sports
Academy, but the city employs more than 100 on a part-time basis (working from
two to 20 hours weekly) in athletics, concessions and community education. When
a new community center opens in autumn, 1995 or early 1996, a variety of new
positions will be created. For information about current part-time opportunities,
contact Eric Hanson, who handles outdoor and sports activities, or Anne McGill,
who handles community education and other special interests.

City of Kent
220 4th Ave. S., Kent WA 98032
Human Resources: 859-3328
Jobline: 859-3375
This city of 40,000 employs 535 regular employees, almost all full-time, plus about
150 temporary, part-time and seasonal. Part-time and temporary jobs are most
often found in parks (for example, as a referee), in day care or the senior center.
Seasonal jobs are available in public works, parks and maintenance; most are
appropriate for college students. Teenagers 16 and older can apply for some
summer day camp jobs. Openings are posted in the human resources office.

King County
Human Resource Management
500 Fourth Ave., Room 450, Seattle WA 98104
296-7340
Jobline:
296-5209 (24 hours),
800-325-6165 (in-state, between 8 and 4:30 weekdays)
800-624-0875 (outside Washington, between 8 and 4:30 weekdays)
In 1993 the Municipality of Metropolitan Seattle (METRO) became a department
of King County. METRO's purpose was always water pollution control and public
transit. County employees have much broader responsibilities: jobs range from
AIDS prevention to Kingdome management. The county may hire as many as
4,000 during the summer—but usually as direct hires by specific departments,
without the positions going through Human Resources. Each department maintains its own file of temporary workers; these departments need to be contacted
individually. Openings for permanent positions are posted in the personnel office,
at entrances to the King County Courthouse and at the Fourth Avenue entrance to
the King County Administration Building. The human resources office has a
clipboard with METRO job announcements, but you must pick up applications for
these jobs at METRO's offices at 821 Second Ave. (See METRO later in this
chapter.) At this time, separate applications are required for METRO and King
County positions.

King County Library System
Personnel Office
300 Eighth Ave. N., Seattle WA 98109
684-6601
Serving communities from Algona, Bellevue and Maple Valley to Carnation, North Bend and Skykomish, the King County system operates 40 branch libraries, with several facilities scheduled to be added or expanded in the next five years. Total employment: about 750. Professional openings are posted in all branch libraries and on the Pacific Northwest Library Association jobline, 543-2890. To work part-time as an assistant (20 hours per week) or as a page (a support position of no more than 16 hours per week), apply at the branch in your area.

King County Parks Division
2040 84th Ave. S.E., Mercer Island WA 98040
296-4232
The parks department employs about 250 full-time; all permanent hiring is handled by King County Human Resource Management (see above). Summer positions are filled directly; depending on budget, there may be 1,000 or more. Jobs are offered by three divisions: Maintenance (physical park clean-up), Aquatics (lifeguards and swim instructors) and Recreation (day camp leaders). All jobs are appropriate for students, especially those in college. Minimum age for some jobs: 16. Some jobs run March-September. Some are full-time, some are part-time. Summer employees will often work several different tasks or at different facilities in a work week. To apply for a summer job, call the Parks Division receptionist and indicate both the geographic area and division in which you'd like to work. You'll be directed to the appropriate facility or branch office, where you can apply directly with the manager for whom you'd work. It's best to apply between Christmas vacation and March 1 and then follow up with either a note or phone call. The Recreation Division's four districts also hire seasonal workers year around for such tasks as teaching (for example, pottery). And there are project opportunities; people are often hired on a temporary basis for such assignments as computer programming.

King County Department of Public Safety (Police)
Headed by the sheriff, this agency employs 843 full-time, including 599 commissioned and 244 in administrative and clerical positions. Unpaid internships are available for community college and university students; they often work in vice or crime analysis, seldom on patrol. For more information, call the recruiter at 296-4069.

Department of Public Works
King County Public Administration Building
400 Yesler Way, #600, Seattle WA 98104
296-6500
This department hires temporary workers in a variety of positions, many dependent on budget. In 1993, for example, it employed 80 to 100 (many professional engineers) on an ongoing basis with an additional 200 (many laborers) during the summer.

City of Kirkland
123 Fifth Ave., Kirkland WA 98033
Personnel: 828-1119
Jobline: 828-1161
Employs 300 in permanent full-time and part-time positions. As many as 150 may be hired for summer maintenance, day camp and aquatics programs. All openings are posted at the front desk at City Hall.

Kitsap County
Personnel and Human Services
Mailing Address
614 Division St., Mailstop-23, Port Orchard WA 98366
876-7169
Jobline: #1
You can use the jobline or look outside the Personnel and Human Services office, located in the Public Works building at Division and Austin, to learn of job openings. The county employs about 880 in permanent positions, with as many as 200 "temporary extras." Most temp positions, including the summer lifeguard, laborer and fair worker jobs, are filled directly by the hiring department, so check with such offices as public works and fairs and parks.

Kitsap County P.U.D.
P.O. Box 1989, Poulsbo WA 98370
779-7656
Lynn Meikle, the accountant, handles personnel for this water district, which employs 29 full-time. There's one unpaid intern. The occasional seasonal jobs are in grounds maintenance. Openings are advertised in the Bremerton *Sun*.

Kitsap Regional Library
1301 Sylvan Way, Bremerton WA 98310
377-7601
This library employs 150 in nine facilities that serve such communities as Bremerton, Bainbridge Island, Little Boston, Silverdale and Poulsbo. The work force is split between full-time and part-time. Openings are posted at each branch.

Kitsap Transit
234 S. Wycoff, Bremerton WA 98312
479-6962
The Kitsap County bus service employs nearly 160, of whom 88 are drivers, both part-time and full-time. No internships or seasonal hiring. Job openings are posted at the front desk.

City of Lacey
P.O. Box B, 420 College St. S.E., Lacey WA 98503
491-3214
Jobline: 491-3213
This city of 22,800 near Olympia employs 150 plus seasonal hires. It posts openings on the jobline and at the personnel office counter in City Hall.

City of Lake Forest Park
17711 Ballinger Way N.E., Seattle WA 98155
364-7711
This city of 7,500 employs about 30, including some part-timers. No seasonal positions. Openings are posted on a bulletin board outside City Hall.

Lighting Design Lab
400 E. Pine St., Seattle WA 948122
325-9711
Funded mostly by Bonneville Power Administration and Seattle City Light, this research and education facility employs nine; three are hired by the city and the balance are on contract. Contract positions include lighting designers, the person who builds lighting mockups and interns, usually students in architecture. Other unpaid internships are possible. Manager: Diana Campbell.

Lummi Indian Business Council
2616 Kwina Rd., Bellingham WA 98226
647-6249
Although outside the five-county area emphasized in this book, the LIBC offers jobs that may be of interest to those in western Washington. Located on the Lummi Indian reservation, it employs 300, in positions ranging from day care and K-12 education to fisheries to gaming casino cash clerks, security staff and business managers.

City of Lynnwood
19100 44th Ave. W., Lynnwood WA 98036
Personnel: 775-1971
Jerry Witzel is personnel director for this city of 29,000, which employs about 250 full-time and an additional 20 on a permanent part-time basis. Many of the 100 seasonal jobs are appropriate for students. Job openings are posted in the City Hall reception area. A jobline may be installed soon.

City of Marysville
514 Delta Ave., Marysville WA 98270
659-8477
About a dozen seasonal positions, usually in the parks. Openings are posted at City Hall and some are advertised.

City of Medina
501 Evergreen Pt. Rd., P.O. Box 144, Medina WA 98039
454-9222
A community of 3,000, Medina employs 16 full-time, eight on a seasonal basis and five on a consulting or contractual basis. Openings are advertised.

City of Mercer Island
9611 S.E. 36th, Mercer Island WA 98040
236-3561
Jobline: 236-5326
About 155 work full-time for this city of 21,000. An additional 60, usually students, are hired for such summer positions as day camp leaders, lifeguards,

tennis instructors and park maintenance. Throughout the year, work-study students are hired for clerical jobs. Openings are posted at the Employee Services office counter (simply ask one of the staff for help).

METRO
Self-Service Application Office
821 Second Ave., Fourth Floor, Seattle WA 98104
684-1175
Jobline: 684-1313
Formerly the Municipality of Metropolitan Seattle, the regional transit and water pollution control programs are now merged into King County government as the county Department of Metropolitan Services, still abbreviated as "METRO." However, for at least the next year, METRO and King County will continue to recruit separately. Of the 4,000-plus METRO employees, nearly 85 per cent work in the transit division, half of them as bus or trolley drivers. About 900 work part-time. Student internships, usually in areas such as engineering and planning, are available for both undergraduate and graduate students.

Metropolitan Park District
4702 S. 19th, Tacoma WA 98405
305-1000
Jobline: 305-1009
Runs the City of Tacoma's parks, playgrounds, pools, zoo, wildlife park, golf course and conservatory. Year around, employs 300 to 400 part-time in such positions as lifeguard. During summer, depending on weather and budget, may add 300 to 600 more jobs. Besides maintenance, there are jobs in day camps (for such special populations as the mentally handicapped as well as regular camps) and at the pools. Summer jobs are appropriate for high school and college students; those as young as 15 can be hired for the locker room attendant position. The jobline lists both permanent and seasonal positions.

Meyenbauer Center
11101 N.E. 6th St., Bellevue WA 98004
637-1020
This convention and 410-seat theater facility is owned by the Bellevue Convention Center Authority. Opened in late 1993, it maintains a 250-person pool of part-timers who work on-call. Internships may be possible. Applications are accepted only for open positions. Openings are posted in the reception area.

City of Mill Creek
15728 Mill Creek Blvd., Mill Creek WA 98012
745-1891
Part-time and temporary positions include project engineers and recreation instructors. Openings are posted in the city hall lobby.

City of Monroe
806 W. Main, Monroe WA 98272
794-7400
A few part-time and summer positions. Betty King is the city clerk.

City of Mountlake Terrace
23204 58th Ave. W., Mountlake Terrace WA 98043
776-1161
Employs about 25 summer helpers. Openings are posted on a clipboard in City Hall.

Muckleshoot Housing Authority
38037 158th Ave. S.E., Auburn WA 98002
833-7616
This agency receives federal funding to provide low-income housing for Muckleshoot Indians. Employs three on a permanent basis; adds others on a part-time and project basis, especially when houses are being renovated. Indian hiring preference. The MHA has taken interns, including teenagers, for summer clerical work. Personnel contact: Gail Christie.

City of Mukilteo
P.O. Box 178, 4480 Chennault Beach Rd., Mukilteo WA 98275
355-4151
Jobline: 290-5175
This city of 14,000 employs about 75 full-time. Applications are accepted at any time.

City of Normandy Park
801 S.W. 174th St., Normandy Park WA 98166
248-7603
Seasonal opportunities—both paid and volunteer—in parks and recreation. When openings occur, notices are posted in the city hall lobby.

City of North Bend
P.O. Box 896, North Bend WA 98045
888-1211
From Seattle: 340-0928
A city of 2,700 with a staff of 25, North Bend advertises openings in local papers and posts them on a clipboard in City Hall, 211 Main Ave. N.

City of Olympia
Personnel
P.O. Box 1967, Olympia WA 98507
753-8442
Jobline: 753-8383
Job announcements are posted at City Hall, 900 Plum S.E. There's 75 summer positions in parks and public works.

Olympic Air Pollution Control Agency
909 Sleater-Kinney Rd., #1, Lacey WA 98503
438-8768
A regional agency funded by federal, state, county and city governments, the OAPCA enforces, implements and provides public education on the state Clean Air Act. Internships (usually unpaid) are often available for college and technical college students; an engineering background is not required. Contact: Charles Peace, control officer.

Pierce County

Personnel Office
615 S. 9th St., #200, Tacoma WA 98405
591-7480
Jobline: 591-7466
Posts its openings in the personnel office and just outside the office doors.
Temporary positions, including summer jobs in Public Works and Parks and
Recreation, are filled directly by the departments.

Pierce County Library

Processing and Administrative Center
3005 112th St. E., Tacoma WA 98446-2215
Personnel: 536-6500, Ext. 129
This library system has 17 branches in the suburbs of Tacoma as well as such
communities as Bonney Lake, Buckley, Orting, Steilacoom and Sumner. Job
openings are on a clipboard available from the receptionist at the administrative
center and on bulletin boards in each branch. The few professional openings are
also listed on the Pacific Northwest Library Association jobline, 543-2890. Total
employment: 280, including 228 part-time. The library maintains a pool of
storytellers for summer work, but there's little turnover. High school students can
work in the page support position.

Pierce County Parks and Recreation

Lakewood Community Center
9112 Lakewood Dr. S.W., #121, Tacoma WA 98499
593-4176
Hires 60 to 80 each summer, about half to work as recreation leaders and
lifeguards, the balance to work in maintenance. Rec leader applications should be
in before April 1; those 18 and older (except for lifeguards, who can apply at age
17 if properly certified) with recreational or youth experience are preferred.
Openings are advertised in the *News Tribune* and posted at local colleges and in the
county personnel office. Year around the county employs about 40 part-timers in
such positions as gym supervisor and crafts instructor. Applications for these
positions are accepted at any time.

Pierce County Public Works

Public Services Building
2401 S. 35th, Tacoma WA 98409
591-7250
Many opportunities here, too.

Pierce Transit

3701 96th S.W., P.O. Box 99070, Tacoma WA 98499
581-8080
Jobline: 581-8097
This transit authority employs 630, 375 as bus drivers. All bus drivers start as part-
time and work into full-time positions. Most other positions are full-time. No
internships, but college work-study opportunities. All openings are posted on the
jobline and just inside the main entrance.

Pike Place Market Preservation and Development Authority
85 Pike St., #500, Seattle WA 98101
682-7453
Employs 85, including 15 in the administrative office. Most positions are in security and maintenance. Openings are posted in the office and at Employment Security offices and advertised. Internships are unusual, but teenagers are employed every summer through the Summer Youth Employment program.

City of Poulsbo
P.O. Box 98, Poulsbo WA 98370
779-3901
Summer positions in public works, often in park maintenance. Openings are posted on a bulletin board at the City Hall entry, 19050 Jensen Way N.E.

Port of Poulsbo
P.O. Box 732, Poulsbo WA 98370
779-3505
Four work full-time for this Kitsap County port. Another four are hired for summer.

Puget Sound Air Pollution Control Agency
110 Union St., #500, Seattle WA 98101
Human Resources: 689-4041
A regional regulatory agency, the PSAPCA enforces, implements and provides public education on the state Clean Air Act. An occasional summer intern through Environmental Careers. Job announcements are available from the receptionist. Dee Endelman is the human resources manager.

Puget Sound Water Quality Authority
P.O. Box 40900, Olympia WA 98504-0900
407-7300
A state agency established in 1985 to preserve and protect Puget Sound and the waters that flow into it, this office employs about 30. Interns hired directly; usually employed for fewer than nine months on a project, they must have a bachelor's degree or be a master's candidate. Contact: Betty Stewart, administration director.

City of Puyallup
218 W. Pioneer, Puyallup WA 98371
Human Resources: 841-5551
Jobline: 841-5596
About 350 (250 of them "regular") work for this city of 25,000. The 100 temps work in athletics, day camps, public works or as clerical substitutes. Job openings are described in a notebook at the City Hall reception desk.

City of Redmond
15670 N.E. 85th St., Redmond WA 98052
Human Resources: 556-2120
Jobline: 556-2121
Openings (full-time, part-time, temporary and full-time seasonal) are posted in the City Hall lobby and in the first floor Human Resources office.

Redmond Parks and Recreation
15965 N.E. 85th, Redmond WA 98052
556-2300
Hires directly for year around part-time positions and summer jobs. About 25 people work between five and 18 hours a week all year in jobs like building monitor and recreation supervisor. During the 10 or 12-week day camp sessions, another 50, usually students, work 30 to 40 hours weekly as camp leaders. Rec classes are taught all year by people who often work on personal services contracts.

Regional Transit Authority
Formed in 1993 as a cooperative government between King, Pierce and Snohomish counties to design and propose an intercounty transit system, this agency is staffed primarily by people lent by the member counties. Through 1995, the RTA's own staff is expected to be limited to the executive director, Tom Matoss, and a few other positions. If the RTA's proposal is approved by voters, hundreds of additional positions may be created in the last half of this decade. If the proposal is not approved, the agency may be eliminated. For current job opportunities, check with transit systems in member counties.

City of Renton
200 Mill Ave. S., Sixth Floor, Renton WA 98055
235-2500
Jobline: 235-2514
This city of 43,000 employs 510 full-time. Besides part-time jobs, there are seasonal positions, usually in the parks. Openings are posted in the personnel department.

Sauk Suiattle Indian Tribe
5318 Chief Brown Lane, Darrington WA 98241
436-0131
Fisheries, law enforcement, housing, child care and early childhood education and community health care are among the programs of this tribe, which employs 25. Indian hiring preference for some positions. Personnel contact: Paula Lurs.

City of SeaTac
17900 International Blvd., SeaTac WA 98188
241-9100
Employs 150 plus about 25 seasonal workers in parks, pools and after-school programs.

City of Seattle
Job Information Center
710 Second Ave., 12th floor, Seattle WA 98104
684-7664
Jobline: 684-7999
Except for civil service positions, most of the City of Seattle's 10,000 jobs are filled through this office. (Some exceptions are noted below.) You can review openings weekdays. The city has implemented a computerized resume-screening program which will eventually eliminate application forms. To ensure that your resume can easily be scanned, the personnel staff recommends that you use white

paper and a single type face with type set ragged right (no justification or centering). Use a chronological format that indicates each job title and the years worked for each employer. You need not include an objective; that can be mentioned in the required cover letter.

If you're a student interested in work-study or internship opportunities, contact the Special Employment Programs office (see below). Internships may be paid or volunteer. Paid positions are available for undergraduates participating in cooperative education programs. Municipal government interns are usually graduate students and occasionally seniors. For information on volunteer internships, for which you may receive academic credit, call 684-7996.

To temp for the city, contact:

Special Employment Programs
710 Second Ave., 12th floor, Seattle WA 98104-1793
684-7986
Through the SEP office, you can be referred to temporary positions in city departments. Most jobs are full-time and most openings are in office support. Many require such word processing programs as WordPerfect and Word. Good customer service skills are necessary, too. Assignments average two to six weeks in length, but can range from a few days to six months or more. In lieu of benefits, temps are paid a slight premium (starting at five per cent) over the standard wage for a given position. Depending on the department for which you temp, you may be required to pay union service fees. The SEP office does not post openings, but you can begin the application process at any time by completing an information form. If you appear qualified for the kinds of jobs filled through the SEP, you'll be asked to schedule an interview. At this time, bring your professional references, resume, original Social Security card and proof of eligibility to work in the U.S. Through the interviews, candidates are selected for the temporary pool. Once in the pool, you may be referred to temp assignments within several weeks.

Seattle Center
Center House, 305 Harrison, #112, Seattle WA 98109
684-7221
Jobline: 684-7218
A city facility, Seattle Center hires most of its staff through the city personnel office. Permanent employment, full-time and part-time: as many as 300. In addition, there are 650 intermittent and on-call positions, including ushers, security guards, parking attendants, janitors and office workers; these people may work two hours a week—or 20. Some work every day, others only once a month. Temp and on-call jobs are filled by the center human resources staff. All positions are listed on the Seattle Center jobline. Applications are accepted only when openings exist: apply at the Job Information Center on the first floor of the Center House. Remember that other job opportunities exist with the nonprofits located in the Center and with the private companies that provide food services and operate the Fun Forest. A few examples:

Fun Forest Amusements
To apply for a job operating rides: 728-1672
To apply for a job operating games: 728-1626
On a permanent basis, the Fun Forest employs only 30, but during the summer, the

work force increases to as many as 400. You can work weekends in the spring and then, during the summer, 40 hours a week. Most employees are students.

Service America Corp.
Personnel: 448-9319
Because the Coliseum is scheduled to be closed from June, 1994 until September, 1995, Service America is reducing both its local permanent staff of eight and its part-time workers for concessions and catering. Some jobs will continue at the Opera House, the Arena and in catering for Seattle Center conference rooms. Requirements include good math skills and an outgoing manner. Some jobs are appropriate for high school students.

Seattle City Light
Personnel
1015 Third Ave., #1111-500A, Seattle WA 98104
684-3273
Jobline: 233-2181
Most of City Light's 2,000 jobs are filled through the city personnel office (see earlier). Summer jobs are offered at:

Skagit Youth Camp
1015 Third Ave., Room 809, Seattle WA 98104-1198
Each summer City Light hires counselors, program leaders and a nurse to work with the 28 low-income youth who attend each session of this camp at Newhalem. Interested? Contact Mary McKinney at 233-2531 in January or February for an application. Positions are filled by late April.

Seattle Fire Department
Personnel
301 Second Ave. S., Fourth Floor, Seattle WA 98104
386-1470
The fire department employs more than 1,000, including 53 civilians, who work in such functions as finance, public education, public information, personnel and administrative support. For information about firefighting and the civil service test necessary for firefighter applicants, this office has an information sheet.

Seattle Housing Authority
120 6th Ave. N., Seattle WA 98109
443-4400
Jobline: 443-4376
A public corporation created by the City of Seattle and funded primarily by the federal government, SHA manages housing developments for the low-income, elderly and disabled; administers the federal voucher program for privately-owned housing; and manages the Seattle Senior Housing Program. Internships are reserved for high school students living in the projects.

Seattle-King County Department of Public Health
110 Prefontaine Pl. S., #600, Seattle WA 98104
296-4618
The health department employs about 1,800, in positions ranging from paramedics and counselors to lab technicians and statistical analysts. Most permanent

positions are filled through the King County Human Resource Management office. This office accepts applications for permanent work in two positions, dentists and nurses, as well as for all temporary or "extra help" positions. There are many professional temp positions (for example, public health nurses, inspectors and even some managers) as well as temp support jobs.

Seattle Law Department, Criminal Division
710 Second Ave., #1414, Seattle WA 98104-1712
684-7736
Although all permanent staff for this agency are hired through the city personnel office, it's a valuable source of unpaid internships. In the past, many interns have gone on to paid positions in law enforcement, advocacy and the law. Opportunities exist in four positions: advocates, those who advocate for victims of and witnesses to domestic violence and other misdemeanor crimes; paralegals, including those who have recently graduated from paralegal training; clerks, who support the staff; and law students, either before or during law school. The family violence program uses as many as 30 volunteers and interns at a time; those earning college credit usually work 12 to 20 hours weekly for two quarters or one semester. Work-study may be available in the future. Internship contact: Karen Dufour Deschamps.

Seattle Parks and Recreation
Employment Services
100 Dexter Ave. N., Seattle WA 98109
684-0991
Most of the park department's 1,000 permanent jobs (of which about 75 per cent are full-time) are filled through the city personnel office. About 800 temporary and seasonal positions are filled through this office; many are summer positions. A few examples: supervisors and assistants for the 38 city playgrounds, cashiers, zookeepers and lifeguards. For specifics on jobs, every rec facility will in spring have a copy of a jobs bulletin. It describes requirements (including certification) and provides pay ranges. For summer employment, apply early; for some positions, applications are accepted only in January. If you'd like to work in a community center, apply directly with a center. You'll find them listed in the blue pages of the Seattle telephone book, under "Seattle Parks and Recreation." Parks and Recreation uses many seasonal volunteers—as many as 4,000 some years—in the zoo, the aquarium, community centers, playgrounds and maintenance. Some positions are short-term; other volunteers work for several months. Volunteer work for the city is an excellent way to obtain experience that will help you in obtaining a paid position. For information on volunteering, call the recreation information office at 684-4075.

Seattle Police Department
610 Third Ave., 15th Floor, Seattle WA 98104
Personnel: 684-5470
The police department employs 632 in civilian positions and approximately 1,250 as officers. All civilian positions are filled through the city personnel office. For police officer positions, the civil service exam must be taken; pick up an application at the police department or call the Seattle civil service commission at 386-1303.

Port of Seattle

Pier 69, 2711 Alaskan Way, P.O. Box 1209, Seattle WA 98111
728-3000
Jobline: 728-3290
About 1,300 work at Seattle-Tacoma International Airport, at the piers, at Shilshole Marina, Fisherman's Terminal or in the port offices. To learn of openings, visit the application area in the Port reception area or use the jobline. For students, there are summer internship opportunities; some require that you apply early in the calendar year. (For example, a part-time trade and economic development internship for graduate students was to pay $12.30 an hour in 1994.)

Seattle Public Library

Personnel Office
1000 Fourth Ave., Fifth Floor, Seattle WA 98104
386-4121
Jobline: 386-4120
All of the library's 510 positions are filled through this office. Openings are posted at the office and in each branch. Besides the positions that require master's degrees, there are administrative and managerial positions and a variety of "library associate" (support) positions; some are technical and involve no public interaction. More than 60 per cent of the total staff is part-time.

City of Snohomish

116 Union Ave., Snohomish WA 98290
568-3115
Seasonal opportunities: park maintenance and public works, plus Youth Employment jobs for high school students.

Snohomish County

Human Resources
3000 Rockefeller, First Floor, Everett WA 98201-4046
388-3411
Jobline: 388-3686
Snohomish County employs more than 2,000, with only about 50 working part-time. However, hundreds work on a seasonal basis: for example, there are 100 positions in gyms, summer camps and other park programs; 400 at the county fair; and 30 to 40 in public works. Poll workers, who may work only a day or two a year, can number as many as 900. There are also 286 "Extra Help," temps who provide supplemental help, usually in support positions. For permanent positions, job descriptions and official application forms are in the HR office. Some seasonal hiring is done directly by departments:

Parks and Recreation: 339-1208

Evergreen Fairgrounds (part of Parks and Recreation): 339-3309

Public Works: 388-6446

Extra Help: 388-3946

Snohomish County P.U.D.
Employee Resources
P.O. Box 1107, Everett WA 98206
258-8655
Toll-free within Washington: (800) 562-9142, Ext. 8655
Jobline: 347-5599
This public utility district provides electric and water service. The "summer hire" program for high school and college students provides as many as 50 positions. Job openings are posted in the personnel office, located at 2401 Hewitt.

Housing Authority of Snohomish County
3425 Broadway, Everett WA 98201
259-5543
A public corporation supported with federal funding and bond issues, HASCO employs 15 maintenance or as resident managers in low-rent housing projects. Students are hired for summer work; temps are used for support jobs. Personnel contact: (Ms.) Rickie Bates.

Sno-Isle Regional Library
Service Center
7312 35th Ave. N.E., Marysville WA 98271-7417
659-8447
Brier, Edmonds, Lynnwood, Mill Creek, Mountlake Terrace, Mukilteo and Sno-homish are examples of the communities served by this 19-branch library system. Employment: 336, with about 70 per cent of the positions part-time. Some part-time jobs are filled by high school students, senior citizens and entry-level workers. Job openings are posted at the service center and in each branch. Professional positions are also listed on the Pacific Northwest Library Association jobline, 543-2890.

City of Stanwood
10220 270th St. N.W., Stanwood WA 98292
629-2181
About 2,400 live in this Snohomish County city, which employs 46, including the police crew and volunteer firefighters. There are 28 full-time positions. Openings are posted in City Hall.

Town of Steilacoom
1715 Lafayette St., Steilacoom WA 98388
581-1900
For recreation programs and maintenance, there are about 20 seasonal positions appropriate for students. Job openings are posted in the administrative building and on the bulletin board by the local bank branch.

City of Sumner
1104 Maple, Sumner WA 98390
863-8300
When this city of 7,500 has openings in its staff of 89, you'll find the jobs posted on the City Hall bulletin board. The city hires one or two college students for park maintenance; the recreation program is co-sponsored by Sumner Schools, which hires all the staff.

City of Tacoma

Human Resources
747 Market St., #1336, Tacoma WA 98402
591-5400
Jobline: 591-5795
Tacoma has a population of 179,000 and a staff of 2,800. There are also internships; see below. For those who prefer to work part-time, there's a "temporary file." You'll find openings for permanent positions listed in the personnel office; for temping, you can submit an application that'll be kept for a year. The best way to get temporary or part-time work, advises the personnel staff, is to get on the eligibility list for a permanent position in your field and then, if not hired, indicate you'll accept temp or part-time assignments. Summer temp jobs include public works.

City of Tacoma Internships

747 Market St., #1430, Tacoma WA 98402
591-5436
Almost all city departments provide unpaid academic internships, usually three months in length. Each quarter a catalog listing intern opportunities is sent to local universities. Copies are also available from Lee Feldhaus at the number above. Volunteer opportunities are very limited and are usually initiated by a department. If there's a particular department in which you'd like to volunteer, you might contact its staff. The manager can then work with Human Resources to set up a program for you.

Tacoma Public Library

1102 Tacoma Ave. S., Tacoma WA 98402
Personnel: 591-5602
The library handles its own recruiting. Openings are posted in the personnel office and on the third floor of the main branch. Employs 200, about half of those part-time. All librarians work full-time; most part-timers work in support positions.

Port of Tacoma

P.O. Box 1837, Tacoma WA 98401
383-5841
From Seattle: 838-0142
Jobline: Ext. 244
Openings are posted in the human resources office of Port headquarters, 1 Sitcum Plaza (on East 11th Street, directly north of Brown & Haley). Summer hires include about 10 college students who work in administration or maintenance.

Thurston County

Employee and Administrative Services
921 Lakeridge Dr. S.W., Olympia WA 98502
786-5498
Jobline: 786-5499
Employs 900 in temporary, permanent and civil service jobs. In addition, there are seasonal positions with Parks and Recreation and the Thurston County Fair. All openings, including seasonal jobs, are listed on the jobline and postings can be reviewed at the courthouse information desk, located at Bldg. 1, 2000 Lakeridge Dr.

Thurston Regional Planning Council

2404 Heritage Ct. S.W., #B, Olympia WA 98502

786-5480

Provides land use, transportation and growth management planning for Thurston County and several of its cities. Openings are posted at the courthouse. Both paid and unpaid internships for students in environmental studies, statistics, planning or transportation. Contact: Angie Dorian, assistant director, administrative services.

Timberland Regional Library

Service Center

415 Airdustrial Way S.W., Olympia WA 98501

943-5001

Operates 28 libraries in five counties (Thurston, Pacific, Grays Harbor, Mason and Lewis). Employs 310, about half part-time or substitutes. When vacancies occur, notices are posted in branches. Professional openings are also listed on the Pacific Northwest Library Association jobline, 543-2890.

City of Tukwila

6200 Southcenter Blvd., Tukwila WA 98188

Personnel: 433-1831

Jobline: 433-1828

About 20 or 30 are hired during the summer for park maintenance and youth leader positions. All positions are listed on the jobline.

City of Tumwater

555 Israel Rd. S.W., Tumwater WA 98501

754-5855

Employs about 120. Also eight summer positions for students, three seasonal jobs and two engineering internships. Openings are posted in City Hall.

U.S. Department of Agriculture

Forest Service

Mount Baker-Snoqualmie National Forest

21905 64th Ave. W., Mountlake Terrace WA 98043

775-9702

One of three national forests in western Washington. At press time, a hiring freeze had been imposed.

Student internships, called "co-op programs," are for natural resources and engineering students who wish to make careers of the forest service. They're administered in Mount Baker-Snoqualmie by Judy Mooney, at the address above.

If you're interested in a summer job in a national forest, Mount Baker-Snoqualmie hires more than 100 natural resource technicians each year. Recruiting is handled by Job Service Centers: Mount Vernon Job Service Center for the Mount Baker Ranger District; Everett Job Service Center for the Darrington and Skykomish Ranger Districts; Bellevue Job Service Center for the North Bend Ranger District; Auburn Job Service Center for the White River Ranger District; Lynnwood Job Service Center for the Mountlake Terrace forest headquarters; and Seattle Rainier Avenue Job Service Center for the Pacific Northwest Research Station.

U.S. Air Force

McChord Air Force Base
There are two kinds of civilian jobs—and two personnel offices—at McChord.
Those jobs funded by the Department of Defense are subject to freezes; other
positions are supported by user fees and, although not subject to the freezes, may
not offer civil service benefits.

Department of Defense-funded Positions

Although at press time a freeze had been imposed, some civil service opportunities
existed for current and previous federal employees. Applicants must be U.S.
citizens. Openings can be reviewed and official application forms picked up at the
personnel office, located inside the front gate of the base, which adjoins Tacoma.

Civilian Personnel Office
Bldg. 773, McChord AFB WA 98438
984-3803
Jobline: 984-2277

Nonappropriated Fund Personnel

These are the people who handle fee-supported activities at McChord—for example, the golf course, officers' club and child care center. Some jobs are
permanent full-time or part-time with full benefits. Others are "flexible;" they may
offer regular work schedules but no benefits. Many positions are appropriate for
students; the minimum age is 16. You need not be a U.S. citizen. About 150
openings occur each year. Examples: recreational aide, food service, maintenance
mechanic, clerk and golf pro. You can walk in the office and check the bulletin
boards.

Human Resources Office
Nonappropriated Fund Personnel
Bldg. 100, Room 1007, McChord AFB WA 98438
984-3838

U.S. Department of the Army

Corps of Engineers

4735 E. Marginal Way S., Seattle WA 98124
Human Resources: 764-3416
Jobline: 764-3739
Most positions are filled through the U.S. Office of Personnel Management (see
below). All positions are listed on the corps jobline and in its human resources
office. High school and college students interested in the "Stay-in-School" work
program for those with financial need can contact Carolyn Coleman, 764-3735.

Fort Lewis

Logistics Center
Bldg. 9503, Room 100-A, Fort Lewis WA 98433
967-5091
Jobline: 967-5377
Despite the civilian hiring freeze imposed at press time, some openings existed at
Fort Lewis, which adjoins Tacoma. Some jobs are part-time, temporary, seasonal
or intermittent (select the correct option on the jobline or visit the Nonappropriated
Funds personnel office in the basement). Openings for the finance office and the

commissaries are posted here, although hiring is handled in Indianapolis (for finance) and Ogden, Utah (for commissaries). You can review postings in the personnel offices weekdays 9 to 4. To reach the Logistics Center, take the Tillicum exit (#123) from Interstate 5. This office handles about 3,000 positions, including those at Madigan Army Medical Center.

U.S. Department of Commerce

Western Administrative Support Center
Human Resources Division
Bin C15700, 7600 Sand Point Way N.E., Bldg. 1, Seattle WA 98115-0070
526-6053
General personnel information (taped message): 526-6053
Jobline: 526-6294
Interested in the Economic Development Administration? The Census? Minority Business Development? This is where you'll learn about opportunities in these agencies and many others in several western states.

National Oceanic and Atmospheric Administration (NOAA)
Personnel Office, Bldg. 1, 7600 Sand Point Way N.E., Seattle WA 98115
Joblines:
General personnel information (taped message): 526-6053
Shipboard jobs: 526-6051
This office handles openings in the weather service, fisheries and National Ocean Service. Some positions are in Seattle, others are aboard vessels.

U.S. Environmental Protection Agency (EPA)
Human Resources Management Branch
1200 Sixth Ave., Seventh Floor, Mailstop MD-077, Seattle WA 98101
553-2959
Jobline: 553-1240
To learn of openings, visit the EPA or Office of Personnel Management (OPM) offices. Applications must be submitted using the SF 171 available in either office. For students, there are co-op positions through colleges; other internships are occasionally available. Temps are hired both directly and through OPM; they may be clerical or technical staff.

Equal Employment Opportunities Commission
901 First Ave., #400, Seattle WA 98104-1061
Personnel: 220-6877
Sixty, mostly attorneys and investigators, work in Seattle for this federal agency, which is responsible for investigating charges of discrimination in the private sector. Unpaid legal internships are possible. Contact: Joanne Cantrell.

U.S. Federal Aviation Administration (FAA)
Northwest Mountain Region
1601 Lind Ave. S.W., Mailstop ANM-14R, Renton WA 98055
Recruiter: 227-2079
Jobline: 227-2014
Test pilots, engineers, airport planners and, of course, air traffic controllers are examples of FAA jobs. Many positions are filled from registers maintained by the Office of Personnel Management (OPM). At press time, there was a hiring freeze.

U.S. Federal Trade Commission, Seattle Regional Office
915 Second Ave., #2806, Seattle WA 98174
220-6350
Consumer protection and anti-trust regulations are the responsibility of this
agency, which employs 20, mostly attorneys. Unpaid internships may be possible;
contact Robert J. Schroeder, assistant regional director.

U.S. Department of Justice
Federal Bureau of Investigation (FBI)
915 Second Ave., #710, Seattle WA 98174
622-0460
FBI internships are available in Washington, D.C. for those between their junior
and senior years of college; you'll find information at the local office.

U.S. Federal Emergency Management Agency (FEMA)
130 228th St. S.W., Bothell WA 98021
487-4600
Jobline: 487-4783
FEMA Region X activities include disaster assistance, which has both full-time
permanent and full-time intermittent employees. The permanent staff establishes
disaster assistance programs which are implemented by experienced personnel
who work on-call, often on two- to four-month assignments. FEMA has about 65
permanent employees and approximately 200 intermittent. Intermittent employees are hired directly; you can apply at any time. All FEMA internships are in
Washington, D.C., but this office can refer you to the appropriate contact.

U.S. Government Services Administration
400 15th St. S.W., Auburn WA 98001
Personnel: 931-7542
Jobline: (415) 744-5182, (800) 347-3378
Internships are competitive and open only to federal employees; co-op programs
offering part-time work during the school year and full-time work during breaks
are open to community and vocational college students, including those at Green
River and Renton Vocational Institute. Temps are hired through CASU (see
earlier).

U.S. Department of Health and Human Services
Regional Personnel
2201 Sixth Ave., Mailstop RX-05, Seattle WA 98121
615-2033
This federal agency has about 750 full-time and part-time positions in this area.
Some hiring is done directly; other positions are filled from registers maintained
by the Office of Personnel Management. Openings are posted at the HHS office,
OPM, Job Service Centers and sometimes on the federal jobline. You must use the
SF 171.

U.S. Department of Housing and Urban Development
909 First Ave., #200, Seattle WA 98104-1000
220-5125
Jobline: 220-5132

HUD positions include jobs in loan management, where you would work with VA and FHA loans, and property management, where you might oversee the management or rehabilitation of government-owned property. At press time there was a hiring freeze.

U.S. Department of the Interior

National Park Service
Pacific Northwest Regional Office
909 First Ave., Seattle WA 98104-1060
220-4000
Jobline: 220-4000
Like to be a park ranger? It's a great job—and there are very few openings. You may have a better chance at a ranger job if you start with a summer seasonal position. To apply, request a "seasonal packet" between Sept. 1 and Jan. 15. You may also be interested in the seasonal park jobs available from the concessions that provide food, lodging and tourist services. These jobs do not lead to park service positions. Concessionaires can be reached during the winter at:

Mount Rainier National Park Concessions

Guest Services, Inc.
Elizabeth Marzano, General Manager
Star Route, Ashford WA 98304

North Cascades National Park (Ross Lake National Recreational Area)

Ross Lake Resort
Hal Tye
Yakima WA 98908

North Cascades National Park (Lake Chelan National Recreational Area)

North Cascades Lodge
Steve Gibson
P.O. Box 1779, Chelan WA 98816

Olympic National Park Concessions

Kalaloch Lodge
Tom McFadden
Star Route 1, P.O. Box 1100, Forks WA 98331

Log Cabin Resort
Bette Linenkugel
6540 E. Beach Road, Port Angeles WA 98362

Lake Crescent Lodge
HC 62, Box 11, Port Angeles WA 98362-9798

Sol Duc Hot Springs Resort
Steve Olsen
P.O. Box 2169, Port Angeles WA 98362-0283

U.S. Department of Labor

1111 Third Ave., #815, Seattle WA 98101-3212
Personnel: 553-4172
Jobline: (800) 366-2753
Employs about 300 in Seattle, in such positions as auditor, attorney, budget analyst, economist, safety specialist and vocational rehabilitation specialist. Temps—hired directly—usually do clerical work, but there are occasional professional assignments. Openings are posted in the Labor Department office.

U.S. Department of Treasury

Internal Revenue Service (IRS)

915 Second Ave., #2392, Seattle WA 98174
220-5725
Jobline: 220-5757
You'll find permanent and seasonal positions at the IRS, which employs 1,200 statewide, with 800 in the Puget Sound area. The IRS seeks bilingual candidates, especially those who speak Spanish or such Asian languages as Korean, Chinese or Vietnamese. Occasional internships. Seasonal positions include those who handle telephone inquiries (called "contact reps") and tax examiner assistants. The contact reps often work full-time October through April and then may be switched to part-time or laid off; benefits are limited. Minimum requirements: a bachelor's degree or a year of related experience. Examiner assistants need a background (although not a C.P.A.) in accounting or collections.

U.S. Office of Personnel Management, Seattle Service Center

915 Second Ave., Seattle WA 98174
Jobline: 220-6400
Many Seattle area federal government positions are filled through this office, which accepts applications in two different ways. For those positions in which openings occur frequently, the government maintains registers, lists of people with the necessary qualifications. For those positions in which openings seldom occur, the government occasionally issues a vacancy announcement and then creates a short-term list. Getting on a register may require taking a test. There is no one exam for all federal positions.

For information, call the jobline or visit the Job Information Center in Room 110 (First Avenue lobby) of the Henry M. Jackson Federal Building. (There is no telephone service.) You can also write the Job Information Center using the address above. Job openings are posted and detailed announcements are compiled in notebooks. There's also computerized information. For many jobs, you'll contact the hiring agency directly.

The Job Information Center also provides information about Administrative Careers with America, which recruits for registers for entry-level positions in six general occupational areas. You also can obtain information from the Career America Connection, (912) 757-3000.

OPM itself employs only 17 people full-time in the Seattle office. The occasional openings are usually for students and are filled through state Job Service Centers.

U.S. Department of the Navy

Fleet and Industrial Supply Center

Human Resources Field Office
467 W St., Bremerton WA 98314
476-7276
Jobline: 476-2889
This office handles recruiting for 14 defense printing operations. Employs about 500. Positions include purchasing, budgeting and contract administration. Openings are posted in the office foyer. Applicants must be U.S. citizens. Personnel for the six navy commissaries (grocery stores) is now consolidated in Ogden, Utah at the Defense Commissary Agency; to learn of openings locally, check the notebook at the commissary.

Puget Sound Naval Shipyard

Reception Center
223 First St., Bremerton WA 98314-5000
476-2958
Jobline: (800) 562-5972
The shipyard has both permanent and temporary positions. Applicants must be U.S. citizens. Reception center hours are limited; check the jobline for the schedule.

U.S. Naval Stations Puget Sound and Everett

There are different kinds of civilian jobs—and different personnel offices—at the Sand Point Naval Station and in Everett. Those jobs funded by the Department of Defense are subject to freezes; other positions are supported by user fees and, although not subject to the freezes, may not offer civil service benefits. The naval station has begun relocating personnel to Everett; note the human resources office addresses and move dates.

Department of Defense-funded Positions

Although at press time a freeze had been imposed, some permanent opportunities existed for current federal employees. Employment: about 200. Check the jobline or the notebook on the front desk in the office:

Human Resources Field Office
Naval Station Everett, Administration Bldg., 2000 W. Marine View Dr., Everett WA 98207-5001
304-3895
Jobline: 304-3598

Morale, Welfare and Recreation (MWR)

This department employs about 160 who handle many fee-supported activities. When the naval station move to Everett is complete, employment may reach 200. About a third of the jobs are permanent full-time with Bureau of Naval Personnel benefits. The balance are "flexible;" they may offer regular work schedules but no benefits. Many are appropriate for students. Examples of MWR positions: lifeguard, recreational specialist, child care worker, chef, waiter, purchasing agent, public affairs specialist and personnel specialist. The MWR personnel office is expected to remain at the following address until early 1995:

Naval Station Puget Sound
7500 Sand Point Way, Bldg. 224, Seattle WA 98115
524-0828

The new address will be:

Naval Station Everett, Administration Bldg., 2000 W. Marine View Drive, Everett WA 98207

Navy Exchange
The exchange operates retail stores, so most of the 200 jobs are for clerks and cashiers. Many are part-time and appropriate for students. You must be at least 16 years old; U.S. citizenship is not required. Applications are accepted at all times, both for Seattle and for the new Smokey Point facility that will serve Naval Station Everett. For information about openings, visit the office, which is expected to remain in Seattle until summer, 1995:

Navy Exchange Personnel Office
Naval Station Puget Sound
7500 Sand Point Way, Bldg. 193, Seattle WA 98115-5006
527-7836

U.S. Postal Service
Personnel Services
415 First Ave. N., #240, P.O. Box 9000, Seattle WA 98109
442-6242
Joblines:
Seattle and Everett positions: 442-6240
Tacoma, Bremerton and Olympia positions: 756-6148
Not everyone who works for the U.S. Postal Service sells stamps or carries mail, but that's where most of the openings are today. And due to postal service automation, at press time the only jobs being filled were "transitional," meaning employees have no tenure and can be laid off at any time.

U.S. Department of Transportation
Coast Guard
915 Second Ave., #3402, Seattle WA 98174
Civilian Personnel: 220-7074
Coast Guard civilian employment includes a variety of positions (for example, architects, engineers, vessel traffic controllers, field secretaries), but only a few positions of each type. Unpaid interns are welcome.

Washington State Convention and Trade Center
800 Convention Place, Seattle WA 98101
447-5000
Jobline: 447-5039
The convention center is a state facility, but employees are not part of the state merit system, which means they do not have seniority when applying for positions in other state agencies. There are 70 on-call positions in such areas as maintenance, admissions, parking and security. During the busy spring and autumn seasons, on-call employees may work as much as a week a month—or as little as a day a month. Openings are posted at the service entrance at the southeast corner of Pike and Ninth, where job applications are available. Unpaid interns are also welcome.

State of Washington
Personnel Office
600 S. Franklin, Olympia WA 98504
753-5368 (Touchtone telephone required)
Joblines:
From Seattle: 464-7378
From Spokane: (509) 456-2889
From Olympia: 586-0545
Olympia is the state capital, but that isn't where all the state jobs are. Positions—some part-time, many full-time—range from accountant and affirmative action officer to fish biologist, social worker, truck driver and volunteer resource coordinator. Review the personnel announcements at Job Service Centers, libraries, community colleges and in the Olympia personnel office. Applications can be picked up at Job Service Centers or the state personnel office and mailed directly to the state personnel office in Olympia. A separate application is required for each position. Some agencies hire directly, usually because they have positions unique to their agencies, or because they're recruiting managers, those "exempt" from the civil service system.

Governor's Internship Program
406 Legion Way S.E., Third Floor, P.O. Box 43123, Olympia WA 98504-3123
Program coordinator: 664-3647
Created to recruit managers for state agencies, this management training program provides valuable experience for undergraduate and graduate students in any discipline and permanent state employees. If you are not a state employee, you must be in school to apply. There are usually 25 to 75 positions ranging in length from three to six months for undergraduates. Most are in Olympia. Most recruiting takes place between March and June. There are 15 to 20 executive fellowships for graduate students, ranging in length from one to two years. Internships are advertised with other state jobs, usually on the green sheet at the end of the job announcements. These are paid positions; those lasting more than six months include full benefits. However, interns are exempt from the state merit system and so have no seniority for other state positions.

Commodity Commissions
You may also be interested in the commodity groups funded by farmers. The larger Puget Sound-area commodity commissions established by the state but funded by farmers on a mandatory basis are listed below. Commissions range in size from the Seed Potato Commission, with no paid staff, to the Apple Commission, which employs several in the state and has trade representatives across the U.S. and overseas. If you work for a commodity commission, you may be a state employee—but not part of the state merit system. This means you do not have seniority when applying for other state positions. Commission openings are not included in the general state listings; you'll need to contact each commission separately. Some commodity commissions contract out their management to related industry groups. In this case, staff members are employees of the industry associations, not the state.

Washington Beef Commission
2200 Sixth Ave., #105, Seattle WA 98121
464-7403
Executive director: Patti Brumbach. Employs five. Purpose: promotion.

Washington Dairy Products Commission
(Dairy Farmers of Washington)
4201 198th St. S.W., Lynnwood WA 98036
545-6763
General manager: Stephen Matzen. Employs six. Purpose: promotion.

Washington Fryer Commission
2003 Maple Valley Highway, Renton WA 98055
226-6125
Manager: Pam Williams. Employs two; internships possible. Purpose: promotion.

Washington Egg Commission
(Northwest Egg Producers)
P.O. Box 1038, Olympia WA 98507
754-4401
Regional coordinator: Helen Tomicic. Employed two at press time.

Washington State Department of Corrections
Human Resources Division
410 W. 5th St., Eighth Floor, Olympia WA 98504-1102
753-0297
This department has several divisions. Two, Community Corrections and Prisons, have positions around the state. Although most hiring is handled by the state personnel office, you can learn about both permanent and temporary positions by contacting these offices:

Division of Community Corrections, Northwest Area
2401 Fourth Ave., Sixth Floor, Seattle WA 98121
Personnel: 464-6301

Division of Prisons
Each correctional institution in the state fills many positions directly. Other positions are filled through Olympia or by other state agencies; for example, the state library may hire librarians who are based at prisons and nearby community colleges may hire instructors who conduct classes for inmates. To learn of openings, visit or call the headquarters HR office, check the bulletins at state job service centers or contact the personnel office at each prison.

Indian Ridge Corrections Center (Arlington)
339-1860

McNeil Island Corrections Center (near Tacoma)
588-5281

Washington Corrections Center for Women (Gig Harbor)
858-9101

Washington State Reformatory (Monroe)
Personnel: 794-2714

Special Offender Center (Monroe)
794-2200

Twin Rivers Corrections Center (Monroe)
794-2400

Cedar Creek Corrections Center (near Olympia)
753-7278

Council for the Prevention of Child Abuse and Neglect
318 First Ave. S., #310, Seattle WA 98104
464-6151
An agency of the Governor's office. Executive director: Kip Tokuda. Staff of four
is supplemented with interns and VISTA volunteers.

Department of Transportation
Washington State Ferries
801 Alaskan Way, Pier 52, Seattle WA 98104-1487
Human Resources: 464-6834
All ferry system employees work either in Seattle or on vessels. Almost 90 per cent
of the 1,500 staff members work on the vessels and so are hired through unions.

Washington State Historical Society
315 N. Stadium Way, Tacoma WA 98403
593-2830
Limited turnover; when openings occur, they're filled through the state personnel
office. Announcements are available at all Job Service Centers. The staff of 30,
of which only nine are full-time, includes photographic and exhibition curators,
volunteer and education coordinators, a publicist, librarians and museum assistants. Unpaid interns are welcome. A new, larger facility is scheduled to be
constructed in 1996.

Washington State Library
P. O. Box 42460, Olympia WA 98504-2460
Personnel: 753-3038
Employs about 135. Most work full-time. Temporary positions are filled directly;
apply at any time to Debbie Chavira, personnel assistant.

Washington State Parks
7150 Cleanwater Lane, Olympia WA 98504-2650
Personnel: 753-5760
Like to know more about openings with state parks? Ask to be on a mailing list for
announcements. Or you can visit the parks office and read the postings. About 40
people work around the state as seasonal park rangers, serving five to nine months
a year. These are Civil Service positions that require law enforcement and first aid
training. During summer, about 500 work as park aides; to apply, contact the park
where you'd like to work or the regional offices in Auburn or Burlington. A
complete list of state parks and an application packet is available by calling the
number above.

Washington Technology Center
Established by the legislature in 1983 to facilitate the transfer and commercializa-
tion of new technology. Sponsors research in five areas, including computer
systems and software, biotechnology, human interface (virtual reality), microelectronics and advanced materials. Most research is conducted at the University of
Washington and Washington State University. In Seattle, the WTC employs 10;
openings are posted at the UW Staff Employment Office. (See *Employers:*

Education.) Paid internships are available, usually for business students (graduate and undergraduate). For more information, call the tech center at 685-1920.

City of Woodinville
13203 N.E. 175th St., Woodinville WA 98072
489-2700
Incorporated in early 1993, this northeast King County community employs about 16, four of whom work part-time. No seasonal hiring. Occasional temps, usually for clerical work. Openings are posted in City Hall. Population is about 9,000.

11. Employers:
Education

Work in a school? Yes, thousands of people in the Puget Sound area do—and they don't all have teaching certificates or graduate degrees. Education offers a wide variety of positions—and schedules. You can teach in hands-on vocational programs or noncredit continuing education courses where expertise and the ability to teach are more important than degrees. You can tutor children in alternative programs or after school. Or you can work far from classrooms—in accounting, admissions, food service, facilities, transportation, public relations or fund-raising. For those with degrees, there are part-time teaching and nursing jobs as well as sub positions, in public and private schools.

If you're considering a job in the academic world because you'd like every summer off, check job descriptions carefully. Today many positions, especially in administration, operate on a business schedule; there are no extended summer or Christmas vacations.

This chapter begins with organizations that serve educational institutions: for example, cooperatives and legislative groups. On page 224, you'll find descriptions of colleges, universities and other post-secondary programs. Note that colleges define "adjunct" as a part-time instructor, without tenure track. Listings for community schools and other noncredit continuing education programs, elementary and secondary schools, educational service districts and in-service programs start on page 235.

EDUCATION-RELATED ORGANIZATIONS

Council of Presidents' Office
P.O. Box 40932, Olympia WA 98504-0932
753-5107
This state agency carries out projects of benefit (for example, legislative liaison) to the university presidents as a group. Internships are possible. Terry Teale is executive director.

Public Schools Personnel Cooperative
601 McPhee Rd. S.W., Olympia WA 98502
753-2855
Organized by Educational School District 113, this agency posts openings and accepts applications for jobs at ESD 113 as well as 10 school districts, including Olympia, Griffin (located in Olympia), Tumwater, North Thurston, and Yelm. Districts with openings screen the applications and conduct their own interviews. Applications can be submitted at any time. The co-op itself employs three full-time, two part-time; internships (probably unpaid) are definitely possible. Contact: Carolyn Vaughn-Young, executive director.

Washington School Information Processing Cooperative
2000 200th S.W., Lynnwood WA 98036
775-8471
Provides data communication services for 276 of the state's 296 public school districts. Its 95 employees (all full-time) include people who work in programming, hardware maintenance and product development. Internships may be possible. Although job openings are posted in the co-op's office, at press time hiring was being coordinated by the Edmonds School District.

Washington State Council on Vocational-Technical Education
P.O. Box 40920, Olympia WA 98504-0290
753-3715
Although a state agency, this office is mandated and funded by the federal government and the two employees are hired directly, not through the state personnel office. They serve as staff for the 13 community volunteers who make up the council. Activities for 1994 included recommending higher standards for vocational education, showcasing good programs and instructors and generating funds for additional student support services. Executive director: Susan Longstreth.

Washington State Higher Education Coordinating Board
917 Lakeridge Way, P.O. Box 43430, Olympia WA 98504
753-2210
A staff of 52, including policy associates, program managers and systems analysts, supports the nine-member volunteer higher ed board. Classified employees are hired through the state personnel system; exempt (or professional and managerial) employees are hired directly. Few part-time opportunities exist; occasional paid internships for college students. Personnel officer: Karen Tate.

COLLEGES, UNIVERSITIES AND OTHER POST-SECONDARY SCHOOLS

Here are the public and private institutions that provide education for those who have completed high school or the equivalent. Some of these schools are very small and offer few employment opportunities. Others are huge and employ more staff than faculty.

If you'd like to teach, you'll need an advanced degree for most academic programs and specialized skills for most vocational programs (for example, the vo-tech courses in upholstery and auto mechanics). Many schools offer part-time, temporary teaching jobs (often in evening courses) as well as full-time, permanent positions.

Antioch University-Seattle
2607 Second Ave., Seattle WA 98121-1211
441-5352
Joblines:
For unsolicited applications: Ext. 5033
For general openings: Ext. 5031
For adjunct faculty applications: Ext. 5032
This branch of a midwestern university offers a baccalaureate completion and four master's degree programs. Most classes meet evenings or weekends. Employs about 85 plus 50 adjunct faculty. About half of the staff positions are half or three-

quarter time. Applications are accepted only for open positions. Human resources manager: Mary T. Hodgson.

Art Institute of Seattle
2323 Elliott Ave., Seattle WA 98121
448-0900
Offers several day and evening programs: examples include visual communications, photography, interior design, industrial design technology and fashion merchandising and illustration. Employs nearly 250; 96 are part-time, mostly in faculty positions. Human resources director: Amy Collis.

Bastyr University
144 N.E. 54th, Seattle WA 98105
523-9585
Includes schools of naturopathic medicine, acupuncture and nutrition. Also affiliated with a natural medicine clinic. For the Leadership Institute of Seattle (LIOS), provides registration and financial aid services. Exclusive of LIOS, employs as many as 300 in a year's time because many specialized medical courses are taught on a part-time basis by doctors. Some support and technical positions are part-time. Jennifer Brown, human resources manager, handles recruiting for both the college and the Natural Health Clinic of Bastyr College.

Bates Technical College
1101 S. Yakima, Tacoma WA 98405
Human Resources: 596-1598
Jobline: 596-1652
A vocational school now part of the community college system. Offers training, apprenticeships and home and family life education. Two campuses: downtown Tacoma and Lakewood. Examples of courses: automobile mechanics, boat building, bookkeeping and medical transcription. Employs 640 total, including 250 full-time. Part-time positions range from work-study student jobs to part-time teaching assignments. Contact Sally Cofchin, personnel director, or her assistant, Kathy Flores.

Bellevue Community College
P.O. Box 92700, Bellevue WA 98009
Human Resources: 641-2271
Jobline: 643-2082
Offers university-transfer and Associate of Arts programs and continuing education. Official applications are available in the personnel office. (Enter the campus at Landerholm Circle from 148th Avenue Southeast.)

Business Computer Training Institute
Administrative Office
6695 Kimball Dr., Bldg. A, Gig Harbor WA 98335
851-8858
(800) 752-2284, (800) 752-0441
BCTI operates eight schools in the Northwest, six of them in the Puget Sound area. The 20-week courses, offered both days and evenings, are in office automation/computer applications. Some teaching jobs are six hours daily. You can inquire

about a teaching position by contacting the Curriculum Department at the administrative office or by calling a school location.

Capitol Business College
5005 Pacific Highway E., #11, Fife WA 98424
926-2382
About 120 are enrolled in this vocational school, which offers day and evening courses in the Tacoma area and in Olympia in such fields as accounting, paralegal, computer information systems and secretarial science. About 20 faculty, two-thirds adjunct. Openings are posted in the school and advertised.

Cascadia Community College
The state's 30th community college was established by the legislature in 1994 and is expected to begin offering classes in 1995. However, until a campus is built in the late 1990s (on the same location at the University of Washington's permanent Bothell campus), most administrative services (including personnel) will probably be provided on contract with Shoreline Community College. Cascadia is also expected to use the Canyon Park classroom facility opened by Shoreline.

Central Washington University
Extended Degree Centers
Although based in Ellensburg, this regional state university offers selected programs on the South Seattle Community College and Edmonds Community College campuses. Both locations have part-time and full-time faculty. Faculty members are hired by Ellensburg administrators in two different ways: full-time instructors are hired by the appropriate department (for example, education or psychology) while part-time instructors are recruited by the individual program directors. For more information, contact the coordinator at:

Central Washington University, South Seattle, 764-6422

Central Washington University, Lynnwood, 640-1574

Chapman University
This Orange, Calif. institution provides classes on four Puget Sound military bases. Each location averages two or three teaching openings each term. For information:

Chapman University-Bangor
P.O. Box 2120, Silverdale WA 98383-2120
779-2040

Chapman University-McChord/Fort Lewis
P.O. Box 4039, McChord AFB WA 98434
584-5448

Chapman University-Whidbey
Building 126, Room 137, Oak Harbor WA 98278
257-1277

City University
335 116th Ave. S.E., Bellevue WA 98004
Personnel: 643-2000, Ext. 4016
Jobline: 649-4625

Most teaching positions are part-time, usually evenings. At least a master's degree is required. Subject areas include business, management, liberal studies and education. Contact: Nancy Johnson.

Clover Park Technical College
4500 Steilacoom Blvd. S.W., Tacoma WA 98499-4098
Human Resources: 589-5834
Employment includes 350 permanent plus 100 part-time (mostly adjunct faculty) positions. If you'd like to teach through the continuing education program, contact Roger Mueller, continuing education director, 589-5833, or Regina Lawrence, continuing education coordinator, 589-5668.

Community College District 6
The administrative office for the three Seattle community colleges (see "Seattle Community Colleges") and Seattle Vocational Institute.

Cornish College of the Arts
Human Resources
723 Harvard Ave. E., Seattle WA 98102
323-1402
Jobline: Ext. 312
This four-year college offers degrees in art, dance, design, music, performance production and theater. Employs 165 faculty (92 are part-time); 40 full-time and 30 part-time staff.

Dominion College
P.O. Box 98947, Seattle WA 98198
878-1010
This new (1994-95 is its fifth year) liberal arts college offers general studies, theology and ministry degrees. Employs fewer than 10 full-time. Occasional openings for adjunct faculty. Contact Bruce Norquist, academic dean.

Edmonds Community College
20000 68th Ave. W., Lynnwood WA 98036
Human Resources: 640-1400
Jobline: 640-1510
Most openings are posted in the registration area and the Human Resources/ Student Employment office, located at 196th in Building A of the North Campus complex. Applications accepted only for open positions. Employment: about 750, including full-time, part-time and adjunct faculty.

Eton Technical Institute
Corporate Office
1516 Second Ave., #410, Seattle WA 98101
621-1899
This vocational school has three Seattle-area programs: Federal Way, Port Orchard and Everett. All offer both day and evening classes, so many opportunities exist for part-time teaching positions. Programs include medical and dental assistant, health office management, computerized business management and pharmacy assistant level A. Contact: James K. Martin, president.

Everett Community College
801 Wetmore, Everett WA 98201
388-9100
Jobline (Live voice): 388-9229
You'll find most openings (staff and faculty) posted outside the college personnel office. Employ about 150 staff (most positions are full-time) and 350 part-time and full-time faculty. Some internships exist in counseling.

The Evergreen State College
Human Resources Services
Library 3238, Olympia WA 98505
866-6000
Jobline: Ext. 6361
Employs about 650 full-time and part-time. Posts openings in the Human Resources office.

Golden Gate University
1326 Fifth Ave., #310, Seattle WA 98101
622-9996
This satellite of the San Francisco school has offered a master's degree in taxation in Seattle since 1974. The program offers as many as 18 evening courses a semester. All faculty positions are part-time and require an advanced degree in taxation.

Green River Community College
12401 S.E. 320th, Auburn WA 98002
833-9111
From Seattle: 464-6133
From Tacoma: 924-0180
Jobline: Ext. 99
Part-time instructors are hired directly by departments at this public two-year school. If you'd like advice on which dean to contact, ask the switchboard operator for the office of the Vice President of Instruction. Total employment: about 150 staff, 115 full-time faculty and 100 part-time faculty. Some internship opportunitities.

Highline Community College
P.O. Box 98000, MS 9-7, Des Moines WA 98198
Personnel: 878-9751
At this public two-year college, the personnel staff can refer you to the appropriate division chairperson if you're interested in a part-time teaching job. Openings are posted at the HCC personnel office reception desk, 2400 S. 240th, Bldg. 9. Employment: 350 full-time faculty and staff plus 350 adjunct faculty.

Lake Washington Technical College
11605 132nd Ave. N.E., Kirkland WA 98034
Human Resources: 828-2307
Now part of the community college system, this vo-tech school offers vocational programs, continuing education and several classes for job-seekers. If you'd like

to teach, call the personnel office; you'll be referred to the appropriate academic department. Full-time employment: 180. Part-time employment (mostly adjunct instructors): 150.

Leadership Institute of Seattle
1450 114th S.E., Bellevue WA 98004
635-1187
Provides a B.S. completion program for working adults and a M.A. in applied behavorial sciences. Enrollment: about 320. Administrative staff of 18. Faculty: about 15 full-time, 15 adjunct. Associated with LIOS Consulting, which provides in-house training for regional firms. Many faculty members are used for the consulting; to apply, contact Brenda Kerr, president.

Lutheran Bible Institute
4221 228th Ave. S.E., Issaquah WA 98027
392-0400
This school offers several programs, most with a religious orientation. The 45 employees include a few part-time staff and some adjunct faculty. If you'd like to teach, contact the Rev. Bob Moylan, academic dean.

Northwest College of Art
16464 State Highway 305, Poulsbo WA 98370
779-9993
Established in 1982, this college enrolls 100 in two B.A. and two Associate of Occupational Science programs. Four staff and about 15 instructors, many of them adjunct. To inquire about teaching, send a cover letter and samples of your work to Craig Freeman, president, or Willo Huard, education director.

Northwest College of the Assemblies of God
5520 108th Ave. N.E., Kirkland WA 98033
822-8266
Offers both associate of arts and bachelor's degrees. Employs more than 100, including part-timers and students. For a support position, pick up an application at the front desk. Regarding teaching positions, contact Academic Affairs.

Olympic College
1600 Chester Ave., Bremerton WA 98310-1699
Human Resources: 478-4980
Jobline: 792-2078
This public two-year college posts its nonacademic job openings in the Administration Building near the first floor mailroom. If you'd like to teach, complete a faculty application and submit it to the personnel office with a cover letter indicating whether you're interested in full-time or part-time positions. Employs about 300 plus more than 200 adjunct faculty.

Pacific Lutheran University
121st and Park Ave., Tacoma WA 98447
Personnel: 535-7185
Jobline: 535-8598
Private liberal arts college affiliated with the Lutheran church. Employs about

750, including adjunct faculty; about 25 per cent of the positions are part-time. Applications can be picked up in the personnel office in Rosso House.

Pacific Oaks College Northwest
2812 116th N.E., Bellevue WA 98004
889-0909
This outreach program of a California college enrolls about 150 in two programs, human development, headed by Barbara Daniels, and teacher education, headed by Jeanne Strong-Cvetich. Occasional adjunct teaching opportunities. You'll need a minimum of a master's degree.

Pierce College
Personnel Services, Room 324
9401 Farwest Dr. S.W., Tacoma WA 98498
964-6585
Jobline: 964-7341
This public two-year college operates two campuses, Fort Steilacoom and Puyallup, and employs 375 plus part-time faculty. Classified openings are posted outside the personnel office. To be considered for a part-time teaching position, submit your resume to Personnel Services.

Pima Medical Institute
1627 Eastlake Ave. E., Seattle WA 98102
322-6100
Offers medical training courses. Enrollment: about 500. Staff: 15, all full-time. Faculty: about 30, including many adjunct instructors. Contact: Walt Greenly, director.

Puget Sound Christian College
410 4th Ave. N., Edmonds WA 98020
775-8686
Glen R. Basey is president of this school affiliated with the Churches of Christ. Employment: about 25, including part-time faculty.

Renton Technical College
3000 N.E. 4th St., Renton WA 98056
Human Resources: 235-2296
TTD: 235-2359
Jobline: 235-2354
Offers day, evening and continuing education classes. Job announcements are posted near the cafeteria on the first floor of the administration building. If you submit a letter and resume regarding teaching to the personnel office, your materials will be circulated to the appropriate associate dean. Employment: about 700, including full-time and part-time faculty and staff. Work-study opportunities for RTC students, but no internships.

St. Martin's College
5300 Pacific Ave. S.E., Lacey WA 98503-1297
491-4700
This Catholic college enrolls 1,300 total, with 850 at the campus and the balance

attending classes on military bases. The occasional openings are posted at the campus information center. Total employment, full-time and part-time: 250.

Seattle Community Colleges
Administrative Office
1500 Harvard Ave., Seattle WA 98122
587-4155
Jobline: 587-5454
Besides full-time faculty and staff, Seattle Vocational Institute and North Seattle, Seattle Central and South Seattle community colleges employ 235 hourly and temporary staff. The part-time faculty (an estimated 600) is hired by division chairpeople or deans on the respective campuses; call the office of the Dean of Instruction on the campus of your choice for the name of the department to which your resume should be sent. Each community college campus has academic (college-transfer), vocational and continuing education programs.

Seattle Massage School
Corporate Office
7109 Woodlawn Ave. N.E., #5, Seattle WA 98115
525-0101
Employs 120, about 75 of whom are part-time (most in faculty positions). Personnel director: (Ms.) Nondis Barrett.

Seattle Pacific University
502 W. Emerson, Seattle WA 98119
281-2000
Jobline: 281-2065
When this undergraduate and graduate school has staff openings, they're posted inside the personnel office. For information about teaching, contact Academic Affairs, 281-2473. Total employment: 500, of which fewer than 40 are part-time.

Seattle University
Broadway and Madison, Seattle WA 98122-4460
Human Resources: 296-5870
Jobline: 296-6363
This Jesuit school posts openings outside the personnel office, located in the University Services Building. For faculty positions, contact the department in which you'd like to teach. For more information, consult the college catalog or call the office of the Assistant Provost for Academic Administration, 296-6140. Employs 400 faculty, of whom as many as 150 are part-time.

Seattle Vocational Institute
315 22nd Ave. S., Seattle WA 98144
587-4800
Now part of the community college system, SVI provides vocational training for youth and adults. Hiring is done through Seattle Community Colleges (see above).

Shoreline Community College
16101 Greenwood Ave. N., Seattle WA 98133
Personnel: 546-4769
If you'd like to teach, you'll probably need at least a master's degree. All hiring

is handled by the personnel office except the continuing education instructors; for information about this part-time work, call the continuing education office, 546-4561. Employment: 150 full-time faculty, with an additional 180 part-timers, and 200 full-time administrators and classified staff. There are also part-time and temporary classified positions.

South Puget Sound Community College
2011 Mottman Rd. S.W., Olympia WA 98502
754-7711
Jobline: Ext. 360
This public two-year school lists its job openings on a board on the second level of the administrative building, just outside the personnel office. If you're interested in a part-time teaching job, submit a resume and cover letter to the personnel office; it will be retained for review when appropriate openings occur. Employs 175 full-time and an additional 225 part-time.

Tacoma Community College
5900 S. 12th St., Tacoma WA 98465
566-5014
Jobline: 566-5014
At this public two-year college, you'll find classified openings posted in the lobby of Building 4. For faculty positions, full-time or part-time, pick up an application in the personnel office or ask that you be mailed one. TCC employs 170 full-time administrative and classified staff as well as 145 hourly staff; there's 100 full-time faculty and an additional 230 part-time.

University of Puget Sound
1500 N. Warner, Tacoma WA 98416
Personnel: 756-3369
Jobline: 756-3368
This private liberal arts college posts faculty and staff openings in the personnel office at 1218 N. Lawrence. Most staff positions are full-time, although some (such as food service) only for a nine-month period. Some faculty positions are part-time. UPS's law school has been sold to Seattle University.

University of Washington
Jobline: 543-6969
The UW employs nearly 19,000 in the greater Seattle area—on the main campus, in Tacoma and Bothell branch campuses, at KUOW and University Press, in the medical centers and at the Henry Art Gallery and Burke Memorial Washington State Museum. You can learn of many job openings by checking the listings posted at many libraries and public agencies. Some positions are advertised in the Seattle papers.

The university has 13,000 classified (nonacademic or support) positions. In addition, the UW employs about 2,300 in professional staff positions. These include directors (for example, of development or continuing education) and curriculum-related positions such as curriculum developers and research scientists. There are also approximately 3,500 faculty positions. Finally, the UW has many temporary employees, both in staff and teaching positions.

To be considered for a classified position, submit a UW application, available at:

Staff Employment Office, 1320 N.E. Campus Parkway

Harborview Medical Center, 319 Terry Ave.

University Hospital Personnel, BB130 University Hospital, 1959 N.E. Pacific St.

There is no centralized hiring for faculty. You must contact the academic department in which you're interested. All departments and their chairpeople are listed in the UW Bulletin, available for purchase at the University Book Store. (The bookstore accepts telephone orders with bankcards; call 634-3400.) Most departments require doctorates. Some contract-basis teaching opportunities exist, often through continuing education or staff training programs.

Many departments hire temporary and contract staff. Such employees are paid on an hourly basis and have none of the benefits provided to permanent employees. Positions are filled directly, not through Staff Employment. Some examples:

University of Washington Medical Center Interpreter Services
1959 Pacific N.E., Mailstop RC-76, Seattle WA 98195
548-4425
Prefers native speakers, especially those with interpreting experience in a medical environment. Employs about eight people who each average 20 hours of work a week. Languages most in demand: Russian, Spanish, Vietnamese and American Sign Language. Candidates certified by the state of Washington or the courts are preferred. Work schedules vary; interpreters are usually given their assignments only a week in advance. Program coordinator Michael Nielsen emphasizes that the work is mostly interpretation rather than translation. Pay: $15 to $17 an hour.

Disability Services Office: 543-6450
Provides American Sign Language interpreters and real-time captioners for staff functions, including meetings and lectures. No work with students. ASL interpreters are hired through the Community Service Center for the Deaf and Hard of Hearing (see *Employers: Nonprofits*), but disability service specialist Daria Ross is seeking real-time captioners. Applicants must be certified graduates of recognized programs like that at Green River Community College and have their own equipment.

Physical Plant Department

Property and Transport Services
1137 N.E. Boat St., Mailstop HE-25, Seattle WA 98195
685-1522
This office hires for six temporary positions. The best paid, at about $13 per hour, is for a Truck Driver II, a position requiring a commercial license. Temps fill in as bus drivers for the 33-passenger Health Sciences Express. This is on-call work, but there's frequent turnover in the crew and the job may lead to a permanent position. The Truck Driver I position pays about $11; it's a nine-month, part-time job driving the U's disabled person shuttle van. No special license required. Transportation Helpers, who work full-time, but only for six months, earn about $9 an hour collecting waste and recyclables or moving furniture. Often leads to a permanent position. Other temp positions include paper sorting, a part-time job; a half-time clerical position usually filled by a student; and warehouse worker, an occasional part-time job. To apply, contact the office supervisor; for the Truck Driver positions, you'll need a copy of your driving record.

Custodial Services

1103 N.E. Boat St., Mailstop HE-20, Seattle WA 98195
685-1500

Depending on budget, this office may hire between eight and 25 temporaries who work full-time to provide janitorial services in the U District. Some are entry-level, others are retirees (from this office) who have returned to work. Job requirements include the ability to lift at least 40 pounds, to be able to run equipment like floor buffers and to read English. You can apply at any time, but because needs vary so much, the office advises that you call to determine if any openings are anticipated.

Intercollegiate Athletics Event Management: 543-2246

If you're willing to clean gyms and stadiums after sporting events, note that the UW uses between eight and 80 workers per event. Most work days, but sometimes weekends—for example, on the Sunday following a football game. Most of the temps are provided by an agency; at press time, the contract was with General Employment. A handful of other temps are hired directly by the Event Management office; these people work almost full-time during the season. Limited turnover in the direct hires. To learn of possible openings or which agency is currently providing clean-up crews, call the number above.

Primate Center

Mailstop SJ-50, Seattle WA 98195
543-0440

If you're dependable, punctual and don't mind working in a tropical environment, consider one of the occasional openings for temps at the Primate Center, where animals must be fed and watered and cages cleaned on weekends and holidays. The work requires protective clothing (not always comfortable in the hot, steamy space). Some temps work on an on-call basis to cover for full-time employees on leave. Note that this is an animal experimentation project. Contact: Sam Sweeney.

University Temporary Services: 543-5420

The University also runs an in-house "temp" agency. You can work in a support position (possibly while applying for classified positions) through University Temporary Services. This office has jobs (some part-time, some full-time) as short as a half day and as long as 12 months. Computer skills are important: UW departments use a wide variety of programs and Macintosh, DOS and Windows platforms. You'll find it easier to be placed through UTS if you have good word processing, spreadsheet and dictating machine skills and can type more than 55 words per minute. UTS also has frequent calls for medical transcriptionists and for those experienced with UW billing systems. The UTS staff points out that it has difficulty placing people who are not available during the entire UW workday (typically 8 to 5) and all five days of the work week. Applicants should also be available on short notice; it is not unusual for temps to be interviewed one day and on the job the next day. At press time, the UTS office was receiving approximately 300 applications a month; about 15 per cent of the applicants are interviewed. Note that only 25 per cent of UTS placements are on the main UW campus; 50 per cent are at the UW medical center, Harborview or in the Health Sciences complex. The balance are in UW offices at Northgate, on Capitol Hill or in the branch campuses in Bothell or Tacoma. To obtain a UTS application, stop by the UW Visitors Information Center, 4014 University Way N.E., or call 543-5813 weekdays. There is no fee to applicants.

Washington State University
Besides the cooperative extension programs in each county (see *Employers: Government Agencies*), WSU has two offices in Seattle. One is academic, the other administrative.

Washington State University Hotel and Restaurant Administration Program
1108 E. Columbia, Seattle WA 98122
464-6349
Located at 914 E. Jefferson, #B-24, on the Seattle University campus. Offers several undergraduate classes. Some part-time faculty positions. Contact Dr. Carl Riegel, the director.

WSU West
2001 Sixth Ave., #100, Seattle WA 98121-2521
448-1330
Fundraising, alumni special events and the sale of Cougar memorabilia are the primary functions of this office, which employs eight, mostly full-time. You can call the office; if an opening exists, you'll be sent a position description.

Western Washington University
The Bellingham-based regional state university offers two programs in the Puget Sound area.

Western Washington University, Seattle Urban Center
1801 Broadway, NP 101, Seattle WA 98122
464-6103
At Seattle Central Community College, WWU offers programs in human services, school administration, adult education and secondary teacher certification. Prospective instructors must submit applications to the Faculty Vacancy Pool, which is opened each spring. Division directors screen the applications and then select candidates for interviews.

Western Washington University, Everett Educational Center
801 Wetmore, Everett WA 98201
388-9438
Both day and evening classes are offered on the Everett Community College campus. Programs include elementary teacher certification, and master's degrees in elementary education and human services. A Faculty Vacancy Pool is opened each spring.

NONCREDIT CONTINUING EDUCATION PROGRAMS
If you can teach dance, drama or Thai cooking, lead a discussion of small business problems or tell people how to tour Europe economically, consider contacting organizations such as the following. Also see "Education" in the index.

Community Schools:
Several school districts in this area make their facilities available for noncredit courses taught by volunteers and part-timers. Some programs (as in Tacoma) are run by the districts; others (as in Seattle) are operated by independent nonprofits, but use school classrooms. A few Seattle community school sponsors:

Nathan Hale Community Night School
10750 30th Ave. N.E., Seattle WA 98125
365-0280
Some 85 programs each quarter are offered by this school, established in 1972. To apply, call and discuss your course proposal and credentials with coordinator Frank Lynch before submitting anything in writing.

Powerful Schools
3301 S. Horton St., Seattle WA 98144
722-5543
After-school and evening classes for children and adults are offered in four Rainier Valley schools by this program, which pays instructors as much as $15 per classroom hour. It also uses volunteers as teachers. Most popular classes at press time: computer programs. Offers about 40 classes each quarter. Contact: Brenetta Ward, community education coordinator.

Magnolia Community School
4000 27th Ave. W., Seattle WA 98199
251-1079
Offers courses (including one by the author of this book) at Blaine and Lawton schools. Executive director (at press time): Susan Lundh.

Other Noncredit Classes:

Discover U
2601 Elliott Ave., #4305, Seattle WA 98121
443-0447
Established in 1992, this for-profit noncredit school uses independent contractors, many of them already self-employed, as instructors. Pay depends on the number of students enrolled; for three-hour workshops, pay can range between $100 and $500. Classes are held in the Seattle Trade Center. By 1995, more than 200 programs will be offered. The most popular classes: those that discuss how to start a small business and how hobbies can turn into paid employment (for example, how travelers can become travel writers). Contact: Debbie Mellen.

The Experimental College
543-4375
An Associated Students activity of the University of Washington which offers noncredit classes, many taught by community members. Call to receive the information packet for prospective instructors.

EDUCATIONAL SERVICE DISTRICTS

Washington has nine regional agencies that serve as liaison between the schools in their geographic areas and the state Superintendent of Public Instruction. In the Puget Sound area, the ESDs are:

Puget Sound Educational Service District
400 S.W. 152nd, Burien WA 98166
439-3636
This ESD's service area includes the 35 school districts and all state-approved private schools in King and Pierce counties and on Bainbridge Island. Programs: in-service training, direct services to children (including Head Start and Indian

education), teacher certification, technical assistance to school districts on both administrative and curriculum questions, and insurance co-ops. Total employment: 145. Dr. Sonja Hampton handles personnel. You'll find openings described in a book at the reception desk.

Olympic Educational Service District 114
105 National Ave. N., Bremerton WA 98312
479-0993
About 125 work for this ESD, which serves Kitsap County (except Bainbridge Island), the North Mason School District, Jefferson and Clallam counties. Because several member districts are small, there is an emphasis on providing direct services—in working directly in the schools. For 11 districts, the ESD also operates a personnel co-op. In the ESD offices, most positions are full-time and year around; however, many Head Start and school-based positions are five hours daily, 180 days a year. Contact Anna Alexander, executive secretary and personnel manager.

Educational Service District 113
601 McPhee Rd. S.W., Olympia WA 98502
586-2933
Depending on the season, as many as 110 work for this ESD, which serves 45 school districts in Grays Harbor, Mason, Lewis, Thurston and Pacific counties. Through a youth employment program, the district also provides work for as many as 800 students. For employment information, contact the Public Schools Personnel Cooperative.

Northwest Educational Service District 189
205 Stewart Rd., Mount Vernon WA 98273
424-9573
Snohomish County, as well as Island, San Juan, Skagit and Whatcom counties, are the areas served by this ESD. Employs 115, mostly in Mount Vernon. However, the district does run a satellite providing classes in Everett for behaviorally disabled children and a second Everett program for court-adjudicated youth as well as the Northwest Environmental Education Center in Seattle. Contact Kathleen Harmon, personnel officer.

HOME-SCHOOLING RESOURCES

Hundreds of children in the Puget Sound area are home schooled—taught at home by their parents. Parents who need advice on developing curricula can call on the teachers who serve as parent consultants through programs such as Family Academy. A private school extension program, it offers education services rather than correspondence courses. Most of the 35 parent consultants work on a part-time basis. For information about working as a parent consultant, contact Candace Oneschak or Diane McAlister at

Family Academy
146 S.W. 153rd, #290, Seattle WA 98166
246-9227

ELEMENTARY AND SECONDARY SCHOOLS
Here you'll find many of the public school districts and the state-approved

private schools in Seattle, Tacoma, Bremerton, Olympia, Everett and Bellevue. For more information about public and private schools, especially those more distant from Seattle, consult the Washington Education Directory, available from Barbara Krohn and Associates, 835 Securities Building, Seattle WA 98101-1162, 622-3538. Cost: $13 plus shipping plus tax.

Many current job openings for administrators, teachers and support staff are listed in bulletins available by subscription from the WEA Position Listing Service, telephone 941-6700 or, within Washington, (800) 622-3393.

A similar listing is available from the University of Washington career center. Contact: Center for Career Services, 301 Loew Hall FH-30, University of Washington, Seattle WA 98195, 543-9104.

Another list of openings for certified staff is published by Seattle Pacific University. (See *Where Are Jobs Listed?*) Contact: Education Vacancy Bulletin, Career Development Center, Seattle Pacific University, Seattle WA 98109, 281-2018.

A listing of openings in Catholic schools is also available to teachers registered with the Archdiocese of Seattle. See Catholic Schools in the Private Schools section of this chapter.

If you have questions about your certification, either because you are coming from another state or because your credentials may have lapsed, contact the state Superintendent of Public Instruction. You'll learn how to certify in Washington or, if your certification has lapsed, what additional education is necessary. If you have been certified in this state, it's helpful if you have your certification number; otherwise your Social Security number will be needed. Contact:

Executive Services, Professional Education and Certification
Old Capitol Bldg., P.O. Box 47200, Olympia WA 98504
753-6773

PUBLIC SCHOOLS

What part-time, seasonal or temporary opportunities do public schools offer? You can be a lifeguard, playground monitor, nurse, therapist, librarian or secretary. Perhaps you' ll work mornings, getting kids to school on the bus—or afternoons, teaching a class or two. After school, you might be a coach or a child care supervisor. You might work the academic calendar or year around, a few hours each day or full-time for nine months. Or you may work on-call, substituting in the classroom, office or kitchen or on the bus route. You may spend all of your time in one office or classroom—or you may switch assignments and desks in midday.

As you review the employers listed below, remember that "administrative" positions in schools are usually management jobs; "certified" (or "certificated") positions are faculty jobs usually requiring a Washington state teaching certificate; and "classified" positions are technical, professional and clerical jobs.

Arlington School District
P.O. Box 309, Arlington WA 98223
435-2156
Employs 390 full-time. There's also a substitute pool which includes teachers and such classified positions as classroom aides and secretaries. Openings are posted in the district office at 600 E. 1st St.

Auburn School District
915 4th St. N.E., Auburn WA 98002
Personnel: 931-4916
You'll find both certified and classified positions posted in the personnel office.
Employment: 1,200, including about 300 part-time classified positions.

Bainbridge Island School District
8489 Madison Ave. N.E., Bainbridge Island WA 98110-2999
842-4715
Jobline: 842-2920
Employs 380.

Bellevue School District
P.O. Box 90010, Bellevue WA 98009-9010
Human Resources: 455-6096
Jobline: 455-6009
For the necessary district application forms, visit the human resources office at
12111 N.E. 1st, reached from 120th Northeast. Total employment: nearly 1,700.

Bethel School District
Educational Service Center
516 E. 176th, Spanaway WA 98387
536-7272
Jobline: 536-7270
You'll find certified and classified openings as well as summer opportunities on
the jobline. Applications are available in the service center. Employs 1,200,
including 600 part-time positions.

Bremerton School District
300 N. Montgomery, Bremerton WA 98312
Employee Relations: 478-5107
This Kitsap County district enrolls about 6,000 and employs about 750. Openings
are seldom advertised, but they're posted on a bulletin board near the personnel
office.

Central Kitsap Schools
P.O. Box 8, Silverdale WA 98383
Personnel: 692-3118
Jobline: 698-3470
Certified, classified, administrative and coaching openings are listed on the jobline
and posted in the personnel office (located at 9210 Silverdale Way N.W.) and in
district schools. Employment: 1,450, including 650 nonteaching positions, many
of which are part-time.

Clover Park School District
10903 Gravelly Lake Dr. S.W., Tacoma WA 98499
Personnel: 589-7433
Jobline: 589-7436
Employment: about 1,500. Many employees—for example, food service workers,
bus drivers and para-educators—work nine months of the year, but with shifts

varying from two to eight hours daily. Those involved with special programs may work four days weekly.

Darrington School District
P.O. Box 27, Darrington WA 98241
436-1323
From Everett: 258-2036
About 75 are employed in this district. There are three half-time certified positions and about 20 part-time classified positions. Openings are posted in the administration building, located at 1065 Fir St. next to the schools.

Dieringer School District
1320 178th Ave. E., Sumner WA 98390
862-2537
872-6370
This growing K-8 district enrolls about 975 in two schools. You'll find openings in the staff of 100 posted in the district office.

Eatonville School District
P.O. Box 698, Eatonville WA 98328
832-4766
Employment: more than 200. Openings are posted in the administration building at 208 Lynch St.

Edmonds School District
20420 68th Ave. W., Lynnwood WA 98036
670-7000
Jobline: 670-7021
You'll need official district application forms for both certified and classified positions. If you cannot pick up a form, request one by sending a large self-addressed, stamped envelope to the address above. Part-time positions include about 350 teacher assistants, 50 food service workers, 50 bus drivers and 50 clerical workers. There are also part-time teachers—often retirees—who may teach as little as one class daily. The district also has a pool of about 350 substitute teachers, bus drivers, secretaries and other workers.

Enumclaw School District
2929 McDougall Ave., Enumclaw WA 98022
825-2588
Job openings are posted in the administrative office. Employment: about 450.

Everett School District
4730 Colby Ave., Everett WA 98203
339-4200
Jobline: 339-4346
Employment: 1,700. Part-time positions are available in food service, noon duty and educational assisting. Many secretaries, nurses and educational assistants also work full-time, but only during the academic year. There are also some part-time teaching assignments. The district always uses substitutes and the human resources staff calls this an excellent means of obtaining experience; besides teachers, there's a sub pool for custodians, secretaries and educational assistants.

Federal Way School District
31405 18th Ave. S., Federal Way WA 98003
941-0100
From Tacoma: 927-7420
Jobline (Certified): 941-2058
Jobline (Classified): 941-2273
Employs about 2,200.

Fife Public Schools
5802 20th St. E., Tacoma WA 98424
922-6697
You'll find openings in the staff of 240 posted in the school administration building.

Fircrest School
15230 15th Ave. N.E., Seattle WA 98155
Personnel: 364-0300, Ext. 371
Jobline: 364-0300, Ext. 244
This residential state program for the developmentally disabled employs about 900, some part-time.

Franklin Pierce School District
315 S. 129th St., Tacoma WA 98444
Personnel: 535-9896
Jobline: 535-8829
Employment: more than 700.

Granite Falls School District
P.O. Box 9, Granite Falls WA 98252
691-7717
Employs 130. Openings are posted in the administration building at 307 N. Alder.

Griffin School District
This Olympia district, which enrolls about 600 in one elementary school, does its hiring through the Public Schools Personnel Cooperative (see earlier in this chapter).

Highline School District
15675 Ambaum Blvd. S.W., Seattle WA 98166
Personnel: 433-2281
Jobline: 433-6339
Job openings (teaching, coaching, classified and substitute) are listed on the jobline and posted in the district office. Employment: 2,000.

Issaquah School District
565 N.W. Holly St., Issaquah WA 98027
557-7000
Jobline: 557-5627
This fast-growing Eastside district employs about 1,200.

Kent School District
12033 S.E. 256th, Kent WA 98031-6643
Human Resources: 859-7209
Jobline (Classified): 859-7508
The fifth largest district in the state. Employment: 2,500. Only nonacademic positions on the jobline; all positions are posted in the personnel office. All certified applications are entered (not scanned) into a database and retrieved when appropriate positions open; candidates do not apply for specific openings.

Lake Stevens School District
2202-A 123rd Ave. N.E., Lake Stevens WA 98258
335-1500
This north end district employs 500. Openings are posted in the administrative office.

Lake Washington School District
P.O. Box 2909, Kirkland WA 98083
Personnel: 828-3220
Jobline: 828-3243
Total employment: about 2,500. Classified openings are posted in schools and in the personnel office at 10903 N.E. 53rd. Certified openings are usually filled from applications on file.

Lakewood School District
P.O. Box 220, Lakewood WA 98259-0220
652-7519
Employs about 200. Openings are posted in the administration building, located at 17110 16th Dr. N.E., Arlington.

Marysville School District
4220 80th St. N.E., Marysville WA 98270-3498
653-7058
Jobline: 653-0807
Employs about 1,000. There are 50 part-time teaching positions and most educational assistants, food service workers and bus drivers work only part-time during the school year; for example, educational assistants may work from one to five and a half hours daily. Openings are posted in the administration building.

Mercer Island School District
4160 86th Ave. S.E., Mercer Island WA 98040
Personnel: 236-3331
Jobline: 236-3302
Employs about 350, of whom about 100 work part-time (less than eight hours daily).

Monroe School District
P.O. Box 687, Monroe WA 98272-0687
794-7777
From Seattle: 745-2677
Toll-free: (800) 282-7818
Employs about 500. Openings posted in the district office at Ferry and Fremont.

Mukilteo School District
9401 Sharon Dr., Everett WA 98204
356-1217
Jobline: 356-1237
Employment: 1,175. There's also a sub pool of about 300.

North Kitsap School District
18360 Caldart Ave. N.E., Poulsbo WA 98370
Personnel: 779-3352
Jobline: 779-8914
Enrolls 6,000 from the communities of Poulsbo, Kingston, Hansville, Central Valley and Suquamish.

Northshore School District
18315 Bothell Way N.E., Bothell WA 98011
Personnel: 489-6356
Jobline (Operates May-September): 489-6381
Serves such communities as Bothell, Woodinville and Kenmore. Employs 1,800. You'll find classified positions announced on the bulletin board outside the personnel office.

North Thurston School District
This Lacey district enrolls about 13,000; all hiring is done through the Public Schools Personnel Cooperative.

Olympia School District
About 1,000 are employed by this district, which enrolls about 8,000. All hiring is done through the Public Schools Personnel Cooperative.

Orting Schools
P.O. Box 460, Orting WA 98360
893-6500
All openings are posted in the administrative office located at 120 N. Washington. Employment: about 160. Teaching positions are also advertised through the Washington Education Association and in college placement offices.

Peninsula School District
Educational Service Center
14015 62nd Ave. N.W., Gig Harbor WA 98332
857-6171
Jobline: 857-3565
Both certified and classified job openings are posted in the educational service center. Employment: 840.

Puyallup School District
P.O. Box 370, Puyallup WA 98371
841-1301
Jobline: 841-8666
To learn of openings, stop at the main desk in the administration building, 109 E. Pioneer, and check the notebooks. Total employment: 1,700.

Rainier School District
P.O. Box 98, Rainier WA 98576
446-2207
Employs 95. Openings are posted in the district office and in several locations in the community.

Renton School District
435 Main Ave. S., Renton WA 98055
Personnel: 235-2385
Jobline: 235-5826
Openings in the staff of 1,300 are posted in the administration building. If you live outside the Renton area and wish to apply for a teaching position, you can ask that an application be mailed to you.

Riverview School District
32240 N.E. 50th St., Carnation WA 98014-6332
Personnel: 333-6114
From Seattle: 788-6610
Jobline: 883-0854
Employs about 300.

Rochester School District
P.O. Box 457, Rochester WA 98579
273-5536
From Olympia: 586-6349
This district enrolls 1,800, including the youth detained at Maple Lane High School, a state institution. Total employment: 180. Job openings are posted in the district office at 9917 Highway 12 S.W.

Seattle Public Schools
815 Fourth Ave. N., #140, Seattle WA 98109
Employment Services: 298-7365
Jobline: 298-7382
The state's largest district, Seattle employs more than 5,700. The three sub pools—certified, paraprofessional and support—include about 550 who work on call; such work is an excellent way to introduce yourself to the district, noted one personnel staffer. All classified and administrative job openings are posted in the personnel office.

Shoreline School District
18560 1st Ave. N.E., Seattle WA 98155
Personnel: 361-4223
Jobline: 361-4367
Official application forms can be picked up at the office. Applications are also mailed to those who provide self-addressed, stamped business-size envelopes. Employment: 600 certified, 550 classified and 400 substitutes (both certified and classified).

Snohomish School District
1601 Avenue D, Snohomish WA 98290
568-3151

Employs about 740. Job openings are in a notebook in the administration office and in each district school.

Snoqualmie Valley School District
P.O. Box 400, Snoqualmie WA 98065
888-2334
When openings occur in the staff of 435, announcements are posted in each school and in the district office at 211 N. Silva St.

South Central School District
4640 S. 144th, Seattle WA 98168
244-2100
Jobline (Live voice): 244-2100
Serves the Tukwila/Southcenter area. Openings in the staff of 230 are posted in the district office.

South Kitsap School District
1962 Hoover Ave. S.E., Port Orchard WA 98366
876-7300
Jobline: 876-7389
You'll need an official district application form to be considered for South Kitsap positions. If you live outside the area, ask that an application be mailed to you. Specify certified (academic) or classified (nonacademic). Employment: 1,000.

Stanwood School District
P.O. Box 430, Stanwood WA 98292
629-9575
When openings occur in the staff of 350, notices are posted in the schools and the district office, located at 9307 271st St. N.W.

Steilacoom Historical School District 1
510 Chambers, Steilacoom WA 98388
588-1772
Posts openings in the district office. Employment: 220.

Sultan School District
P.O. Box 399, Sultan WA 98294
793-9800
Employs 195. Openings are posted in the schools and the district office, located at 514 4th.

Sumner School District
1202 Wood Ave., Sumner WA 98390
863-2201
Jobline: 863-2232
Posts certified and classified job openings in the personnel office. Provides staff for city' s summer recreation programs. Employment: 760.

Tacoma School District
P.O. Box 1357, Tacoma WA 98401
Personnel: 596-1250
Jobline (Certified, operates June-August): 596-1300
Jobline (Classified): 596-1265
To apply for a classified position, you'll need the official school district application distributed only on Wednesdays. Applications for certified positions are available any weekday; if you're outside Pierce County, you can ask that an application be mailed. All openings are posted in the personnel office, located at 601 S. 8th St. Employment: 3,500. Part-time opportunities for certified staff include both half-time teaching and "itinerant" nursing jobs.

Tahoma School District
25720 Maple Valley-Black Diamond Rd. S.E., Maple Valley WA 98038
432-4481
Employment: nearly 500. Notices of faculty openings are routed to the Washington Education Association and area colleges. Limited classified openings. All openings are posted in the administration building.

Tenino School District
P.O. Box 4024, Tenino WA 98589
264-4123
Employs 145. Openings are posted in all buildings, including the district office, located at 301 Old Highway 99 N.

Tumwater School District
More than 600 are employed by this district, which enrolls about 5,500. All hiring is done through the Public Schools Personnel Cooperative.

University Place School District
8805 40th St. W., Tacoma WA 98466
566-5600
Jobline: 566-5605
Posts openings in the district office and publicizes them through the Washington Education Association. Employment: 500.

Vashon Island School District
20414 Vashon Highway S.W., Vashon WA 98070
463-2121
No unsolicited resumes accepted. Many openings are advertised in the Vashon Island paper. You can also call the district personnel office for information. Employment: 140.

White River School District
P.O. Box G, Buckley WA 98321
Personnel: 829-0600, Ext. 115
Employs 400. Openings are posted in the administrative office, located in the high school annex at 240 N. A.

Yelm Community Schools

P.O. Box 476, Yelm WA 98597
458-1900
Employs 500. Teachers and administrators are recruited through the Public School Personnel Cooperative; classified staff are hired directly. You'll find openings announced on a bulletin board in the district office, located at 404 Yelm Ave. W.

PRIVATE SCHOOLS

Some private schools seldom hire subs for short teacher absences; they combine classes or use teacher aides to cover for a day or two. Few have food or bus service. Many schools, however, have part-time positions, ranging from teaching and after-school care to admissions to fund-raising. Only those most likely to have opportunities are listed here. For jobs in Catholic schools, see that general reference.

Achieve Educational Services

8117 240th St. S.W., Edmonds WA 98026
672-1451
Organized in the early 1980s as a tutoring service for elementary through high school students, this program now includes a 55-student school. The school staff is stable and small, but there are tutoring opportunities for those who wish to work part-time, usually between 3 and 9 p.m. Educational certification is preferred, but not required. More important: expertise in your subject area and good interpersonal skills. Contact: Mark Selle, director.

Adventist Schools

For the 27 Seventh Day Adventist schools in western Washington, resumes are accepted and teachers recommended to individual schools by the conference office:

Education Department
Washington Conference of Seventh Day Adventists
20015 Bothell-Everett Highway, Bothell WA 98012
481-7171

Annie Wright School

827 N. Tacoma Ave., Tacoma WA 98403
272-2216
Coeducational Lower and Middle schools and a girls' college prep program. Enrolls 432.

Bellevue Christian School

1601 98th Ave. N.E., Clyde Hill WA 98004-3499
454-4028
Administrative office for three-campuses including Three Point Elementary, Bellevue (enrolls 365 plus preschool), Mack Elementary, Woodinville (enrolls 180 plus preschool) and Bellevue Christian junior and senior high school, enrolling 460. Each campus hires its own teachers; for information, contact Chuck Pasma, superintendent.

Bertschi School
2227 10th Ave. E., Seattle WA 98102
324-5476
Prekindergarten-5 independent school. Enrolls 175.

Bright and Early School
21316 66th Ave. W., Lynnwood WA 98036
672-4430
Preschool-4 program. Enrolls 185.

The Bush School
405 36th Ave. E., Seattle WA 98112
322-7978
K-12 program. Enrolls 520.

Cascade Christian School
District Office
306 N. Meridian, Puyallup WA 98371
841-1776
Hiring is handled here for three programs, including the preschool-12 Tacoma campus (formerly Peoples Christian School), enrolling 500; the preschool-6 Puyallup program (formerly Puyallup Christian), enrolling 300; and the preschool-6 Spanaway campus (formerly Spanaway Christian), enrolling 140.

Catholic Schools
To apply for positions in Puget Sound Catholic schools, contact the Archdiocese of Seattle for an application packet. The education office serves as a clearinghouse, maintaining applicants' files and notifying applicants of openings with a weekly bulletin. When an opening occurs, you'll contact the school principal, who can then request your file from the Archdiocese. For more information:

Office of Superintendent of Schools
Archdiocese of Seattle
910 Marion, Seattle WA 98104
382-4861

Cedar Park Christian School
16300 112th Ave. N.E., Bothell WA 98011
488-9778
Preschool-grade 10. Enrolls 350.

Charles Wright Academy
7723 Chambers Creek Rd. W., Tacoma WA 98467
564-2171
Preschool-12. Enrolls 630.

Chief Leschi Schools/Puyallup Tribal School System
2002 E. 28th, Tacoma WA 98404
593-0219
Elementary and secondary, enrolls 550. Most students are enrolled tribal members.

Christian Faith School
P.O. Box 98800, Seattle WA 98198
878-6036
Preschool-12, enrolls 480.

Christian Life Prep School
629 S. 356th St., Federal Way WA 98003
661-7340
Prekindergarten-6, enrolls about 375.

Christ the King Academy
P.O. Box 2460, Poulsbo WA 98370
779-9189
K-9, enrolls 180.

Concordia Lutheran School
7040 36th N.E., Seattle WA 98115
525-7407
Preschool-grade 8, enrolls 250.

Concordia Lutheran School
202 E. 56th, Tacoma WA 98404
475-9513
Preschool-grade 8, enrolls 500.

Cornerstone Christian School
21705 58th Ave. W., Mountlake Terrace WA 98043
776-0760
Prekindergarten-8, enrolls 180.

Cougar Mountain Academy
5410 194th Ave. S.E., Issaquah WA 98027
641-2800
Prekindergarten-4 program, enrolls 100. Designed for children "with high expectations."

Eastside Academic Institute
12503 N.E. Bellevue-Redmond Rd., #103, Bellevue WA 98005
455-2778
Established for college-bound students who have difficulty in traditional school settings, the program serves about 120 in grades 8-12. Some are full-time students; others receive tutoring. The faculty of 20 includes many part-timers. Contact: Sherrill O'Shaughnessy, director.

Epiphany School
3710 E. Howell, Seattle WA 98122
323-9011
Prekindergarten-6, enrolling 135.

Eton School
2701 Bellevue-Redmond Rd., Bellevue WA 98008
881-4230
Ages 3-14. Enrolls 325.

Everett Christian School
2221 Cedar St., Everett WA 98201
259-3213
K-8, enrolls 100.

Evergreen Academy
16017 118th Pl. N.E., Bothell WA 98011
488-8000
Preschool-5, enrolls 290.

Evergreen Christian School
1010 Black Lake Blvd., Olympia WA 98502
357-5590
Prekindergarten-8 program, enrolls 250 in K-8.

The Evergreen School
15201 Meridian Ave. N., Seattle WA 98133
364-2650
Preschool-8, enrolls 272.

Fairview Christian School
844 N.E. 78th, Seattle WA 98115-4202
526-1880
Preschool-6, enrolls 140.

Faith Lutheran School
7075 Pacific Ave. S. E., Olympia WA 98503
491-1733
Preschool-8, enrolls 185.

Gig Harbor Christian School
9911 Burnham Dr. N.W., Gig Harbor WA 98332
851-5156
Preschool-8, enrolls 210.

Grace Academy
8521 67th Ave. N.E., Marysville WA 98270
659-8517
K-12, enrolls about 250.

Hamlin Robinson School
10211 12th Ave. S., Seattle WA 98168
763-1167
Grades 1-6 for those with such learning disabilities as dyslexia. Enrolls about 100.

Heritage Christian School
19527 104th Ave. N.E., Bothell WA 98011
485-2585
Preschool-9. Enrollment: 550.

Heritage Christian School
5412 67th Ave. W., Tacoma WA 98467
564-6276
K-8, enrolls 190.

Hope Lutheran School
4446 42nd Ave. S.W., Seattle WA 98116
935-8500
Preschool-8. Enrolls 220.

Jewish Day School of Metropolitan Seattle
15749 N.E. 4th St., Bellevue WA 98008
641-3335
 K-8, enrolls 245.

Kent View Christian Schools
930 E. James, Kent WA 98031
852-5145
Preschool-12, enrolls 600, including 120 in the preschool.

King's Schools
19303 Fremont Ave. N., Seattle WA 98133
546-7241
Jobline (Live voice): 546-7533
Preschool-12, enrolls more than 1,000. Operated by Crista Ministries. Also operates:

King's West School
4012 Chico Way N.W., Bremerton WA 98312
377-7700
K-12 program, formerly Bremerton Christian.

Lakeside School
14050 First Ave. N.E., Seattle WA 98125
368-3600
Middle and Upper schools offering grades 5-12. Enrolls 670.

Life Christian School
1717 S. Puget Sound, Tacoma WA 98405
756-5317
Preschool-10, enrolls about 700.

The Little School
2812 116th Ave. N.E., Bellevue WA 98004
827-8708
Ungraded school for children 3-12. Enrolls 170.

Maple Valley Christian School
16700 174th Ave. S.E., Renton WA 98058-9599
226-4640
K-6, enrolls 265.

Master's Touch Christian School
9610 48th Dr. N.E., Marysville WA 98270
653-8976
K-12, enrolls about 110.

Montessori Schools of Snohomish and Spokane Counties
1804 Puget Dr., Everett WA 98203
347-1000
Prekindergarten-8, enrolls 150 in Snohomish County.

Neighborhood Christian School
625 140th Ave. N.E., Bellevue WA 98005
746-3258
Day care and preschool-8. Enrolls 140 exclusive of day care.

New Hope Christian School
25713 70th Ave. E., Graham WA 98338
847-2643
Preschool-6, enrolls 100.

A New School for Children
4649 Sunnyside Ave. N., Seattle WA 98103
632-8445
K-5, enrolls 65. Unpaid internships possible.

North Seattle Christian School
12351 8th N.E., Seattle WA 98125
365-2720
K-8, enrolls 120.

The Northwest School
1415 Summit Ave., Seattle WA 98122
682-7309
Grades 6-12, enrolls 290.

The Overlake School
20301 N.E. 108th St., Redmond WA 98053
868-1000
Grades 5-12. Enrolls 290.

Pacific Crest Schools
600 N.W. Bright St., Seattle WA 98107
789-7889
Headed by Jackie Maughan, this program includes a Montessori school for about
75, ages 2 1/2 to 10, and a middle school, enrolling 50 sixth-eighth graders.

Parkland Evangelical Lutheran School
P.O. Box 44006, Tacoma WA 98444
537-1901
Larry Rude is the principal of this preschool-grade 8 program. Enrolls 100.

Peace Lutheran School
1234 N.E. Riddell Rd., Bremerton WA 98310
373-2116
Preschool-8, enrolls 130.

Perkins Elementary School
4649 Sunnyside Ave. N., Seattle WA 98103
632-7154
Grades 1-5, enrolls 167. No longer affiliated with the Perkins School for Children, which operates a preschool and kindergarten.

Puget Sound Christian School
1740 S. 84th, Tacoma WA 98444
537-6870
Preschool-7, enrolls 100.

Renton Christian School
221 Hardie Ave. N.W., Renton WA 98055
226-0820
Preschool-8, enrolls 280.

St. Christopher Academy
318 3rd Ave. S., Kent WA 98032
852-1515
K-12, enrolls 130. No church affiliation. Focus is on L.D. and A.D.D. students.

St. Thomas School
P.O. Box 124, Medina WA 98039
454-5880
Episcopal, preschool-6, enrolls 190.

The Seabury School
1801 N.E. 53rd St., Tacoma WA 98422
952-3111
From Seattle: 838-1912
About 100 are enrolled in this prekindergarten-6 program for the gifted. Director: Barbara Field.

Seattle Academy of Arts and Sciences
1432 15th Ave., Seattle WA 98122
323-6600
Grades 6-12, enrolls 166.

Seattle Christian School
19639 28th Ave. S., SeaTac WA 98188
824-1310
K-12, enrolls 500.

Seattle Country Day School
2619 4th Ave. N., Seattle WA 98109
284-6220
K-8, enrolls about 300. For gifted children.

Seattle Hebrew Academy
1617 Interlaken Dr. E., Seattle WA 98112
323-5750
Preschool-8, enrolls 270.

Seattle Lutheran High School
4141 41st Ave. S.W., Seattle WA 98116
937-7722
Grades 9-12, enrolls 185.

Seattle Preparatory School
2400 11th Ave. E., Seattle WA 98102
324-0400
Catholic high school, enrolls 630.

Seattle Waldorf School
2728 N.E. 100th, Seattle WA 98125
524-5320
Preschool-8, enrolls about 200.

Silver Lake Christian School
2027 132nd S.E., Everett WA 98208
337-6992
K-12, enrolls 320.

Silverwood School
8551 Dicky Pl. N.W., Silverdale WA 98383
692-7504
Montessori, grades 1-6, enrolls 100.

Snohomish County Christian School
Administrative Office
23607 54th Ave. W., Mountlake Terrace WA 98043
774-7773
K-12, enrolls 500.

South Kitsap Christian School
1780 S.E. Lincoln Ave., Port Orchard WA 98366
876-5594
K-9, enrolls about 190.

Spring Valley Montessori School
36605 Pacific Highway S., Federal Way WA 98003
From Tacoma: 927-2557
From Seattle: 874-6003
Preschool-8, enrolls about 230. Through the University of Puget Sound, also offers Montessori teacher training.

Tacoma Baptist Schools
2052 S. 64th, Tacoma WA 98409
475-7226
K-12, enrolls 480.

Thomas Academy
8207 S. 280th St., Kent WA 98032
852-4438
Prekindergarten-9, formerly known as St. James of Thomas School. Enrollment: about 200.

University Child Development School
5062 9th N.E., Seattle WA 98105
547-5059
Preschool-5, enrolls about 200. For gifted children.

University Preparatory Academy
8000 25th N.E., Seattle WA 98115
525-2714
Grades 6-12, enrolls 346.

Valley Christian School
1312 2nd St. S.E., Auburn WA 98002
833-3541
Preschool-6, enrolls 180.

Watson Groen Christian School
2400 N.E. 147th St., Seattle WA 98155
364-7777
Preschool-12. Enrolls 350.

West Seattle Christian School
4401 42nd Ave. S.W., Seattle WA 98116
938-1414
Preschool-8, enrolls 260.

West Seattle Montessori
4536 38th Ave. S.W., Seattle WA 98126
935-0427
Preschool-6, enrolls 130.

Woodinville Montessori School
13965 N.E. 166th, Woodinville WA 98072
481-2300
Preschool-6, enrolls 130. Takes teacher interns from the Montessori Educational
Institute of the Pacific Northwest. Other unpaid internships possible.

Zion Lutheran School
3923 103rd Ave. S.E., Everett WA 98205
334-5064
Preschool-8, enrolls 250.

Zion Preparatory Academy
620 20th S., Seattle WA 98144
322-2926
Christian, preschool-8, enrolls more than 450.

12. Employers:
Nonprofits

What do nonprofits offer you? Experience, responsibility, autonomy...and the chance to support an important cause or program. Whether you work full-time, part-time, as an intern, free-lancer or consultant, on a temporary or volunteer basis, the low budgets and lean staffs typical of nonprofits mean you'll probably get to tackle a variety of tasks. That translates to hands-on skills and a resume with quantifiable accomplishments.

Volunteers are important to most of the groups listed. If you haven't worked in years, are making a career change or are a recent graduate, you may need work experience in a particular field or job function to increase your marketability. Consider contacting one of these organizations regarding an assignment. Besides getting valuable experience, you'll make industry contacts and earn the references you need for the next job. If your academic program is one of those that requires field work, you'll see that many of the organizations listed here take student interns. In most cases, internships are unpaid or involve only modest stipends.

Allied Arts of Seattle
105 S. Main, #201, Seattle WA 98104
624-0432
Focused on support of the arts, historic preservation and urban design, this nonprofit and its affiliate, the Allied Arts Foundation, have only a one-person staff supplemented by contract employees. But if you're interested in the arts, Allied Arts offers unpaid internships. Usually the same length as an academic quarter, these provide exposure to the Seattle arts community.

ALS Support Services of Washington
12043 35th N.E., Seattle WA 98125
364-4667
A local organization that serves those across the state with Lou Gehrig's disease, this group provides client outreach, referrals and education and client networking. Formed in 1979, it employs one full-time, executive director Leslie Lytle, and uses volunteers and interns. Health-care professionals who can provide outreach services would be the best interns; for example, students in speech pathology, social work, occupational or physical therapy and nursing. There's also a possible internship for a grantwriter.

Alzheimer's Association of Puget Sound
120 Northgate Plaza, #316, Seattle WA 98125
365-7488
One of 220 chapters of a national, this group covers 22 western and central Washington counties with seven paid positions. Nearly 300 volunteers are also

involved—and occasionally, volunteer positions do become part-time or full-time paid jobs. Sandra Lewis, association director, said volunteers are especially welcome on publications projects (newsletters and brochures) and for office support; some positions are appropriate for teenagers.

American Cancer Society, Washington Division
2120 First Ave. N., Seattle WA 98109
283-1152
The cancer society offers educational programs; services to cancer patients and their families; and fellowships and grants to research institutions. Employs 35. Contact: Sylvia Cummings, director, administrative services.

American Cancer Society, Northwest Area Office
14450 N.E. 29th Pl., #220, Bellevue WA 98007
869-5588
Contact: Kevin Williams, area vice president. Staff: 17. Occasional interns.

American Cancer Society, Southwest Area Office
1551 Broadway, #200, Tacoma WA 98402
272-5767
Contact: (Ms.) Kelly Morken, area vice president. Staff: 14.

American Civil Liberties Union (ACLU)
705 Second Ave., #300, Seattle WA 98104
624-2184
Kathleen Taylor is executive director of the ACLU, which employs 13. Interns can be students in law or other disciplines.

American Cultural Exchange
200 W. Mercer St., #504, Seattle WA 98119
217-9644
A nonprofit educational company specializing in teaching languages, ACE operates four major programs. It offers intensive English As A Second Language institutes on college campuses; runs a foreign language service that offers classes for children and adults as well as ACE Translation; provides technical and cross-cultural training and teachers' in-service programs through the International Training and Development Institute (IDDI); and operates a travel service and small publisher. Full-time employees: about 70. Part-time: about 180, including teachers who may work as little as two hours a week. In addition, there's a 250-person "language bank" of people who work on contract. For IDDI, a database is kept of qualified candidates who are available to work full-time on a temporary basis on consulting projects; most such positions require foreign language skills, usually in Spanish, as well as technical expertise (for example, in forestry, chemical engineering or small business management). ESL teaching candidates must have master's degrees in teaching ESL. Interpreter and translator applicants are interviewed to determine proficiency; most are native speakers. Many positions are added during the summer, so many openings are posted in the spring; there's no jobline, but you can ask the receptionist about vacancies. Or write Linda Harris, vice president, human resources.

American Diabetes Association, Washington Affiliate
557 Roy St., Seattle WA 98109
282-4616
Toll-free within Washington: (800) 628-8808
Statewide programs are coordinated by this office, which employs 10. Interns can work in public relations, special events management or youth activities. Resumes can be directed to Carl Knirk. There are smaller chapter offices in Everett and Olympia. The Tacoma group, not affiliated with the ADA, is the Diabetes Association of Pierce County.

American Heart Association, Washington Affiliate
4414 Woodland Park Ave. N., Seattle WA 98103
632-6881
More than 30 work in this facility, which houses both the state and Northwest area offices. Mark Rieck is executive director of the state association; Lori Gangemi is the area executive director of the Northwest area office. Most hiring and intern selection is done by department heads. Volunteers are welcome, especially for office jobs. There are internships, especially for students majoring in communications, business or health care.

American Lung Association of Washington
2625 Third Ave., Seattle WA 98121
441-5100
In Washington the association has both a state office and three regional offices (in Tacoma, Yakima and Spokane). Seattle is the state headquarters: Astrid Berg is executive director. Internships require good writing skills and computer literacy; many interns are liberal arts or public relations majors. Wide range of volunteer opportunities. Kathy Rexford, office manager, routes job applications and volunteer inquiries to the appropriate departments.

American Red Cross, Seattle-King County Chapter
1900 25th Ave. S., Seattle WA 98144-4708
323-2345
David Siebert manages this agency, which offers disaster preparedness and relief, health and safety education, aid to aging and military and senior volunteer recruitment and placement (RSVP). Employs 63 full-time. Classes such as first aid, CPR, HIV-AIDS education, swimming and water safety are taught by "per diem" employees, who may work as much as three days a week or only occasionally, and by volunteers. Teaching ability is as important for these jobs as the ability to be certified. Internships are possible for students in public affairs, social work, health care and human resources. Human resources director: Patricia VandenBroek.

American Red Cross, Tacoma-Pierce County Chapter
1235 S. Tacoma Way, Tacoma WA 98409
572-4830
About 65 work for this chapter, which also has contract opportunities. Nancy Mendoza, development director, handles personnel. Internships are available throughout the agency.

American Red Cross, Snohomish County Chapter
2530 Lombard Ave., Everett WA 98206
252-4103

Besides disaster preparedness and relief and health and safety education, this chapter's programs include Project Pride, which helps those in need with payment of utility bills, and emergency housing. Employs 12 full-time; also part-time and "per diem" opportunities.

American Red Cross, Kitsap-North Mason County Chapter
605 Washington Ave., Bremerton WA 98310
377-3761
Employs six full-time, two part-time staff. Internships are possible. Manager: Joe Elmore III.

American Red Cross, Thurston-Mason County Chapter
P.O. Box 1547, Olympia WA 98507
352-8575
Executive director: Kay Walters. Full-time staff: four. Internships are possible.

American Youth Hostels, Washington State Council
419 Queen Anne Ave. N., #102, Seattle WA 98109
281-7306
Part of Hosteling International. Oversees eight hostels in Washington and serves as liaison to the national and international hostel programs. Employs three; volunteers are welcome, especially for special events, data entry and office support. Contact Naida Lavery, administrative and travel center manager. Job opportunities also sometimes occur at:

Seattle International Hostel
84 Union St., Seattle WA 98101
622-5443
Louise Kipping, manager, accepts resumes at all times. Most positions are for front desk or maintenance people. Customer service skills are important; fluency in foreign language is not required, but it's a significant asset.

APPLE (A Positive Parenting Learning Experience)
1102 J St. S.E., Auburn WA 98002
833-7002
About 30 teach part-time in this organization's parenting training programs. Uses interns in social services and early childhood education. Executive director: Cherie Sigrist.

Arthritis Foundation, Washington State Chapter
100 S. King St., #330, Seattle WA 98104
622-1378
Fund-raising, public relations and program administration are examples of the positions at this nonprofit. Employs seven full-time, one part-time. Unpaid internships available, especially in communications, health care and nonprofit management. President: Carl Jones.

Artists Unlimited
158 Thomas St., #14, Seattle WA 98109
441-8480
Founded in 1981 to help disabled artists reach their creative potential, this program now employs six and uses 50 volunteers. Interns are welcome. Contact: Julianne Jaz, executive director.

Artist Trust

1402 Third Ave., #415, Seattle WA 98101
467-8734
Administers fellowship and grant programs that fund individual artists and issues the Artist Trust newsletter (see *Where Are Jobs Listed?*). Volunteers and interns welcome. Contact: (Ms.) Marschal Paul, executive director.

Ashley House

40903 236th Ave. S.E., Enumclaw WA 98022
825-6525
Provides transitional and respite care for medically fragile children. Internships possible for nursing students. Executive director: Thelma Struck.

Asian Counseling and Referral Service

1032 S. Jackson, #200, Seattle WA 98104
461-8414
Provides services to the King County Asian and Pacific Island community. Primary programs: mental health counseling, including a semi-independent housing program; and help for the elderly. Most interns are M.S.W. candidates. Personnel director: Jodi Haavig.

A Territory Resource

603 Stewart St., #221, Seattle WA 98101
624-4081
A foundation that makes grants for projects involving "social change," ATR is funded by private donations. Serves five Northwestern states. Employs three full-time, two part-time. Executive director: Carol Pencke.

Atlantic Street Center

2103 S. Atlantic, Seattle WA 98144
329-2050
Provides social services to low-income minorities in central and southeast Seattle. Programs for children and teenagers, counseling and the Family Center on Beacon Hill are among the services offered. Interns should be M.S.W. candidates; volunteers are used for academic tutoring. Executive director: David Okimoto.

Bathhouse Theater

7312 W. Green Lake Dr. N., Seattle WA 98103
783-0053
Employs 15-20 permanent staff, 15 on an hourly basis, interns (some paid), work-study students, on-call people and, of course, actors. Volunteers are always needed. Regarding internships or volunteer work, contact Susan Taylor, office manager; for production or technical jobs, Rod Pilloud, production manager; for managerial positions, Phil Peters, managing director.

Bellevue Art Museum

301 Bellevue Square, Bellevue WA 98004
454-3322
Staff of 13. Unpaid internships are available in nearly every department. Linda Krouse, chief financial officer, handles personnel.

Bellevue Philharmonic Orchestra
P.O. Box 1582, Bellevue WA 98009
455-4171
R. Joseph Scott, general manager, founded this arts group in 1967. Today it has a paid staff of six, supplemented by volunteers.

The Benefit Gang
2708 Elliott Ave., Seattle WA 98121
443-3277
Founded in 1989 to encourage community involvement by young adults, this group now places 3,800 trained volunteers in 225 nonprofits. Call for a copy of the newsletter listing volunteer opportunities. Director: Will Hewett.

Big Brothers/Big Sisters
Merged on the national level, these organizations operate local programs that are sometimes combined—and sometimes separate. Based on the concept of one-to-one relationships between adult volunteers and a child or teenager (often from a single-parent family), Big Brothers matches men with boys and Big Sisters matches women with girls. The goal is to provide positive role models for youth.

Big Brothers of King County
608 State St. S., Kirkland WA 98033
822-6687
Recruiting and screening adult volunteers, recruiting young participants, matching volunteers with boys, monitoring the matches, fund-raising (through special events and a bingo operation), working with a board of volunteers and general administration are examples of the responsibilities handled by this unit. Internships possible. Employs 25 permanent, full-time employees in addition to the bingo staff. Executive director: Keith Padgett.

Big Sisters of King County
1100 Virginia, #210, Seattle WA 98101
461-3636
Serves girls from both two-parent and single-parent homes. Besides matching girls with women, the program matches teen mothers and pregnant girls with older volunteers. Employs 24 program staff members and an additional 14 in the bingo operation. Interns are welcome; there are opportunities for social work students and for those interested in public relations and development. The chapter also employs high school students in paid clerical positions. Executive director: Venetia Magnuson.

Big Brothers/Big Sisters of Tacoma/Pierce County
8200 Tacoma Mall Blvd., Tacoma WA 98409
581-9444
Besides matching boys with men and girls with women, this chapter has a Sisters Plus program to pair teenage girls, especially young mothers or pregnant teenagers, with adult women. Employs 14 in addition to the 30 who work on bingo. Social work interns welcome. If you're interested in working in social services, contact Linda Mason; Sylvia Anderson handles inquiries regarding administrative positions.

Boy Scouts of America, Chief Seattle Council
3120 Rainier Ave. S., Seattle WA 98114
725-5200
Character development, physical fitness and citizenship are the programs for youth
and young adults provided by this council. Seasonal positions in the camps for
youth members. Contact: Dean Lollar, scout executive.

Boy Scouts of America, Pacific Harbors Council
1722 S. Union St., Tacoma WA 98405
752-7731
Employs 22 in the office, with an additional three working as camp caretakers/
rangers. Scout executive: Norman Stone.

Boy Scouts of America, Pacific Harbors Service Center
P.O. Box 1308, Olympia WA 98507
357-3331
Formerly the Tumwater Area Council. Employs seven. All hiring done in Tacoma.

Boy Scouts of America, Mt. Baker Council
1715 100th Pl. S.E., Everett WA 98208
338-0380
Scout executive: James Martin. Staff: 15.

Boys & Girls Clubs of King County
107 Cherry, #200, Seattle WA 98104
461-3890
Part of a national organization for those between 6 and 18, the Boys & Girls Clubs
help youth develop self-esteem, values and skills. Quincy Robertson is the
personnel and training director for the Seattle-based affiliate, which has internships and part-time and seasonal positions, especially in the summer camp
program.

Bellevue Boys & Girls Club
209 100th Ave. N.E., Bellevue WA 98004
454-6162
The 15 to 20 seasonal jobs include day camp counselors, who must be 18 or older.
Executive director: Rob Parker.

Boys & Girls Clubs of Tacoma
4301 S. Pine, #519, Tacoma WA 98409
474-3590
Hires seasonal help (for day camp) and interns.

Boys & Girls Clubs of Snohomish County
P.O. Box 5224, Everett WA 98206
258-2436
Thirty work full-time and 40 part-time for the Snohomish organization, which adds
another 20 during the summer. Internships are available. Contact: Bill Tsoukalas,
executive director.

Broadway Center for the Performing Arts
901 Broadway, Tacoma WA 98402
591-5890
Formerly the Pantages Centre for the Performing Arts, this arts center is now one

of three theaters operated by the nonprofit Broadway Center Corp. in City of Tacoma facilities. Department managers in finance, development, marketing and operations select their own interns. The staff is supplemented by more than 100 volunteers.

Camp Fire Boys and Girls, Central Puget Sound Council
8511 15th Ave. N.E., Seattle WA 98115
461-8550
Provides personal development programs for boys and girls ages 5-18. Has full-time, part-time and seasonal positions. Day camp leaders must be at least 18 and enrolled in college. Unpaid interns are welcome in public relations; they work 10-15 hours weekly for an academic term. Executive director: Lee Drechsel.

Camp Fire Boys and Girls, Orca Council
3555 McKinley Ave., Tacoma WA 98404
597-6234
Employs nine full-time and others on a seasonal basis. The program for the developmentally disabled employs both specialists and high school students who work with participants. Internships are available on a project basis or for an entire academic term. Executive director: Larry Conrad.

Camp Fire Boys and Girls: Snohomish County Council
11627 Airport Rd., #F, Everett WA 98204-8714
355-9734
Employs 22, with additional positions during the summer. Executive director: David Surface.

Catholic Archdiocese of Seattle
Office of Lay Personnel
910 Marion St., Seattle WA 98104
382-4570
Jobline: 382-4564
About 2,000 lay personnel are employed by the Archdiocese of Seattle. Many work in Catholic schools, some in parishes and others at the Archdiocese offices. Some positions must be filled by Catholics. The jobline includes positions in schools, Catholic colleges, parishes and affiliated agencies like Catholic Community Services. If you are a teacher, contact the Catholic School Department. (See *Employers: Education*)

Catholic Community Services, Seattle/King County
100 23rd Ave. S., Seattle WA 98144-2302
323-6336
This social service agency, one of King County's largest, employs 1,000 and offers such programs as adoption, foster care, counseling, in-home day care for the elderly and disabled, meal programs, a shelter for the homeless, chore services, legal services for the elderly and disabled and day care. Human resources director: Mary Hatch.

Catholic Community Services, Pierce and Kitsap Counties
5410 N. 44th, Tacoma WA 98407
752-2455
From Seattle: 838-2073

Offers counseling, children's programs (including foster care and help for the developmentally disabled) and the family crisis program at the headquarters as well as a downtown Tacoma program for senior citizens and refugees and a Spanaway program on substance abuse. Employment: 250, including part-time. Human resources director: DeLayne McDanold.

Catholic Community Services, Snohomish County
1918 Everett, Everett WA 98201
259-9188
From Seattle: 622-8905
Employs about 65; the independent living program employs as many as 80 in field positions. Most interns are candidates for master's degrees and work in counseling. Human resources director: Sharon Paskewitz.

Center for Human Services
17018 15th N.E., Seattle WA 98155
362-7282
Offers substance abuse prevention and treatment, individual and family counseling, drop-out prevention, youth employment, a Shoreline family support center and a University District youth center. Employs 45 plus volunteers and interns (often M.S.W. candidates). Personnel director: Irwin Batara.

Center for the Prevention of Sexual and Domestic Violence
1914 N. 34th, #105, Seattle WA 98103
634-1903
Mission: to end sexual and domestic violence by working through churches. Services include training, a speakers' bureau, sexual abuse prevention curricula, workshops, videos and publications. Internships possible. Executive director: the Rev. Marie Fortune.

Center on Contemporary Art
P.O. Box 1277, Seattle WA 98111
682-4568
Established in 1980, the center promotes visual and performing arts. It has a gallery at 1309 First Ave. Employs two full-time, two part-time and uses both volunteers and unpaid interns. Interns should have a background in art and commit to a minimum of eight hours weekly for three months. Interns might work in accounting, fund-raising or show installation. Executive director: Katherine Marczuk.

Central Area Motivation Program
722 18th Ave., Seattle WA 98122
329-4111
A social service agency providing a food bank, employment program, home repairs, emergency shelter and a program for at-risk youth, CAMP employs 53, with occasional volunteers and interns. Executive director: Leon Brown.

Central Area Youth Association
119 23rd Ave., Seattle WA 98122
322-6640
Employs 26 and uses 1,200 volunteers each year to deliver programs for youth,

including teen parents. Job applicants should have youth social services experience. Unsolicited job applications are discouraged; written inquiries regarding
unpaid internships are welcome.

Chicken Soup Brigade
1002 E. Seneca, Seattle WA 98122
328-8979
Provides food (groceries and prepared meals), transportation and home chore
services to those living with AIDS. Uses volunteers (800-plus) and student interns.
Executive director: Carol Sterling.

Childbirth Education Association of Seattle
10021 Holman Rd. N.W., Seattle WA 98177
789-0883
No full-time staff; the two directors each work 30-hour weeks. Small administrative staff; limited turnover. However, if you are a nurse or physical therapist
interested in teaching prenatal courses, there are six to eight openings each year.
CEAS also offers courses for new parents in mother-baby care, child safety and
breast-feeding; trains hospital childbirth educators; and sells a childbirth education textbook. Contact: Janet Whalley, administrative director.

Children's Home Society of Washington
P.O. Box 15190, Seattle WA 98115
524-6020
D. Sharon Osborne, president, heads this statewide agency, which provides child-
and family-related programs in 22 locations. Emphasis: preventive and crisis-
intervention services. M.S.W. candidates and those working on related master's
degrees can work as interns in direct services; students in public relations or similar
fields can intern in administrative departments. To apply at the corporate headquarters or Northwest regional office (both at this location), write Personnel.

Children's Kitchen
6208 60th, Seattle WA 98115
528-0806
A cooperative not-for-profit catering program, the Kitchen provides meals for 20
Seattle-area child care programs. Interns are welcome. So are inquiries from
skilled food service candidates. Director: Lenore Emery Neroni.

Children's Museum at Seattle Center
305 Harrison St., Seattle WA 98109-4695
441-1768
The museum expects to enlarge its space—and its staff—by summer, 1995.
Currently employs 15 full-time, 10 part-time. Two or three times a year there's a
call for artists to submit applications to teach six afternoons weekly on a short-term
basis; applicants must be visual artists, good with children (the museum's focus is
on those 8 and younger) and have innovative suggestions for projects (for example,
with clay, textiles or handmade paper). Pay for such assignments: $12-$15 an
hour. Interns usually work in public relations, marketing, exhibits, programs and
development; applicants should contact Alice Caballero, volunteer coordinator.
Director: Michael Herschensohn.

Children's Museum of Tacoma
925 Court C, Tacoma WA 98402
627-6031
This hands-on museum in downtown Tacoma employs 10; most positions are part-time.   Consultants are hired as needed for projects such as exhibit design, development and special events. The expansion being considered for 1995 may result in additional positions. Internships and work-study assignments may be possible. Contact Jackie Gretzinger or Jacquie Boyd, directors.

Children's Services of Sno-Valley
P.O. Box 969, Snoqualmie WA 98065
888-2777
From Seattle: 392-3762
Early childhood programs for special needs children and education and support for the children's families are the services of this nonprofit. Employs 13. Volunteer opportunities. Interns are welcome, especially in early childhood education, special education, language therapy or social work. Executive director: Joan Sharp.

Chinese Information and Service Center
409 Maynard Ave. S., #203, Seattle WA 98104
624-5633
Access, an Asian bilingual outreach program that serves newcomers who live within King County, is one of the programs of this nonprofit. Other programs serve at-risk youth. Of the 22 employees, many are social workers. Interns are sometimes accepted; bilingual applicants are preferred. Executive director: Rita Wang.

Citizens Education Center
310 First Ave. S., #330, Seattle WA 98104
624-9955
Established in 1979, this statewide group employs seven. Volunteers and interns are welcome, especially in such areas as research, marketing and program support. The CEC's primary focus is community involvement in education. Executive director: Judith McBroom.

CityClub
1111 Third Ave., #260, Seattle WA 98101
682-7395
A membership group that sponsors forums on local and national issues, CityClub employs three and uses student interns. Executive director: Deborah Swets.

Coalition for Charitable Choice
219 First Ave. S., Seattle WA 98104
527-1103
Promotes workplace giving for 10 umbrella organizations representing more than 300 nonprofits. Executive director: Leslie Fritchman. At press time, internship opportunities only with coalition members (for example, Earth Share, Northwest AIDS Foundation, Arts Unlimited of Puget Sound); by mid-1995, however, the coalition itself may be able to offer an internship.

Common Meals
1902 Second Ave., Seattle WA 98101
443-1233
Established in 1991 to meet two needs: to provide food service for homeless shelters and Head Start programs and to offer vocational training in the food services industry for those living in shelters or transitional housing. Common Meals also runs a public cafeteria and catering service. Enrolls as many as 22 food service students at a time. Employs five full-time, three part-time. Unpaid internships possible, especially for students completing university hospitality programs who could teach in the food services program. Other internship opportunities for grantwriters and office support personnel. Executive director: Bob Sarbiewski.

Community Service Center for the Deaf and Hard of Hearing
1609 19th Ave., Seattle WA 98122
322-4996
Provides services, support and advocacy for the deaf and hard of hearing, both children and adults. Employs fewer than 10, all of whom can use American Sign Language. It's also important that volunteers and interns can sign. Executive director: Janet E. Johanson. Those seeking work as ASL interpreters can apply for the center's Interpreter Referral Service; applicants are interviewed and qualified candidates are placed in the pool, which receives 200-300 requests a month, for assignments ranging from one hour to several days. Placement frequency and pay rates depend on skills, experience and certification; for example, some jobs require ASL, others require coded English. Pay for free-lance assignments starts at $20 to $35 per hour, with the more specialized (for example, legal or medical) and most experienced being paid more.

Community Technology Institute
P.O. Box 61385, Seattle WA 98121
441-7872
Interns (probably at the graduate level in schools such as public affairs or government) interested in sophisticated research projects may want to contact Patricia Barry or Richard Feldman, co-founders of this new nonprofit. Projects may include how technology is used to help the homeless or jobless. Barry and Feldman, while at the Worker Center (see later), won a national award for their work with a community voice-mail program for the jobless.

Co-Motion Dance Company
206 First Ave. S., Seattle WA 98104
382-0626
Established in 1979, this repertory modern dance company employs two in its office and six dancers. Its three programs: professional performance, arts in education, and guest artist residencies and workshops. Interns (unpaid or work-study) can work in arts management.

Concilio for the Spanish-Speaking of King County
157 Yesler Way, #400, Seattle WA 98104
461-4891
Employs three full-time; the staff includes the editor of *La Voz* and the coordinator

of Fiestas Patrais, an annual festival. Volunteers are welcome. Internships may be available. Fluency in Spanish is important. Executive director: Raquel Orbegozo.

Consumer Credit Counseling Service
4220 Aurora Ave. N., Seattle WA 98103
545-4300
An independent not-for-profit affiliated with the National Foundation for Consumer Credit. Serves more than 12,000 people a year from Bellingham to Oak Harbor to Kent. It offers budget and debt counseling, debtor payment plans and workshops. Interns are accepted only in the education department, which provides workshops on money management, surviving layoffs and wise use of credit.

Consumer Credit Counseling Service
11306 Bridgeport Way, Tacoma WA 98499
588-1858
Laura Johnson is executive director of this not-for-profit, another affiliate of the National Foundation for Consumer Credit. Occasional interns (work-study).

Corporate Council for the Arts
1420 Fifth Ave., #475, Seattle WA 98101
682-9270
Raising funds from corporations for professional visual and performing arts in the Seattle and Tacoma area is the responsibility of this organization. Employs five; virtually no turnover. Typical intern assignments: grantwriting, volunteer coordination, public relations or special events coordination. Peter Donnelly is president.

Council for the Prevention of Child Abuse and Neglect
10230 N.E. Points Dr., #110, Kirkland WA 98033
803-0689
Founded in 1975 to raise money and public awareness to prevent child abuse. Employs two full-time, one part-time. Interns (unpaid or work-study) welcome. Executive director: Laurie Sorensen.

Country Doctor
500 19th Ave. E., Seattle WA 98112
461-4503
A community supported clinic that provides low-cost medical services. Employs more than 60, including doctors, nurse practitioners, RNs, physician assistants and medical assistants. The administrative staff includes only nine. Some doctors rotate on a quarterly schedule, working only for three months at a time. Some employees work three or four-day weeks. Personnel is handled by the finance manager.

Crisis Clinic
1515 Dexter Ave. N., #300, Seattle WA 98109
461-3210
This nonprofit, which employs about 25 full-time in addition to part-timers, operates a 24-hour telephone service for people in emotional distress. It also offers referral to social, health and welfare services. Interns may include students in social work (M.S.W. candidates), psychology, counseling, library science, public relations and development. The volunteers who help staff the telephone lines

receive a 40-hour training course recognized for its thoroughness; many human services students use their volunteer work at Crisis Clinic for valuable practical experience. Volunteer work with the Crisis Clinic is also valuable for those new to the Northwest and those considering a career change to human services. Some volunteers work into paid positions. Executive director: Susan Eastgard.

Crisis Pregnancy
1416 State Ave. N.E., Olympia WA 98506
753-8023
A Christian organization funded by churches and United Way, this group employs three. Volunteers and interns are provided training. Services include pregnancy testing, counseling, prenatal support groups, childbirth and parenting education and an abstinence education program in the public schools. Director: Judy Perry.

Crista Ministries
19303 Fremont Ave. N., Seattle WA 98133
Human Resources: 546-7525
Jobline: 546-7202
This nonprofit interdenominational Christian service organization employs 1,000 in its radio stations, a nursing home, foster care and adoption programs, schools, camps, conference centers, Third World relief and Christian job placement service. Some jobs are part-time (for example, school bus driver or nursing home podiatry aide); others are temporary seasonal (for example, a groundskeeper). Interns may be unpaid or stipended; opportunities often exist in computing, radio broadcasting, summer camp counseling (for recreation students) and in such administrative departments as human resources and public relations. Human resources director: Roy Parnell.

Cross-Cultural Health Care Program
c/o Pacific Medical Center
1200 12th Ave. S, Seattle WA 98144
Funded only until early 1996, this program serves ethnic communities. Because improving interpreter services is one of its goals, it maintains a list of agencies that hire interpreters, provides information on interpreter certification and makes interpreters aware of job openings. If you are an interpreter, you can contact Cynthia Roat, 326-4161, for detailed information.

Dance on Capitol Hill
340 15th Ave. E., Seattle WA 98112
325-6697
All the teachers are part-time at this nonprofit, which provides dance classes, performances and rental space for other performing groups. Artistic director: Shirley Jenkins.

Deaconess Children's Services
4708 Dogwood Dr., Everett WA 98203
259-0146
Founded in 1898 by a Methodist group, this organization today says its mission is to serve at-risk children and families. Offers such programs as Parents Anonymous. Employs about 44, many part-time. Can use high school and college students as interns in public relations, program development and other administra-

tive departments; uses M.S.W. candidates in direct services. Contacts: for paid employment, Mary McLaughlin, office manager; for internships, Ginger Whelan, volunteer coordinator.

Denny Place Youth Shelter
210 Dexter Ave. N., Seattle WA 98109
328-5772
Established in 1991, this program for street youth employs full-time, part-time and on-call youth workers, a volunteer coordinator, a director and support staff. Student interns can work both with youth and as assistants to administrators (for example, to the volunteer coordinator). Located in Denny Park Lutheran Church but run on contract by Catholic Community Services.

Diabetes Association of Pierce County
1722 S. J St., Tacoma WA 98405
272-5134
This organization, which offers public education on diabetes, free diabetes screening and a referral service, offers volunteer opportunities. Executive director: Ruth Ann Ruff.

Discovery Institute
1201 Third Ave., 40th Floor, Seattle WA 98101
287-3144
Bruce Chapman, a former Census Bureau director, is the president of this think tank, which focuses on national and international issues. Employs seven staff. Of the 13 fellows, some are salaried, others volunteer. Several internship opportunities, usually for students with a background or interest in economics or international affairs. Requires a minimum commitment of five hours per week. Some interns are paid, others volunteer.

Domestic Abuse Women's Network (DAWN)
P.O. Box 1521, Kent WA 98035
656-4305
A United Way agency founded in the early 1980s to combat domestic violence, DAWN offers a crisis line, confidential shelter, community education on abuse, legal advocacy, support groups, referrals to other agencies and an educational program for abused women and children. Employs 64, of whom 23 are full-time. Volunteer attorneys staff the legal clinic, which provides advice, but no legal processing. Unpaid interns are welcome. Executive director: Linda Rasmussen.

Earth Share of Washington
1402 Third Ave., #825, Seattle WA 98101
622-9840
Affiliated with Earth Share International, the local chapter was founded in 1987. Its mission: collaborative fund-raising for environmental organizations. It seeks workplace solicitation campaigns and wants to be a stable source of funding for environmental nonprofits. Employs three, with an occasional volunteer and intern. Executive director: Maria Denny.

Easter Seal Society of Washington
521 2nd Ave. W., Seattle WA 98119
281-5700
Executive director: Paul Sorensen. Serves children and adults who are disabled
mentally or physically. At camps in Vaughn (Pierce County) and Coeur d'Alene,
Idaho, the society employs a few paid senior counselors to supervise volunteers.

Eastside Domestic Violence Program
P.O. Box 6398, Bellevue WA 98008
746-1940
EDVP's staff of 27 provides services to victims of domestic violence and offers
community education regarding domestic violence. Executive director: Aggie
Sweeney.

Economics America, Washington Council on Economic Education
1305 Fourth Ave., #1000, Seattle WA 98101-2401
622-0965
Training teachers about economics is the mission of this group, which was
established in New York some 50 years ago and opened a Washington affiliate in
the mid-1970s. A private nonprofit funded with grants and some user fees,
Economics America develops curriculum for use in K-12 programs. One example:
a personal finance course for high school students. Executive director Rose Yu
heads a staff of four. Volunteers are important; an informal internship could be
designed, especially for someone who could upgrade the software used for
curricula or tackle the accounting and inventory management systems.

Environmental Works
402 15th Ave. E., Seattle WA 98122
329-8300
Founded in 1970, this nonprofit architectural design center serves disadvantaged
communities with services like economic development, provides architectural
design for nonprofits and helps handicapped and low-income people with design
issues. Employs 10, including six architects. Most interns are architectural
students who are unpaid or receive only stipends. Contacts: Cynthia Richardson,
executive director, or Gary Oppenheimer, senior architect.

Epilepsy Association of Western Washington
200 W. Thomas, #105, Seattle WA 98119
286-4440
Information referral, especially for those recently diagnosed with epilepsy; counseling; public education; and advocacy are among the programs of this group,
which employs eight. Interns are welcome. Executive director: Cherie Kearns.

Equifriends Therapeutic Horseback Riding Program
22610-A Highway 2, Monroe WA 98272
794-5688
Therapeutic horseback riding lessons for children and adults with disabilities are
offered by this group, which has no full-time paid staff. It uses 60-80 volunteers
for each 10-week program as well as interns. Established in 1989. Program
director: Evie Bredeson.

Family Services

615 Second Ave., #150, Seattle WA 98104
461-3883
At six locations, this agency provides counseling, education and support services
for families. A master's degree in social work or counseling is required for many
of the 110 positions. Interns are welcome; most work in counseling and so should
be candidates for a master's degree. Information on openings is available from the
receptionist. Contacts: Gail Jackson, human resources director, and Ruth Ann
Howell, president.

The 5th Avenue Theatre

1326 Fifth Ave., Second Floor, Seattle WA 98101
625-1468
The 5th Avenue has two operations: The 5th Avenue Musical Theatre Company,
which presents a four-show season each year; and theater rental. Some temporary
jobs on a show-by-show basis; for example, in the box office. Internships may be
possible. Actors should watch for the general audition call each summer. Managing director: Marilynn Sheldon.

First Place

P.O. Box 22536, Seattle WA 98122-0536
323-6715
Carolyn Pringle is executive director of this school for homeless children, founded
in 1989. Employs nine full-time, three part-time. M.S.W. candidates supplement
the counseling staff and some 60 volunteers help in the classrooms and with
clerical tasks.

Food Lifeline

15230 15th Ave. N.E., Seattle WA 98155
545-6600
Solicits contributions primarily from the food industry and then distributes the
food to 258 food banks and emergency feeding programs. An affiliate of Second
Harvest, a national food bank network. Volunteer opportunities. Interns welcome,
especially in public relations, development or accounting. Contact: Winifred
Nazarko, executive director.

45th Street Clinic

1629 N. 45th St., Seattle WA 98103
633-3350
The only community clinic in North Seattle, this private nonprofit provides
medical and dental services to about 7,000 low-income people each year. Uses
interns as medical and dental assistants and volunteers. Executive director:
Elizabeth Swain.

Fremont Public Association

2326 Sixth Ave., Seattle WA 98121
441-5686
Jobline: 727-0331
Established in 1974 in the Fremont neighborhood; now serves 35,000 people
throughout King County. Programs range from the annual Fremont Fair to a food

bank and soup kitchen, legal clinic, food stamp assistance, welfare rights counseling, emergency and transitional housing, employment and housing counseling, and home care and transportation for the elderly and disabled. It employs 350 (240 as hourly home health aides). Administrative staff: 15. Examples of internships: housing development (especially graduate students in planning or public administration) and welfare rights counseling (law students). Interns may be unpaid or stipended. Volunteer opportunities. Contact: Kathy Crumlish, personnel director.

Girl Scouts, Totem Council
3611 Woodland Park Ave. N., Seattle WA 98103
633-5600
The Girl Scouts offer educational group activities for girls 5-17. This council employs about 60 on a permanent, full-time basis. Also summer positions. Interns are welcome. Executive director: Pamela Sanchez.

Girl Scouts, Pacific Peaks Council
5326 Littlerock Rd S.W., Tumwater WA 98512
572-8950
Serve most of southwest Washington. Employs about 30. Interns welcome. Contacts: Cecilia Kayano and Kay Bridges, public involvement directors.

Girls, Inc. of Puget Sound
708 Martin Luther King Jr. Way, Seattle WA 98122
720-2912
Provides programs and classes for girls 6-18 in such subjects as career planning, health, leadership and community action, sports and self-reliance. Some seasonal opportunities, especially with the summer day camps. Interns welcome, especially in social services and recreation.

Goodwill
All Goodwill programs are autonomous, but 176 of them, including the one in Tacoma, belong to a national Goodwill organization. Many in this organization continue to focus on training and rehabilitation of the handicapped. Seattle Goodwill's program, which does not belong to the national group, emphasizes job readiness through paid vocational training.

Seattle Goodwill
1400 S. Lane, Seattle WA 98144
329-1000
The thrift stores that sell donated items provide nearly all the funding for Seattle Goodwill, which runs vocational training programs and operates the Goodwill Community Learning Center, which provides free literacy and adult education classes for about 500. Some of those served by Goodwill are handicapped physically. The approximately 300 employees all work full-time; more than 110 of these are participating in nine-month training programs. The small teaching staff handles the vocational training, high school equivalency training program (G.E.D.) and conversational English; it also trains volunteers who teach or tutor at the Learning Center. Personnel director: Jay Cubbage.

Tacoma Goodwill Industries
714 S. 27th, Tacoma WA 98409
272-5166

Although hundreds are employed by Tacoma Goodwill through training programs, the administrative staff totals only about 80. Includes operations in Auburn, Puyallup, Olympia, Lacey, Longview and Yakima. Personnel director: Norma Carolyn.

GoodWorks
4223 Fremont Ave. N., Seattle WA 98103
545-0630
Serves both nonprofit public interest organizations and those who wish to work in such organizations. For nonprofits across the U.S., GoodWorks offers workshops (e.g., on time management and burn-out) and consulting. For job-seekers, it sponsors (usually through the University of Washington student group, the Experimental College) a 13-hour workshop, "Making A Living, Making A Difference." Employs three; some internship opportunities. Executive director: Michael Gilbert. For information on "Making A Living...," send a self-addressed stamped No. 10-size envelope to the address above.

Greenpeace Action
4649 Sunnyside Ave. N., Seattle WA 98103
632-4326
Employs 15 in its regional campaign office. To learn of openings locally or in Greenpeace's other regional, national or international operations, check the office job board. Interns may work on such issues as ocean ecology, international waste trade, the atmosphere or nuclear power and waste. Greenpeace also hires canvassers, those who go door-to-door soliciting volunteers, contributions and signatures for petitions. For information regarding canvass positions: 633-6027.

Hemophilia Foundation of Washington
c/o Ryther Child Center
2400 N.E. 95th, Seattle WA 98115
528-7759
Organized to provide education, advocacy and support for those with bleeding disorders and related conditions (including HIV/AIDS), this foundation's local chapter was established in 1952. Employs only one, but offers unpaid internships, usually in such areas as public relations and family camp organization.

The Homeless Challenge
107 Cherry St., Seattle WA 98104-2223
461-3763
Fund-raising for programs that help families in transition between shelters and affordable housing is the mission of this agency, founded in 1989. No direct services to the homeless. Only one paid staff member. Welcomes interns, especially in business, journalism, public relations or marketing. Intern assignments might be event planning, grantwriting or fund development. Executive director: Rebecca Luke.

HomeSight
4710 32nd Ave. S., #400, Seattle WA 98118
723-4355
Established in 1990, this nonprofit housing development corporation serving

central and southeast Seattle has two missions: to construct new homes in the Interstate 90 area; and to help first-time homebuyers make home purchases. Employs five; uses interns. Executive director: Dorothy Lengyel.

Hospice of Kitsap Co.
1007 Scott Ave., #D, Bremerton WA 98310
479-1749
Nearly 40 patients can be cared for by this hospice, which employs 36 and uses interns, mostly nursing students and M.S.W. candidates. Volunteers receive 40 hours of training. Executive director: Don Tarbutton.

Housing Hope
P.O. Box 7823, Everett WA 98201
258-2214
A United Way agency founded in 1987, this nonprofit provides and promotes affordable housing for the homeless and runs an emergency shelter. Employs 32, including housing developers, building managers, financial counselors, VISTA volunteers and social workers. Interns might work in office management, employee relations, accounting or building construction. Personnel contact: Gail Kogut, operations director.

Human Services Roundtable of King County
811 First Ave., #200, Seattle WA 98104
623-7134
A coalition of elected officials and United Way representatives. Employs no one; all staff is provided on contract. Founded in 1988, its goal is to create more effective human service agencies; it encourages the development of services not already provided. Also provides legislative advocacy. Opportunities for student interns, especially graduate students in public affairs, social work or public administration; contact Judith Clegg.

International Service Agencies, Northwest Regional Office
3433 E. Florence Ct., Seattle WA 98112
329-4423
Raises funds through workplace giving for 55 American nonprofits (for example, CARE, Save the Children, Oxfam and the U.S. Committee for UNICEF) that provide relief and development worldwide. This office covers 13 states. No employment opportunities; there's only one staff member. Interns, especially graduate students in communications and international affairs, and volunteers are welcome.

Intiman Playhouse
P.O. Box 19760, Seattle WA 98109
626-0775
Thirty work full-time on the administrative staff of this theater, with another 15 or 20 joining the organization on a full-time basis during the May-December season. Also temporary and free-lance opportunities on a show-by-show basis for technicians and designers. Only the acting staff is union. Internships are possible in such fields as production, marketing and general administration. All acting internships are filled through audition. Personnel contact: Julie Dearman, business manager.

Jack Straw Foundation

4261 Roosevelt Way N.E., Seattle WA 98105
634-0919
Two operations: Jack Straw Productions, a noncommercial audio production and training center managed by Stephen Malott; and KSER-FM, a Lynnwood radio station run by James Witmer. Employs 12, with opportunities for interns in recording, engineering and administration.

Jewish Family Service

1214 Boylston Ave., Seattle WA 98101
461-3240
Social service agency. Offices in Seattle and Bellevue and group homes for the mentally ill and developmentally disabled. The staff of 50 includes more than 25 part-time positions. Interns are welcome; most are graduate students in clinical counseling programs. Personnel contact: Joel Neier, associate director.

Jewish Federation of Greater Seattle

2031 Third Ave., Seattle WA 98121
443-5400
Raises funds for Jewish agencies, including Jewish Family Service, the Jewish Community Center, the Jewish schools, the Kline-Galland Home and for social services in Israel. Staff: 20. Interns are usually graduate students in public affairs or social work. Contact: Michael Novick, executive director.

Junior Achievement of Greater Puget Sound

600 Stewart St., #212, Seattle WA 98101
296-2600
Provides children and teenagers with economic-based educational experiences through business and school partnerships. Employs 20; uses consultants and volunteers. Contact: Gloria Studer, office manager.

Kirkland Center for the Performing Arts

220 Kirkland Ave., Kirkland WA
828-0422
Steve Lerian, formerly managing director of the Bathhouse Theater, is developing this facility, which will occupy the former Kirkland library. At press time, fund-raising efforts were underway; construction may start early in 1995. Now employs two; internships available in administration and fund-raising.

Lesbian Resource Center

1808 Bellevue Ave. E., #204, Seattle WA 98122
322-3953
A newspaper, community services (including a drop-in center with library), and meeting space are offered by this group, which promotes social and personal networking for lesbians. Employs four; volunteer opportunities. Executive director: Valerie Reuther.

Leukemia Society of America, Washington State Chapter

1001 Fourth Ave., #3714, Seattle WA 98154
628-0777

Provides community education and fund-raising for research and patient care. Staff: seven. Interns are welcome in public relations and development. Executive director: Dixie Welch.

Lifetime Learning Center
160 John St., Seattle WA 98109
283-5523
Established in 1976, this program for people older than 50 employs four part-time. It offers about 50 eight-week noncredit continuing education classes each quarter, most taught by volunteers (often retired university faculty). Executive director: Clyde Fisher.

Lutheran Compass Center
77 S. Washington, Seattle WA 98104
461-7835
Offers transitional housing, a representative payee program for those unable to manage their own finances, case management and shelters. Employs 40 full-time plus a part-time staff. Interns welcome. Openings are posted at the center. Executive director: the Rev. Jim Fergin.

Lutheran Social Services of Washington and Idaho
Northwest Area Office
6920 220th St. S.W., Mountlake Terrace WA 98043
672-6009
Programs include counseling, adoption services, a Family Support Center, refugee services, pregnancy counseling, divorce support groups, Divorce Lifeline, the Seamen's Center and a social ministry. Employs 31 plus 45 counselors, many of whom work part-time. Internships possible for graduate students in social work or counseling. Personnel contact: Candace Reed.

Lutheran Social Services of Washington and Idaho
Southwest Area Office
223 N. Yakima, Tacoma WA 98403
272-8433
Serves Pierce County. There are approximately 25 staff. Executive director: Bernard Meyer.

Lutheran Social Services of Washington and Idaho
Olympic Area Office
5610 Kitsap Way, Bremerton WA 98312
377-5511
Serves the Olympic peninsula with a staff, including counselors, of approximately 25.

March of Dimes/Birth Defects Foundation, Western Washington Chapter
1904 Third Ave., #230, Seattle WA 98101
624-1373
"Healthier babies" is how the March of Dimes describes its mission. Local programs include prenatal health care, school programs to help children understand handicaps and video training materials. Interns are welcome, especially in such fields as development, communications and public health. Executive director: Andrew Ballard.

Marine Science Center
P.O. Box 2079, Poulsbo WA 98370
779-5549
This museum employs six and uses staff from the North Kitsap School District. Internships possible for those with science backgrounds; projects might include public relations, fund-raising or grantwriting. Executive director: Jim Colb.

Mediation Services for Victims and Offenders
1305 Fourth Ave., #606, Seattle WA 98101
621-8871
Mediation regarding property crimes committed by juveniles is the focus of this group. Uses volunteers trained in mediation. Executive director: Kate Hunter.

Medina Children's Service
123 16th Ave., P.O. Box 22638, Seattle WA 98122
461-4520
Offers adoption services, counseling for unplanned pregnancies and school-based services for pregnant teenagers, expectant fathers and teenage parents. Internships possible for graduate students in social work. Executive director: Dini Duclos.

Metropolitan Development Council
622 Tacoma Ave. S., #6, Tacoma WA 98402
383-3924
Offers such programs as treatment for alcohol and substance abuse; housing development and rehabilitation; early childhood education, foster care, health care and employment assistance for the homeless. Interns, usually college freshmen and sophomores, can work in both educational counseling and substance abuse programs. Some work-study opportunities. Director: Shirley Payne.

Mothers Against Drunk Driving (MADD)
1511 Third Ave., #801, Seattle WA 98101
624-6903
Employs two. Volunteers and interns welcome. Mission: advocacy for the victims and the families of victims of drunk driving crashes; and public, corporate and school education to promote the awareness of the dangers of drunk driving. Executive director: Jeanette Greenfield. May relocate in late 1994.

Multiple Sclerosis Association of King County
753 N. 35th, #208, Seattle WA 98103
461-6914
Programs include rehabilitation and social services. Locally-based provider of direct services to those with multiple sclerosis. Not affiliated with the National Multiple Sclerosis Society. Interns welcome, especially graduate students in social work. Executive director: Ruth Scott.

Multi-Service Centers of North & East King County
P.O. Box 3577, Redmond WA 98073-3577
869-6000
A community action agency that helps low-income residents of Bothell, Kirkland, Redmond, Bellevue and the Snoqualmie Valley. Employs 150. Volunteers are

welcome. Internships may be available. Human resources manager: Cathy Capers.

Municipal League of King County
810 Third Ave., #604, Seattle WA 98104-1651
622-8333
A nonpartisan citizens' organization that calls itself a "good government watch-dog," the Municipal League employs four. Interns are welcome. President: Eileen Quigley.

Muscular Dystrophy Association
701 Dexter Ave. N., #106, Seattle WA 98109-4339
283-2183
Education and fund-raising for patient services and research are the major respon-sibilities of this MDA office, the only one in western Washington. Interns welcome. Contact: (Mr.) Alex Dieffenbach, western Washington district director.

Museum of Flight
9404 E. Marginal Way S., Seattle WA 98108
764-5700
Located on the edge of Boeing Field, this museum incorporates the original Boeing factory. However, the museum is private, supported by the Museum of Flight Foundation. Mission: preservation of Pacific Northwest flight history. There are 70 full-time employees in addition to part-timers and volunteers. Interns welcome in such departments as marketing and programs. Resumes are accepted only for open positions.

Museum of History and Industry
2700 24th Ave. E., Seattle WA 98112
324-1126
Focuses on Northwest history. Employs 30 full-time. As many as 15 may work part-time in the museum store, at the front desk, in exhibit construction and to set up for meetings and facility rental. Interns can work in public relations (contact Mary Ann Barron, PR director) or development (contact Maggie Blackburn). The education department trains volunteers to lead school and senior citizen tours of specific exhibits and to assist with "family fun days" (contact Tori Smith). Executive director: Wilson O'Donnell.

National Campaign for Freedom of Expression
1402 Third Ave., #421, Seattle WA 98101
340-9301
A national advocacy group formed to protect and extend freedom of artistic expression and fight censorship. Employs three. Welcomes volunteers and interns. Executive director: David Mendoza.

National Multiple Sclerosis Society, Western Washington Chapter
192 Nickerson St., #100, Seattle WA 98109
284-4236
Provides community education, fund-raising and direct services to MS patients and their families in 18 counties. Employs nine in Seattle and two in its branch office in Tacoma. Internships possible in development and direct services,

especially information referral. Executive director: Norman Schwamberg.

Nature Conservancy
217 Pine St., #1100, Seattle WA 98101
343-4344
Goal: preserving biological diversity by protecting habitats for rare and endangered species. One office and 27,000 members in Washington. Employs 19. Internships possible. Executive director: Elliot Marks.

Neighborhood House
905 Spruce St., #213, Seattle WA 98104
461-8430
Offers a variety of services in Seattle's low-income housing developments and runs day care centers, Head Start and senior programs. Interns can work in substance abuse programs, finance, human resources and general human services. Executive director: Brent Crook. Personnel director: (Ms.) Perry Welch.

New Beginnings for Battered Women and Their Children
P.O. Box 75125, Seattle WA 98125
783-4520
Provides a confidential shelter for battered women and their children, a 24-hour crisis line, support groups and community advocacy. The staff of 20 is supplemented by volunteers, who complete a training program. Occasional interns. Personnel contact: Donnetta Vessel.

911 Media Arts Center
117 Yale Ave. N., Seattle WA 98109
682-6552
Executive director: Robin Reidy. Interns are welcome and can sometimes work into paid positions. The only media arts center in the state; it maintains a film and video-editing facility and screening room and offers video and film workshops.

Nordic Heritage Museum
3014 N.W. 67th, Seattle WA 98117
789-5707
This museum in Ballard is devoted to the preservation and interpretation of Scandinavian heritage. Interns and volunteers are welcome. Contact: Marianne Forssblad, director.

Northwest AIDS Foundation
127 Broadway E., Seattle WA 98102
329-6923
Provides case management, housing and education for AIDS patients, fundraising, grant administration, advocacy services and technical assistance to smaller nonprofits. The paid staff is supplemented with 1,000 volunteers. Interns can work in such departments as education, communications, housing and direct services. Human resources manager: (Ms.) Shamim Jiwa-Kassam.

Northwest Chamber Orchestra
1305 Fourth Ave., #522, Seattle WA 98101
343-0445

Offers a dozen concerts during its September-May season and a musical education program that tours schools and provides teacher-training materials. The two-member permanent staff is supplemented by volunteers and interns. Managing director: Louise Kincaid.

Northwest Harvest/E.M.M.
P.O. Box 12272, Seattle WA 98102
625-0755
Functions as a center for food collection and distribution. Serves more than 300 hunger programs. Interns can work in communications or public relations, finance and accounting or development. Contact: Rosemary Boyle, office administrator. An affiliate is

Northwest Caring Ministry
P.O. Box 12272, Seattle WA 98102
625-7524
This agency offers referrals and advocacy on issues other than hunger. The Rev. Steven Bauck, the supervisor, welcomes interns, especially M.S.W. candidates.

Northwest Interpretative Association
909 First Ave., #630, Seattle WA 98104-1060
220-4140
Publishes and sells interpretative materials for the National Park Service. Unpaid internships available in editing and office support. Executive director: Mary Ellen Rutter. At the same address and telephone number you can reach the affiliate:

Pacific Northwest Field Seminars
Headed by Jean Tobin. She employs instructors as needed for the programs, which are intended to enhance individual knowledge and enjoyment of natural resources.

Northwest Renewable Resources Center
1411 Fourth Ave., #1510, Seattle WA 98101-2216
623-7361
Purpose: the resolution of disputes over the use of natural resources. Works at a policy level with tribes, state agencies, environmental groups and industry. Internships may be possible. Executive director: Amy Solomon.

Northwest Women's Law Center
119 S. Main St., #330, Seattle WA 98104-2515
682-9552
Purpose: advancing legal rights for all women. Besides litigation, it provides education, public policy and a telephone referral service. Uses interns, especially paralegals and law students. Volunteers welcome. Contact: Peggy Lynch, office manager.

Odyssey Contemporary Maritime Museum
318 First Ave. S., Seattle WA 98104
623-2120
Scheduled to open in 1996 on Seattle's Pier 66, this nonprofit already employs three. Interns can be used now in public relations, marketing, exhibit design and research. The museum's purpose: a focus on contemporary maritime trade, fisheries and the environment.

One Church, One Child
6419 Martin Luther King Jr. Way S., Seattle WA 98118
723-6224
Mission: recruiting adoptive families for waiting children. Also offers parenting preparation for foster and adoptive parents. Volunteers and interns welcome. Executive director: Gwendolyn Townsend.

Pacific Arts Center
305 Harrison St., Seattle WA 98109
443-5437
Provides arts education for children and youth from practicing professional artists. If you're an artist who'd like to work on contract (at $21 an hour) leading activities at children's birthday parties, send your resume with activity ideas to (Ms.) Pat Crace. Contract employees are also used for Saturday Artsploration (contact Laura Posten, center director), Artsreach (contact Carmita Abrigo) and SKIT (contact Celina Knight). Interns can work in marketing. Volunteers are welcome.

Pacific Northwest Ballet
301 Mercer St., Seattle WA 98109
441-9411
Interns are welcome in development, public relations or marketing. Crew positions are union. Human resources manager: Judy Porterfield.

Pacific Northwest Pollution Prevention Research Center
1326 Fifth Ave., #650, Seattle WA 98101
223-1151
Madeline M. Grulich is executive director of this group, which uses interns (especially students in environmental studies) and an occasional volunteer. Offers grants and organizes conferences on different kinds of pollution.

Pacific Science Center
200 Second Ave. N., Seattle WA 98109
443-2001
A private educational and museum foundation that promotes the understanding of science, mathematics and technology through interactive exhibits and programs. Employs 300, about 170 part-time. Many part-timers work as science demonstrators and explainers, demonstrating science principles and explaining exhibits. Openings for these positions are often advertised in the University of Washington *Daily*, a free paper available on campus. There's also a summer volunteer program for those 14 and older. The part-time professional opportunities are often on a project basis. No formal internships. Job openings are posted in the science center offices, located under the IMAX theater. No unsolicited resumes.

Paramount Theater (Seattle Landmark Association)
911 Pine St., Seattle WA 98101
467-5510
Closed for renovation at press time, but expected to re-open by early 1995. At that time the staff will be expanded with both full-time and part-time postions. Internships will be available in such marketing functions as public relations and advertising; there'll also be opportunities for students in audio-visual communica-

tions, theater production and business administration. General manager: Douglas Gray.

Parents Anonymous Washington State
1305 Fourth Ave., #310, Seattle WA 98101
233-0156
Offers free weekly parent support groups across the state and a family helpline. Employs six (two are part-time). Interns can work on the helpline or on special projects. Executive director: Sylvia Meyer.

People for Puget Sound
1326 Fifth Ave., #450, Seattle WA 98101
382-7007
This group's 16,000 members strive to protect and restore Puget Sound. Interns can work in the Kids for Puget Sound education program, on public policy issues or in communications. Executive director: Kathy Fletcher.

People of Color Against AIDS Network
1200 S. Jackson, #25, Seattle WA 98144
322-7061
Mission: AIDS prevention and education. Provides street outreach, health presentations and peer education. Serves as the umbrella for the Puget Sound Indian AIDS Task Force, LUCES (formerly the Washington State Latino AIDS Coalition) and the Asian Pacific AIDS Council. Uses interns and volunteers (training is provided).

Performance Support Services
1625 Broadway, Seattle WA 98122
328-5548
Sponsors the Allegro Dance Festival, runs the Foundation for Choreographers and co-sponsors Leap Into Art, a summer art festival for children. Employs three plus performers. Executive director: Peter Staddler.

Planned Parenthood of Seattle-King County
2211 E. Madison, Seattle WA 98112
328-7734
Jobline: 328-7721
Provides quality reproductive health care to men and women in King, Island, Mason, Lewis and Thurston counties. Employs 98 full-time, 70 part-time and 65 on a per dium basis. Job openings are posted in the personnel office on East Madison, in each clinic, at the University of Washington and at community colleges and in community service centers. Applications are accepted only for open positions.

Planned Parenthood of Pierce County
813 Martin Luther King Jr. Way, Tacoma WA 98405
572-6955
Employs 40. Internships possible in such fields as counseling. Openings are posted in the building and advertised. Unsolicited resumes are discouraged.

Planned Parenthood of Snohomish County

P.O. Box 1051, Everett WA 98206

339-3392

Employs 50. Openings are advertised. Unsolicited resumes are discouraged. Prospective interns can contact Karrie Evans, lead clinician, regarding work in direct services. Executive director: Ann Markewitz.

Plymouth Housing Group

1305 Fourth Ave., #417, Seattle WA 98101

343-7838

An offshoot of Plymouth Congregational Church; provides low-income housing. Unpaid internships are available half-time or full-time for an academic term. Executive director: Cheryl DeBoise.

Pratt Fine Arts Center

1902 S. Main St., Seattle WA 98144

328-2200

Offers classes to adults and children. Employs 10 in addition to the artists who teach. Work-study opportunities; internships may be offered in 1995. Contact: Risa Morgan, executive director.

Professional Ski Instructors of America, Northwest

11204 Des Moines Memorial Dr., Seattle WA 98168

244-8541

Provides certification and recordkeeping for more than 100 ski schools. At press time, executive director Barbara Darrow supervised two part-time employees. Internships for administrative tasks are possible.

Program for Early Parent Support (PEPS)

4649 Sunnyside Ave. N., Seattle WA 98103

547-8570

Local parent-support organization; employs two full-time, five part-time. Interns are used occasionally in public relations, development or human services. Executive director: Jane White-Vulliet. Volunteer coordination is handled by Sandra Wallace.

Powerful Schools

3301 S. Horton St., Seattle WA 98144

722-5543

Operates noncredit after-school and evening classes in Rainier Valley elementary schools, runs a "parent involvement incentives" program and offers teacher training programs. Uses volunteers and interns. Executive director: Greg Tuke. Also see *Employers: Education.*

Puget Sound Neighborhood Health Centers

905 Spruce St., #201, Seattle WA 98104

461-6935

Runs medical and dental clinics in southeast and southwest Seattle and in the Georgetown neighborhood. Employs 130, including doctors, nurse practitioners, medical assistants, dentists and dental assistants. Small administrative staff. Many part-time opportunities. Interns can work in clinics or administration.

Personnel specialist: Theresa Norris. Intern contacts: for medical, Colin Romero, medical director (461-6961); for dental, John McFatridge, dental director (461-6981); and for administration, Annette Neilson, administrative assistant (461-6935).

Puyallup Tribe of Indians
2002 E. 28th, Tacoma WA 98404
597-6200
Provides social and medical services, housing, employment counseling and a property buying program for members of the Puyallup tribe and other Native Americans. Job openings are posted at several locations in the complex, including the personnel office, JPTA office and the reception area of the health authority, located at 2209 E. 32nd. Resumes can be submitted at any time to the appropriate personnel director: Dennis Johnson for the health authority and Dianne Ward for tribal administration.

Resource Institute
2319 N. 45th St., #139, Seattle WA 98103
784-6762
Offers both land programs and shipboard seminars. Shipboard topics include photography and Northwest Indian art. May use unpaid interns starting in 1995. Administrative director: Paige Tyley.

Rivers Council of Washington
1731 Westlake Ave. N., #202, Seattle WA 98109
283-4988
The oldest river conservation organization in the Northwest. Employs two and uses interns and volunteers. Executive director: Joy Huber.

Rosehedge
P.O. Box 25055, Seattle WA 98125
365-6806
Organized in 1988 as a nursing facility for those living with AIDS, Rosehedge today also provides assisted living and home health care for those with HIV/AIDS. Will take nursing students as interns. Executive director: Linda Chelotti.

Ruth Dykeman Children's Center
P.O. Box 66010, Seattle WA 98166
242-1698
Thomas E. Rembiesa is the executive director of this program, which serves emotionally and behaviorally dysfunctional youth and families. Employs more than 100, most full-time. Opportunities for interns.

Ryther Child Center
2400 N.E. 95th, Seattle WA 98115
525-5050
Runs alcohol and substance abuse programs for youth as well as a Parents Anonymous support group and parenting classes. Total employment: 140, with about 50 working part-time. Internships may be available for drug and alcohol abuse counselors. Executive director: Frances Hume.

Salvation Army
Northwest Divisional Headquarters
P.O. Box 9219, Seattle 98109
281-4600
You need not be a Salvation Army member to work at this nonprofit, which
provides emergency help for the needy (including alcohol/drug abusers and abused
women), counseling and holiday programs. Internships are possible in the
administrative office in finance, public relations, development and youth programs. Local Salvation Army programs have different emphases and thus different
opportunities; for example, the north Seattle office offers day care, the West
Seattle office a youth center.

Scandinavian Language Institute
3014 N.W. 67th, Seattle WA 98117
771-5203
Ed Egerdahl directs this program established in the 1970s. It provides four levels
of training in Norwegian, Danish and Swedish for hundreds of students (mostly
adults) each year. No full-time staff employees; all instructors are hired on a per-
class basis. Some teach one class a week, others teach 10 or 11. Compensation is
on a per-student basis. The institute also offers tutoring and provides translators
and interpreters to clients ranging from tour companies to public libraries to law
firms. Some instructors translate software documentation for foreign editions of
local software programs. In selecting instructors, Egerdahl looks for personality,
competency and concern for curriculum (those completing a year of Institute
classes may accomplish the equivalent of a academic year at the college level).

Seattle Art Museum
Human Resources Office
P.O. Box 22000, Seattle WA 98122-9700
654-3189
Employs 180, most full-time; the part-time jobs are mostly in security. Some job-
share opportunities. The studio art program hires people to work on a series basis.
Interns are usually hired by department heads to work in curatorial, public
relations, education (programs), development or accounting. No unsolicited
resumes. Openings are advertised in the Seattle Sunday paper and the *Seattle
Weekly*. Inquiries regarding internships can be mailed to Cynthia Miles, human
resources manager.

Seattle Audubon Society
8028 35th Ave. N.E., Seattle WA 98115
523-4483
Employs two full-time, with several part-timers. Volunteers welcome. Interns can
work in administration (for example, managing the Nature Shop), accounting,
customer relations or special events. Contact: Michelle McLaughlin, operations
director. An affiliate at the same address is the grant-funded:

Washington Wetlands Network
524-4570
Employs two part-time. Welcomes volunteers and interns. Coordinator: Christi
Norman.

Seattle Center Academy

305 W. Harrison, Seattle WA 98109

233-3959

Funded in part by the Seattle Center Foundation, this program uses staff from the Seattle Center nonprofits (for example, the Pacific Science Center, KCTS/9 and the Seattle Symphony) to teach two-week arts and sciences summer programs for middle-school students. Employs only two, but uses volunteers as assistants to the master teachers. Volunteers, who by 1995 may be able to receive academic credit for their work, are usually college students; experience in teaching, an understanding of teenagers and interest or ability in the arts or sciences is desired. Also hires youth aged 14-18 (usually disadvantaged) to write and perform plays at community centers. A conflict resolution program for high school students is being developed; participants will receive stipends for the one-week program. Executive director: John Merner.

Seattle Chamber Music Festival

2618 Eastlake Ave. E., Seattle WA 98102

328-5606

Presents internationally known musicians in its summer series of concerts and recitals. Employs three in administration; volunteers are welcome. Interns can work in arts administration. No open auditions for performers. Contacts: Cheryl Swab, executive director, and Toby Saks, artistic director.

Seattle Children's Home

2142 10th Ave. W., Seattle WA 98119

283-3300

Provides specialized care and treatment for mentally ill children, youth and young adults. Graduate degrees are necessary for those who provides direct services to patients. Internships sometimes possible. Job openings are posted in the administration building; resumes can be directed to Stacy Young, personnel specialist.

Seattle Children's Theatre

P.O. Box 9640, Seattle WA 98109

443-0807

Equity theater. Employs 50 full-time as well as part-timers, free-lancers and interns. Three major operations: the main stage theater; an education program; and a touring program. Kathy Alm, associate director, handles personnel. Internships may be available in administrative functions by late 1995. All acting internships are arranged only through drama programs at the University of Washington and Cornish College of the Arts.

Seattle Counseling Service for Sexual Minorities

200 W. Mercer St., #300, Seattle WA 98119

282-9314

Provides help for sexual minority youth in crisis, the chronically mentally ill and homeless mentally ill, AIDS services and same-sex domestic violence counseling. Employs 14 full-time plus 45 therapists. Interns are M.S.W., M.A., B.S.W. or B.A. (social services or human services) candidates. Interim executive director: Ann Malain.

Seattle Emergency Housing Service
905 Spruce St., Seattle WA 98104
461-3660
The largest agency in the state providing services to homeless families, assisting nearly 2,000 annually with emergency, interim and permanent housing. M.S.W. candidates serve as interns; a few volunteers are used in the food bank and for clerical support. Each year the agency also receives staff, often counselors, from the Jesuit Volunteer Corps. Executive director: John Braden.

Seattle Housing Resources Group
500 Union St., #320, Seattle WA 98101
623-0506
Rehabs, constructs and manages buildings for low- and moderate-income tenants. Employs 50. Internships are usually available during the summer. Deputy director and HR contact: Marcia Almquist.

Seattle Indian Center
611 12th Ave. S., #300, Seattle WA 98144
329-8700
Services include adoption, education, employment, child care, emergency services, SSI application assistance, a mail stop service for the homeless and a food bank and hot meal program. Volunteers and interns welcome. Executive director: Camille Monzon.

Seattle International Children's Festival
305 Harrison St., Seattle WA 98109
684-7338
A multi-cultural performing arts organization that each May organizes several days of performances at Seattle Center. Employs six full-time. Uses volunteers (150 the week of the festival) and consultants. Interns can work in writing and research. Executive director: Marilyn Raichle.

Seattle/King County Housing Development Consortium
107 Pine St., #103, Seattle WA 98104
682-9541
Represents 25 nonprofit developers of low-income housing. Executive director Carla Okigwe heads a staff of three. Unpaid interns, work-study students and volunteers are welcome.

Seattle Opera
P.O. Box 9248, Seattle WA 98109
389-7600
Employs about 50 in nonperforming positions; besides the full-time positions, there are part-time jobs, especially in telemarketing, and seasonal opportunities, mostly in production (for example, the costume and scene shops). Some seasonal box office work. Interns, usually college graduates, can work full-time in production; summer interns, usually hired on a work-study basis, can work in such areas as public relations or marketing. Human resources director: Julie Tatum.

Seattle Rape Relief
1905 S. Jackson, Seattle WA 98144
325-5531
Offers short-term counseling, legal and medical advocacy, education and a 24-hour crisis line. Volunteers receive an 80-hour training program before starting on the crisis line. Co-directors are Ellen Hurtado and Ann McGettigan.

Seattle Repertory Theatre
155 Mercer St., Seattle WA 98109
443-2210
You'll find full-time positions, a few part-time jobs, free-lance opportunities and a formal internship program at the Rep, which employs 150 during its season. Many positions do not require a theater background. For example, free-lancers design the costumes and create scenic art and some props for the theater productions. Assistance is provided by volunteers and by interns, who usually join the Rep for a season after completing college. If you have a theater background and expect to make the arts your career, you can apply for the internships by writing the Professional Arts Training Program. Regarding administrative positions, write Ben Moore, managing director.

Seattle Symphony Orchestra
305 Harrison St., Seattle WA 98109
443-4740
Offers classical concert music in a variety of concert series. Interns can work in public relations, marketing and development as well as in music operations; if you have a classical music background, you can help with such projects as greeting guest artists and writing program notes. Volunteers are always welcome. Contact: Sharon King, executive assistant.

Seattle Treatment Education Project
127 Broadway E., #200, Seattle WA 98102
329-0064
An AIDS/HIV information provider, STEP serves both those living with AIDS and health care providers with a newsletter, hotline, health-management seminars and fact sheets. Employs two full-time. Interns might work in fund-raising, writing and editing publications or inventory management of publications. Administrative director: Michael Auch.

Senior Services of Seattle/King County
1601 Second Ave., #800, Seattle WA 98101
448-5757
Provides counseling, home sharing, nutrition, advocacy, home repair, home-delivered meals, adult day care, transportation, recreation and health services for senior citizens. Volunteers are welcome. Internships are possible, especially for M.S.W. candidates. Human resources contact: Tom Rasmussen.

Senior Services of Snohomish County
8225 44th Ave. W., #O, Mukilteo WA 98275
355-1112
From Seattle: 745-1112
· Offers information and referral, a monthly newspaper, respite care, low-income

housing, home repair, Meals on Wheels, adult day care and transportation. Uses volunteers. Interns might work in social work or public administration. Executive director: Keith Spelhaug. Human resources contact: Jennifer Harbo.

Senior Services for South Sound
222 N. Columbia, Olympia WA 98501
943-6181
Serves Thurston and Mason counties. Executive director: Katherine Davis Delaney.

Snohomish County Arts Council
P.O. Box 5038, Everett WA 98206
259-0380
Maintains a visual arts gallery in the Everett Center for the Arts. Offers, with the city parks and recreation staff, an arts education program. Employs four plus project artists. Volunteers and interns welcome. Executive director: Robyn Johnson.

Stroum Jewish Community Center
3801 E. Mercer Way, Mercer Island WA 98040
232-7115
Employs 40 full-time and 200 part-time. Offers classes, day care, preschool and summer day camp. There's also a professional (Equity) theater that employs three and hires as many as 10 additional (including actors) on a show-by-show basis. The youth theater employs three full-time, two part-time. Job openings are usually advertised and posted at the center. Interns might work in health and fitness or cultural arts. Volunteers are welcome; contact Ann Meisner, membership services director.

Stroum Jewish Community Center, North End Branch
8606 35th Ave. N.E., Seattle WA 98115
526-8073
Offers preschool, child care, summer day camp and some classes. Employs six administrative staff and 23 full-time and 12 part-time teachers. Contact: Patricia Schwartz, director.

Student Conservation Association
2524 16th Ave. S., Seattle WA 98144
324-4649
A national nonprofit that employs 100 across the U.S., SCA has a four-person permanent staff in Seattle with additional people on a seasonal basis. Internships include the resource assistant position for those 18 and older. This stipended position does not require that you be in college; available year around, it involves three months of hands-on conservation work (for example, trail construction). About 30 resource assistants are hired in Seattle each year. Occasional administrative internships for graphic design or special event organization. Northwest coordinator: Peter Sanborn.

Tacoma Actors Guild
901 Broadway Plaza, #600, Tacoma WA 98402
272-3107
Tacoma's resident professional theater company, TAG is the only Equity house

outside Seattle. Presents at least six plays between October and May and in 1990 initiated a Summer Conservatory Program. Permanent staff: 11. Seasonal staff: 30 plus actors, directors and musicians. Temps are also hired to work on props and costumes and sometimes as a carpenter's helper. Opportunities for interns in both production and administration. Contact: Nancy Hoadley, company manager.

Tacoma Art Museum
1123 Pacific Ave., Tacoma WA 98402
272-4258
Volunteers are welcome and internships are possible; work might be clerical, as docents or in public relations, special events or development. Director: Chase Rynd.

Tacoma Little Theatre
210 N. I St., Tacoma WA 98403
272-2481
Presents six shows during its September-June season. Employs four; interns are welcome in public relations, marketing or technical theater fields. People who have acted, directed and worked with youth can apply for the contract faculty positions with the Young Actors Program. Managing director: David Fisher.

Tacoma Symphony
P.O. Box 19, Tacoma WA 98401
272-7264
Five classical music concerts are offered by this group. About 80 musicians are part of the symphony; auditions are held each August for open positions in the non-union group. Interns might work in public relations, marketing, grantwriting or arts administration; for many assignments, a music background is a prerequisite. Executive director: Carlene Garner.

Travelers Aid Society
909 Fourth Ave., #630, Seattle WA 98104
461-3888
Offers emergency and transitional services to the homeless and protective travel services to children, senior citizens and the disabled or ill. Volunteers supplement the paid staff. Internships may be possible. Executive director: Jane McKinley-Chinn.

The Trust for Public Land
506 Second Ave., #1510, Seattle WA 98104
587-2447
The Northwest regional office for a national land conservation organization. Interns welcome. Regional manager: Craig Lee.

United Cerebral Palsy Association of King and Snohomish Counties
4409 Interlake Ave. N., Seattle WA 98103
632-2827
Rehabilitation is the focus of this agency, which provides direct services and community education. Employs more than 150 plus volunteers and, in the dental clinic, interns. Executive director: Greg Payton.

United Indians of All Tribes Foundation
1945 Yale Pl. E., Seattle WA 98102
325-0070
Offers job placement, youth, human services and economic development programs. Interns might work in data entry, in early childhood education classrooms or in the drug and alcohol abuse counseling programs. Contact: Mary Allen, employment specialist.

United Ways of Washington
615 Second Ave., #350, Seattle WA 98104
461-3717
Assists 27 local United Way chapters. Internships are possible, especially for students interested in working on public policy during the legislative session (requires a January-May commitment). You should contact the local organizations listed below regarding most opportunities. United Way organizations operate autonomously; all hiring is handled at the county level.

United Way of King County
107 Cherry, Seattle WA 98104
Human Resources: 461-7843
Internships are available, especially for students doing field work. Unpaid summer internships may also be available. Human resources manager: John Mack.

United Way of Pierce County
P.O. Box 2215, Tacoma WA 98401-2215
272-4263
Includes a volunteer center, the Center for Nonprofit Development. Interns are welcome. Contact: Marcia Walker, vice president, community and human resources.

United Way of Snohomish County
917 134th St. S.W., #A-6, Everett WA 98204
258-4521
From Seattle: 742-5911
Unpaid interns are welcome in market research, fund-raising, volunteer training and coordination, nonprofit management or public administration. President: Patrick Soriconi.

United Way of Kitsap County
2135 Sheridan Rd., #D, Bremerton WA 98310
377-8505
Volunteer Center: 377-0059
Employs six. Interns are welcome. Executive director: Barbara Stephenson.

United Way of Thurston County
1401 4th Ave. E., Olympia WA 98506
943-2773
Employs five. Volunteers welcome. Occasional interns for clerical assignments. Executive director: Dean Hanks.

Union Gospel Mission
P.O. Box 202, Seattle WA 98111-0202
723-0767

Provides food and shelter, a drug and alcoholism program, youth programs, a clothing and household item bank and retail second-hand stores. Employs 105 plus interns and volunteers. Executive director: Herbert Pfiffner.

Virginia V Foundation
901 Fairview Ave. N., #A-100, Seattle WA 98109
624-9119
Maintains the landmark 73-year-old Virginia V, the last of the Pacific Northwest's "mosquito fleet." Offers charters, public cruises and dockside events. Employs two. Uses volunteers; internships possible. Executive director: Karen Laverdiere.

Volunteers of America
6559 35th Ave. N.E., Seattle WA 98115
523-3565
Runs seven programs in King County, including low-income housing, food banks, an outreach center, companions to the homebound, and programs for youth in south King County neighborhoods. Employs 40 and uses volunteers. Interns can work in fund development, public relations or as assistants to program developers. President: Connie Devaney.

Washington Association of Churches
4759 15th Ave. N.E., Seattle WA 98105
525-1988
Employs three full-time. Staff supplemented with part-time employees, interns and volunteers. Focus: ecumenical dialog, legislative advocacy, refugee advocacy, economic justice, civil rights and farm worker justice. Executive minister: John Boonstra.

Washington Business Week
P.O. Box 658, Olympia WA 98507
943-1600
Toll-free within Washington: (800) 521-9325
This three-employee group organizes week-long educational programs for high school students. Responsibilities: fund-raising, faculty and student recruitment, volunteer coordination, conference planning and development of teaching materials. Volunteers are welcome; internships may be possible. Executive director: Beverlee Hughes.

Washington Center for the Performing Arts
512 Washington St. S.E., Olympia WA 98501
753-8585
This center serves as a rental facility for touring shows and also presents about 20 of its own programs each year. Employs 14 permanent staff plus part-timers for backstage work. Uses interns and volunteers. Executive director: Tom Iovanne.

Washington Corporate Council for the Environment
P.O. Box 21071, Seattle WA 98111
781-3552
Established in 1992 to help business and environmentalists work together. A primary function: obtain corporate donations for selected environmental nonprofits.

No paid staff at this time; volunteer opportunities only for the one special event organized each year.

Washington Commission for the Humanities
615 Second Ave., #300, Seattle WA 98104
682-1770
Supports the humanities and humanities education with several programs, including grants, a speakers' bureau, an exhibit touring service and forums for community groups considering the establishment of humanities programs. The full-time staff of six includes positions in grants, programs, development and finance. Internships are available. Contact: Hidde Van Duym, executive director.

Washington Institute for Policy Studies
999 Third Ave., #1060, Seattle WA 98104
467-9561
A public policy think tank that focuses on greater accountability of government spending and development of private sector solutions for social problems. Small staff, but offers part-time internships; students can receive academic credit and a small stipend. Assignments: conduct research and perform administrative tasks. Contact: Dann Mead Smith.

Washington Literacy
2209 Eastlake Ave. E., Seattle WA 98102
461-3623
Helps develop community literacy programs rather than conducting its own reading classes. Employs eight. Interns are welcome. Contact: Christine Cassidy, executive director.

Washington Special Olympics
2150 N. 107th, Seattle WA 98133
362-4949
Organizers of year around athletic games for the developmentally disabled. Few entry-level opportunities, although internships are occasionally available. The ability to work with volunteers and good organizational skills are important for all employees. Contact: Bonnie Benofski, office manager.

Washington State Democratic Central Committee
506 Second Ave., #1701, Seattle WA 98104
583-0664
Even during presidential elections, this staff is very small; at press time, employed three plus contract workers. Most positions require some experience in politics. Volunteers and interns are important; students majoring in political science or public affairs are especially valuable. Executive assistant: Mary Eversole.

Washington State 4-H Foundation
7612 Pioneer Way E., Puyallup WA 98371
840-4560
Raises funds for 4-H programs; the 4-H clubs work with the cooperative extension staff in each county. John Engen is executive director of the foundation, which has a staff of three. Internships available.

Washington State Grange
P.O. Box 1186, Olympia WA 98507
943-9911
Grange News, the monthly, is one of the projects of this group, supported by some 62,000 members statewide. Employs six full-time. Student internships possible. State master: Robert Clark.

Washington State Jewish Historical Society
2031 Third Ave., #400, Seattle WA 98121
443-1903
Charna Klein is the executive director of this group, which employs two part-time. Volunteers and interns are welcome. Maintains archives in cooperation with the University of Washington libraries, issues a newsletter, organizes exhibits and presentations and offers speakers.

Washington State Republican Party
16400 Southcenter Parkway, #200, Seattle WA 98188
575-2900
Executive director: Lance J. Henderson. Part-time and intern positions, especially during campaigns. Interns can work year around on such projects as the convention or in communications (writing). Political experience, either paid or volunteer, is helpful.

Washington Toxics Coalition
4516 University Way N.E., Seattle WA 98105
632-1545
A local organization founded in the early 1980s to reduce toxics, the coalition provides publications and speakers; it often responds to as many as 7,000 information requests each year. Uses volunteers. Unpaid interns might work on special projects, often research, involving industrial or household toxics or pesticides; they might also assist in lobbying. Administrative director: Jeff Cohn.

Washington Trails Association
1305 Fourth Ave., #512, Seattle WA 98101-2401
625-1367
Preserves and enhances existing trails and extends the trails network. Employs two, executive director Greg Bull, and magazine editor Dan Nelson. Each takes interns; for example, in administration and in journalism. The monthly magazine, *Signposts for Northwest Trails*, established in 1966, accepts free-lance writing and photography.

Washington Women's Employment and Education
841 N. Central, #232, Kent WA 98032
859-3718
Provides an intensive three-week program and then a year of follow-up for low-income individuals pursuing training or job placement. Together, the Kent and Tacoma offices employ fewer than 20. Both employ directors, education directors, employment specialists and transition coordinators. Volunteers handle many functions in both operations and interns are welcome. For more information about this office, contact Lynn Roberts, director.

Washington Women's Employment and Education
3516 S. 47th St., #205, Tacoma WA 98409
474-WWEE
Contact: Margo Fleshman, executive director.

Washington Zoological Park
19525 S.E. 54th, Issaquah WA 98027
391-5508
Volunteers/Internships: 391-6278
A teaching zoo specializing in endangered and threatened species. Employs three.
Uses volunteers (you must be at least 18) as docents, to prepare animal meals and
clean habitats, in the office, in fund-raising and special events and in the Washington Zoological Supply, a retail operation. Interns are often veterinary students who
work in the zoo. Executive director: Peter Rittler.

WashPIRG
340 15th Ave. E., Seattle WA 98112
322-9064
A citizen outreach lobby that works on environmental and consumer legislation.
Employs fewer than 10 in the office; the field staff ranges between 20 and 70.
Volunteers and interns are welcome. Interns can be trained to work in campaigns,
community organizing or with the media. Contact: Rebecca Levison, field
organizer.

Wing Luke Asian Museum
407 7th Ave. S., Seattle WA 98104
623-5124
Specializes in Asian and Asian-American folk art and history. Its staff is very
small and most positions are part-time. Volunteers are always needed. A variety
of internships (all unpaid) are available. Intern assignments can be designed to
meet academic requirements; although most students work part-time in the museum for three months, internships ranging in length from two weeks to one year
have also been arranged. Contact: Ron Chew, director.

Wolf Haven
3111 Offut Lake Rd., Tenino WA 98589
264-4695
Toll-free: (800) 448-9653
A research and education center. Besides offering tours, it provides classroom
programs, supports field research and trains field biologists and wildlife agents.
Internships may be possible. Executive director: Maureen Greeley.

The Women's Building
Hotline: 781-7787
This nonprofit coalition is working to purchase a building, with office, retail and
meeting space, child care facilities and common resources like a library and
computer equipment, for nonprofits and women-owned businesses. No paid staff
at press time, but opportunities for interns and volunteers, especially in grantwriting.
Staff jobs may be created when funding is secured.

Women's Funding Alliance
219 First Ave. S., #120, Seattle WA 98104
467-6733
A fund-raising organization for several nonprofits that offer health and human services programs for women and children. Employs three. Volunteer opportunities. Interns might work in grantwriting, fund drives or research for speechwriting, depending on the agency's need.

Woodland Park Zoological Society
601 N. 59th, Seattle WA 98103
789-6000
A nonprofit that supports the Woodland Park Zoo by raising funds. Employs 25 plus five at the Zoo Store. Positions include accounting, public relations, fund-raising, data processing, membership and special events. Interns can work as assistants to department heads.

The Worker Center
115 Battery, Seattle WA 98121
461-8408
Started as a community-wide coalition during local factory closures in the mid-1980s, the center has become a model for re-employment support centers across the U.S. Not a direct services provider, it facilitates the delivery of services by others. Employs five full-time, with occasional additional staff on a project basis. Interns can work in project evaluations (for example, women in trades); students should be upper division, with good quantitative skills. Acting director at press time: Rich Feldman.

World Association for Children and Parents (WACAP)
P.O. Box 88948, Seattle WA 98138
575-4550
Recruits adoptive parents, provides home studies for adoption, provides support to adopting parents, arranges with child care agencies in the U.S. and abroad to place children for adoption and runs an Options for Pregnancy program. Unpaid internships possible. Janice Neilson is executive director.

YMCA of Greater Seattle
909 Fourth Ave., Seattle WA 98104
382-5022
Jobline: 382-5335
Serves King and part of Snohomish County. Includes the Metrocenter Y; camping services, which operates two residential camps; and the administrative office. Operates 250 guest rooms, providing opportunities for hospitality industry jobs. The child care program for school-age children is one of the Y's largest areas. Full-time, employs about 240; in addition, there are about 800 part-time jobs. Another 300-400 join the staff for summer, many working in the day and residential camps. Recruiting for the summer positions starts in winter. The Y welcomes both volunteers and interns. Interns can work in business administration, public relations, development, child development, recreation, physical education and aquatics, often as assistants to department heads. Openings are posted in most Y

offices and listed in *Sound Opportunities* and the United Way monthly, *For Your Information.* Contact: Sheila Tiemens, human resources director.

YMCA of Snohomish County
2720 Rockefeller, Everett WA 98201
258-9211
Offers health and fitness, child care and preschool, and youth leadership programs. Leadership programs for junior and senior high school students. Employs 206, with about half working full-time. Interns welcome. Contact: Lorrie Hermanson, personnel.

Kitsap Family YMCA
60 Magnuson Way, Bremerton WA 98310
377-3741
Offers activities for children and teenagers, before- and after-school care in school buildings, health and fitness programs and a program for the military. The full-time staff of 12 is supplemented with approximately 80 part-timers. Interns welcome. Contact: Jane Erlandsen, associate director.

YMCA of Tacoma-Pierce County
Metropolitan Office
1002 S. Pearl, Tacoma WA 98465
564-9622
More than 120 are employed full-time at this Y; there's also a large part-time staff. Programs include health and fitness, day, residential and family camps, employment preparation, international programs and community school. Interns welcome. Contact: Rollin Mills, human resources director.

YWCA of Seattle-King County
1118 Fifth Ave., Seattle WA 98101
461-4871
About 135 work for the Seattle YWCA. Job opportunities administrators and teachers in the day care centers, summer day camp staff, maintenance and housekeeping workers and the administrative staff. Employs counselors in its emergency shelter and transitional housing and contract instructors for the health and fitness classes. Job openings are posted in the Y employment services wing. Human resources director: (Ms.) Lynn G. Perry.

YWCA of Kitsap County
P.O. Box 559, Bremerton WA 98310
876-1608
Offers a confidential shelter for battered women and their children; an after-school program for girls; a school-based educational program on domestic violence and a women's financial information service. The staff of 15 is supplemented with volunteers, many of whom receive training in domestic violence programs so that they can work in the shelter, and with interns. Executive director: Carolyn French.

YWCA of Tacoma-Pierce County
405 Broadway, Tacoma WA 98402
272-4181
Operates a shelter, health and fitness center, youth programs, thrift store and career resource center. When openings occur, they're advertised and announced in the resource center.

YWCA of Thurston County

220 Union Ave. S.E., Olympia WA 98501

352-0593

Pat McGreer is the executive director of this Y, which has two permanent staff members and two on contract for the displaced homemakers program. Interns are welcome.

YouthCare

333 1st Ave. W., Seattle WA 98119

282-1288

Established in 1974, this local organization works with homeless and at-risk youth. Contacts about 14,000 youth annually. Employs 65 (nearly all full-time). Internships possible in social work, public administration and grantwriting. Personnel contact: (Ms.) Kelly Nolan, administrative manager.

Youth Eastside Services

16150 N.E. 8th, Bellevue WA 98008

747-4937

Serves some 10,000 annually with counseling, sexual abuse prevention and treatment, drug and alcohol treatment, and consultation and training for children, adolescents, parents, teachers and others working with youth. Employs 48, including part-time and contract employees. Uses more than 175 volunteers. Serves as a training facility for M.S.W. candidates; other internships may be possible for master's level students desiring counseling experience. Executive director: Clifford Warner.

13. Employers: Business and Tourism Organizations

Business and tourism organizations can serve as valuable resources in your job search. Some chambers of commerce offer directories of members or major area employers. Most welcome nonmembers to meetings. The larger organizations offer a variety of job opportunities; even the smaller chambers often have intern positions. (Some chambers, however, have such space constraints that they cannot accommodate additional staff, even on an unpaid basis.) A reminder: none of these groups run employment services; don't expect them to provide job-search counseling or to circulate your resume to their members.

Greater Seattle Chamber of Commerce
1301 Fifth Ave., #2400, Seattle WA 98101-2603
389-7200
Jobline: 389-7300, Ext. 506
Employs about 75 in its departments and affiliated programs (for example, Business Volunteers for the Arts and the King County Housing Partnership). Student interns (undergraduate and graduate) are welcome in both the affiliates and chamber departments. There is a formal internship program, Chamber Business Fellows, for graduate students. Human resources manager: Evelyn Lemoine.

Bellevue Chamber of Commerce
10500 N.E. 8th, #212, Bellevue WA 98004
454-2464
Advocacy for business, information (including publications and educational seminars) and networking are the three major goals of the Bellevue chamber, which employs 15. Interns are welcome. Contact: Jo Ann Curley, controller.

Everett Area Chamber of Commerce
P.O. Box 1086, Everett WA 98206
252-5181
Includes a convention and visitors bureau. Employs 10. Interested in an internship in the visitors' bureau? Write Jean Hale, acting president.

Tacoma-Pierce County Chamber of Commerce
950 Pacific Ave., #300, P.O. Box 1933, Tacoma WA 98401-1933
627-2175
Employs 18 in such departments as business and trade development, member services, neighborhood area councils and small business programs. Contact: Cynthia Spry, business manager.

Other area chambers with part-time positions or internships include:

Arlington Chamber of Commerce
P.O. Box 102, Arlington WA 98223
435-3708
Employs one part-time. Unpaid interns welcome.

Auburn Area Chamber of Commerce
228 1st N.E., Auburn WA 98002
833-0700
Employs three full-time, one part-time. Internships possible.

Bainbridge Island Chamber of Commerce/Visitor Center
590 Winslow Way E., Bainbridge Island WA 98110
842-3700
Employs one full-time, four part-time. Internships possible. Volunteers welcome.

Ballard Chamber of Commerce
2208 N.W. Market St., Seattle WA 98107
784-9705
Employs one full-time, one part-time. Internships possible.

Bremerton Area Chamber of Commerce
P.O. Box 229, Bremerton WA 98310
479-3579
Employs four full-time, three part-time. Internships possible.

Central Area Chamber of Commerce
2108 E. Madison St., Seattle WA 98112
325-2864
No permanent staff; however, interns (especially in grantwriting) are welcome. For several years the chamber has produced a weekly television program for a local cable station; community college and art institute students are also sought as interns for this project. Other volunteer opportunities exist in clerical positions. Contact: DeCharlene Williams or Althea McAfee.

Greater Des Moines Chamber of Commerce
P.O. Box 98672, Des Moines WA 98198
878-7000
Employs one. Internships possible.

Edmonds Chamber of Commerce
P.O. Box 146, Edmonds WA 98020
670-1496
Employs one. Internships possible.

Enumclaw Chamber of Commerce
1421 Cole St., Enumclaw WA 98022
825-7666
Employs one full-time, one part-time. Unpaid internships possible. Volunteers welcome.

Greater Federal Way Chamber of Commerce
34004 16th Ave. S., Federal Way WA 98003
838-2605
Employs two full-time, two part-time.

Greater Greenwood Chamber of Commerce
P.O. Box 30715, Seattle WA 98103
789-1148
Employs one part-time. Internships possible.

Greater Issaquah Chamber of Commerce/Issaquah Festivals
155 N.W. Gilman Blvd., Issaquah WA 98027
392-7024
Employs four full-time, three part-time. Internships possible.

Kent Chamber of Commerce
P.O. Box 128, Kent WA 98035
854-1770
Employs four full-time, two part-time. Internships possible.

Greater Kirkland Chamber of Commerce
356 Parkplace Center, Kirkland WA 98033
822-7066
Employs five. Internships possible.

Lacey/Thurston County Chamber of Commerce
701 Sleater-Kinney Rd. S.E., #7, Lacey WA 98503
491-4141
Employs one full-time, two part-time. Internships possible.

Lake City Chamber of Commerce
2611 N.E. 125th, #102, Seattle WA 98125
363-3287
Employs one. Internships possible.

Lakewood Chamber of Commerce
P.O. Box 98690, Tacoma WA 98498
582-9400
Employs two. Internships possible.

Greater Marysville Chamber of Commerce
4411 76th N.E., Marysville WA 98270
659-7700
Employs two full-time. Internships possible.

Mercer Island Chamber of Commerce
7601 S.E. 27th, Mercer Island WA 98040
232-3404
Employs one. Internships possible. Volunteers welcome.

Monroe Chamber of Commerce
P.O. Box 38, Monroe WA 98272
794-5488
Employs two part-time. Interns welcome.

Northshore Chamber of Commerce
10410 Beardslee Blvd., Bothell WA 98011
486-1245
Employs four full-time, one part-time. Internships possible.

Olympia-Thurston County Chamber of Commerce
P.O. Box 1427, Olympia WA 98507
357-3362
Employs six full-time, two part-time. Interns welcome.

Port Orchard Chamber of Commerce
839 Bay St., Port Orchard WA 98336
876-3505
Employs two. Internships possible.

Greater Poulsbo Chamber of Commerce
P. O. Box 1063, Poulsbo WA 98370
779-4999
Employs one full-time. Internships possible.

Puyallup Area Chamber of Commerce
P.O. Box 1298, Puyallup WA 98371
845-6755
Employs four. Interns welcome.

Greater Redmond Chamber of Commerce
P.O. Box 791, Redmond WA 98073
885-4014
Employs four full-time. Interns welcome.

Greater Renton Chamber of Commerce
300 Rainier Ave. N., Renton WA 98055
226-4560
Employs two full-time, one part-time. Internships possible.

Shoreline Chamber of Commerce
P.O. Box 55066, Seattle WA 98155
361-2260
Employs one full-time, one part-time. Internships possible.

Silverdale Chamber of Commerce
P.O. Box 1218, Silverdale WA 98383
692-6800
Employs three. Volunteers welcome.

Smokey Point Area Chamber of Commerce
15414 Smokey Point Blvd., #A, Arlington WA 98223
659-5453
Employs one part-time. Internships possible. Volunteer opportunities.

South Snohomish County Chamber of Commerce
3400 188th St. S.W., #102, Lynnwood WA 98037
774-0507
Employs four full-time. Internships possible.

Southwest King County Chamber of Commerce
P.O. Box 58591, Seattle WA 98138
244-3160
Employs seven. Internships possible.

Tumwater Area Chamber of Commerce
488 Tyee Dr., Tumwater WA 98512
357-5153
Employs two full-time.

Greater University Chamber of Commerce
4714 University Way N.E., Seattle WA 98105
527-2567
Employs two full-time. Interns welcome.

West Seattle Chamber of Commerce
4151 California Ave. S.W., Seattle WA 98116
932-5685
Employs one full-time. Unpaid internships possible.

White Center Chamber of Commerce
P.O. Box 46223, Seattle WA 98146
763-4196
Employs one. Volunteers welcome. Internships possible.

Woodinville Chamber of Commerce
13205 N.E. 175th, Woodinville WA 98072
481-8300
Employs three. Unpaid internships possible.

DOWNTOWN ASSOCIATIONS

Downtown Seattle Association
500 Union St., #325, Seattle WA 98101
623-0340
President: Kathleen Joncas. Employs 10. Internships possible.

Bellevue Downtown Association
500 108th Ave. N.E., #210, Bellevue WA 98004
453-1223
Employs six full-time and one part-time on the administrative staff and four as
parking monitors. Internships possible.

Kirkland Downtown Association
220 Kirkland Ave., #10, Kirkland WA 98033
822-5158
Employs one full-time and two part-time. Internships possible.

Greater Bothell Association
P.O. Box 1203, Bothell WA 98041
485-4353
Only one staff member, program manager Randy Flesher. Internships possible.

Bremerton Main Street Association
245 4th St., #201-B, Bremerton WA 98310
377-3041
Staff: one full-time, one part-time. Unpaid internships possible. Executive
director: Don Atkinson.

CONVENTION AND VISITORS BUREAUS

Seattle-King County Convention and Visitors Bureau
Administrative Office
520 Pike St., #1300, Seattle WA 98101
461-5800
This tourism development office, which is not part of the government-operated
Washington State Convention and Trade Center, employs about 140. Some
positions are part-time or seasonal. Turnover is limited; unsolicited resumes are
not accepted. An affiliate :

Seattle-King County News Bureau
461-5805
Provides media relations liaison to out-of-state media. Employs two. Internships,
especially for students in journalism, public relations or marketing. Contact: Barry
Anderson, news bureau manager.

Tacoma-Pierce County Visitor and Convention Bureau
906 Broadway, Tacoma WA 98401
627-2836
Recruits and trains 60 volunteers to staff the county's seven visitor information
centers. Interns are welcome. Contact: Nancy Watkins, executive director.

East King County Convention and Visitor Bureau
520 112th Ave. N.E., #101, Bellevue WA 98004
455-1926
Employs 11. Internships possible, especially for students in hotel administration
or hospitality. Volunteer opportunities, especially for senior citizens interested in
providing visitor information.

Bremerton/Kitsap Visitor and Convention Bureau
120 Washington Ave., #101, Bremerton WA 98310
479-3588
Employs seven. Internships possible.

Snohomish County Visitor Information Center
101 128th S.E., #5000, Everett WA 98208
745-4133, 338-4437
Employs two. Uses 50 volunteers. Internships possible.

14. Getting to the Job

How can you reach an interview—or your job? For help with public transportation, call:

METRO: 553-3000
King County rider information available 24 hours a day.

Community Transit: 778-2185, 353-RIDE
Snohomish County information available from 5:30 a.m. to 9 p.m. weekdays and from 8 to 4:30 weekends.

Pierce Transit: 581-8000
Pierce County information available from 6 a.m. to 6 p.m. weekdays and from 9 to 5 weekends.

Kitsap Transit: 373-2877
Kitsap County information available from 6 a.m. to 6 p.m. weekdays and from 10 to 2 Saturdays.

Intercity Transit: 786-1881
Thurston County information available from 7 a.m. to 7 p.m. weekdays and from 8 to 5 Saturdays.

Directions
When you schedule an interview, don't hesitate to ask for directions. You'll find some companies are so accustomed to the question that they have taped instructions on their telephone systems.

A good map is also valuable. Some suggestions:

Thomas Bros. Maps, available from many map dealers and bookstores in King, Snohomish and Pierce county versions.

King of the Road Maps, available in many book, drug and grocery stories in several different versions. By mail the maps are $2.50 each. Contact King of the Road Map Service, 6325 212th S.W., #E, Lynnwood WA 98036, (800) 223-8852 or 774-7112.

Seattle Best Places includes a detailed map of downtown Seattle and *The Seattle Survival Guide* includes a list of downtown buildings with parking garages. Both are available in bookstores and from the publisher (see Sasquatch Publishing).

Index

How To Save Money On
Your Next Copy Of This Book

To make the next edition of **989 Great Part-time Jobs in Seattle** even better, we'd appreciate your comments. You need not identify yourself, but if you do, we'll send you a discount coupon good for $5 off on another copy of this book—or a discount on a copy of the 408-page **How To Find A Good Job In Seattle: Your Best Guide to 1,600 Puget Sound Employers**.

Your completed survey should be sent to:

Barrett Street Productions
P.O. Box 99642
Seattle WA 98199

Please tell us where you bought your copy of **989 Great Part-time Jobs in Seattle**:

_____bookstore _____ by direct mail from_____

Other:_____

Your home ZIP code:_____

If you are not a Puget Sound area resident, do you plan to move here?

___ yes

___ no

Please describe yourself:

_____ seeking professional/technical work

_____ seeking interim or part-time middle management position

_____ seeking secretarial/clerical/administrative position

_____ seeking seasonal work

_____ student seeking part-time work

_____ seeking internship

_____ retiree considering a "second" career

_____ employed, seeking sales leads

_____ job-search counselor

Other:_____

Your age:

____ younger than 18

____ 18-25

____ 25-34

____ 34-45

____ older than 45

Your education level:

____ high school graduate

____ vocational/technical training

____ some college

____ college graduate

____ postgraduate education

Your annual household income:
____ less than $10,000
____ $10,000-$24,999
____ $25,000-$40,000
____ more than $40,000

What did you find most valuable about **989 Great Part-time Jobs in Seattle**?

The chapter you found most valuable?

How would you suggest we improve this book?

To obtain your discount coupon, please enclose:

    your sales receipt or other proof of purchase and

    a stamped, self-addressed envelope.

Name_____

Address_____

Discount coupons are sent upon receipt of completed surveys only. Please submit the original of this page; **no photocopies can be accepted**. One coupon per household. Publisher reserves the right to limit recipients of coupons. Coupons are valid only on books ordered directly from publisher; discounts may not be combined. This offer expires Dec. 31, 1995.

More Help for the
Seattle Job Search

Linda Carlson has also written a comprehensive guide to managerial and professional positions, **How To Find A Good Job In Seattle**. The 1995 edition includes 1,600 employers, 300 joblines, 325 professional associations, alumni and civic organizations—and a special resume critique offer. To order, send a check for $24 to

Barrett Street Productions
P.O. Box 99642
Seattle WA 98199
(206) 284-8202

Both this book and **How To Find A Good Job In Seattle** are available at a discount when purchased in quantity. The minimum discount is 20 per cent. Call for specifics.

You may also be interested in the job-search workshops Linda Carlson teaches at North Seattle and Seattle Central Community Colleges. For more information, call either school's continuing education office.